Studies in Computational Intelligence

Volume 1228

The series "Studies in Computational Intelligence" (SCI) publishes new developments and advances in the various areas of computational intelligence—quickly and with a high quality. The intent is to cover the theory, applications, and design methods of computational intelligence, as embedded in the fields of engineering, computer science, physics and life sciences, as well as the methodologies behind them. The series contains monographs, lecture notes and edited volumes in computational intelligence spanning the areas of neural networks, connectionist systems, genetic algorithms, evolutionary computation, artificial intelligence, cellular automata, self-organizing systems, soft computing, fuzzy systems, and hybrid intelligent systems. Of particular value to both the contributors and the readership are the short publication timeframe and the world-wide distribution, which enable both wide and rapid dissemination of research output.

Indexed by SCOPUS, DBLP, WTI AG (Switzerland), zbMATH, SCImago.

All books published in the series are submitted for consideration in Web of Science.

Vu Phi Ho Pham · Andrew Lian · Ania Lian ·
Jeremy White
Editors

Empowering Educators: Integrating AI Tools for Personalized Language Instruction

Springer

Editors
Vu Phi Ho Pham
Industrial University of Ho Chi Minh City
Ho Chi Minh, Vietnam

Andrew Lian
Institute of Social Technology, School of Foreign Languages
Suranaree University of Technology
Nakhon Ratchasima, Thailand

Ania Lian
Faculty of Arts and Society
Charles Darwin University
Winnellie, NT, Australia

Jeremy White
Department of Information
Ritsumeikan University
Kyoto, Japan

ISSN 1860-949X ISSN 1860-9503 (electronic)
Studies in Computational Intelligence
ISBN 978-3-032-01347-7 ISBN 978-3-032-01348-4 (eBook)
https://doi.org/10.1007/978-3-032-01348-4

This Springer imprint is published by the registered company Springer Nature Switzerland AG
The registered company address is: Gewerbestrasse 11, 6330 Cham, Switzerland

Contents

Editors and Contributors

About the Editors

Assoc. Prof. Dr. Vu Phi Ho Pham Industrial University of Ho Chi Minh City, Vietnam, is used to be Vice-President of Ba Ria—Vung Tau University and Vice-President at Van Hien University, Vietnam. Pham has published more than 70 research articles in both local and International journals (17 Scopus/14 ISI), such as Computer-Assisted language Learning, SAGE Open, System, and Journal of Psycholinguist Research, 10 books and course-books, and two edited books. He is Vice-President for Administrative Affairs of AsiaCALL and Managing Editor of its online journal. He is now Editor-in-Chief of the International Journal of TESOL and Education. He is Editorial Staff for the Suranaree Journal of Social Science (Scopus) and Peer Reviewer for some international journals indexed in ISI/Scopus such as Computer-Assisted Language Learning, Open Sage.

Prof. Dr. Andrew Lian is Professor of Foreign Language Studies, School of Foreign Languages, Suranaree University of Technology, Thailand. He specializes in the methodology of teaching foreign/second languages and has had a special interest in the uses of modern technology to enhance learning since the late 1970s. He is one of the pioneers of Technology-Enhanced Language Learning in Australia. Previous to this appointment, he was Professor and Chair of the Department of Foreign Languages and Literatures at Western Illinois University in the USA. Prior to that, he had been Professor of humanities and Director of the Center for the Study of Languages at Rice University, Houston, TX, USA, and Professor and Head of the School of Languages and International Education at the University of Canberra in Australia. He has held further professorial appointments and been Head of Department in two other universities in Australia (James Cook University and Bond University). His current research interests are in the area of self-adjusting and self-organizing (language/culture-) learning environments based on rhizomatic approaches to (language/culture-) learning and the generation of personal learning environments within a twenty-first-century perspective. As a consequence, he is also interested in the development and use of multimedia databases in (language/culture) teaching and learning.

Dr. Ania Lian is Senior Lecturer in education (teaching and learning), Charles Darwin University, Australia, Vice-President for research and innovation, and Chief Editor of the AsiaCALL online journal. Since 1993, Ania has held positions at various universities in Australia, with her work focusing on the uses of technology in second language learning and in education in general, including software development. She has also worked at the National Policy Office of the Council on the Ageing in Canberra and has a history of working on a voluntary basis with the wider community on sustainability projects within the framework of the Queanbeyan Business Council, NSW. Ania has been a keynote speaker at a number of academic conferences both in Australia and in Asia, where she engages in building collaborative networks between CDU and other universities, with the aim of expanding the international focus of all involved. The leading objective of her teaching and research is to explore the concept of inclusive learning environments, with a specific focus on learner-centredness. Her recent interest in graduate attributes developed from these concerns which form the framework of her approach.

Prof. Dr. Jeremy White is Professor in the College of Information Science and Engineering at Ritsumeikan University, Japan. He has taught English as a Foreign Language (EFL) in Japan for the past 20 years. He earned his Ph.D. from Kyoto University; his dissertation research was related to Minecraft and task-based learning to encourage English language communication. Prof. Dr. Jeremy White is Editor-in-Chief of the CALL-EJ (Computer-Assisted Language Learning Electronic Journal) (Scopus-Q1). Prof. Dr. Jeremy White is also Editor-in-Chief of the International Journal of AI in Language Education (IJAILE) published by the ICTE Press.

Contributors

Kujaimah Abdul Kahar Faculty of Arabic Language, Universiti Islam Sultan Sharif Ali, Begawan, Brunei

Rafidah Abdullah Faculty of Arabic Language, Universiti Islam Sultan Sharif Ali, Begawan, Brunei

Rafizah Abdullah Faculty of Arabic Language, Universiti Islam Sultan Sharif Ali, Begawan, Brunei

Mansour Amini School of Languages, Literacies and Translation, Universiti Sains Malaysia, Penang, Malaysia

Norhakimah Khaiessa binti Ahmad Faculty of Educational Studies, Universiti Putra Malaysia, Serdang Selangor, Malaysia

Ahmad Halimah binti Jamil Faculty of Educational Studies, Universiti Putra Malaysia, Serdang Selangor, Malaysia

Tin T. Dang Ho Chi Minh City University of Technology and Education, Ho Chi Minh City, Vietnam

Le Trong Nhan Dao Faculty of Foreign Languages, Saigon University, Ho Chi Minh City, Vietnam

Pham Thanh Dieu Bui Huu Nghia High School, Can Tho, Vietnam

Chao Du Faculty of Educational Studies, Universiti Putra Malaysia, Serdang Selangor, Malaysia

Doan Minh Hue Industrial University of Ho Chi Minh City, Ho Chi Minh City, Vietnam

Que Quan Huynh Van Lang University, Ho Chi Minh City, Vietnam

Amalena Jarudin Faculty of Arabic Language, Universiti Islam Sultan Sharif Ali, Begawan, Brunei

Bao Kham University of Foreign Languages and International Studies, Hue University, Hue City, Vietnam

Mengly Ky Charles Darwin University, Casuarina, Australia

Nguyen Le Ngoc Anh Can Tho University, Can Tho, Vietnam

Truong Bach Le University of Foreign Languages and International Studies, Hue University, Hue City, Vietnam

Andrew Lian Suranaree University of Technology, Nakhon Ratchasima, Thailand

Ania Lian Charles Darwin University, Casuarina, Australia

Hai Linh Nguyen FPT University, Hanoi, Vietnam

Hoang Lan Thi Nguyen Saigon University, Ho Chi Minh City, Vietnam

Ngoc Hoang Vy Nguyen University of North Texas, Denton, USA

Thi Luong Nguyen FPT University, Hanoi, Vietnam

Hoang Ngoc Quynh Nhu Industrial University of Ho Chi Minh City, Ho Chi Minh City, Vietnam

Yongjing Peng Henan Sport University, Henan, China

Vu Phi Ho Pham Industrial University of Ho Chi Minh City, Ho Chi Minh City, Vietnam

Le Thi Ngoc Phan VNU University of Languages and International Studies, Vietnam National University, Hanoi, Vietnam

Nguyen Truong Sa Industrial University of Ho Chi Minh City, Ho Chi Minh City, Vietnam

Vo Nhat Sinh Industrial University of Ho Chi Minh City, Ho Chi Minh City, Vietnam

Alif Sismat Faculty of Arabic Language, Universiti Islam Sultan Sharif Ali, Begawan, Brunei

Phi The Tran Saigon University, Ho Chi Minh City, Vietnam

Jeremy White Ritsumeikan University, Kyoto, Japan

Wang Yiqiu Faculty of Social Sciences and Liberal Arts, UCSI University, Federal Territory of Kuala Lumpur, Malaysia;
Organization Department, Zhejiang Chinese Medical University, Hangzhou, People's Republic of China

Ali Zahabi School of Liberal Arts, King Mongkut's University of Technology Thonburi, Bangkok, Thailand

Overview of Empowering Educators: Integrating AI Tools for Personalized Language Instruction

Vu Phi Ho Pham, Andrew Lian, Jeremy White, and Ania Lian

Abstract With an eye toward ethical, pedagogical, and cognitive consequences, this edited volume explores the integration of artificial intelligence (AI) tools—especially ChatGPT—into English language education. Inspired by empirical research from Vietnam and abroad settings, it explores the transforming possibilities and difficulties of artificial intelligence in regard to academic integrity, learner autonomy, teacher identity, and writing growth. Three components comprise the collection: AI in language teaching and learning; AI-enhanced language learning strategies; and AI in translation and support systems. Results show that, especially in underfunded environments, artificial intelligence runs the danger of overreliance, shallow engagement, and ethical uncertainty even when it promotes motivation, grammatical progress, and tailored instruction. To fully harness the advantages of artificial intelligence, educators want ethical integration and professional growth. The volume advocates long-term, multidisciplinary research to guarantee inclusive, reflective, and sustainable language education in the AI era and offers a cooperative human-AI educational approach.

Keywords Artificial intelligence in education · ChatGPT · Language instruction · Learner autonomy · Ethical integration

V. P. H. Pham (✉)
Industrial University of Ho Chi Minh City, Ho Chi Minh City, Vietnam
e-mail: phamvuphiho@iuh.edu.vn

A. Lian
Suranaree University of Technology, Nakhon Ratchasima, Thailand

J. White
Ritsumeikan University, Kyoto, Japan

A. Lian
Charles Darwin University, Casuarina, Australia

V. P. H. Pham et al. (eds.), *Empowering Educators: Integrating AI Tools for Personalized Language Instruction*, Studies in Computational Intelligence 1228,
https://doi.org/10.1007/978-3-032-01348-4_1

1 Background of Integrating AI Tools for Personalized Language Instruction

A new era of individualized, interactive, and self-directed learning has begun with the introduction of Artificial Intelligence (AI) into language instruction. Because they provide real-time feedback, content creation, and conversational simulation, AI-powered systems such as ChatGPT have become essential to teaching English as a foreign language (EFL) (Lo, 2023; Zawacki-Richter et al., 2019). As new technologies proliferate around the world, critical scholarly attention is required to address their educational, cognitive, and ethical implications.

The advantages of AI-enhanced language learning have been shown in a substantial amount of recent research, particularly with regard to learner engagement, writing improvement, and instructional efficiency. For example, Pham and Le (2024) found that students in the United States and Vietnam thought ChatGPT was a useful tool for boosting writing confidence and reducing fear. Similarly, Ho (2024) discovered that while IT students valued AI tools for paraphrase and grammatical guidance, they still needed teacher input for more in-depth critical learning. Sari (2024) demonstrated that Upscore.ai produced IELTS scores that were most similar to human raters in the context of exam preparation, highlighting AI's potential to democratize access to writing feedback, but with limits in terms of argument coherence and nuance (Yan, 2023; Yang et al., 2024).

Notwithstanding these benefits, academics have warned against depending too much on generative artificial intelligence techniques. Pham and Cao's (2025) methodical evaluation found improvements in student autonomy and vocabulary but also noted major concerns including instructor readiness, shallow engagement, and ethical uncertainty. From a pedagogical perspective, including artificial intelligence into language training calls for ethical awareness and intentional instructional design. Nguyen (2023) emphasizes that although many teachers have worries about using AI technologies like ChatGPT even if they offer great improvements in writing education. Though they were excited about ChatGPT's possibilities, teachers underlined the need of professional training to prevent abuse and promote educated, sensible classroom integration.

The literature review by Pham and Cao (2025) shows that although ChatGPT greatly helps to improve vocabulary development and writing efficiency in Vietnam, widespread concerns remain over academic dishonesty, critical thinking degradation, and teachers' lack of preparedness. This calls for a similar call to direction and balance. Tran et al. (2025) research emphasizes even more these difficulties. Their mixed-methods study with MA students at IUH found that although AI technologies promote idea generation, grammar correction, and paraphrase, students often grew overly dependent on these tools. Sometimes this overuse resulted in shallow engagement with writing and challenges assessing the originality and credibility of AI-generated content. This is consistent with those of Nguyen et al. (2025), who noted comparable problems with plagiarism, citation accuracy, and a drop in independent thought among postgraduate students.

These investigations expose a complex reality: although artificial intelligence has great potential for EFL teaching, its fast technical development has exceeded institutional adaption and pedagogical preparedness. While short-term, task-specific benefits including better grammar, fluency, and learner engagement are frequently recorded, long-term effects on writing development, learner autonomy, and academic integrity are still mostly unknown. Underfunded environments like Vietnam show especially this disparity. Many teachers lack sufficient instruction to properly and ethically leverage artificial intelligence, and students sometimes rely on these tools without fully acquiring critical and reflective learning abilities. Thus, teacher development, ethical frameworks, and curriculum design that promotes human-AI cooperation rather than substitution must all help to construct sustainable AI inclusion in language instruction.

Combining regional and worldwide data via empirical and conceptual research examining how artificial intelligence technologies are changing writing education, academic integrity, learner identity, and professional growth, this collection therefore meets a vital need. It makes a balanced argument: artificial intelligence should be seen as a cooperative, ethically integrated partner in enhancing transformative language learning opportunities rather than a replacement for pedagogical knowledge.

2 Section I: AI Integration in Language Teaching and Learning

In EFL/ESL (Chapter 2), Mansour Amini, Ali Zahabi, and Wang Yiqiu offer a thorough analysis of how artificial intelligence could inspire moral feelings. Emphasizing the incorporation of emotional and moral intelligence into curriculum design, they look at AI techniques such sentiment analysis, adaptive learning systems, and virtual emotional intelligence coaches. Emphasizing the need of morally and culturally sensitive instruction, the chapter advocates a whole framework supporting both verbal and emotional growth.

In Chap. 3, Tran The Phi and Nguyen Thi Hoang Lan investigate how a redesigned rubric and the Tree-of- Thought architecture may be combined to improve ChatGPT's assessment of research proposals. Particularly in complicated methodological components, the study shows better intra- and inter-rater reliability; it also highlights difficulties assessing simple criteria. This creative approach provides insightful analysis for improving the position of artificial intelligence in research education and greatly helps AI-assisted academic assessment.

In Chap. 4, Nguyen Le Ngoc Anh and Pham Thanh Dieu looked at how artificial intelligence techniques enable individualized instruction in IELTS writing. With thirty-two students, conducted in a Vietnamese language center, their quasi-experimental study examined conventional and AI-assisted instruction. Teacher interviews and pre/post-test data were subjected both statistically and conceptually. Grammar, vocabulary, and cohesiveness all showed notable improvement. From mistrust to hope, teachers' opinions changed to support artificial intelligence as a complementing tool for instruction.

In Chap. 5, Dao Le Trong Nhan looks at how Vietnamese undergraduate students use ChatGPT to help with English writing. With 61 participants, the study applied a mixed-methods approach including writing assignments, surveys, and interviews. Data analysis turned up strong usage of social, memory, and compensatory techniques. Students had subject and communication difficulties; they were frequently lessened by quick improvement. Results show how students want teacher support and ChatGPT training to improve tailored writing teaching including AI integration.

In Chap. 6, using the Human-AI Collaboration framework, Truong Bach Le and Bao Kham looked at how Vietnamese EFL students interacted with an artificial intelligence writing assistance. Using combined methods—questionnaires, journals, and interviews—the study with 95 students revealed AI helpful for enhancing structure, grammar, and writing autonomy. Over-reliance, contextual flexibility, and trust become issues, though. Results support merging ethical grounded, learner-centered academic writing with AI tools under teacher direction.

Under AI integration (Chapter 7), Chao Du, Yongjing Peng, Norhakimah Khaiessa Binti, and Ahmad Halimah Binti Jamil investigate identity conflicts among Chinese university EFL professors. Ten participants in a qualitative case study had data from story frames and interviews thematically examined. The study notes tensions from opposing, novel, and limited I-positions. Teachers negotiated these under developing Intelligent-TPACK, emotional resilience, and adaptive strategies. Future policy and teacher development informed by a triadic teacher-AI-student paradigm guides both.

In Chap. 8, forty Vietnamese rookie EFL instructors' use of AI-powered tools for lesson planning was examined by Nguyen Truong Sa, Hoang Ngoc Quynh Nhu, Vo Nhat Sinh, and Doan Minh Hue. They looked at questionnaire and interview data using a mixed-methods technique. Although teachers underlined the requirement of content modification, findings revealed artificial intelligence aids creative activity design and resource development. The paper emphasizes the need of artificial intelligence literacy, institutional training, and careful integration to guarantee successful, customized instruction.

3 Section II: AI-Enhanced Language Learning Skills and Practices

In Chap. 9, Nguyen Thi-Luong and Nguyen Hai-Linh investigate how Vietnamese EFL teachers see utilizing Diffit for AI-assisted reading assignments. Eighteen university professors took part; pre/post questionnaires and interviews helped to compile data. Conducted in Hanoi, the survey showed generally favorable opinions on the advantages of Diffit's automation, while some difficulties with implementation like The report provides insightful analysis for integration of artificial intelligence into education.

In Chap. 10, Vu Phi Ho Pham and Que Quan Huynh looked at how Vietnamese high school pupils saw artificial intelligence technologies for autonomy and vocabulary acquisition. The study using survey data from 185 twelfth graders revealed tools like ChatGPT and Google Translate improved learner motivation, goal-setting, and self-regulation. Though there were advantages, questions about overreliance and limited participation surfaced. Results underline the possibility of artificial intelligence in encouraging autonomy and the requirement of educational direction and ethical integration.

In Chap. 11, Tin T. Dang probes closely how GenAI products like ChatGPT and Google Translate are used in EFL classrooms by Vietnamese university students. By encouraging passive engagement, overreliance, and avoidance of critical thinking, AI use frequently compromises learner autonomy, the study finds via instructor surveys and classroom observations. Results highlight the requirement of pedagogical scaffolding, teacher feedback, and controlled integration to turn artificial intelligence from a shortcut into a tool for sustained, reflective language acquisition.

In Chap. 12, Alif Sismat and colleagues looked at how ChatGPT helps seven Malay undergraduates in Brunei learn Arabic. Strong student performance in translation, summarizing, and sentiment analysis was discovered by using a qualitative approach including eight NLP activities and focus groups. But accuracy problems caused major difficulties with grammar and morphology. Effective, tailored AI-assisted Arabic language learning depends on quick quality, ethical use, and AI literacy, the paper emphasizes.

Using Python and ChatGPT, Vu Phi Ho Pham and Ngoc Ho Vy Nguyen (Chap. 13) offer a useful road map for language teachers creating artificial intelligence-powered chatbots. The report emphasizes how chatbots might replicate meaningful dialogues and provide tailored, real-time comments. Emphasizing NLP and machine learning integration, it tackles pedagogical restrictions of conventional approaches and provides a detailed implementation step-by-step guide. The study advocates immersive, autonomous, chatbot-enhanced language learning opportunities.

4 Section III: AI in Translation and Support Systems

In Chap. 14, With 100 students at Vietnam National University, Phan Thi Ngoc Le looked at how artificial intelligence tools might be included into translation instruction. The study found using mixed methods—questionnaires, interviews, and translation assessments—that artificial intelligence techniques improved translation speed, accessibility, and efficiency. Still, difficulties continued in naturalism, contextual awareness, and cultural sensitivity. Emphasizing human control, students appreciated AI's support but stayed critical. The work offers educational ideas for ethical, efficient AI-assisted translation education.

To evaluate academic support services at an Australian institution, Mengly Ky and Ania Lian (Chapter 15) created a three-layer assessment system with an eye toward inclusion, academic achievement, and student satisfaction. By use of desk-based research and qualitative document analysis, the study revealed design flaws and suggested AI-enhanced solutions like learning analytics and chatbots. The framework provides doable suggestions for ethically integrating artificial intelligence, enhancing service responsiveness, and directing next data-informed academic support evaluations in digital learning environments.

5 Conclusion

Finally, this collection synthesizes innovative research from Vietnamese and international EFL settings to critically investigate how artificial intelligence technologies—especially generative tools like ChatGPT—are changing the field of language instruction. From helping IELTS preparation, vocabulary growth, and grammar improvement to supporting research writing and teacher identity transformation, the examined papers show a wide spectrum of educational uses. Crucially, this study emphasizes the educational, ethical, and cognitive conflicts as well as the great possibilities accompanying artificial intelligence integration.

Although AI tools can democratize access to writing criticism, improve student autonomy, and lower language anxiety, these advantages are sometimes outweighed by concerns including overreliance, academic dishonesty, and less critical engagement. Particularly in underfunded environments like Vietnam, the results repeatedly expose deficiencies in institutional policy frameworks, student digital literacy, and teacher preparation. Particularly the research by Tran et al. (2025) as well as Nguyen et al. (2025), underline students's increasing reliance on AI-generated ideas and the challenges in validating AI outputs, so stressing the immediate necessity of educational scaffolding and ethical integration.

Three main themes—AI Integration in Language Teaching and Learning, AI-enhanced Language Learning Skills and Practices, and AI in Translation and Support Systems—formulate the framework of the next chapters. Taken together, they show a comprehensive view of how artificial intelligence should be understood in terms of changing instructional techniques, learner identities, and educational support systems as well as in terms of language competency. From investigating Intelligent-TPACK systems and rubric-based AI evaluation to chatbot-enhanced practice and identity issues in AI adoption, the papers show how instructors and students are adjusting—often blindly, sometimes creatively—to this changing digital environment.

This volume demands a redesigned education where artificial intelligence is a strategic partner rather than a replacement. Future investigations on the long-term effects of artificial intelligence on writing development, learner cognition, and teacher agency must transcend isolated, transient interventions toward longitudinal, multidisciplinary studies. We can only guarantee that artificial intelligence satisfies its potential in creating inclusive, ethical, and transforming language learning environments by means of such ongoing research and responsible innovation.

References

Ho, P. X. P. (2024). Using ChatGPT in English language learning: A study on I.T. students' attitudes, habits, and perceptions. *International Journal of TESOL & Education, 4*(1), 55–68. https://doi.org/10.54855/ijte.24414

Lo, C. K. (2023). What is the impact of ChatGPT on education? A rapid review of the literature. *Education Sciences, 13*(4), 410. https://doi.org/10.3390/educsci13040410

Nguyen, T. T. H. (2023). EFL teachers' perspectives toward the use of ChatGPT in writing classes: A case study at Van Lang University. *International Journal of Language Instruction, 2*(3), 1–47. https://doi.org/10.54855/ijli.23231

Nguyen, T. Y. P., Nguyen, N. T., & Phan, N. K. H. (2025). The challenges of applying ChatGPT in the academic writing of postgraduate students in English major at IUH. *International Journal of AI in Language Education, 2*(1), 20–37. https://doi.org/10.54855/ijaile.25212

Pham, M. T., & Cao, T. X. T. (2025). The practice of ChatGPT in English teaching and learning in Vietnam: A systematic review. *International Journal of TESOL & Education, 5*(1), 50–70. https://doi.org/10.54855/ijte.25513

Pham, V. P. H., & Le, A. Q. (2024). ChatGPT in language learning: Perspectives from Vietnamese students in Vietnam and the USA. *International Journal of Language Instruction, 3*(2), 59–72. https://doi.org/10.54855/ijli.24325

Sari, A. N. (2024). Exploring the potential of using AI language models in democratising global language test preparation. *International Journal of TESOL & Education, 4*(4), 111–126. https://doi.org/10.54855/ijte.24447.

Tran, H. N., Le, T. T. N., & Tran, V. B. U. (2025). AI tools in learning academic writing: Benefits and challenges for MA students in the english language studies at the Industrial University Of Ho Chi Minh City. *International Journal of AI in Language Education, 2*(1), 74–91. https://doi.org/10.54855/ijaile.25215

Yang, K., Raković, M., Liang, Z., Yan, L., Zeng, Z., Fan, Y., Gašević, D., & Chen, G. (2024). Modifying AI, enhancing essays: How active engagement with generative AI boosts writing quality. arXiv:2412.07200. https://doi.org/10.48550/arXiv.2412.07200

Yan, D. (2023). Impact of ChatGPT on learners in an L2 writing practicum: An exploratory investigation. *Education and Information Technologies, 28*(11), 1–25. https://doi.org/10.1007/s10639-023-11742-4

Zawacki-Richter, O., Marín, V. I., Bond, M., & Gouverneur, F. (2019). Systematic review of research on artificial intelligence applications in higher education–where are the educators? *International Journal of Educational Technology in Higher Education, 16*(1), 1–27. https://doi.org/10.1186/s41239-019-0171-0

Vu Phi Ho Pham Faculty of Foreign Languages, Industrial University of Ho Chi Minh City, Vietnam, was Vice-President of Ba Ria–Vung Tau University and Vice-President at Van Hien University, Vietnam. Pham has published more than 70 research articles in both local and International Journals, such as Computer-Assisted Language Learning, SAGE Open, System, and Journal of Psycholinguist Research (*20* Scopus/*14 ISI*), and 10 books/course books, and 2 edited books (Springer and IGI Global). He is the Vice President for Administrative Affairs of AsiaCALL. He is the Editor-in-chief of the International Journal of TESOL & Education. He is now the managing editor of CALL-EJ (Scopus-Q1).

Professor Dr. Andrew Lian is Professor of Foreign Language Studies, School of Foreign Languages, Suranaree University of Technology, Thailand, He specializes in the methodology of teaching foreign/second languages and has had a special interest in the uses of modern technology to enhance learning since the late 1970s. He is one of the pioneers of Technology-Enhanced Language-Learning in Australia. Previous to this appointment, he was Professor and Chair of the

Department of Foreign Languages and Literatures at Western Illinois University in the United States. Prior to that, he had been Professor of Humanities and Director of the Center for the Study of Languages at Rice University, Houston, TX, USA, and Professor and Head of the School of Languages and International Education at the University of Canberra in Australia. He has held further Professorial appointments and been Head of Department in two other universities in Australia (James Cook University and Bond University). His current research interests are in the area of self-adjusting and self-organizing (language/culture-) learning environments based on rhizomatic approaches to (language/culture-) learning and the generation of personal learning environments within a 21st-century perspective. As a consequence, he is also interested in the development and use of multimedia databases in (language/culture)-teaching and learning.

Professor Dr. Jeremy White is a professor in the College of Information Science and Engineering at Ritsumeikan University, Japan. He has taught English as a Foreign Language (EFL) in Japan for the past 20 years. He earned his PhD from Kyoto University; his dissertation research was related to Minecraft and task-based learning to encourage English language communication. Prof. Dr. Jeremy White is the editor-in-chief of the CALL-EJ (Computer-Assisted Language Learning Electronic Journal) (Scopus-Q1). Professor Dr. Jeremy White is also the editor-in-chief of the International Journal of AI in Language Education (IJAILE) published by the ICTE Press.

Ania Lian is a Senior Lecturer at Charles Darwin University, where she plays a leading role in supervising PhD and research students and contributes to the development of a vibrant and inclusive research culture.

AI Integration in Language Teaching and Learning

Employing Artificial Intelligence to Foster Moral Emotions in English Language Education: A Review

Mansour Amini, Ali Zahabi, and Wang Yiqiu

Abstract Moral emotions are pivotal in shaping learners' development and influencing their learning behaviors. Artificial intelligence (AI) technologies offer innovative opportunities to enhance both language proficiency and emotional awareness by integrating moral and emotional intelligence into language learning frameworks. This chapter reviews the role of AI tools in incorporating moral emotions within English as a Foreign Language (EFL) and English as a Second Language (ESL) educational contexts. The chapter focuses on the significance of the theoretical underpinning of moral emotions, emotional intelligence in teaching and learning, integrating AI into curriculum design, various AI-driven tools including sentiment analysis, adaptive learning platforms, AI-Powered Feedback Systems, and Virtual Emotional Intelligence (EQ). This review emphasizes the transformative potential of AI in bridging the gap between cognitive and emotional learning, enabling educators to create more emotionally responsive and morally aware EFL and ESL classrooms. Future research directions are proposed, with particular attention to technologies that can be culturally and ethically tailored to fit diverse educational settings. The implications for moral and emotional development are discussed, along with recommendations for integrating AI tools in curriculum design.

M. Amini (✉)
School of Languages, Literacies and Translation, Universiti Sains Malaysia, Penang, Malaysia
e-mail: mansour@usm.my

A. Zahabi
School of Liberal Arts, King Mongkut's University of Technology Thonburi, Bangkok, Thailand
e-mail: ali.zaha@kmutt.ac.th

W. Yiqiu
Faculty of Social Sciences and Liberal Arts, UCSI University, Federal Territory of Kuala Lumpur, Malaysia

Organization Department, Zhejiang Chinese Medical University, Hangzhou, People's Republic of China

W. Yiqiu
e-mail: 1002165223@ucsiuniversity.edu.my

V. P. H. Pham et al. (eds.), *Empowering Educators: Integrating AI Tools for Personalized Language Instruction*, Studies in Computational Intelligence 1228,
https://doi.org/10.1007/978-3-032-01348-4_2

Keywords Artificial intelligence · EFL · Emotional intelligence · ESL · Moral emotions · Tool

1 Introduction

The evolving landscape of education, supported by groundbreaking advancements in Artificial Intelligence (AI), underscores the critical need to incorporate moral emotions into learning frameworks for students. The integration of AI tools in EFL and ESL education may enhance linguistic proficiency and offer unique opportunities for moral and emotional development.

Moral emotion, a significant area of study in the field of Psychology, refers to emotional experiences arising from individuals' judgments of their own or others' behaviors and thoughts according to specific moral standards (Amini et al., 2025). This complex emotion encompasses feelings such as disgust, empathy, guilt, admiration, gratitude and shame (Haidt, 2001; Haidt, 2003; McCullough et al., 2001). For example, two typical behaviors influenced by moral emotions are moral purity and moral compensation (Ren & Gao, 2011) which could also be relevant to language learning, for example in terms of learner motivation, identity, and classroom behavior.

The intersection of second or foreign language learning and emotional development is particularly significant, as it allows educators to harness AI's capabilities to create immersive environments where moral emotions can be actively engaged and explored. The nature of language learning in these contexts emphasizes the significance of interpersonal interactions and cultural nuances (Ha & Ho, 2025; Ho & Ha, 2025; Pham & Cao, 2025). Fostering moral emotions is not limited to mere emotional acknowledgement; it plays a crucial role in facilitating collaboration, intercultural communication, and social responsibility among learners.

Furthermore, moral emotions are crucial in shaping learners' developmental trajectories and influencing their interactions, motivation, and engagement in the learning process (Giner-Sorolla, 2013). For example, when students participate in group activities, feelings of empathy can encourage them to support their peers, share ideas, and engage in meaningful discussions. This enhances not only their language skills but also their intercultural competence, which is vital in EFL and ESL contexts (Amini et al., 2024a, 2024b). Fostering positive emotions, such as happiness, contentment, and satisfaction, can significantly enhance student motivation, creativity, and a sense of belonging (Fredrickson, 2001). Engagement, motivation, and academic success all correlate with students' emotional experiences (e.g., Pekrun & Linnenbrink-Garcia, 2012). This necessitates a nuanced understanding of how emotions interact with cognitive processes within educational settings. For instance, emotional regulation plays a foundational role in cognitive development, significantly influenced by the interplay of emotional states and effective learning strategies. According to Li et al. (2019), the ability to manage one's emotions is crucial as it enhances concentration, facilitates task completion, and improves overall academic performance. This relationship underscores the necessity for implementing emotional support systems within educational contexts, especially as learners increasingly navigate complex academic environments to construct more emotionally responsive and morally aware environments for language learners (Amini & Amini, 2017) across diverse cultural backgrounds.

The chapter critically explores the benefits of various AI-driven tools, including sentiment analysis, adaptive learning platforms, and virtual emotional intelligence (EQ) coaches, noting their capability to identify, track, and cultivate moral emotions in students. Furthermore, it elucidates the significance of automated feedback mechanisms, which analyze students' emotional tones and the moral implications of their communications, thereby contributing to both language and ethical development. By synthesizing the existing literature, this chapter highlights the extensive potential of AI to bridge the gap between cognitive learning and emotional engagement, and construct more emotionally responsive and morally aware environments for language learners. Additionally, it addresses the need for culturally and ethically relevant research focusing on how AI technologies can be tailored to diverse educational settings. Through a detailed discussion of the implications for emotional and moral development among EFL and ESL learners, alongside recommendations for integrating AI tools into curriculum design, this chapter emphasizes the necessity of a holistic educational approach that recognizes the intertwined nature of linguistic and moral education in facilitating well-rounded student development.

2 Theoretical Underpinning of Moral Emotions

Research in moral psychology provides a comprehensive framework for examining how moral emotions influence decision-making and social interactions in various contexts. For example, Kim and Johnson (2013) reported that moral emotions significantly influenced purchase intention for a social-cause product. Haidt's domains of moral psychology illuminate these emotional dynamics, while Weiner's (2007) Attribution Theory adds depth by explaining how social norms shape emotional responses. This theory highlights twelve moral emotions that significantly affect individuals' perceptions and learning outcomes (Rudolph & Tscharaktschiew, 2014). Understanding how students attribute their successes and failures can guide educators to enhance motivation and emotional well-being. Students with stable external attributions might develop maladaptive emotional states. Maymon et al. (2018) found that students who blamed stable causes for tech problems felt more negative emotions, while online learners benefited emotionally from seeing minor issues as external or within their control. Student with internal attributions could improve their self-efficacy and engagement (e.g., Geng et al., 2024). Understanding the epistemological foundation of moral emotions and the significance of these emotions are significant both in facilitating language learning, and in shaping a positive classroom atmosphere, as well as language learners' emotional growth and ethical development.

For instance, emotions such as guilt, shame, empathy, and compassion significantly impact students' educational behaviors and outcomes. These self-conscious emotions play crucial roles in influencing students' perceptions of their academic responsibilities and their interactions with both peers and instructors (Wu & Kabilan, 2025). Delayed progress happens when a language learner might feel guilty for not dedicating enough time to their studies (Arnold, 1999), especially if they are aware of others who are working hard and making progress; while a student may feel guilty for not helping a fellow learner who is struggling, especially if they have already mastered some concepts or vocabulary (Eisenberg et al., 2014). A learner may feel grateful toward a teacher who goes above and beyond to provide resources, encouragement, or personalized feedback, motivating the student to engage more deeply with the language (e.g., Emmons & McCullough, 2004; Froh et al., 2008).

Moreover, empathy involves recognizing and sharing the feelings of others and is a powerful moral emotion that encourages supportive relationships among students (Eisenberg et al., 2014). For example, Li et al. (2024) found that behavior empathy is positively correlated with prosocial behavior among college students. According to Van de Vyver and Abrams (2017), elevation is more effective at promoting benevolence-oriented outcomes, while outrage is more effective at promoting justice-oriented outcomes. When empathy is cultivated in educational settings, it promotes cooperative learning environments where students are more likely to assist and motivate one another, fostering a sense of community. Empathetic students are more likely to engage in collaborative tasks (Silke et al., 2024) offering support that can significantly improve overall academic performance. For example, role-playing and group discussions centered around moral dilemmas, may promote peer support and enrich classroom dynamics (Alavi & Amini, 2024). Therefore, students skilled in empathetic engagement are more likely to contribute to a classroom atmosphere where emotional well-being is prioritized alongside academic achievement (e.g., Aldrup et al., 2022; Mercer, 2016). Empathy can help learners appreciate the values and emotions of speakers from diverse backgrounds, making interactions more meaningful (Kramsch, 2009). A learner's admiration for fluent speakers, accomplished language learners, or the literature, music, and traditions of the associated culture can inspire them to improve their skills and motivate them to emulate certain practices or attitudes, fostering a deeper connection and engagement with the language (Dörnyei, 2009).

Closely related to empathy, compassion extends the emotional experience beyond empathy to active caring and support for others. It fosters a supportive learning environment where students feel safe, connected, and willing to take risks in their learning endeavors (e.g., Jennings & Greenberg, 2009). Research indicates that compassionate classroom practices are linked to improved student outcomes, including higher levels of engagement and motivation (Roeser, 2017).

Moreover, according to Curtis (2023), moral and self-conscious emotions such as guilt and shame can act as internal negative feelings that discourage or penalize undesirable behavior. People vary in their propensity to feel guilt and shame. Those who are more likely to experience these emotions might anticipate how they would emotionally react to participating in unethical actions, like academic misconduct, which in turn could discourage them from pursuing such behavior (Curtis, 2023, p.743). For instance, guilt arises when individuals perceive that they have failed to meet their moral standards or obligations (Baumeister et al., 1994). In educational contexts, students who experience guilt over academic misconduct, such as cheating or not fulfilling collaborative responsibilities, are often motivated to adhere more closely to academic integrity (Curtis, 2023). This reflection prompts them to evaluate and adjust their behaviors, leading to enhanced accountability and self-regulation. The guilt-driven contemplation can also lead to reparative actions (Tangney et al., 2007), where students seek to make amends, ultimately fostering a culture of honesty and ethical behavior within the classroom.

Furthermore, shame is characterized by a negative evaluation of the self rather than the behavior (de Azevedo et al., 2022). It can result in feelings of worthlessness and disconnection, which may hinder academic performance. While shame can serve as a deterrent against unethical behaviors, it can also lead to withdrawal and avoidance, resulting in reduced engagement and motivation (Tangney et al., 2007). Therefore, while shame can lead to reflection, educational strategies must promote awareness of guilt rather than shame to foster a constructive emotional response to academic challenges.

These emotions significantly shape not only individual behavior but also the collective atmosphere of learning environments, proving essential in promoting a nurturing and cooperative classroom culture. Implementing educational practices that recognize the significance of moral emotions and emotional intelligence ultimately creates nurture-rich environments where all students can thrive both academically and socially.

3 Significance of Emotional Intelligence in Teaching and Learning

Emotional intelligence (EI), which involves managing one's own and others' emotions, is closely related to moral emotions as both influence behavior, but EI encompasses a broader set of emotional abilities beyond moral reasoning. While moral emotions provide key insights into student behavior, EI plays a crucial role in shaping educational outcomes. Emotional intelligence refers to the ability to identify, understand, manage, and utilize emotions effectively, both in oneself and in others (Goleman, 1995; Salovey & Mayer, 1990). The interplay between emotional and cognitive processes has garnered increased attention in educational research, emphasizing their significance in enhancing learning experiences (e.g., Alavi et al., 2017). Studies have highlighted a positive correlation between high emotional intelligence and academic achievement (e.g., MacCann et al., 2020). Students who demonstrate stronger emotional intelligence through skills in self-regulation, social awareness, and relationship management tend to have better academic and social outcomes (e.g., Durlak et al., 2011). Rezvani et al. (2019) reported that team emotional intelligence is positively associated with team performance, while, trust and conflict in the team mediate the association between team emotional intelligence and team performance.

Self-regulation, a key component of emotional intelligence, equips students with the ability to manage their emotional responses effectively. A study revealed that emotional intelligence has a notable impact on self-regulated learning, showing a 28.6% positive correlation in junior high school students (Dianah & Oktariza, 2024). Students who can regulate their emotional states are less likely to experience overwhelming anxiety or frustration during challenging academic tasks, enabling them to persist and perform well under pressure (Sam et al., 2022). Improved self-regulation strategies can help students remain focused, avoid procrastination, and maintain motivation throughout their academic pursuits. In this regard, AI can significantly enhance self-regulation by providing tailored feedback, progress tracking, and personalized resources (Zawacki-Richter et al., 2019). This support fosters the development of essential cognitive and emotional skills among students. The connection between self-regulation and emotional regulation indicates that emotional states profoundly influence decision-making processes (Carmona–Halty et al., 2019). For example, emotional stability, characterized by positive feelings and contentment, accelerates cognitive processing, particularly in subjects that require critical thinking, such as linguistics (Brandt et al., 2020). Conversely, negative emotional responses, such as anxiety and depression, can impede cognitive function and lead to decreased academic achievement (Brandt et al., 2020).

In some literary studies, the analysis revealed lessons on deep reflections and creativity that could be incorporated in language learning (e.g., Tee et al., 2022; Wan & Amini, 2020). For example, AI-driven storytelling or interactive narratives can similarly engage learners in moral and ethical discussions.

Emotional intelligence also influences students' intrinsic motivation to engage with their learning material (Ibrahim & AL-Ali, 2016). When students understand and appreciate the emotional aspects of their learning experiences, they become more motivated to participate actively in classroom discussions and activities. This motivation is further enhanced when educators employ emotionally aware pedagogical techniques, allowing students to connect learning objectives with their emotional landscapes. For example, Rahman et al (2024) found that emotional self-awareness and empathy in educators are closely linked to students' motivation for academic achievement, indicating that teachers with high emotional intelligence can foster increased student engagement. Moreover, achieving academic success remains a central focus of educational research (Neroni et al., 2019). Several studies reveal a positive correlation between students' emotional intelligence and their academic performance (Trigueros et al., 2019). When students feel recognized and valued, their self-efficacy increases (Shawky & Badawi, 2018). Emotional regulation, alongside emotional rehearsal and the maintenance of appropriate arousal levels, serves as a vital component of academic success (Amengual-Pizarro, 2018). By providing real-time support and resources tailored to students' individual emotional needs, educational institutions can foster more equitable learning environments. AI tools can enhance this recognition by analyzing student interactions, delivering constructive feedback, and fostering a learning environment wherein students feel validated and engaged. Interpersonal skills cultivated through emotional intelligence contribute to enhanced social relationships among students and teachers. Stronger relationships lead to open communication, creating an environment where students feel comfortable expressing their thoughts and asking for help. This sense of belonging and support helps mitigate feelings of isolation, ultimately improving academic performance. Students' emotional states significantly shape the learning process and outcomes (Tyng et al., 2017).

An essential facet of integrating moral emotions into educational settings is understanding how these emotions influence students' motivation and learning processes. For instance, feelings of guilt and shame can profoundly impact a learner's drive for self-improvement (Tangney & Dearing, 2002). Experiences of guilt, especially when performance falls short of expectations, often spur a desire for enhancement and personal growth. Such dynamics illustrate that emotional experiences are not only peripheral; they form the core of the overall learning process (Dörnyei & Ushioda, 2011; Shohamy, 2022). Recognizing the significance of these emotions can lead educators to foster environments that promote constructive emotional experiences, ultimately enhancing students' academic engagement and persistence. For example, Misailidi (2018) reported that children who show a better understanding of guilt also tend to perform better on theory of mind tasks, regardless of age. Likewise, integrating moral emotions significantly improves classroom dynamics, fostering engagement and cultivating an environment in which students feel valued and understood (Devi, 2024). Bandura's social cognitive theory underscores the importance of reinforcement in learning, demonstrating that the likelihood of replicating positive behaviors increases with adequate emotional engagement (Bandura & McClelland, 1977; Shawky & Badawi, 2018). Emotional engagement stemming from educational content has been shown to correlate significantly with learning efficiency (Burroughs & Barkauskas, 2017). Here, AI can play a pivotal role by utilizing data analytics to gauge levels of emotional engagement, thereby suggesting targeted interventions or modifications to learning materials. Such adjustments can enhance emotional resonance and help mitigate loneliness, reinforcing connections that are often weakened in virtual settings.

Incorporating moral emotions into teaching methodologies also enhances language learning effectiveness by fostering empathy, moral responsibility, and a supportive classroom atmosphere.

4 The Role of AI in Understanding Moral Emotions

As the educational landscape shifts towards more online and hybrid models, the integration of AI represents a significant advancement in nurturing the emotional dimensions of learning. Leveraging moral emotions through AI interventions can enhance academic performance while fostering a culture of emotional intelligence that benefits students beyond formal education (e.g., Vistorte et al., 2024). AI's multifaceted role includes real-time monitoring and assessment of students' emotional states through algorithms that analyze engagement patterns, facial expressions, and participation levels in online platforms (Picard et al., 2001). Such tools provide immediate feedback, helping educators adapt their teaching strategies based on students' emotional cues. For instance, if an AI system detects disengagement or frustration, it can suggest personalized interventions like additional resources or emotional support via chatbots or virtual counselors. This prompt response to emotional signals is crucial for maintaining a positive learning environment, which is essential for fostering student motivation and commitment.

Moreover, AI plays a pivotal role in bridging cognitive and emotional learning through the principles of affective computing, which involves developing systems that can recognize, interpret, and simulate human emotions (Picard, 1997). AI tools can create emotionally attuned learning environments by recognizing and responding to students' emotional cues (Khadimallah et al., 2020). When a student shows signs of frustration, affect-aware intelligent tutoring systems can recommend reviewing key concepts or offering motivational materials, fostering a supportive atmosphere (Woolf et al., 2009). This nuanced interaction empowers language learners to develop both linguistic skills and moral awareness, encouraging the growth of self-regulation strategies as students learn to manage their emotional responses (Bandura & McClelland, 1977; Broadbent, 2017). This integrative approach not only enhances academic and professional skills but also cultivates emotionally resilient, socially responsible individuals ready to navigate a complex world.

Furthermore, AI aids the creation of personalized learning experiences by analyzing data on students' interactions and assessments (Sajja et al., 2023). This process helps educators identify which moral emotions, such as empathy, compassion, or gratitude should be nurtured in specific groups or individuals to provide enriched feedback via Generative AI tools (Alsaiari et al., 2024). This targeted support optimizes academic outcomes while promoting emotional engagement within the learning community, ensuring students receive tailored resources to thrive. AI also enhances collaborative learning by facilitating meaningful engagement among peers (Kővári, 2025). Likewise, digital games and virtual environments can provide immersive, emotionally rich scenarios that promote both language acquisition and socio-emotional development, particularly for EFL/ESL learners (Reinders, 2012). The synergy of emotional intelligence and AI capabilities equips students to excel academically while nurturing resilience and empathy, qualities vital for thriving in diverse and dynamic social contexts. Research suggests that students with higher emotional intelligence are more receptive to AI-enhanced learning environments, leading to improved learning experiences (Alenezi, 2024).

Enhancing these qualities can empower students to tackle challenges with confidence and insight, ensuring they emerge as individuals capable of contributing positively to society (Amin et al., 2018). AI-driven platforms can strengthen language learners' understanding of ethical issues and nurture a commitment to principled behavior among peers. Additionally, AI tools can promote reflective practices through various mechanisms (Holmes et al., 2019), encouraging ESL/EFL students to share insights on moral dilemmas or collaborative projects. This sharing enriches their understanding of diverse perspectives, ultimately enhancing their emotional intelligence.

5 The Role of Intercultural Competence and Academic Achievement

Emphasizing moral emotions can help students appreciate cultural differences, fostering the moral sentiments necessary for navigating today's interconnected world. The integration of humanistic-oriented instruction along with AI support is correlated with increases in student motivation, engagement, and ownership of learning outcomes (Syafira et al., 2024). AI can support inclusive, personalized, and culturally aware learning environments, promoting values like empathy, collaboration, and global competence (Luckin et al., 2016). Several studies illustrate a strong link between moral emotions and intercultural competence, asserting that emotions like empathy, respect, and openness are essential for effective intercultural engagement (Calloway-Thomas et al., 2017). AI systems can support this by providing analytics on students' interactions while suggesting personalized activities that enhance intercultural sensitivity. These initiatives not only deepen understanding and connection across cultures but also create a classroom atmosphere rich in sensitivity and awareness of varying social contexts.

Research increasingly connects emotional intelligence with academic achievement. A meta-analysis conducted by MacCann et al. (2020) revealed that individuals with higher emotional intelligence tend to perform better academically. This success correlates with superior emotional regulation capabilities that facilitate effective academic decision-making, underscoring the importance of integrating emotional intelligence training into the curriculum—especially in a rapidly changing educational environment. In this regard, AI-driven interventions can monitor and respond to these emotional states by offering resources, and coping strategies, and fostering positive emotional experiences. For instance, gratitude and sympathy has been linked to outstanding academic performance, serving as vital motivational factors (Carmona–Halty et al., 2019). Interestingly, while emotions such as guilt and shame are typically associated with negative experiences, recent research indicates a positive correlation between these emotions and improvements in academic performance. Manganelli et al. (2019) discovered that when effectively managed, high levels of shame can act as motivators for enhanced performance despite the challenges they may present to self-esteem. This points to the transformative potential of AI in education: by helping educators understand the complexities of students' emotional experiences, these systems can navigate the intricacies of emotional intelligence, facilitating an educational landscape that enriches both academic performance and emotional well-being.

6 Transformative Potential of AI in Education

AI emerges as a transformative element capable of bridging the gap between emotional and cognitive learning. AI technologies can be designed to recognize and respond to students' emotional states, offering tailored support that addresses their unique needs. For example, AI-driven platforms can utilize natural language processing and sentiment analysis to assess students' written interactions, identifying emotional cues that indicate frustration, confusion, or disengagement. By analyzing these signals, educators can employ targeted interventions, providing reassurance or additional resources to enhance students' emotional well-being. AI chatbots, as highlighted by Wu and Yu, can create a relaxed learning atmosphere by detecting students' emotions and providing emotional support, thus alleviating anxiety and fostering a more conducive learning environment (Wu & Yu, 2023). As traditional educational frameworks have often prioritized cognitive processes, including knowledge acquisition and memory retention, the essential role of emotions has been overlooked (Tyng et al., 2017). This oversight has resulted in a growing recognition of the affective dimensions of learning environments, emphasizing the need for pedagogical strategies that incorporate emotional frameworks into curriculum design. Jafari notes that leveraging AI to detect and address students' emotions allows educators to optimize engagement and comprehension, thereby enhancing the overall learning experience (Jafari, 2024). These findings suggest that AI tools can effectively bridge the gap between cognitive and emotional learning, fostering an environment conducive to moral development. Several categories of AI tools in language learning are briefly explained here.

7 Sentiment Analysis and Adaptive Learning Platforms

AI-driven sentiment analysis tools have shown promise in assessing and responding to students' emotional states, thereby facilitating a more emotionally responsive learning environment. For example, utilizing Natural Language Processing (NLP), these tools assess the emotional tone of students' spoken and written language. By tracking emotional expressions, educators can promote moral emotions, ultimately enhancing empathy and gratitude among learners. Vistorte emphasizes that AI technologies can significantly enhance the accuracy of emotion classification in educational settings, which is vital for tailoring pedagogical approaches to individual learner needs (Vistorte et al, 2024). In an EFL/ESL classroom, sentiment analysis can be applied to enhance feedback provided to students on their writing assignments (e.g., Phoophuangpairoj, & Pipattarasakul, 2022). The sentiment analysis software processes the assignments to identify not only the overall sentiment (positive, negative, or neutral) but also the specific emotional content related to the language used (Shaik et al., 2023). A student whose essay reflects high levels of enthusiasm may receive feedback that acknowledges and encourages their engagement.

Furthermore, adaptive learning platform systems personalize educational experiences based on students' individual needs. By integrating elements of emotional intelligence, they adapt content according to learners' emotional states and learning preferences (Halkiopoulos & Gkintoni, 2024). Some adaptive learning platforms are designed for ESL and EFL students. They utilize AI to customize learning experiences according to the individual needs, emotional states, and learning preferences of each student. Such platforms can provide real-time feedback on students' emotional tones and the moral implications of their communication, which is essential for developing both language proficiency and emotional intelligence. For example, Akintayo discusses how AI systems can deliver personalized feedback and adaptive learning experiences that enhance students' emotional intelligence and social competence (Akintayo, 2024). This capability is particularly beneficial in EFL and ESL contexts, where learners often face anxiety and stress related to language acquisition.

8 Virtual Emotional Intelligence Coaches and AI-Powered Feedback Systems

Virtual emotional intelligence coaches are AI-driven tools like chatbots designed to enhance emotional awareness and regulation by interpreting user inputs and offering personalized, emotion-based feedback (Bilquise et al., 2021; Casheekar et al., 2024). They are designed to assess, develop, and enhance users' emotional intelligence. These tools utilize technologies such as natural language processing, sentiment analysis, facial expression recognition, and behavioral data tracking to provide personalized feedback and training on emotional competencies like self-awareness, empathy, emotional regulation, and interpersonal communication (Wu & Amini, 2025). They are often used in educational, corporate, and therapeutic settings to foster emotional growth and social-emotional learning. Essentially, it functions as a virtual coach, capable of recognizing emotional response patterns and recommending ways to improve, all without the necessity for a human coach. In other words, AI-driven EQ coaches facilitate discussions that demand moral reasoning (Keshishi & Hack, 2023). They enable students to explore and understand moral emotions through role-playing and guided scenarios, creating enriching learning experiences.

Moreover, AI-driven feedback tools provide immediate insights into language use and communication styles, analyzing the emotional and moral dimensions of students' expressions (Zawacki-Richter et al., 2019). This functionality supports the development of more empathetic and constructive communication skills. By integrating these tools, AI enhances the learning experience while fostering a deeper understanding of moral emotions, equipping students with the emotional and cognitive abilities necessary for success in an interconnected world. The multifaceted role of AI extends beyond mere language support; it actively cultivates an emotionally intelligent learning community. Educators can harness AI's potential to enhance both linguistic and moral development, ensuring that students are prepared for future challenges. Additionally, in online learning environments where social interaction may be limited (Heng et al., 2024), AI can help create a sense of community among students. AI-driven platforms can facilitate collaborative projects and group discussions, fostering peer-to-peer engagement. These interactions promote shared emotional experiences and strengthen interpersonal relationships, which are essential for building social skills and emotional intelligence. Through navigating emotional dynamics in collaborative settings, students can develop a more nuanced understanding of social interactions (Ravindran et al., 2023). Therefore, the implications of AI tools for creating emotionally responsive and morally aware EFL/ESL classrooms are significant. They not only support language learning but also influence moral and emotional development, enriching the educational experience for students.

9 Integrating AI into Curriculum Design and the Potential Challenges in EFL and ESL Contexts

Integrating AI into EFL and ESL curriculum design necessitates a focused approach that emphasizes strategies for enhancing emotional intelligence. Educators should utilize AI tools to create interactive and engaging learning experiences. For example, AI-driven platforms can curate content that specifically addresses students' emotional needs and learning styles. By analyzing student interactions, these tools can deliver personalized feedback that encourages self-reflection on emotional responses to diverse learning situations. Incorporating AI-based moral emotion analysis into classroom activities can take practical forms, such as utilizing AI chatbots that simulate ethical dilemmas. This setup encourages students to engage in meaningful discussions about moral choices. Such interactions can be structured to support assessments, reflective exercises, and collaborative projects centered around understanding emotions in the learning context. Research shows that these reflective practices not only enhance critical thinking (Zeng et al., 2023) but also promote self-awareness, both of which are vital components of emotional intelligence. Active collaboration between AI developers, linguists, and educators is essential for constructing AI-supported frameworks that integrate linguistic skills with emotional development. Curriculum developers can partner with AI experts to design learning modules that assess language proficiency alongside students' emotional engagement, leading to a more comprehensive evaluation of their overall capabilities. Moreover, educators should integrate emotional competence directly into subject content through methods such as role-playing and scenario-based learning. These techniques contextualize academic lessons within real-world emotional interactions, ensuring students gain academic knowledge while also honing essential emotional skills necessary for personal and professional growth. As suggested by Abd Aziz (2024), integrating emotional intelligence training into the curriculum can be achieved through initiatives such as workshops focusing on emotional regulation and communication skills. This dual emphasis on cognitive and emotional development will enrich learning experiences and cultivate a more compassionate, interconnected educational community. To effectively integrate AI tools into EFL and ESL curricula, a reassessment of instructional strategies aimed at nurturing emotional intelligence is crucial. Educators should explore the technical capabilities of AI while ensuring these tools fit within transformative pedagogical frameworks. Incorporating AI-driven moral emotion analysis into assessments and reflective exercises can deepen engagement with moral emotions (Shawky & Badawi, 2018). Such practices promote critical thinking (Ravindran et al., 2025; Zeng et al., 2023) and self-awareness as students learn to evaluate their emotional responses in learning contexts. Ultimately, it is imperative that curriculum designers and educators embed emotional competence within subject content and teaching methodologies, facilitating students' acquisition of both academic knowledge and the emotional skills needed for holistic development. This dual focus on cognitive and emotional learning not only enhances individual educational experiences but also fosters a more empathetic, responsible, and connected learning community. Integrating emotional intelligence training into curricula, as advocated by Abd Aziz (2024), empowers students to navigate their emotional landscapes effectively and prepares them for the multifaceted challenges of modern life by combining social-emotional learning with academic skills.

On the other hand, despite the potential benefits, the integration of AI tools in EFL and ESL contexts is not without challenges. One significant concern is the current limitations of AI in replicating the empathy and emotional intelligence inherent in human educators. While AI can perform certain coaching functions, it lacks the nuanced understanding and emotional depth that human coaches provide (Plotkina & Sri Ramalu, 2024). This limitation raises questions about the effectiveness of AI in fully addressing the moral and emotional needs of learners. Moreover, the ethical implications of using AI in education must be carefully considered, as highlighted by Schuller and Schuller (2018), who discuss the importance of emotional intelligence in AI systems to ensure they are used responsibly and effectively. Furthermore, some unique challenges can be posed in the cases of online education, including the lack of in-person interaction, exacerbating emotional strain on students (Kebritchi et al., 2017). This has been shown to negatively impact academic performance, as feelings of loneliness, anxiety (Sam et al., 2022), and disconnection can significantly diminish motivation and engagement (Erzen, 2017). To counteract these adverse emotional states, AI tools can be leveraged to monitor emotional indicators such as participation, writing tone, or engagement levels. By facilitating timely interventions based on these insights, educators can nurture a more supportive online learning atmosphere, thereby improving students' emotional well-being and academic outcomes. For example, participating in role-play or situational exercises can allow learners to practice empathy and moral reasoning in a safe space, effectively preparing them for real-world interactions and challenges.

Therefore, it is essential to recognize how AI interventions can specifically address the emotional challenges faced by learners in online environments. As outlined, moral emotions significantly shape student engagement and learning outcomes; thus, understanding these dynamics in the context of digital education becomes paramount. In online settings, where traditional support systems are often diminished, the integration of AI tools offers unique advantages. AI can help cultivate a more socially responsive learning atmosphere. The enhanced capacity of AI to promote self-regulation skills allows learners to better navigate the emotional complexities that arise in isolation while tackling academic challenges. Consequently, this intersection highlights the transformative potential of AI not only in fostering language proficiency but also in nurturing the moral and emotional development of students. As we move forward, research and curriculum design must prioritize these emotional dimensions, ensuring that AI technologies are deployed in ways that recognize and enhance the unique emotional experiences of learners in digital and online settings.

10 Emotional Dynamics in Digital and Online Learning

The significance of understanding emotional dynamics is particularly pronounced in online learning scenarios, where traditional support structures often become less accessible. In such environments, students may confront academic challenges (Mailizar et al., 2020) in isolation, devoid of the immediate social feedback and encouragement typically provided in physical classrooms. Comparative studies show that students engaged in online learning tend to employ self-regulation strategies more often than their counterparts in blended learning environments (Allen & Seaman, 2014; Broadbent, 2017; Yli-Piipari et al., 2009). Thus, online learning can create conditions that promote independence in reflection and critical thinking. Such self-awareness and cognitive autonomy enable students to effectively navigate academic challenges and achieve satisfactory outcomes. Addressing these emotional components of learning, particularly through AI interventions, becomes critical in fostering a supportive online educational atmosphere.

11 Conclusion

The application of AI tools in incorporating moral emotions within EFL and ESL contexts presents significant opportunities for enhancing learners' emotional and language development. While AI technologies can facilitate personalized learning experiences and provide valuable insights into students' emotional states, the challenges related to empathy and ethical considerations must be addressed. As AI technologies continue to evolve, their capacity to enrich both cognitive and emotional dimensions of language learning will become increasingly significant. Future research and curriculum development efforts must focus on optimizing the ethical and cultural relevance of AI tools, ensuring that language learners receive a holistic and socially responsible education. In this transformative era, integrating moral emotions into educational practices, amplified by AI, establishes a critical shift that equips students with the resilience, empathy, and ethical understanding necessary to navigate the complexities of contemporary life successfully. Exploring how AI-driven emotional intelligence can be customized to meet the unique needs of various learners will enhance the cultivation of moral emotions across different backgrounds and cultural settings. Additionally, it is crucial to consider the ethical implications of AI in education, such as data privacy and the potential for bias in emotion recognition algorithms. Investigating the long-term effects of AI-assisted emotional learning on moral development can provide deeper insights into the educational potential of these innovations, highlighting academic outcomes for language learners.

Acknowledgements This work was supported by a Universiti Sains Malaysia, Short-Term Grant with **ProjectNo:304/PBAHASA/6315692.**

AI Declaration In writing process of this article, an AI tool (Google Gemini) was used for language editing and proofreading of the final manuscript.

References

Abd Aziz, N. S. (2024). Exploring the state of mental well-being among b40 women. *Journal of the Malaysian Parliament, 4*, 293–306. https://doi.org/10.54313/journalmp.v4i.132

Akintayo, O. (2024). Integrating AI with emotional and social learning in primary education: Developing a holistic adaptive learning ecosystem. *Computer Science & IT Research Journal, 5*(5), 1076–1089. https://doi.org/10.51594/csitrj.v5i5.1116

Alavi, M., Mehrinezhad, S. A., Amini, M., & Kaur A/P Parthaman Singh, M. (2017). Family functioning and trait emotional intelligence among youth. *Health Psychology Open*, 1–5. https://doi.org/10.1177/2055102917748461

Alavi, S., & Amini, M. (2024). The ethical dilemma of academic integrity and job security: A quantitative study on moral obligations in competitive academic environments in Thailand. *Asia Social Issues, 17*(5), e267154. https://doi.org/10.48048/asi.2024.267154

Aldrup, K., Carstensen, B., & Klusmann, U. (2022). Is empathy the key to effective teaching? A systematic review of its association with teacher-student interactions and student outcomes. *Educational Psychology Review, 34*(3), 1177–1216. https://doi.org/10.1007/s10648-021-09649-y

Alenezi, A. (2024). The effect of Emotional Intelligence on higher education: A pilot study on the interplay between Artificial Intelligence, Emotional Intelligence, and E-Learning. *Multidisciplinary Journal for Education, Social and Technological Sciences, 11*(2), 51–77. https://doi.org/10.4995/muse.2024.21367

Allen, I. E., & Seaman, J. (2014). *Grade change: Tracking online education in the United States*. Babson Survey Research Group. https://www.bayviewanalytics.com/reports/gradechange.pdf

Mailizar, Almanthari, A., Maulina, S., & Bruce, S. (2020). Secondary school mathematics teachers' views on Elearning implementation barriers during the COVID-19 pandemic: The case of Indonesia. *Eurasia Journal of Mathematics, Science and Technology Education, 16*(7), em1860. https://eric.ed.gov/?id=EJ1272650

Alsaiari, O., Baghaei, N., Lahza, H., Lodge, J., Boden, M., & Khosravi, H. (2024). Emotionally enriched feedback via Generative AI. *ArXiv*. https://arxiv.org/abs/2410.15077

Amengual-Pizarro, M. (2018). Foreign language classroom anxiety among English for Specific Purposes (ESP) students. *International Journal of English Studies, 18*(2), 145–159. https://revistas.um.es/ijes/article/view/323311

Amin, A., Zolkifeli, Z., Latib, M. F. A., & Som, A. P. M. (2018). Relationship between social capital and mental health on quality of life among low-income group (b40) in Terengganu. *International Journal of Academic Research in Business and Social Sciences, 8*(9), 1309–1320. https://doi.org/10.6007/ijarbss/v8-i9/4698

Amini, D., & Amini, M. (2017). Integrating emotional, motivational and cognitive engagement to create state of flow in language learning tasks. *Journal of Language and Communication, 4*(1), 27–41. https://journalfbmk.upm.edu.my/ojs3/index.php/jlc/article/view/45

Amini, M., Alavi, M., Alavi, S., Sadacharam, J., Alipour, M., & Amini, D. (2024a). A review on the role of moral emotions in EFL learning. *International Journal of Academic Research in Progressive Education and Development, 13*(1), 2533–2544. https://doi.org/10.6007/IJARPED/v13-i1/21133

Amini, M., Ravindran, L., & Lee, K-F. (2024b). Implications of using AI in Translation Studies: Trends, challenges, and future direction. *Asian Journal of Research in Education and Social Sciences, 6* (1), 740–754). https://myjms.mohe.gov.my/index.php/ajress/article/view/24617

Amini, M., Wang, Q., Amini, D., Ravindran, L., Tan, A. L. D., Ganapathy, M., & Singh, M. K. M. (2025). The significance of humanistic approach and moral development in English language classrooms. *Discover Education, 4*, 238. https://doi.org/10.1007/s44217-025-00691-4

Arnold, J. (Ed.). (1999). *Affect in language learning*. Cambridge University Press.

Bandura, A., & McClelland, D. C. (1977). *Social learning theory* (Vol. 1). Prentice Hall.

Baumeister, R. F., Stillwell, A. M., & Heatherton, T. F. (1994). Guilt: An interpersonal approach. *Psychological Bulletin, 115*(2), 243–267. https://doi.org/10.1037/0033-2909.115.2.243

Bilquise, G., Ibrahim, S., & Shaalan, K. (2021). Emotionally Intelligent Chatbots: A Systematic Literature Review. *Human Behavior and Emerging Technologies, 2022*(1), 9601630. https://doi.org/10.1155/2022/9601630

Brandt, N. D., Lechner, C. M., Tetzner, J., & Rammstedt, B. (2020). Personality, cognitive ability, and academic performance: Differential associations across school subjects and school tracks. *Journal of Personality, 88*(2), 249–265. https://doi.org/10.1111/jopy.12482

Broadbent, J. (2017). Comparing online and blended learner's self-regulated learning strategies and academic performance. *The Internet and Higher Education, 33*, 24–32. https://doi.org/10.1016/j.iheduc.2017.01.004

Burroughs, M. D., & Barkauskas, N. J. (2017). Educating the whole child: Social-emotional learning and ethics education. *Ethics and Education, 12*(2), 218–232. https://doi.org/10.1080/17449642.2017.1287388

Calloway-Thomas, C., Arasaratnam-Smith, L. A., & Deardorff, D. K. (2017). The role of empathy in fostering intercultural competence. *Intercultural Competence in Higher Education*, 32–42. https://doi.org/10.4324/9781315529257-4

Carmona-Halty, M., Salanova, M., Llorens, S., & Schaufeli, W. B. (2019). How psychological capital mediates between study–related positive emotions and academic performance. *Journal of Happiness Studies, 20*(2), 605–617. https://doi.org/10.1007/s10902-018-9963-5

Casheekar, A., Lahiri, A., Rath, K., Prabhakar, K. S., & Srinivasan, K. (2024). A contemporary review on chatbots, ai-powered virtual conversational agents, ChatGPT: Applications, open challenges and future research directions. *Computer Science Review, 52*, Article 100632. https://doi.org/10.1016/j.cosrev.2024.100632

Curtis, G. J. (2023). Guilt, shame, and academic misconduct. *Journal of Academic Ethics, 21*(4), 743–757. https://doi.org/10.1007/s10805-023-09480-w

Devi, B. D. (2024). Humanistic curriculum by accentuating confluent and consciousness forms—an overview. *Thiagarajar College of Preceptors Edu Spectra, 6*(2), 27–34. https://doi.org/10.34293/eduspectra.v6i2.05

Dianah, L., & Oktariza, S. (2024). The effect of emotional intelligence on student self regulated learning. *Journal Civics and Social Studies, 8*(1), 14–24. https://doi.org/10.31980/journalcss.v8i1.984

de Azevedo, F., Simão André, R., Quintão, A., Jeremias, D., & Almeida, C. (2022). Shame and psychopathology. Its role in the genesis and perpetuation of different disorders. *European Psychiatry, 65*(S1), S703. https://doi.org/10.1192/j.eurpsy.2022.1811

Dörnyei, Z. (2009). *The psychology of second language acquisition.* Oxford University Press.

Dörnyei, Z., & Ushioda, E. (2011). *Teaching and researching motivation.* Pearson Education.

Durlak, J. A., Weissberg, R. P., Dymnicki, A. B., Taylor, R. D., & Schellinger, K. B. (2011). The impact of enhancing students' social and emotional learning: A meta-analysis of school-based universal interventions. *Child Development, 82*(1), 405–432. https://doi.org/10.1111/j.1467-8624.2010.01564.x

Emmons, R. A., & McCullough, M. E. (Eds.). (2004). *The psychology of gratitude.* Oxford University Press. https://doi.org/10.1093/acprof:oso/9780195150100.001.0001

Eisenberg, N., Spinrad, T. L., & Morris, A. S. (2014). Empathy-related responding in children. In M. Killen & J. G. Smetana (Eds.), *Handbook of moral development* (2nd ed., pp. 184–207). Psychology Press.

Erzen, E. (2017). The effect of anxiety on student achievement. In *The factors affecting student achievement* (pp. 75–94). Springer, Cham. https://doi.org/10.1007/978-3-319-56083-0

Fredrickson, B. L. (2001). The role of positive emotions in positive psychology: The broaden-and-build theory of positive emotions. *American Psychologist, 56*(3), 218–226. https://doi.org/10.1037/0003-066X.56.3.218

Froh, J. J., Sefick, W. J., & Emmons, R. A. (2008). Counting blessings in early adolescents: An experimental study of gratitude and subjective well-being. *Journal of School Psychology, 46*(2), 213–233. https://doi.org/10.1016/j.jsp.2007.03.005

Geng, Q., Amini, M., Binti Hashim, S. N. A., & Zhu, M. (2024). The mediating roles of academic self-efficacy and learning interest in the relationship between teaching style and math behavior engagement among junior high school students in China. *PLoS ONE, 19*(10), Article e0311959. https://doi.org/10.1371/journal.pone.0311959)

Giner-Sorolla, R. (2013). *Judging passions: Moral emotions in persons and groups.* Psychology Press.

Goleman, D. P. (1995). *Emotional intelligence: Why it can matter more than IQ.* Bantam Books.

Ha, Y. N., & Ho, N. P. (2025). EFL postgraduate students' perceptions on the use of Grammarly and peer feedback to improve their academic writing skills. *International Journal of TESOL & Education, 5*(1), 25–49. https://doi.org/10.54855/ijte.25512

Haidt, J. (2001). The emotional dog and its rational tail: A social intuitionist approach to moral judgment. *Psychological Review 108* (4), 814–834. https://doi.org/10.1037/0033-295X.108.4.814

Haidt, J. (2003). The moral emotions. In R. J. Davidson, K. R. Scherer, & H. H. Goldsmith (Eds.), *Handbook of affective sciences* (pp. 852–870). Oxford University Press. https://people.stern.nyu.edu/jhaidt/articles/alternate_versions/haidt.2003.the-moral-emotions.pub025-as-html.html

Halkiopoulos, C., & Gkintoni, E. (2024). Leveraging AI in e-learning: Personalized learning and adaptive assessment through cognitive neuropsychology—A systematic analysis. *Electronics, 13*(18), 3762. https://doi.org/10.3390/electronics13183762)

Heng, J. X., Lee, K.F., Amini, M. & Ravindran, L. (2024). Instructors' perceptions and pedagogical approaches to online teaching in selected Malaysian private universities. *International Journal of Evaluation and Research in Education (IJERE), 13*(4), 2650–2658. https://doi.org/10.11591/ijere.v13i4.28718

Ho, N. P., & Ha, Y. N. (2025). Evaluation of the effectiveness of learning outcomes from students' perspectives towards research writing course: A case study. *International Journal of Language Instruction, 4*(1), 33–49. https://doi.org/10.54855/ijli.25413

Holmes, W., Bialik, M., & Fadel, C. (2019). *Artificial intelligence in education: Promises and implications for teaching and learning*. Center for Curriculum Redesign. https://curriculumredesign.org/wp-content/uploads/AIED-Book-Excerpt-CCR.pdf

Ibrahim, I. R. A., & AL-Ali, W. A. (2016). The academic intrinsic motivation and its relationship with the emotional intelligence level with a sample of the academic overachievers and underachievers of Najran university. *Journal of Studies in Education, 6*(2), 1–15. https://doi.org/10.5296/jse.v6i2.9234

Jafari, E. (2024). Artificial intelligence and learning environment: Human considerations. *Journal of Computer Assisted Learning, 40*(5), 2135–2149. https://doi.org/10.1111/jcal.13011

Jennings, P. A., & Greenberg, M. T. (2009). The prosocial classroom: Teacher social and emotional competence in relation to student and classroom outcomes. *Review of Educational Research, 79*(1), 491–525. https://doi.org/10.3102/0034654308325693

Kebritchi, M., Lipschuetz, A., & Santiague, L. (2017). Issues and challenges for teaching successful online courses in higher education: A literature review. *Journal of Educational Technology Systems, 46*(1), 4–29. https://doi.org/10.1177/0047239516661713

Keshishi, N., & Hack, S. (2023). Emotional intelligence in the digital age: Harnessing AI for students' inner development. *Journal of Perspectives in Applied Academic Practice, 11*(3). https://doi.org/10.56433/jpaap.v11i3.579

Khadimallah, R., Abdelkefi, M., & Kallel, I. (2020). Emotion regulation in intelligent tutoring systems: A systematic literature review. In *2020 IEEE international conference on teaching, assessment, and learning for engineering (TALE)* (pp. 363–370). IEEE. https://doi.org/10.1109/TALE48869.2020.9368372

Kim, J. E., & Johnson, K. K. (2013). The impact of moral emotions on cause-related marketing campaigns: A cross-cultural examination. *Journal of Business Ethics, 112*(1), 79–90. https://doi.org/10.1007/s10551-012-1233-6

Kővári, A. (2025). A systematic review of AI-powered collaborative learning in higher education: Trends and outcomes from the last decade. *Social Sciences & Humanities Open, 11*, Article 101335. https://doi.org/10.1016/j.ssaho.2025.101335

Kramsch, C. (2009). *The multilingual subject: What foreign language learners say about their experience and why it matters*. Oxford University Press.

Li, C., Dewaele, J. M., & Jiang, G. (2019). The complex relationship between classroom emotions and EFL achievement in China. *Applied Linguistics Review, 11*(3), 485–510.https://doi.org/10.1515/applirev-2018-0043

Li, P., Jiang, Y., Ye, J., & Xiong, Z. (2024). The impact of empathy on prosocial behavior among college students: The mediating role of moral identity and the moderating role of sense of security. *Behavioral Sciences, 14*(11), 1024. https://doi.org/10.3390/bs14111024

Luckin, R., Holmes, W., Griffiths, M., & Forcier, L. B. (2016). *Intelligence unleashed: An argument for AI in education*. Pearson Education. https://oro.open.ac.uk/50104/

MacCann, C., Jiang, Y., Brown, L. E., Double, K. S., Bucich, M., & Minbashian, A. (2020). Emotional intelligence predicts academic performance: A meta-analysis. *Psychological Bulletin, 146*(2), 150. https://doi.org/10.1037/bul0000219

Manganelli, S., Cavicchiolo, E., Mallia, L., Biasi, V., Lucidi, F., & Alivernini, F. (2019). The interplay between self-determined motivation, self-regulated cognitive strategies, and prior achievement in predicting academic performance. *Educational Psychology, 39*(4), 470–488. https://doi.org/10.1080/01443410.2019.1572104

Maymon, R., Hall, N. C., Goetz, T., Chiarella, A., & Rahimi, S. (2018). Technology, attributions, and emotions in post-secondary education: An application of Weiner's attribution theory to academic computing problems. *PLoS ONE, 13*(3), Article e0193443. https://doi.org/10.1371/journal.pone.0193443

McCullough, M. E., Kilpatrick, S. D., Emmons, R. A., & Larson, D. B. (2001). Is gratitude a moral affect? *Psychological Bulletin, 127*(2), 249–266. https://doi.org/10.1037/0033-2909.127.2.249

Mercer, S. (2016). Seeing the world through your eyes: Empathy in language learning and teaching. *ELT Journal, 70*(2), 171–179. https://doi.org/10.1093/elt/ccv063

Misailidi, P. (2018). Individual differences in children's understanding of guilt: Links with theory of mind. *The Journal of Genetic Psychology, 179*(4), 219–229. https://doi.org/10.1080/00221325.2018.1474848

Neroni, J., Meijs, C., Gijselaers, H. J., Kirschner, P. A., & de Groot, R. H. (2019). Learning strategies and academic performance in distance education. *Learning and Individual Differences, 73*, 1–7. https://doi.org/10.1016/j.lindif.2019.04.007

Pekrun, R., & Linnenbrink-Garcia, L. (2012). Academic emotions and student engagement. In S. L. Christenson, A. L. Reschly, & C. Wylie (Eds.), *Handbook of research on student engagement* (pp. 259–282). Springer. https://doi.org/10.1007/978-1-4614-2018-7_12

Picard, R. W. (1997). *Affective computing*. MIT Press.

Picard, R. W., Vyzas, E., & Healey, J. (2001). Toward machine emotional intelligence: Analysis of affective physiological state. *IEEE Transactions on Pattern Analysis and Machine Intelligence, 23*(10), 1175–1191. https://doi.org/10.1109/34.954607

Pham, M. T., & Cao, T. X. T. (2025). The practice of ChatGPT in English teaching and learning in Vietnam: A systematic review. *International Journal of TESOL & Education, 5*(1), 50–70. https://doi.org/10.54855/ijte.25513

Phoophuangpairoj, R., & Pipattarasakul, P. (2022). Preliminary indicators of EFL essay writing for teachers' feedback using automatic text analysis. *International Journal of Educational Methodology, 8*(1), 55–68. https://doi.org/10.12973/ijem.8.1.55

Plotkina, L., & Sri Ramalu, S. (2024). Unearthing AI coaching chatbots capabilities for professional coaching: A systematic literature review. *Journal of Management Development, 43*(6), 833–848. https://doi.org/10.1108/jmd-06-2024-0182

Rahman, Md. H., Amin, M. B., Yusof, M. F., Islam, Md. A., & Afrin, S. (2024). Influence of teachers' emotional intelligence on students' motivation for academic learning: An empirical study on university students of Bangladesh. *Cogent Education*. https://doi.org/10.1080/2331186x.2024.2327752

Ravindran, L., Lee, KF., & Amini, M. (2023). Pedagogical approaches of ESL educators with an intent-focussing on interaction, time and pace during COVID-19: Lessons learned. In M. So-Sum Wai-Cook, A. Saleh, & K. Bista (Eds.), *Online teaching and learning in Asian higher education* (pp. 101–125). Palgrave Macmillan, Cham: Springer Nature Switzerland AG. https://doi.org/10.1007/978-3-031-38129-4_6

Ravindran, L., Amini, M., & Fong, L. K. (2025). Developing critical thinking skills in EFL teaching: Approaches and trends. In S. Mekala & M. P. Shabitha (Eds.), *Thinking skills in higher education* (pp. 279–294). Springer. https://doi.org/10.1007/978-981-96-5600-4_21

Reinders, H. (2012). *Digital Games in Language Learning and Teaching*. https://doi.org/10.1057/9781137005267

Ren, J., & Gao, X. X. (2011). Moral emotions: The moral behavior's intermediary mediation. *Advances in Psychological Science, 19*(8), 1224–1232. https://journal.psych.ac.cn/xlkxjz/EN/abstract/abstract1986.shtml

Rezvani, A., Barrett, R., & Khosravi, P. (2019). Investigating the relationships among team emotional intelligence, trust, conflict, and team performance. *Team Performance Management: An International Journal, 25*(1/2), 120–137. https://doi.org/10.1108/TPM-03-2018-0019

Roeser, S. (2017). *Risk, technology, and moral emotions*. Routledge.

Rudolph, U., & Tscharaktschiew, N. (2014). An attributional analysis of moral emotions: Naïve scientists and everyday judges. *Emotion Review, 6*(4), 344–352. https://doi.org/10.1177/1754073914534507

Sam, M. M. Y., Siau, C. S., Fitriana, M., Amini, M., Rabbani, M., Prawiromaruto, I. G., & Yahya, A. N. (2022). Internet use and addiction symptoms among young adults during the COVID-19 movement control order: Associations with anxiety and depression. *Kasetsart Journal of Social Sciences, 43*(1), 159–165. https://so04.tci-thaijo.org/index.php/kjss/article/view/257006

Sajja, R., Sermet, Y., Cwiertny, D., & Demir, I. (2023). Integrating AI and learning analytics for data-driven pedagogical decisions and personalized interventions in education. *ArXiv*. https://arxiv.org/abs/2312.09548

Schuller, D., & Schuller, B. (2018). The age of artificial emotional intelligence. *Computer, 51*(9), 38–46. https://doi.org/10.1109/mc.2018.3620963

Shaik, T., Tao, X., Dann, C., Xie, H., Li, Y., & Galligan, L. (2023). Sentiment analysis and opinion mining on educational data: A survey. *ArXiv*. https://doi.org/10.1016/j.nlp.2022.100003

Shawky, D., & Badawi, A. (2018). A reinforcement learning-based adaptive learning system. In *International conference on advanced machine learning technologies and applications* (pp. 221–231). Springer.

Shohamy, E. (2022). Language testing/assessment and linguistic human rights. In Y. Baiza (Ed.), *The handbook of linguistic human rights* (pp. 605–612). https://doi.org/10.1002/9781119753926.ch46

Silke, C., Davitt, E., Flynn, N., Shaw, A., Brady, B., Murray, C., & Dolan, P. (2024). Activating social empathy: An evaluation of a school-based social and emotional learning programme. *Social and Emotional Learning: Research, Practice, and Policy, 3*, Article 100021. https://doi.org/10.1016/j.sel.2023.100021

Salovey, P., & Mayer, J. D. (1990). Emotional intelligence. *Imagination, Cognition and Personality, 9*(3), 185–211. https://doi.org/10.2190/DUGG-P24E-52WK-6CDG

Syafira, N. P., Yusuf, A., Prayuga, N. G. A. P., & Putri, N. H. (2024). Learning theory according to humanistic psychology and its implementation in students. *Progres Pendidikan, 5*(3), 215–221. https://doi.org/10.29303/prospek.v5i3.548

Tangney, J. P., & Dearing, R. L. (2002). *Shame and guilt.* Guilford Press. https://doi.org/10.4135/9781412950664.n388

Tangney, J. P., Stuewig, J., & Mashek, D. (2007). Moral emotions and moral behavior. *Annual Review of Psychology, 58*(1), 345–372. https://doi.org/10.1146/annurev.psych.56.091103.070145

Tee, Y. H., Amini, M., Siau, C. S., & Amirdabbaghian, A. (2022). English to Chinese fansub translation of humour in The Marvellous Mrs. Maisel. *Texto Livre: Linguagem e Tecnologia, 25*, 1–21. https://doi.org/10.35699/1983-3652.2022.37677

Trigueros, R., Aguilar-Parra, J. M., Cangas, A. J., Bermejo, R., Ferrandiz, C., & López-Liria, R. (2019). Influence of emotional intelligence, motivation and resilience on academic performance and the adoption of healthy lifestyle habits among adolescents. *International Journal of Environmental Research and Public Health, 16*(16), 2810. https://doi.org/10.3390/ijerph16162810

Tyng, C. M., Amin, H. U., Saad, M. N., & Malik, A. S. (2017). The influences of emotion on learning and memory. *Frontiers in Psychology, 8*, 1454. https://doi.org/10.3389/fpsyg.2017.01454

Van de Vyver, J., & Abrams, D. (2017). Promoting third-party prosocial behaviour: The potential of moral emotions. In E. van Leeuwen, H. Zagefka, (Eds.), *Intergroup helping*. Springer. https://doi.org/10.1007/978-3-319-53026-0_17

Vistorte, A. O. R., Deroncele-Acosta, A., Ayala, J. L. M., Barrasa, A., López-Granero, C., & Martí-González, M. (2024). Integrating artificial intelligence to assess emotions in learning environments: a systematic literature review. *Frontiers in Psychology, 15*. https://doi.org/10.3389/fpsyg.2024.1387089

Weiner, B. (2007). Examining emotional diversity in the classroom: An attribution theorist considers the moral emotions. In P. A. Schutz & R. Pekrun (Eds.), *Emotion in education: A educational psychology* (pp. 75–88). Academic Press.

Wan, S.Y.C., & Amini, M. (2020). Secondary world infrastructures and Storyworld of The Little Prince novella. *Pertanika Journal of Social Sciences and Humanities, 28*(1), 175–189. http://www.pertanika.upm.edu.my/pjssh/browse/regular-issue?article=JSSH-4478-2019

Woolf, B. P., Burleson, W., Arroyo, I., Dragon, T., Cooper, D. G., & Picard, R. W. (2009). Affect-aware tutors: Recognizing and responding to student affect. *International Journal of Learning Technology, 4*(3–4), 129–164. https://doi.org/10.1504/IJLT.2009.028804

Wu, R., & Yu, Z. (2023). Do AI chatbots improve students learning outcomes? Evidence from a meta-analysis. *British Journal of Educational Technology, 55*(1), 10–33. https://doi.org/10.1111/bjet.13334

Wu, W., & Kabilan, M. K. (2025). Emotion-related theories in classroom language learning: The conceptualization and causation of emotions. *Frontiers in Psychology, 16*, 1551640. https://doi.org/10.3389/fpsyg.2025.1551640

Wu, S. L., & Amini, M. (2025). Emotionally intelligent AI: Redefining wellness in the digital age. In A. Ahadzadeh, M. Amini, & S. Wu (Eds.), *Navigating health information in the age of Artificial Intelligence* (pp. 37–66). IGI Global Scientific Publishing. https://doi.org/10.4018/979-8-3693-5837-5.ch002

Yli-Piipari, S., Watt, A., Jaakkola, T., Liukkonen, J., & Nurmi, J. E. (2009). Relationships between physical education students' motivational profiles, enjoyment, state anxiety, and self-reported physical activity. *Journal of Sports Science & Medicine, 8*(3), 327. https://pmc.ncbi.nlm.nih.gov/articles/PMC3763276/

Zawacki-Richter, O., Marín, V. I., Bond, M., & Gouverneur, F. (2019). Systematic review of research on artificial intelligence applications in higher education—where are the educators? *International Journal of Educational Technology in Higher Education, 16*(1), 1–27. https://doi.org/10.1186/s41239-019-0171-0

Zeng, X., Ravindran, L., & Amini, M. (2023). Teaching critical thinking to Chinese students in English as a foreign language writing class: A review. *International Journal of Evaluation and Research in Education, 12*(3), 1735–1744. https://ijere.iaescore.com/index.php/IJERE/article/view/24699/13675

Mansour Amini is an interdisciplinary researcher and senior lecturer at the School of Languages, Literacies, and Translation, Universiti Sains Malaysia. He holds a Ph.D. in Translation Studies. Dr. Amini has published articles in the fields of Translation and Education. He serves as a reviewer, editorial manager, and editorial board member for several academic journals. In addition, he has conducted workshops on research writing and methodology in various countries.

Ali Zahabi has a PhD in Applied Linguistics and currently is a lecturer at King Mongkut's University of Technology Thonburi, Thailand. He has published articles about different language teaching and learning areas in international peer-reviewed journals.

Wang Yiqiu is a PhD candidate at UCSI University Malaysia. His field of research is education.

Optimizing ChatGPT-Assisted Evaluation of Vietnamese English Majors' Research Proposals: A Tree-of-Thought and Rubric-Based Approach

Phi The Tran and Hoang Lan Thi Nguyen

Abstract This study examines the enhancement of ChatGPT-assisted evaluation in assessing the methodological components of Vietnamese undergraduate English majors' research proposals at Saigon University, Vietnam, by using a more concise rubric and a Tree-of-thought (ToT) framework with a zero-shot learning approach. The evaluation focuses on the research titles, research questions, hypotheses, paradigm, design, and techniques of 40 research proposals. Compared to the detailed rubric with a chain-of-thought prompting style in Experiment 1, results indicate a significant improvement in ChatGPT's intra-rater and inter-rater reliability, particularly in complex reasoning areas such as the justification and effectiveness of the research paradigm, design, and techniques. However, reliability declined in straightforward aspects, likely due to the inherent complexity of ToT. In addition, inconsistency emerged in evaluating research significance, which requires contextualized field knowledge. While these discoveries flag ToT's limitations in evaluating simple aspects and those that require knowledge about the current literature, they also showcase its potential in enhancing ChatGPT's performance in complex reasoning evaluations, rendering it a useful approach in assessing research methodology. Despite these findings, this experiment suffers from limited generalizability and an incomplete demonstration in evaluating research hypotheses, as this section was absent from all samples.

Keywords ChatGPT · Assisted evaluation · Tree-of-Thought (ToT) framework · Research methodology assessment · Zero-Shot learning · Intra-Rater · Intra-Rater reliability

P. T. Tran (✉) · H. L. T. Nguyen
Saigon University, Ho Chi Minh City, Vietnam
e-mail: tranthephi@sgu.edu.vn

H. L. T. Nguyen
e-mail: nthlan@sgu.edu.vn

V. P. H. Pham et al. (eds.), *Empowering Educators: Integrating AI Tools for Personalized Language Instruction*, Studies in Computational Intelligence 1228,
https://doi.org/10.1007/978-3-032-01348-4_3

1 Introduction

Traditionally, the process of evaluating research papers has focused on evaluating their academic quality and rigor, which has usually been done via methods such as peer review. However, traditional peer review has been criticized for its biases, low reliability, especially in assessing interdisciplinary research (Lee et al., 2013; Spaapen et al., 2007). Different authors have proposed alternative evaluation methods such as using artificial intelligence (AI). As recent advances in AI have shown, to an extent, there is potential for tools like plagiarism detection, statistical transparency checks, research rigor and originality assessment (Checco et al., 2021; Kousha & Thelwall, 2022; Lin et al., 2023).

Building on this progress, a study was conducted at Saigon University to pinpoint the potential of ChatGPT-4o in assessing methodological components of research proposals—such as paradigms, designs, and techniques—and their alignment with research titles, questions, and hypotheses, using a standardized rubric (Tran & Nguyen, 2024). To determine ChatGPT-4o's reliability as an evaluation tool, the study measured intra-rater reliability (consistency within ChatGPT's evaluations) and inter-rater reliability (consistency between ChatGPT's and human evaluations). While moderate to high intra-rater reliability and moderate inter-rater reliability were observed in straightforward areas, ChatGPT struggled with abstract criteria requiring deeper reasoning, such as evaluating the relevance of titles and the justification of paradigms and designs. These findings emphasize the need for innovative approaches to address AI's deficiencies in human-like reasoning.

Several authors have confirmed that discrepancies occur when ChatGPT struggles with broader and more abstract criteria that require advanced logical reasoning (Liang et al., 2023; Lin et al., 2023; Syriani et al., 2023; Thelwall, 2024). This diagnosis prompted further research to overcome ChatGPT's reasoning limitations. A recent advancement, the Tree-of-Thought (ToT) framework, has shown promise in enhancing the problem-solving capabilities of large language models (LLMs) by mimicking the human mind's trial-and-error approach to complex reasoning tasks (Long, 2023; Yao et al., 2023). This approach improves AI's ability to tackle tasks requiring deep logical reasoning, making it a promising solution for improving ChatGPT's capacity to evaluate complex aspects of research methodology.

In addition to addressing AI reasoning, the rubric itself plays a crucial role in ensuring the reliability of evaluation. As the effectiveness of any evaluation process depends heavily on the rubric quality, it is necessary to revise and improve the rubric to better reflect the needs of stakeholders (Olson & Krysiak, 2021). The revised rubric incorporates feedback from experts and users to create a more inclusive and adaptive evaluation tool deemed to enhance the reliability of the evaluations (Timmerman et al., 2011). Notably, ChatGPT itself was consulted as a rubric user, providing comments and insights that contributed to its refinement. This marks a novel aspect of the study, leveraging AI feedback to enhance the rubric's structure and effectiveness alongside human expertise.

While the educational applications of ChatGPT have received broad examination throughout Vietnam, especially to help students improve their language proficiency and support teaching activities, research about ChatGPT as an evaluation tool for academic research and specifically for research methodology assessment remains sparse despite its widespread usage. At Vietnamese universities such as Saigon University, faculty members sometimes face the challenge of assessing an overwhelming number of undergraduate research proposals. Due to the fact that research proposal evaluation, especially assessment of methodological components, using AI is underdeveloped in both international and domestic contexts, the lecturers have not yet been able to rely on machine evaluation for this type of task. As previously mentioned, the initial exploratory study conducted at Saigon University provided initial insights into ChatGPT's potential as an evaluation tool, but also highlighted its limitations, emphasizing the need for further research on evaluating research proposals' methodological components, particularly focusing on the modifications of the rubric and the employment of ToT framework.

Saigon University is an ideal research site as a public, interdisciplinary university offering programs across diverse fields while strictly adhering to the Ministry of Education's standards. The university offers a conducive environment for both the initial small-scale study and potential larger-scale applications across disciplines. Additionally, the university's openness to technological innovation in educational practices and student research-orientation generates ample materials and facilitate the implementation of this research (Saigon University, 2018).

Therefore, the present study seeks to build upon the earlier research conducted at Saigon University by addressing its identified limitations through the integration of the modified rubric and the Tree-of-Thought approach. Particularly, this study aims to investigate whether ChatGPT's evaluation of research proposals' methodological components can be improved through the use of the modified rubric and the Tree-of-Thought approach. By addressing AI's reasoning limitations and ensuring the rubric is robust and stakeholder-informed, this research seeks to enhance the reliability and accuracy of AI-assisted evaluations.

2 Literature Review

2.1 Overview of ChatGPT-4o

ChatGPT is a large-scale transformer-based language model created by OpenAI, a well-known research organization in artificial intelligence (AI). ChatGPT is based on the Generative Pre-trained Transformer (GPT) architecture. This deep learning model is pre-trained on large corpora of text data and can be finetuned for specific tasks like language generation, sentiment analysis, language modeling, machine translation, and text classification (Kojima et al., 2023; Yenduri et al., 2023). Deep learning can perform tasks similar to human thinking, such as understanding text, reasoning, and creating new ideas (Russell & Norvig, 2021; UNESCO IELSALC, 2023). The newest version, GPT-4o, builds on these abilities by adding new features allowing it to handle text, audio, images, and videos in one system (OpenAI, 2024).

While GPT-4o still has some limits such as its ineffectiveness in working autonomously and often makes small mistakes, like misusing APIs or hallucination, which usually require trial-and-error debugging (OpenAI, 2024), this model has a lot of potential. It can facilitate both mundane scientific acceleration (in helping scientists do routine tasks faster) and transformative scientific acceleration (by de-bottlenecking intelligence-driven tasks like information processing, writing new simulations, or devising new theories, showing promise on tasks involving specialized scientific reasoning (OpenAI, 2024).

OpenAI has also introduced GPTs, running on GPT-4o, custom versions of ChatGPT tailored for specific purposes, such as learning board game rules, teaching math, or designing stickers (OpenAI, 2023). These GPTs can be easily created without coding by starting a conversation, giving it instructions and extra knowledge, and picking what it can do, like searching the web, making images or analyzing data (OpenAI, 2023). The present research utilized this function with the hope of reducing time and resources as well as increasing consistency between GPT rounds.

2.2 *ChatGPT in Vietnam Education*

As AI is currently an emerging field of research in Vietnam, ChatGPT has become one of the most popular research interests. Numerous studies conducted in Vietnam have explored its applications in various contexts, including education. Thanks to ChatGPT, Vietnamese language and higher education have seen many changes and innovations. Examining language education, various authors have proven ChatGPT's applications in writing skills enhancement through grammar correction, vocabulary expansion, and academic writing feedback (Duong & Le, 2024; Duong et al., 2024). Studies also discovered ChatGPT's positive role in conversation practicing, improving reading comprehension, and cultural learning, allowing students to engage in self-directed and personalized language improvement in English learning (Hoang & Vu, 2024) as well as boosting their productive skills through word-lookup assistance (Mai & Tran, 2024). Beyond language learning, ChatGPT is transforming English teaching and assessment in higher education. ChatGPT has been reported to support language teachers in various teaching tasks such as generating lesson plans, instructional materials, and quizzes (Nguyen, 2024a, 2024b). Lecturers also recognized that ChatGPT has potential in test creation and grading thanks to its versatility in drafting quicker, more diverse, and more detailed types of questions and enhanced time efficiency (Le, 2024).

From students' perspectives, research has also shown that Vietnamese students generally appreciated ChatGPT as a valuable tool for enhancing learning efficiency, providing instant feedback, and supporting academic tasks. Many students appreciated its role in language learning, particularly in grammar correction, research assistance, personalization, and automation (Duong et al., 2024; Nguyen, 2024a; Vu & Le, 2024). In addition, ChatGPT was also recorded to be widely used by post-graduate students of English majors in advanced tasks such as Academic writing (Nguyen et al., 2025; Tran et al., 2025). AI tools like ChatGPT, Grammarly, and Quillbot were reported to provide quick access to ideas, simplify complex concepts, enhance language use, and streamline the overall writing process (Nguyen et al., 2025; Tran et al., 2025). Nonetheless, concerns remain on the over-reliance, lack of creativity, reliability and potential ethical issues like plagiarism (Duong et al., 2024; Nguyen, 2024a; Nguyen et al., 2025; Vu & Le, 2024).

While there is significant interest in ChatGPT's potential in language learning and personalized education in Vietnam, little research has been conducted on its effectiveness in assessing academic research, particularly in areas such as evaluating research methodology. This gap suggests a need for further exploration into how ChatGPT can be utilized in academic research assessment.

2.3 *ChatGPT in Research Evaluation*

Despite the importance of peer review, it has been widely criticized for inefficiency, low reproducibility, limited knowledge and conflicted interests (Lin et al., 2023). Recent advancements in AI have allowed for tools designed to assist in the peer review process. Table 1 shows the assisting tools for peer review (as summarized by Lin et al., 2023).

As one of the most advanced achievements in AI, GPT also has significant potential for improving the research review process. ChatGPT-3.5 was demonstrated by Syriani et al. (2023) to be capable of screening articles. In this study, the researchers compared ChatGPT (GPT-3.5), which received no prior training, with traditional machine learning classifiers, which had already been trained on sampled data sets and discovered that ChatGPT delivered highly consistent decisions with near-perfect agreement across multiple runs (Fleiss' Kappa > 0.8). In addition, while ChatGPT achieved high recall and balanced accuracy across diverse datasets, it still made false positives (including irrelevant articles) and some false negatives (misses relevant ones). This study also placed significant emphasis on prompt engineering, recognizing it as a crucial factor influencing ChatGPT's screening performance. The final prompt was carefully crafted to simulate the role of a human reviewer conducting a systematic review. It consisted of three parts: context which explained the situation for ChatGPT and informed ChatGPT about the specific topic of the systematic review; instructions which explicitly asked ChatGPT to decide whether to *include* or *exclude* an article based on its title and abstract; and task which included the title and abstract of the article. The tool builders were advised to develop functionality that allows researchers to express their desired screening strategy in terms of customizing a common prompt template (Syriani et al., 2023).

Going beyond this, Liang et al. (2023) used ChatGPT-4 for comprehensive evaluations, extracting content from papers and generating feedback on significance,

Table 1 The assisting tools for peer review

Name	Year	Website/Author	Applications
CrossCheck	2008	https://crosscheck.ithenticate.com/	Plagiarism checking, improper reference detection, writing scoring
UNSILO	2012	https://unsilo.ai/	Key concept extraction, linguistic quality assessment, journal match reviewing, reviewer finder, manuscript screening
Recite	2014	https://reciteworks.com/	Citation match checking, reference format checking
Statcheck	2014	http://statcheck.io/	Statistical data extraction, P-values recomputation and consistency checking
Penelope	2016	https://www.penelope.ai/	Matching journal request detection, missing reference checking, figure citation checking, standard format checking
StatReviewer	2016	http://statreviewer.com/	Numerical error checking, statistical tests, integrity and quality checking, methodological reporting
Scholarcy	2018	https://www.scholarcy.com/	Paper summarization, reference extraction, table and figure extraction, chapter segmentation and highlighting
SciScore	2019	https://sciscore.com/	Key resource analyzing, NIH, MDAR, and ARRIVE report generation, journal reproducibility tracking with RTI
AIRA	2020	https://www.frontiersin.org/news/2020/07/01/artificial-intelligence-peer-review-assistant-aira	Evaluating language quality, assessing the integrity of figures, detecting plagiarism and identifying potential conflicts of interest
AI-Powered Initial Screening Tools	2021	Checco et al	Automate preliminary quality assessments by evaluating elements such as language clarity, coherence, logical flow and plagiarism detection
ReviewAdvisor	2021	http://review.nlpedia.ai/	Review comment generation from eight aspects: originality, substance, replicability, clarity, etc.
ASPR Pipeline	2023	Lin, Song, Zhou, Chen, & Shi	Citation analysis, language assessment, novelty detection, reviewing, scoring, SOTA comparison and summarization
			(Lin et al., 2023)

novelty, acceptance, rejection, and improvement. This study also employed zero-shot learning technique with a prompt template where the parsed data from the PDF file of the article is inserted. The prompt template included the overview of the task at hand; the specific parts of the article (e.g., title, abstract, introduction, ...); and the specific tasks to create a review. The last part explicitly instructed ChatGPT to produce a structured outline with four main sections (i.e., Significance and Novelty, Potential Reasons for Acceptance, Potential Reasons for Rejection, Suggestions for Improvement). This prompt allowed ChatGPT to create feedback that significantly aligns with human reviewers in some aspects, especially on prominent issues identified early in reviews and those noted by multiple reviewers. However, the model tended to overemphasize research implications and datasets while the novelty and technical depth were overlooked. This led to unclear or brief reviews without methodological criticism.

Let us also discuss the paper "Can ChatGPT evaluate research quality?" by Thelwall (2024), which explored the potential of ChatGPT-4 to assess research quality using the REF criteria - based on originality, significance, and rigor—in a case study. Thelwall conducted an evaluation of 51 of his own research articles using zero-shot learning on ChatGPT-4, guided by REF criteria. The chatbot was configured with detailed REF scoring criteria, but the prompt itself was minimal ("score this") and did not clearly specify the evaluation steps, leaving ChatGPT to independently determine how to carry out the assessment. While ChatGPT-4 could produce plausible document summaries and quality evaluation rationales that matched the REF criteria, its overall scores had weak correlations with the researcher's evaluation scores and with its own of the same documents, illustrating that it was scoring inconsistently with both human and itself and struggled to make fine-grained evaluation, which can be a result of a general and unspecific prompt. One noteworthy point from this research is that ChatGPT could not distinguish fabricated or implausible research due to its inability to bring wider information into the research evaluation.

This finding agrees with other authors who concluded ChatGPT's lack of in-depth subject-matter expertise to evaluate methodological components and the significance of the articles (Doskaliuk et al., 2025; Ye et al., 2024). Ye et al. (2024) also highlighted a point observed by Thelwall (2024): LLMs such as ChatGPT tend to take the statements in the articles as objective truths rather than by applying externally obtained information to make judgments. The work of Ye et al. (2024) demonstrated that when explicit manipulation (i.e., white texts praising the articles invisible to human eyes) and implicit manipulation (i.e., strategically disclosing minor limitations within the manuscript) were applied, LLM tended to accept these cues uncritically, generating overly favorable reviews by treating the injected or self-reported content as factual rather than independently evaluating the substance of the research, making it vulnerable to bias. Moreover, Ye et al. (2024) revealed that LLMs were prone to hallucination as they could produce detailed and confident reviews for incomplete or entirely empty papers, suggesting that they made up content to comply with the instructions.

A follow-up study on ChatGPT's abilities and limitations in evaluating research by Thelwall and Kurt (2024) determined the extent of consistency to which ChatGPT's predicted scores to human assessments of research quality according to criteria like originality, rigor, and significance using REF criteria. Furthermore, the experiment compared the effectiveness of using different model versions of ChatGPT for research evaluation and suggested that ChatGPT-4o achieved the highest correlation (0.673) with an assigned score. Detailed system prompts, like Strategy 6, significantly improved performance by guiding ChatGPT's reasoning, whereas simpler prompts, such as Strategy 0, were less effective. Strategy 6 encouraged ChatGPT to provide detailed reasoning and structured analysis, aligning with principles of Chain-of-Thought (CoT) prompting and highlighting the potential of CoT prompting.

In conclusion, while ChatGPT, especially GPT-3.5 and GPT-4, was proven to have potential in automating research screening and evaluation, moderately aligning with human judgments when guided by carefully crafted prompts, it still faces limitations. These include a lack of subject-matter expertise, susceptibility to biased or manipulated content, lack of methodological scrutiny and hallucination. In addition, the studies also highlighted the importance of employing well-engineered prompts due to the fact that vague or minimal prompts led to high level of inconsistency. These challenges highlight an urgent need for further research aimed at mitigating ChatGPT's limitations, particularly through strategies that enhance domain-specific reasoning and develop prompting methods that can better guide the reasoning steps of the evaluations. While research on how to evaluate research quality through AI advances internationally, this field shows minimal investigation in Vietnam. Hence, the next step in research needs to be to analyze how ChatGPT can be utilized to best support research quality assessment within Vietnam's higher education system.

2.4 ChatGPT in Evaluating Methodological Components of Research Proposals

Built on the progress of AI in research evaluation, an experiment on using ChatGPT to evaluate Methodological components was conducted. This experiment, titled "Evaluating English Majors' Research Proposals Using ChatGPT: An Experimental Study on Methodological Components at Saigon University" (unpublished) (henceforth referred to as Experiment 1), was conducted in early 2024 with the hope of ultimately replacing human evaluation of research Methodology with AI's. To achieve this ultimate goal, we investigated ChatGPT-4o's effectiveness in assessing the methodological sections of research proposals by measuring intra-rater reliability (ChatGPT's consistency across evaluations) and inter-rater reliability (agreement between ChatGPT and human evaluators). Thirty-seven proposals submitted by English majors at Saigon University in partial fulfillment of the Research Method module were evaluated based on five methodological components: research title, questions, hypotheses, design, and techniques. They were evaluated using a detailed rubric devised by the researchers and lecturers who taught the Research Method module directly. This Rubric consists of 39 evaluation questions, each with 5 distinct levels corresponding to 5 points.

Using zero-shot learning, ChatGPT was fed specific prompts guiding step-by-step evaluation, exhibiting Chain-of-Thought (CoT) prompting characteristics. The prompts covered six sections (Research Title, Research Questions, Research Hypotheses, Research Paradigm, Research Design, and Research Technique), and the steps were systematically repeated for each, with only minor variations specific to certain sections, which resulted in a lengthy prompt set. The steps are as follows:

Step 1. Extract text: For each section (Research Title, Research Questions, Research Hypotheses, Research Paradigm, Research Design, Research Technique), identify and extract the exact text from the proposal.
Step 2. Summarize theories: Summarize relevant theories from the book "How to Research".
Step 3. Evaluate using rubric: Apply the specific evaluating questions from the Rubric to assess each section. Ensure that the questions are used exactly as provided, without alteration.
Step 4. Compare with theories: Compare the text with theories from "How to Research". (for Paradigm, Design and Technique sections).
Step 5. Assign scores: Assign scores using the descriptions in the 'Evaluation Scale' column of the Rubric file.
Step 6. Calculate average score: Compute the average score for each section.
Step 7. Provide comments: For each evaluating question, include the extracted text and detailed comments on the evaluation.
Step 8. Generate evaluation template: Create a table with columns for Section, Details, Evaluating Questions, Score, and Comments. Include all necessary details and leave rows blank where appropriate.
Step 9. Mark N/A: If hypotheses are not explicitly stated, mark the section as N/A.

Cohen's Weighted Kappa analysis revealed moderate to high intra-rater reliability for ChatGPT but only moderate inter-rater reliability with human evaluators. The study found that ChatGPT-4o demonstrated fair intra-rater reliability ($0.2 < k < 0.4$) across most evaluation areas, with higher reliability in simpler tasks like assessing Research Titles and Questions. Research Hypotheses and Paradigm evaluations demonstrated robust intra-rater reliability because they are more structured. Inter-rater reliability between human raters and ChatGPT came in at a lower level because raters disagreed notably on abstract and subjective criteria like title relevance, jargon interpretation, and justifications for paradigms, designs, and techniques. ChatGPT proved efficient at recognizing ethical problems and title wording, suggesting it can mimic human reasoning for clear, objective criteria. While the limitations highlight the need for human oversight in nuanced evaluations, ChatGPT shows promise for tasks with a structured nature, offering efficiency and reducing human workload. This experiment lays the foundation for our present work, which aims to optimize ChatGPT's ability to evaluate methodological components.

2.5 AI Reasoning and Prompting Strategies

2.5.1 AI Reasoning Techniques

The quest to create machines capable of thinking like humans has captivated humanity for centuries, tracing back to ancient Greece (Ovid & Martin, 2004; Sparkes, 1996; Tandy, 1997, as cited in Goodfellow et al., 2016). As early as 400 BCE, philosophers proposed that the mind operates like a machine, processing knowledge through an internal language to inform decisions (Russell & Norvig, 2021). These philosophies indicated machines' capability to simulate the human mind and lay the groundwork for AI.

Today, AI is capable of multiple tasks, from learning, reasoning, and perception to specialized tasks like problem-solving, creative generation, autonomous driving, and medical diagnosis (Russell & Norvig, 2021). Recent advancements in LLMs, including ChatGPT, Gemini, Opus, and LLaMA-3, have marked a significant leap forward, showcasing sophisticated reasoning capabilities that can rival human performance across various domains (Putta et al., 2024). This development is characterized by the diversity of modern AI reasoning techniques which range from rule-based methods to probabilistic and machine learning-driven paradigms.

One of AI's most fundamental reasoning techniques is rule-based reasoning, which relies on predefined if–then rules to make decisions or draw conclusions (Goodfellow et al., 2016; Russell & Norvig, 2021). This reasoning technique is best suited for well-defined and structured domains because all scenarios must be explicitly encoded within the rules. To be free of this limitation, logical reasoning—the process of analyzing and deriving arguments using a set of facts and rules, was devised (Hong et al., 2024). This reasoning technique encompasses deductive (premise-based), inductive (pattern-based), and abductive (explanation-based) methods, enabling flexible decision-making in scenarios where a structured logical framework can guide inferences (Hong et al., 2024; Russell & Norvig, 2021). Built upon logical reasoning techniques, knowledge-based reasoning leverages structured knowledge bases to make inferences and decisions through logical operations (Goodfellow et al., 2016; Russell & Norvig, 2021). Knowledge-based reasoning enables agents to perform actions through a set of operations TELL (update knowledge), ASK (query knowledge), and TELL (report actions) and can achieve competence quickly by being told or learning new knowledge about the environment; and they can adapt to changes in the environment by updating the relevant knowledge (Russell & Norvig, 2021). However, the process of hard-code knowledge about the world in formal languages is excessive, suggesting that AI systems need the ability to acquire their own knowledge, by extracting patterns from raw data. This capability is known as machine learning (Goodfellow et al., 2016). Machine learning broadens reasoning capabilities, using unsupervised, transfer, and semi-supervised learning to infer patterns and relationships from data (Goodfellow et al., 2016). Deep learning, a subset of machine learning where machines learn from experience and understand the world in terms of a hierarchy of concepts (Russell & Norvig, 2021), is now the foundation of many LLMs.

An LLM, is a generative AI system built on advanced deep-learning architectures like the transformer (Esposito, 2024). These models process unstructured text to deduce implicit rules and relationships and can excel in symbolic and commonsense reasoning (Hong et al., 2024). However, despite these advancements, significant challenges persist: LLMs, even some of the strongest still models of the most updated generation, such as ChatGPT-4, struggle to generalize effectively in interactive, multi-step environments (Achiam et al., 2023 as cited in Esposito, 2024; Putta et al., 2024), which highlights the need for more advanced prompting strategies. One such strategy is chain-of-thought (CoT) prompting, which involves guiding the model to outline all the steps (or thoughts) it takes to arrive at a solution. This technique gives the model time to think, and thereby, enhances its reasoning ability by incorporating intermediate reasoning steps (Wei et al., 2023). This strategy has been proven to improve LLM's performance on intricate tasks that demand various reasoning steps with either few-shot or zero-shot prompting (Esposito, 2024; Kojima et al., 2023; Wei et al., 2023; Zhang et al., 2022).

2.5.2 Evolving Reasoning Frameworks: From Chain-Of-Thought to Tree-of-Thought Frameworks

Chain of Thought (CoT)

As previously mentioned, reasoning techniques in AI have seen great advancements, especially in recent years with the popularity of LLM. One reasoning technique that has been proven effective in making multi-step decisions is Chain-of-thought (CoT) (Wei et al., 2023). Earlier works relied on rationale-augmented training from scratch or fine-tuning a pre-trained models to generate natural language intermediate steps (Cobbe, 2021 as cited in Wei et al., 2023). However, as these methods are often costly and complicated, Wei et al. (2023) made use of few-shot prompting technique (Brown et al., 2020) to craft a prompt that consists of input, chain of thought, output, in which a chain of thought is a series of intermediate reasoning steps that lead to the final output (Wei et al., 2023). As demonstrated by Wei et al. (2023), while with few-shot standard prompting technique, the model was provided with a direct query and generates a single, concise response without explaining its reasoning process, chain-of-thought prompting displayed its reasoning process step by step in natural language before arriving at a final answer. The empirical assessments on three LLMs showed that chain-of-thought prompting improved performance on a range of arithmetic, commonsense, and symbolic, sometimes surpassing even fine-tuned LLM with a verifier (GPT-3).

In an attempt to avoid having to hand-craft specific exemplars for separate cases, Kojima et al. (2023) devised a simpler yet highly effective zero-shot CoT prompting technique. By adding a generic prompt like "Let's think step by step", the user allowed LLMs to reason in steps and to achieve state-of-the-art performance in symbolic and arithmetic reasoning tasks. Built upon this prompting technique, Zhang et al. (2022) proposed Auto-CoT which used the AI itself to automatically generate demonstrations (examples) through clustering and reasoning prompts in the reasoning process. Wang et al. (2023) further introduced a self-consistency decoding strategy, which enhanced CoT prompting by generating diverse reasoning paths and selecting the best answer. Using this method resulted in better performance since complex problems usually require multiple thinking paths which produce their specific correct answers (Wang et al., 2023). Similarly, Shum et al. (2024) proposed an augment-prune-select three-phase procedure that first produces various chain-of-thought candidates (augment) before filtering them against ground truths (prune). A policy gradient algorithm selects the best sequence of rationale chains within the generated candidate pool (select). This laid the foundation for more complex chain reasoning in AI like Tree-of-thought.

Tree-of-Thought (ToT)

ToT, introduced by Long (2023), is a paradigm that allows LLMs to explore multiple reasoning paths, allowing prompt branching at any point of the chain of thoughts (Besta et al., 2024; Long, 2023; Yao et al., 2023). This technique identifies every problem as a search over a tree, where each node is a state representing a partial solution to the input and the sequence of thoughts so far (Long, 2023; Yao et al., 2023). It is inspired by the human mind's approach for solving complex reasoning tasks through trial and error, allowing for backtracking when necessary (Long, 2023). This framework enhances the problem-solving capabilities of LLMs by enabling systematic backtracking, correctness checks, and the exploration of larger solution spaces, addressing the limitations of linear reasoning models. Additional core elements such as memory modules, checker modules and ToT controllers enable long-range reasoning and evaluating their potential through heuristic-based strategies, which can adapt to diverse tasks. Successes in varied tasks that exceed linear-think capabilities (i.e., Sudoku puzzle solving and Game of 24 and Creative Writing and Mini Crossword) proved the achievement of this technique when employed by LLMs GPT-4 or GPT 3.5 (Long, 2023; Yao et al., 2023).

The original ToT devised by Long (2023) includes 4 components. The "Prompter Agent" generates prompts for the LLM, encouraging it to produce intermediate solutions rather than solve the entire problem simultaneously. The "Checker Module" verifies the correctness of the LLM's responses, either using explicit rules for well-defined tasks or a neural network-based classifier. If a response passes validation (valid), it is stored in the "Memory Module", which records the conversation history, intermediate states, and supplemental data essential for problem-solving. Overseeing the process is the "ToT Controller", which uses information from the memory to guide the prompter agent in generating the next prompt. An invalid response prompts the controller to trigger backtracking, encouraging the LLM to explore alternative directions. This dynamic process prevents the system from getting stuck by leveraging predefined rules or advanced monitoring mechanisms. However, this model requires high technical overhead, cost management, and development effort as it interacts with the LLM through API and involves the development of complicated and dynamic modules. The present research develops a ToT-style set of prompts to be fed directly as prompts or instructions into user interface, which evades complications with raw API calls, token limits, or coding. Hence, the model from Yao et al. (2023) is adopted as the core framework. In this model, ToT frames any problem as a search over a tree, where each node is a state. According to Yao et al. (2023), a specific ToT framework involves four components.

(1) Thought Decomposition: This is the first component of the framework which divides the problem-solving process into "thoughts". These thoughts are represented nodes of a tree. The nodes can branch out and explore multiple problem-solving states.
(2) Thought Generator: This part generates candidate thoughts for each node in the tree which are possible steps in the problem-solving process. This generator can either sample thoughts generated independently using CoT technique or propose thoughts sequentially using a "propose prompt".
(3) State Evaluator: This component assesses the quality of the tree nodes or states (intermediate thoughts). The evaluation from this component allows search algorithm to determine which states to keep exploring and the order to explore them. The assessment can be done by the model assigning scores based on their potential toward the final solution (Value) or comparing and selecting the most promising state through voting (Vote).
(4) Search Algorithm: This algorithm, employing quality assessment from State evaluator, guides the model to systematically explore possible solutions. Different algorithms such as Breadth-First (BFS) (maintains a set of the most promising states at each level of the tree) and Depth-First Search (DFS) (focuses on exploring the most promising state to its conclusion before backtracking) can be integrated into the framework.

While CoT enables linear, interpretable reasoning and improves performance in tasks requiring logical steps (Wei et al., 2023), it is limited by its inability to revise previous steps and its reliance on single-path reasoning which can result in subsequent errors. In contrast, Tree-of-Thought (ToT) generalizes CoT by introducing a structured, search-based approach that allows for branching, looking ahead, evaluating, and backtracking (Long, 2023; Yao et al., 2023). ToT significantly boosts performance in complex and long-range reasoning tasks. Hence, researchers find the ToT framework to be the most appropriate method for resolving complex problems including research paper assessment. The decomposition feature combined with path exploration and systematic backtracking provides the ToT framework with an extensive and sophisticated reasoning ability, which enables it to manage the complexities involved in research methodology evaluation.

2.6 Evaluating the Research Proposal's Methodological Components

As the research title sets the stage and guides the methodological approach (Paltridge & Starfield, 2020; Thomas, 2003), it is necessary that before any part of the research is evaluated, its title is first assessed to ensure the alignment of the project parts. In addition, it was emphasized that quality of research questions or hypotheses, the alignment of methodology with these inquiries, and the logic of their justification are features prioritized in research quality assessment (Paltridge & Starfield, 2020). Therefore, similar to the previous paper, in order to fully evaluate a research proposal's methodological components, we must first evaluate its title, research questions or hypotheses.

According to Blaxter et al. (2010), and Booth et al. (2018), Tcherni-Buzzeo and Pyrczak (2024), a good research title must be specific, clear, concise, name key variables, and communicate both topic and conceptual framework. In addition, the title and the research questions must align closely to ensure clarity and relevance for the audience (Creswell, 2014). While Tcherni-Buzzeo and Pyrczak (2024) provide a list of evaluative questions for good research titles, we have decided to retain criteria emphasizing specificity, clarity, conciseness, inclusion of key variables, and alignment with the research questions or hypotheses.

A research question attains effectiveness through multiple necessary conditions. A research question should demonstrate feasibility by using available resources such as time, funding, and human effort (Fraenkel et al., 2022) which must be carefully defined (Cohen, 2000, as cited in Andrews, 2003). This is often achieved by specifying participants, research sites, and a specific phenomenon or concept (Creswell, 2012). Additionally, the research question needs to use specific terms and keywords that both readers and researchers understand, allowing for precise definitions for measurement or identification (Fraenkel et al., 2022). The significance of the research question is another key feature, as it must address issues that contribute valuable knowledge and are worth investigating (Fraenkel et al., 2022).

Research questions may be framed as hypotheses in quantitative studies. The features of a good research hypothesis share much resemblance with a good research title. A hypothesis must be precise, specific, and clearly defined to guide the research methods effectively (Andrews, 2003). These are achieved by specify the participants, the research site and focusing on a single phenomenon or concept as the research question. Moreover, as hypotheses are meant to be proven or disproven (Blaxter et al., 2010), it must be formulated to allow empirical testing, which means the variables can be precisely defined and measured.

As research is carried out within particular paradigms that shape the entire process (Blaxter et al., 2010), evaluating the alignment of research design with its questions or hypotheses involves considering the underlying paradigm. As emphasized by Paltridge and Starfield (2020), the methodology and methods section of a proposal needs to put forward a logical justification for the choice of research paradigm and research methods, with references support, that will assure readers that the study is both viable and feasible within the time available. Blaxter et al. (2010), identified three main paradigms—quantitative, qualitative, and mixed methodologies—limiting proposals in this paper to these methodological frameworks. Tcherni-Buzzeo and Pyrczak (2024) also emphasized the importance of evaluating the specification of the design and techniques for data collection and the justification of why the design and techniques solicit data that will address the research questions or hypotheses. In other words, other than the specification and justification of the research paradigm, design, and techniques that need evaluating, the practicality of the design and techniques are also subject to examination to establish the logic and feasibility of the proposal.

2.7 Research Objectives and Hypotheses

As synthesized above, despite its potential, ChatGPT-4o has shown limitations in handling criteria that demand complex reasoning, particularly in assessing methodological alignment. Up-to-date research has shown that it had only moderate agreement with human evaluators, struggled with nuanced judgments, and relied heavily on detailed prompts. Additionally, it lacked subject-matter expertise, showed limited methodological scrutiny, was vulnerable to biased content, and occasionally produced hallucinated information. These shortcomings highlight the need for further research with different materials and approaches to render the model more reliable for methodological components evaluation.

Built upon the results of Experiment 1, this follow-up study aims to investigate whether the application of the ToT reasoning technique in AI and rubric modifications can enhance the intra-rater and inter-rater reliability of ChatGPT-4o's evaluation of Research Titles, Questions, Hypotheses, Paradigms, Design, and Techniques.

Hypotheses:

H1: The implementation of the modified rubric will improve the intra-rater reliability of ChatGPT-4o's evaluations when employing the ToT reasoning technique with zero-shot learning.

H2: The modified rubric will result in higher inter-rater reliability between ChatGPT-4o (utilizing the ToT reasoning technique with zero-shot learning) and human raters compared to the original rubric.

3 Methods

3.1 Research Design

In light of ChatGPT's limitations in evaluating research methodological components, there is a pressing need to examine whether ToT reasoning technique and rubric enhancements can improve the reliability of AI-assisted evaluations in research methodology. To test the research hypotheses mentioned, a quasi-experimental design was employed, since it enables examination of whether a specific intervention (ChatGPT) influences the evaluation of research proposals (Shadish et al., 2002). Random assignment was not feasible in this context—only one group of proposals was available—so quasi-experimental rather than true experimental methods was adopted. This design allowed for a direct comparison between the scores assigned by human lecturers (control group) and those generated by ChatGPT (experimental group).

3.2 Research Context

Saigon University (SGU) is a public, interdisciplinary university, offering programs across diverse fields such as Economics, Technology, Social Sciences, Law, Politics, Art, and Pedagogy in Vietnam (Saigon University, n.d.). The Department of Foreign Languages (DFL) at Saigon University offers undergraduate programs in English Language Teaching and English linguistics (for Commerce and Tourism), equipping students with the skills needed for education, business, and the service industry (Saigon University, 2024). The authors of proposals employed in this research are junior students of DFL who have completed four modules covering the four English language skills. These modules are designed to achieve an IELTS equivalency of 6.5–7.0, making it reasonable to estimate that their English proficiency is at a B2 level or higher on the CEFR scale. The proposals were composed as the final project of a 30-period Research Methods module. The module provides students with crucial research abilities through lessons about selecting study interests, formulating research questions and reviewing literature. It also covers the selecting and designing of research as well as data collection and analysis. The module also provides instructions about literature reviews while it covers academic writing and methods to structure research projects. The textbook How to Research by Blaxter et al. (2010) functions as the basis for this course to deliver both practical and theoretical knowledge for independent research to students.

3.3 Research Procedures

The experiment was conducted in three stages—preparation, implementation, and data collection—repeated for both Research Methods module lecturers and ChatGPT-4o.

3.3.1 Stage 1: Preparation

In this stage, three resources required for the evaluation were designed, namely, Scoring rubric, customized GPT and Student proposals.

Scoring Rubric

A rubric is a structured tool that outlines the key components of an assignment and the levels of performance for each component (Arcuria & Chaaban, 2019; Goodrich, 1997; Popham, 1997; Suskie, 2018; Wiggins, 1998, as cited in Olson & Krysiak, 2021). It generally consists of three main elements: a scoring strategy (e.g., scales, points, or percentages), the dimensions of the task, and the descriptive criteria that define performance levels in observable manner (Popham, 1997; Reddy & Andrade, 2010; Wolf & Stevens, 2007, as cited in Olson & Krysiak, 2021). As there is no single right way to construct a rubric (Goldberg, 2014 as cited in Olson & Krysiak, 2021), the present research adopted a procedure that not only included the review of theoretical framework but also took into account the practical viewpoints of stakeholders who directly use the Rubric. This was said to improve the consistency of assessment (Olson & Krysiak, 2021). Following the developing procedure from Timmerman et al. (2011), the Rubric used in this paper was developed in 3 stages:

Stage 1: The authors reviewed existing literature on the criteria for evaluating research title, questions, hypotheses, paradigm, design and techniques. This aimed to identify and integrate commonly valued aspects of scientific reasoning and writing. This stage also involved examining the Rubric employed in Experiment 1.

Stage 2: Experts holding advanced degrees in English linguistics and education—both master and doctoral-level lecturers and researchers—were consulted in iterative cycles to refine the rubric's criteria and performance levels.

Stage 3: To ensure that the rubric met both its practical and educational goals, we collected multiple rounds of feedback from the intended users—lecturers employed to score the papers. These lecturers were the same experts consulted during the previous step. Concordantly, we tested the rubric with ChatGPT as it is also an evaluator, to confirm that it could interpret the rubric's structure, concepts, and level descriptors effectively.

The final Rubric includes 6 sections: the Research Title, Questions, Hypotheses, Paradigms, Designs, and Techniques. Each section includes a series of evaluation questions that guide the evaluator in considering clarity, alignment, feasibility, comprehensibility, significance, reasoning and logic of the sections in the proposal. For each question, a five-point scale from "Very unsatisfactory" to "Very satisfactory" is defined, with detailed descriptors for each level from 1-point to 5-point (Appendix A).

Customized GPT

Adapting the ToT framework from Yao et al. (2023), the model employed in this research also involves 4 components: Thought Decomposition, Thought Generator, State Evaluator and Search Algorithm. However, as previously mentioned, in order to avoid complex technical modification to the GPT model as well as complicated hand-crafted examples, the present research deployed the framework as prompts. In addition, as Zero-shot CoT's capabilities have been demonstrated by Kojima et al. (2023), in this experiment, we attempted the Zero-shot ToT prompting technique.

Zero-shot training requires fewer resources than methods like Few-shot or One-shot training while producing comparable or superior results. A Zero-shot prompting technique was explored by Reynolds and McDonell (2021), emphasizing methods like Direct task specification and Behavior constraint. These methods generate Metaprompts—general templates that expand into specific prompts when combined with task-specific information.

In practice, prompts are crafted to describe precise actions required for specific tasks. These actions are guided by "signifiers," actions derived from human evaluators' practices, ensuring alignment with human evaluators.

Below shows a prompt set to evaluate a proposal's methodological components, using Zero-shot prompting and detailed how they were deployed. The prompt set was built upon the ToT framework, on the basis of prompt chaining and adheres to the key elements of effective prompts as outlined by Baars (2024), namely clarity, context, specificity, conciseness and relevance. In addition, the prompt also includes an exit strategy (Esposito, 2024), for instances where the model cannot locate the relevant section in the text. The exit strategy instructs the model to either mark N/A (not applicable) for Hypotheses or assign a score of 1 for other sections when evidence is missing.

As shown in the Table 2, all steps in the evaluation process are interconnected with Thought Decomposition and Thought Generator. Each step involves breaking down the evaluation task (decomposition) and generating potential actions for assessment (thought generation). The Search Algorithm is applied in Steps 3 and 4, where the model searches through the pool of point descriptors to match the extracted evidence. The process includes a backtracking feature, if the evidence does not match the current point descriptor, the process moves to the next scoring level and repeats the comparison. The State Evaluator confirms whether the extracted evidence aligns with the next higher and lower level of point descriptors in Step 4.2. If the evidence matches a higher point descriptor ($X + 1$) or lower point descriptor ($X - 1$), the process returns to Step 3 to reassess and continue with the new point level. In Step 5, the model is asked to repeat the same process for the next evaluating question and so on. Step n mark the end of the evaluating process where the model is prompted to create an Evaluation Form summarizing the Evaluating Questions. A detailed diagram illustrating the ToT process for evaluating the methodological components of research proposals is shown in Appendix B.

Students' Proposals

Forty research proposals were collected from English majors at Saigon University, each prepared by groups of four to five students as the final project for their Research Methods course. These proposals, drawn from four classes taught by four different lecturers—who also served as Control group raters—followed departmental guidelines specifying both the paper's format and English-language-focused topics. In

Table 2 ChatGPT prompt's structure for proposal evaluation

Prompt name	Function	Instructions	Deployment method
Identity	Define the role of GPT	You are a proposal reviewer	Placed into the GPTs' 'Instructions' box to steer the evaluation process
Task specification	Initiate the evaluation process	Review proposals adhering strictly to the following procedure [*The ToT process of Evaluating Methodological components of research proposals*] and Rubric	
	Specify actions to be taken and constraints	Assign score based on the highest matching level Made no assumption or inference on the text or the Rubric	
The ToT process of evaluating methodological components of research proposals	Thought decomposition Thought generator	**Step 1: Present Question and Level Descriptors** • Step 1.1: Clearly state the question being evaluated (e.g., Question Y) • Step 1.2: List the level descriptors (1 to 5) for the question, as provided in the rubric	
	Thought decomposition Thought generator	**Step 2: Extract Relevant verbatim** • Step 2.1: Identify and extract verbatim text directly addressing the question • Step 2.2: If no explicit information exists (e.g., hypotheses under a dedicated heading), mark the section as N/A	

(continued)

Table 2 (continued)

Prompt name	Function	Instructions	Deployment method
	Thought decomposition Thought generator Search algorithm	**Step 3: Compare Excerpts to Level Descriptors** • Step 3.1: Start comparing the extracted excerpt against the descriptors for 1 point • Step 3.2: If no match is found, incrementally proceed to compare it to the next level (2, 3, 4, 5) • Step 3.3: Mark the level of application for each level	
	Thought decomposition Thought generator Search algorithm State evaluator	**Step 4: Tentatively Assign and Immediately Validate the Score** • Step 4.1: Assign a tentative score based on the best match between evidence and descriptors • Step 4.2: Validate the score immediately: • Step 4.2.1: Compare evidence against the next higher level (X + 1) and the next lower level (X-1) • Step 4.2.2: Adjust the score if needed to ensure it aligns most closely with the descriptors	
	Thought decomposition Thought generator	**Step 5: Move to the Next Question** • Step 5.1: Repeat the above steps for the next question, always presenting the question and descriptors first	

(continued)

Table 2 (continued)

Prompt name	Function	Instructions	Deployment method
	Request for structured output	**Step n:** Create a structured Evaluation Form summarizing the Evaluating Questions (1 to 26), assigned scores, and corresponding comments, formatted in table form	
Conversation starter	Outline the evaluation process and constraints prior to conducting the assessment	Display the evaluating procedure and its constraints	Deployed as initial guidance in the chat environment
Confirmation prompts	Confirm the next step suggested by GPT	Specified question numbers Step n	Subsequently introduced into the chat environment to lead the evaluation process

accordance with the official template of the faculty, each proposal included a clear research title, table of contents, introduction (200–400 words), literature review (300–1500 words), research significance (300–500 words), objectives/research questions (≈100 words), research methods (500–1000 words), data analysis (≈300 words), proposed chapter outline (≈200 words), research limitations (100–300 words), proposed time scale (100–300 words), and references in APA (7th edition).

3.3.2 Stage 2: Implementation

Human Evaluation

Four lecturers from the Faculty of Foreign Languages at Saigon University, specializing in Research Methodology, were responsible for scoring the research proposals. These lecturers possess extensive expertise in the materials, assessment criteria, and requirements of the Research Methodology modules. The evaluation panel comprised two PhD holders and two Master's degree holders in English Linguistics or English Language Teaching (ELT), ensuring a well-rounded and academically rigorous assessment process.

Each proposal was rated by two raters, that is, one with a PhD and one with a Master's diploma. They conducted the evaluations based on 26 questions specified in the Rubric. All rater pairs contained one researcher and one unexposed rater who had no prior knowledge of ChatGPT's scoring patterns. The proposals were scored individually, and the results were compared. In cases where discrepancies between scores were observed, the raters engaged in discussions to reach a consensus. The final output for each proposal was a single evaluation form that included the agreed-upon scores for all 26 questions.

ChatGPT-4o Evaluation

The "Context," "Task Specification," and "The ToT Process of Evaluating Methodological Components of Research Proposals" were directly inserted into the Instructions box of GPT to create a customized model named ToT Proposal Evaluator. Additionally, the Rubric document was uploaded as the knowledge base for the customized evaluator. A detailed "Conversation Starter" prompt was also included to guide the evaluation process.

To initiate the evaluation process, the "Conversation Starter" prompt was deployed in the chat environment of the ToT Proposal Evaluator. After outlining the evaluation procedures and restrictions as described in the Instructions, individual proposals were uploaded for assessment. ChatGPT then sought confirmation before beginning the evaluation process.

Each evaluation commenced with Question 1 alone to test the procedure. Subsequent questions were evaluated in batches (2–5, 6–11, 12–16, 17–21, and 22–26), with the relevant question numbers manually provided in the chat environment.

Upon completing the evaluation of Question 26, the "Step n" prompt was used to initiate the generation of an Evaluation Form, which included the evaluation questions, corresponding scores, and comments. The process which started with the deployment of "Conversation starter" was then repeated for the proposals.

3.3.3 Stage 3: Data Collection

Human Evaluation

The proposals were distributed to the raters. 2 weeks later, the data was collected in the form of 80 Evaluation forms. The researchers then conducted comparison of the scores and arranged for consensus meetings to finalize the scores. The final data set was 40 Evaluation forms with scores agreed upon by both raters. No qualitative data was collected for the proposals.

ChatGPT-4o Evaluation

The process of collecting ChatGPT evaluation was conducted after the finalized human evaluation forms were collected to minimize biases as 2 of the raters were researchers who directly deploy the ChatGPT's evaluations. Each proposal was evaluated twice on separate occasions (the first and second GPT rounds were conducted at different times) to minimize hallucinations and inferences. The results were 80 Evaluation Forms provided directly in the Chat environment which were later stored in Excel file.

3.4 Ethical Concerns

The research addresses the following practices to confidentiality, fairness, and evaluator well-being. The authors protected student privacy by anonymizing research proposals prior to distribution. As these proposals were pre-existing and have already been graded and reported by the lecturers, their usage in this research has no impact on the students' academic performance. However, informal permission was obtained from the Dean of the Faculty of Foreign Languages to use these proposals.

In addition, before participation, human evaluators received information about the study and consent to participate. To avoid stress and encourage accurate and reliable scoring from the human evaluators, the workload was evenly distributed over the 14 days with maximum 2 proposals scored and reported per day.

3.5 *Data Analysis*

Similar to Experiment 1, to calculate the intra- and inter-rater reliability between ChatGPT-4o and human raters, we applied Cohen's weighted Kappa, a common statistic for ordinal data (Cohen, 1968). Weighted Kappa considers both the level of agreement and the severity of disagreements, assigning smaller penalties to minor score differences (e.g., 4 vs. 5) and larger penalties to major ones (e.g., 1 vs. 5) (Maclure & Willet, 1987, as cited in Berry & Johnston, 2008), which is suitable for our Rubric using 5-point evaluation scale. We also used Quadratic Kappa (Sim & Wright, 2005), which increases weights quadratically, to further highlight these differences, and then categorized results according to (Landis & Koch, 1977).

After collection, the data was stored in an Excel file. This file includes (1) the evaluation score of human evaluators, (2) the evaluation score of the first round of ChatGPT and (3) the evaluation score of the second round of ChatGPT. Each Excel tab was dedicated for the 3 sets of scores for the 26 Rubric questions of 1 proposal. These scores were later input into SPSS in appropriate format for analysis. The statistics test was conducted using the built-in function of Quadratic Weighted Kappa in SPSS (version 27) program. 3 pairs of Quadratic Weighted Kappa scores and their significant level were calculated: (1) between the two rounds of ChatGPT evaluations, (2) between Humans and the first set of ChatGPT evaluations, and (3) between Humans and the second set of ChatGPT evaluations.

4 Results

This section presents the results of the study by analyzing the reliability of GPT-generated evaluations compared to human assessments. The findings focus on both intra-rater reliability (consistency between GPT-1 and GPT-2) and inter-rater reliability (alignment between GPT and human raters) across various research components. By examining agreement levels using Quadratic Weighted Kappa statistics, this analysis highlights areas of strong consistency, as well as key discrepancies that require further refinement.

4.1 *Reliability Between Human and GPT Evaluations of Research Title*

Table 3 evaluated agreement levels between GPT-1, GPT-2, and human raters on five questions evaluating Research title on five criteria: Ambiguity, Conciseness, Comprehensibility, Coverage, and Alignment.

The two rounds of GPT achieved a moderate level of consistency, with an average Cohen's kappa (K) value of 0.497. The k values of all evaluation questions fell

Table 3 Comparison of Intra-rater and Inter-rater reliability between human and GPT evaluations of research title

	GPT 1 versus GPT 2		Human versus GPT 1		Human versus GPT 2	
Evaluating question	Weighted Kappa[a]	Sig.	Weighted Kappa[a]	Sig.	Weighted Kappa[a]	Sig.
Q1 (Ambiguity)	0.543	0.001	−0.035	0.765	0.059	0.618
Q2 (Conciseness)	0.533	0.001	0.205	0.116	0.309	0.018
Q3 (Comprehensibility)	0.417	0.003	0.000	1.000	0.179	0.256
Q4 (Coverage)	0.552	0.000	0.429	0.004	0.320	0.033
Q5 (Alignment)	0.442	0.005	0.199	0.194	0.321	0.035
Average Q1 to Q5	0.497		0.159		0.238	

into the moderate range, with Coverage having the highest agreement (0.552) and Comprehension having the lowest agreement (0.417). All agreements were statistically significant (p-values ≤ 0.005), indicating the consistency between GPT 1 and GPT 2 did not happen due to chance. This value was notably higher than the average k value from GPT versus GPT in Experiment 1 (0.354) (see Appendix C), suggesting that the method and Rubric used here enhanced consistency between GPT rounds.

The inter-reliability between human and GPT 1 was lowest with average k value of 0.159, falling into the slight range. Similar to intra-reliability, Coverage had the highest agreement (0.429, $p = 0.004$, significant), falling into the moderate range. However, Ambiguity and Comprehensibility had considerably low values (k = −0.035 and k = 0.0), which indicated no agreement existed when humans and GPT evaluated whether the research titles had ambiguous words or were understandable. It is worth noting that except for Coverage, none of the criteria was statistically significant. This meant GPT-1's ratings diverged substantially from human judgment, with meaningful overlap when evaluating whether the titles covered all variables.

The average agreement of GPT2 with human raters was 0.238, low but better than Human versus GPT-1. Coverage, Alignment, and Conciseness not only showed fair k values (0.320, 0.321, and 0.309, respectively) but were also statistically significant. This meant there was fair consistency between humans and GPT-2 in evaluating whether the titles covered all variables, its alignment with research questions/hypotheses, and conciseness and this consistency was not due to random variation. Similar to GPT 1, Ambiguity and Comprehensibility had the lowest agreement (0.059 and 0.179), falling into the slight spectrum and were both not statistically significant.

The statistics on Kappa levels suggested that ChatGPT had better intra-reliability than inter-rater reliability as it had higher k value between rounds. It was also clear that GPT-2 aligned better with human evaluations than GPT-1, especially on Conciseness, Coverage, and Alignment. In addition, GPT struggled to align with human judgment on the criteria of Ambiguity and Comprehensibility, showing low levels of agreement.

For the two pairs, Human versus GPT1 and Human versus GPT2, while both Ambiguity and Conciseness were not statistically significant, similar to Experiment 1, their k values increased slightly. Similarly, k value of question regarding the Coverage increased moderately with statistical significance. Comprehensibility was the only criterion where the new k values were lower than those from Experiment 1, suggesting that the new Rubric and ToT framework did not improve the evaluation of this criterion.

In conclusion, compared to Experiment 1, improvements in Coverage and Conciseness, particularly in GPT2's evaluation, were observed in this new study. Intra-rater reliability also improved significantly for Coverage, Alignment, and Conciseness, with the new rubric enhancing consistency between GPT1 and GPT2. However, Comprehensibility and Ambiguity still exhibited weaker agreement, requiring further refinement for more reliable evaluations.

4.2 Reliability Between Human and GPT Evaluations of Research Questions

Table 4 evaluates agreement levels between GPT-1, GPT-2, and human raters on six questions evaluating Research Questions (RQ) on six criteria: Feasibility, Practicality, Coverage, Comprehensibility, Measurability, and Significance.

The two GPT rounds showed fair agreement overall (average $\kappa = 0.356$). Reliability was strongest for Q8, which evaluated whether the RQ included the variables ($\kappa = 0.499$), indicating the GPT evaluated coverage consistently. Most of the k values fell into the fair and moderate range, from 0.3 to 0.5, and were statistically significant, suggesting that GPT consistently evaluated whether the RQ was scientifically feasible, practical within resources, and included measurable terms.

Table 4 Comparison of Intra-rater and Inter-rater reliability between human and GPT evaluations of research questions

	GPT 1 versus GPT 2		Human versus GPT 1		Human versus GPT 2	
Evaluating question	Weighted Kappa[a]	Sig.	Weighted Kappa[a]	Sig.	Weighted Kappa[a]	Sig.
Q6 (Feasibility)	0.317	0.026	0.320	0.032	0.069	0.558
Q7 (Practicality)	0.470	0.002	0.288	0.034	0.204	0.072
Q8 (Coverage)	0.499	0.002	0.368	0.015	0.123	0.409
Q9 (Comprehensibility)	0.232	0.128	0.159	0.313	0.143	0.352
Q10 (Measurability)	0.344	0.024	0.195	0.118	0.265	0.058
Q11 (Significance)	0.277	0.063	0.159	0.291	0.006	0.966
Average Q6 to Q11	0.356		0.248		0.135	

The weakest agreement was for Comprehensibility and Significance of the RQ ($\kappa = 0.232$ and 0.277, respectively), suggesting significant variation in how the GPT models assessed the clarity and the contribution of the RQ. These results were also not statistically significant, indicating the consistency was due to chance, rendering it not reliable.

Compared to Experiment 1, whose average k value for GPT rounds was 0.341, slight improvement was observed in the intra-reliability of GPT's evaluation using this new Rubric and ToT framework.

The overall average Kappa value for GPT 1 and Human was 0.248, indicating a fair level of agreement between GPT 1 and human evaluators. Similar to intra-reliability, Q8 (Coverage) had the highest k value of 0.368 and was statistically significant ($p < 0.05$). Feasibility and Practicality of the RQ were also fairly consistently evaluated, with statistically significant k values (0.320 and 0.288, respectively).

While Comprehensibility, Measurability, and Significance yielded slight agreement (k = 0.159, 0.195, 0.159, respectively), they were not statistically significant, rendering the agreement unreliable. The same phenomenon was observed in Experiment 1 as well when all three criteria yielded low k values and were not statistically significant. However, significant improvement ranging from 0.118 to 0.231 was recorded in Feasibility, Practicality, and Coverage.

Contrary to Research title, the overall average k value of GPT 2 versus Human was significantly lower than GPT 1 (k = 0.135), indicating weak alignment between GPT 2 and human evaluators. The highest agreement was observed in Measurability (k = 0.265), but with a p-value slightly higher than 0.05, the statistic could be considered not significant to conclude. Most criteria's k values fell into the slight range (k $\leq$ 0.2), with Q11's k = 0.06, indicating virtually no alignment existed for this question, showing severe divergence between GPT 2 and human evaluations. For GPT 2 versus Human, the k value obtained in this experiment was significantly higher than Experiment 1 (average k = 0.099). However, similar to Experiment 1, none of the questions were statistically significant, which meant the agreement might have been due to chance.

While intra-rater reliability between GPT rounds showed fair agreement and slight improvements over Experiment 1, inter-rater reliability, particularly for GPT 2 versus Human, remains weak. Coverage (Q8) emerged as the most consistently aligned criterion across all comparisons, whereas Comprehensibility and Significance continued to be the weakest areas, requiring further refinement in GPT models to align with human evaluations.

4.3 Reliability Between Human and GPT Evaluations of Research Hypotheses

To explore the consistency of evaluations across raters, we attempted to calculate weighted kappa values for intra-rater (GPT 1 vs. GPT 2) and inter-rater (Human vs. GPT) reliability on five key aspects of research hypotheses. However, all evaluating questions returned the same outcome: the statistics could not be computed because each variable had fewer than two valid categories. Upon manual review, we found that for all five questions (Q12 to Q16), weighted kappa values and significance tests were not applicable due to a lack of variability in responses. This was because all evaluated research proposals lacked explicit hypotheses, prompting both human raters and the GPT model to consistently assign "Not Applicable" (N/A) for every item. The uniformity in ratings resulted in insufficient variation in calculating agreement metrics such as kappa.

Nevertheless, this outcome highlights an important finding: ChatGPT consistently recognized the absence of hypotheses in the proposals. This suggests that the model followed instructions carefully by marking "N/A" when appropriate, rather than hallucinating content or inferring meaning implicitly—despite the fact that the instructions were less detailed than those used in Experiment 1.

4.4 Reliability Between Human and GPT Evaluations of Research Paradigm

Table 5 evaluates agreement levels between GPT-1, GPT-2, and human raters on 2 questions evaluating Research Paradigm on 2 aspects: Identification and Justification.

The overall average for Q17 and Q18 is 0.509, indicating a moderate level of agreement between the two GPT evaluations.

For Q17 on the identification of the research paradigm, the k value was 0.325, with statistical significance ($p = 0.030$), indicating a fair level of agreement. For Q18 on the justification of the chosen paradigm using relevant literature, the weighted kappa was 0.692, with high statistical significance ($p = 0.000$). This suggested a substantial level of agreement when GPT evaluated these criteria, which was similar to that of Experiment 1 when the k value for the criterion was 0.641. However, the statistic of Q17 in the new experiment was significantly lower than that in Experiment 1 (k = 0.742, $p = 0$), making the average k value of GPT 1 versus GPT 2 lower than in Experiment 1 as well.

Table 5 Comparison of Intra-rater and Inter-rater reliability between Human and GPT evaluations of Research Paradigm

	GPT 1 versus GPT 2		Human versus GPT 1		Human versus GPT 2	
Evaluating question	Weighted Kappa[a]	Sig.	Weighted Kappa[a]	Sig.	Weighted Kappa[a]	Sig.
Q17 (Identification)	0.325	0.030	0.247	0.086	0.448	0.002
Q18 (Justification)	0.692	0.000	0.674	0.000	0.721	0.000
Average Q17 to Q18	0.509		0.461		0.585	

The overall average of Human versus GPT 1 was 0.461, indicating a moderate level of agreement. While the k value for Q17 was 0.247 (not statistically significant, $p =$ 0.086), the k value of Q18 was 0.674 (statistically significant, $p = 0.000$). Compared to the statistic of Experiment 1 on this criterion (k = 0.126, $p = 0.047$), the new experiment displayed substantial improvement in the agreement between human and GPT evaluation of the justification of the paradigm, suggesting the strength in optimizing the Rubric and the ToT framework.

The overall average of Human versus GPT 2 was 0.585, which fell into the moderate range and was significantly higher than that of Experiment 1 (0.326). The k value of Q17 in the second GPT round was significantly higher than the first time (k = 0.448) and was statistically significant ($p = 0.002$). Similarly, the k value of the Justification question (k = 0.721) was not only higher than GPT 1 but also significantly higher than Experiment 1 (k = 0.088, p = 0.179) and was statistically significant ($p = 0.000$).

These statistics showed that while the identification of the research paradigm was less consistent, the evaluation of paradigm justification was considerably improved using the new Rubric and the ToT framework.

4.5 *Reliability Between Human and GPT Evaluations of Research Design*

Table 6 evaluates agreement levels between GPT-1, GPT-2, and human raters on 3 questions evaluating Research Design on 3 aspects: Identification, Justification and Feasibility.

The average k value indicating intra-rater reliability was 0.507, indicating moderate agreement across the criteria. This statistic exceeded that of Experiment 1 (average k = 0.42), suggesting overall improvement in the evaluation of Research Design. Justification (Q20) had the highest k value at 0.558 (statistically significant, $p = 0.00$), reflecting moderate agreement and suggesting that GPT interpreted and assessed the proposals' explanation of the chosen design similarly. The evaluation of the design's feasibility within given resources was also reliably consistent with k =

Table 6 Comparison of Intra-rater and Inter-rater reliability between human and GPT evaluations of research design

	GPT 1 versus GPT 2		Human versus GPT 1		Human versus GPT 2	
Evaluating question	Weighted Kappa[a]	Sig.	Weighted Kappa[a]	Sig.	Weighted Kappa[a]	Sig.
Q19 (Identification)	0.442	0.004	0.118	0.435	0.256	0.069
Q20 (Justification)	0.558	0.000	0.551	0.000	0.493	0.000
Q21 (Practicality)	0.521	0.001	0.382	0.008	0.418	0.003
Average Q19 to Q21	0.507		0.350		0.389	

0.521 ($p = 0.001$). Similar to Paradigm, Identification of design (Q19) had the lowest kappa at 0.442 ($p = 0.004$). However, k values for all criteria in this experiment were sufficiently higher than the previous experiment, especially for Justification, as the k value for this criterion in Experiment 1 was only 0.42.

The average k value for Human versus GPT1 was 0.350, reflecting fair agreement. This was the lowest average among all comparisons, suggesting GPT1 struggled to align with human evaluators. However, it was sufficiently higher than that of Experiment 1 (k = 0.269). Similar to intra-rater reliability statistics, Justification (Q20) achieved the highest k value at 0.551 ($p = 0.00$), indicating moderate agreement between Human and GPT1. Identification (Q19) had the lowest Weighted Kappa at 0.118, reflecting very weak agreement with no statistical significance ($p = 0.435$). While the statistic for Justification showed significant improvement compared to Experiment 1 (k = 0.208, $p = 0.002$), the value for Identification in this experiment was insubstantial compared to that of Experiment 1 (k = 0.383, $p = 0.00$).

The average Weighted Kappa for Human versus GPT2 was 0.389, slightly higher than GPT1 versus Human. Justification (Q20) again had the highest k value at 0.493, with a p value of 0.00, more than tripling that in Experiment 1 (k = 0.144, $p = 0.016$). Identification (Q19) again had the lowest Weighted Kappa at 0.256, which was slightly better than Human versus GPT1 but still reflected fair agreement. This result was borderline significant ($p = 0.069$), indicating GPT2 slightly outperformed GPT1 and Experiment 1 (k = 0.239, $p = 0.009$) in aligning with human evaluators for identification but still fell short overall. Practicality was fairly consistently evaluated with both GPT1 and GPT2 (k = 0.382 and 0.418, respectively), indicating that this criterion was moderately aligned between human evaluators and GPT systems.

Overall, for the evaluation of Design, the consistency between raters improved, but this increase did not extend to the identification criterion. For identification, Experiment 1 showed greater consistency compared to the present study. However, the highlight was justification, which consistently demonstrated improved agreement across both intra-rater and inter-rater reliability.

4.6 Reliability Between Human and GPT Evaluations of Research Techniques

Table 7 evaluates agreement levels between GPT-1, GPT-2, and human raters on 5 questions evaluating Research techniques on 3 aspects: Identification, Theoretical justification *(The proposal's explanation how the chosen techniques facilitate answering the research questions/testing hypotheses using relevant literature*), Practical justification (*The proposal's explanation on the practicality of the techniques)*, Effectiveness and Practicality *(The true practicality of the techniques within resources)*.

The average Weighted Kappa for GPT 1 was 0.526, reflecting moderate agreement and showcasing moderate intra-rater reliability. The authentic practicality of the

Table 7 Comparison of Intra-rater and Inter-rater reliability between human and GPT evaluations of research techniques

	GPT 1 versus GPT 2		Human versus GPT 1		Human versus GPT 2	
Evaluating question	Weighted Kappa[a]	Sig.	Weighted Kappa[a]	Sig.	Weighted Kappa[a]	Sig.
Q22(Identification)	0.379	0.015	0.214	0.167	0.366	0.020
Q23 (Theoretical justification)	0.583	0.000	0.374	0.018	0.393	0.012
Q24 (Practical justification)	0.493	0.002	0.301	0.024	0.299	0.015
Q25(Effectiveness)	0.486	0.002	0.419	0.006	0.446	0.002
Q26 (Practicality)	0.690	0.000	0.282	0.053	0.592	0.000
Average Q22 to Q26	0.526		0.318		0.419	

techniques (Q26) with a k value of 0.690 demonstrated substantial agreement. Most of the evaluation questions' k values fell into the moderate range (0.41 < k < 0.60) and were all statistically significant, indicating overall consistency between GPT rounds. Similar to Paradigm and Design, Q22 (Identification) with a k value of 0.379 had the lowest consistency among criteria. This was the only criterion where this study fell short of Experiment 1 (k = 0.601, p = 0). While most of the criteria witnessed improvement in k value, Effectiveness was the criterion where the most improvement was observed between this study and Experiment 1 (k = 0.252, $p = 0.017$).

The average Weighted Kappa for Human and the first GPT round was 0.318. Despite being the lowest among the pairs, it exceeded that of Experiment 1 (average k = 0.186). Q25 (Effectiveness) with a k value of 0.419 was the most consistent criterion across evaluations. This number was not only statistically significant but also five times higher than that of Experiment 1 (k = 0.086, $p = 0.133$). A similar phenomenon was observed in the Theoretical Justification criterion with a k value of 0.374 ($p = 0.018$), more than six times that of Experiment 1 (k = 0.058, $p = 0.127$). Most of the criteria fell into the fair range with statistical significance. Q22 (Identification) with a Weighted Kappa of 0.214 reflected very weak agreement and a lack of statistical significance ($p = 0.167$). Similar to intra-rater reliability, this criterion fell short of that of Experiment 1 (k = 0.415, $p = 0.00$).

GPT 2 versus Human had a kappa value of 0.419, which showed moderate agreement but was several times higher than that of Experiment 1 (average k = 0.117). Q26 (Practicality) had the highest k value of 0.592, demonstrating moderate to substantial agreement. Except for this criterion and the Effectiveness of the techniques, all criteria fell into the fair range (0.21 < k < 0.4) and were all statistically significant ($p < 0.05$), which meant the agreement recorded was reliable and not due to chance. Q24 (Practical Justification) with a Weighted Kappa of 0.299 had the weakest agreement among criteria. Notably, an improvement in consistency levels was observed across all criteria compared to Experiment 1, with Theoretical Justification showing the most significant increase, as the statistic in the present study was ten times higher than that of Experiment 1 (k = 0.036, $p = 0.196$).

In conclusion, most criteria demonstrated significant improvements in reliability and agreement compared to Experiment 1. Practicality (Q26) and Theoretical Justification (Q23) showed the most notable improvement across both intra-rater and inter-rater reliability. However, Identification (Q22) remained the least consistent criterion, especially in Human-GPT comparisons.

5 Discussion

Overall, the inter-rater and intra-rater reliability between ChatGPT's evaluations and human evaluators' ranged from fair to substantial, with most of the criteria evaluated falling into the moderate range. Similar to Experiment 1, this finding aligns with Syriani et al. (2023) and Lin et al., (2023), who reported that ChatGPT performs well in structured classification tasks without task-specific training. However, this experiment using ChatGPT with the optimized Rubric (26 questions), the Tree of Thoughts (ToT) framework, and a Zero-shot learning approach yielded better results than Experiment 1, where the Rubric consisted of 39 questions and employed detailed Chain-of-Thought (CoT)-style prompts stating evaluation steps for each individual section. This discovery agrees with existing studies that emphasized that ToT's ability to handle complex reasoning tasks is more effective than CoT (Besta et al., 2024; Long, 2023; Yao et al., 2023). It is assumed that the evaluation precision of ToT was improved through its backtracking and lookahead functions combined as the model could reevaluate past decisions while anticipating future results of the path being explored. This led to more informed and accurate global decision-making. However, this finding contradicts the discoveries of Thelwall and Kurt (2024), who stated that more complicated prompts resulted in better ChatGPT reasoning abilities. In our case, replacing CoT's step-by-step style prompt with ToT's branching prompt led to greater reliability across many sections, suggesting that complexity in prompt design must also support structured exploration and reasoning, not just length or detail. This implies that it is not the surface complexity of the prompt that enhances reasoning performance, but rather the underlying structure of the reasoning technique. ToT's evaluation is an improvement compared to CoT's, which, although beneficial for improving interpretability and reasoning transparency, can suffer from error propagation (when a mistake in an early step causes later steps to be incorrect) due to its inability to backtrack (Wei et al., 2023). While CoT relies on detailed prompts for each rubric item, it follows a linear path where a mistake in a previous step inevitably leads to mistakes in subsequent steps. In contrast, ToT enables branching explorations and self-evaluation, allowing the model to evaluate intermediate steps and make timely adjustments. As shown in the findings, despite simpler prompt sets, ToT technique produced more accurate and consistent evaluations, especially in areas requiring nuanced assessment and in-depth logic. In addition, the evaluation made through ToT reasoning technique showed more alignment with that of humans, which is now the benchmark for evaluation. Thus, it is safe to conclude that reasoning success may depend more on strategic exploration than prompt elaboration.

Except for the intra-rater reliability of the evaluations of the Research Title and Research Questions sections, all other sections showed fair to moderate consistency ($0.2 < k < 0.6$). Most evaluation questions were statistically significant, indicating the agreements were unlikely to occur by chance. These findings are consistent with Thelwall (2024), who reported moderate correlation between ChatGPT and human evaluations under structured conditions. Reliability improved across sections compared to Experiment 1, with the most pronounced improvement in the Research Title section, which increased by nearly 0.150. However, the identification of the Paradigm and Techniques scored significantly lower than Experiment 1. In contrast, the consistency of Justification and Effectiveness evaluations for Paradigm, Design, and Techniques improved significantly ($p < 0.05$). This further confirms that the new Rubric and ToT framework enhanced ChatGPT's consistency, particularly in areas requiring deeper analysis. However, it flagged the new model's struggles with the ability to identify research paradigms and techniques, which was a strength of Experiment 1. This implies that ToT better supports deeper critical analysis, but underperforms with straightforward classification tasks.

Examining inter-rater reliability alone, improvements were discovered across most sections, with average k values for Human versus GPT exceeding those from Experiment 1, except for Human versus GPT 1 in the Research Title section. The most notable improvement occurred in the Paradigm and Techniques sections (Human vs. GPT2), which demonstrated an increase of more than 0.250. This highlights ChatGPT's potential for evaluating research methods, partially resolving previously discovered limitations in ChatGPT's ability to critiquing methodological designs (Liang et al., 2023; Thelwall, 2024). However, the identification of Paradigm, Design, and Techniques yielded lower agreement between the evaluations of ChatGPT's rounds and human and ChatGPT. This reinforces that ToT's ability to evaluate straightforward areas may fall short compared to CoT. This feature is also proven in the evaluation of Comprehensibility and Ambiguity of the Research Title which showed less agreement, suggesting more discrepancies in how humans and GPT evaluate these criteria using the new Rubric and ToT framework compared to Experiment 1. Nevertheless, the evaluation of Effectiveness and Justification of Paradigm, Design, and Techniques improved significantly, with statistically significant results confirming these agreements were not due to chance.

As can be seen from the findings, while the ToT framework improved ChatGPT's ability to evaluate complex criteria, its inherent complexity might hinder performance on straightforward tasks. For example, pattern recognition as well as direct verbatim pattern cues are used for identifying sections such as Paradigm, Design and Techniques as well as evaluating the Comprehensibility and Ambiguity of the Research Title. The additional layers of self-evaluation within the ToT framework may lead ChatGPT to overanalyze from straightforward logic, resulting in lower consistency for simpler tasks. This contradicts concerns raised by Ye et al. (2024) and Doskaliuk et al. (2025) that ChatGPT lacked the critical reasoning needed to identify methodological components, often relying on superficial linguistic patterns rather than actual comprehension. In our study, ToT demonstrably enhanced ChatGPT's capacity for such evaluations. However, this result also implies that while the ToT framework is highly beneficial for tasks requiring deep analysis, nuanced judgment and logical scientific reasoning, it may introduce unnecessary complexity for tasks that require direct and structured evaluations. As pointed out Besta et al. (2024), a complicated problem requires decomposing into many sub-problems, but a straightforward one does not benefit from many more subdivisions, as the additional branches then can be either redundant or wrong. ToT's complex exploratory paths and constant self-check may have distracted the model from recognizing simpler pattern-based answers that CoT previously handled more effectively.

Moreover, consistent with Thelwall (2024), Ye et al. (2024), Doskaliuk et al. (2025) and Experiment 1, this study found that, ChatGPT struggled to reliably evaluate the Significance of research questions due to this criteria's demand for broader contextual knowledge. This feature was highlighted by Thelwall (2024) who discovered through the evaluation of a fabricated paper concerning "squirrel surgeon". This proves that while ChatGPT possesses a vast database with knowledge from various fields, it fails to employ this knowledge into the evaluation process. This limitation hinders its ability to evaluate research proposals holistically, as such evaluations often require contextualization within current discoveries in the field.

Another finding worth highlighting is the evaluation Hypotheses. In contrast to prior findings by Ye et al. (2024), which demonstrated that ChatGPT-generated reviews were prone to hallucination and exhibited behaviors such as creating reviews for incomplete or even empty papers, flagging its inability to detect missing methodological components, our study revealed a markedly different behavior. When equipped with a detailed rubric and ToT style prompt set, ChatGPT consistently recognized the absence of hypotheses and appropriately marked all hypothesis-related criteria as "Not Applicable" (N/A), which resulted in uniform ratings across all proposals and rendered Cohen's weighted kappa incalculable. However, rather than indicating a failure, this outcome highlights ChatGPT's capacity to detect missing methodological elements and strictly follow evaluation instructions when the exit strategy is used in the prompts (*mark N/A*) and the instructions of the Rubric are clear (i.e., *The hypotheses are explicitly stated under the HYPOTHESES section: move to question 12. The hypotheses are NOT explicitly stated: mark N/A for Questions 12 to 16*).

6 Conclusion

This research shows that combining Tree of Thoughts (ToT) framework with optimized Rubric and zero-shot instruction allows ChatGPT to perform structured evaluation tasks with superior success when compared to the detailed linear evaluation method Chain-of-Thought (CoT). ToT made evaluations more reliable particularly when evaluating nuanced areas requiring deep-analytic ability such as Methodological components of research articles. However, the research findings show that ToT fails to perform well in basic tasks since its complex approach obscures obvious pattern cues that CoT detects more efficiently. While the results of this study reinforce previous conclusions that ToT supports advanced reasoning capabilities, its success relies on the complexity of the assignment. It is advised that reasoning methods can be task-specific and more complex reasoning techniques does not necessarily result in better performance. ToT should be employed for complex evaluations but basic CoT approach should be considered for standard grading procedures.

While the ToT framework enhanced ChatGPT performance, it still only reached a moderate consistency with human assessments through most evaluation criteria. These shortcomings highlight the model's lack of genuine academic understanding and its tendency to simulate reasoning rather than engage in deep, concept-driven evaluation. The results reinforce the necessity of human involvement in reviewing academic work and that ChatGPT needs further development before its assessment can rival that of humans, especially in texts needing domain-specific expertise, contextual abilities and critical analysis.

Nonetheless, the present research has several limitations. Firstly, the small sample size (n = 40) limits the generalizability of the findings. The samples also uniformly excluded hypotheses, which, while demonstrating that ChatGPT can consistently recognize the absence of hypotheses, fails to demonstrate its ability to evaluate the quality of hypotheses. This limitation signifies a missed opportunity to assess ChatGPT's capacity for deeper analysis into this crucial component of research evaluation. Additionally, the study did not incorporate qualitative data, such as comments from both human and ChatGPT evaluations, which could have provided valuable insights into the sources of discrepancies between the two. Furthermore, two of the four human raters were the researchers who have done similar research in the past (Experiment 1), resulting in the potential for bias in the scoring process.

Future research should address these limitations by increasing the sample size, including proposals with research hypotheses and analyzing qualitative data alongside quantitative results to gain deeper insights into the differences between human and ChatGPT evaluations. Moreover, human raters should ideally have no prior knowledge of ChatGPT's scoring patterns to ensure fairness and minimize potential bias.

Appendix A: Scoring Rubric

Section	Evaluating question	Evaluation scale				
		Very unsatisfactory	Satisfactory	Neutral	Satisfactory	Very satisfactory
Research title	1. Does the title avoid ambiguous words that may be open to different interpretations?	1 point: Contains multiple ambiguous terms open to multiple interpretations	2 points: Contains one or two ambiguous terms that can be understood in different ways	3 points: Avoids major ambiguities but could be clearer in its phrasing	4 points: Clear with no evident ambiguous terms; some minor room for improvement in phrasing or specificity	5 points: Exceptionally clear, with no ambiguity, and the focus is immediately understandable without requiring further interpretation
	2. Is the title concise, avoiding unnecessary words or overly complex phrasing?	1 point: Is excessively long, overly complex, or includes redundant words	2 points: Has unnecessary words or overly complex phrasing that could be simplified	3 points: Moderately concise but could benefit from slight simplification	4 points: Concise with minimal or no unnecessary words, but could benefit from slight refinement	5 points: Exceptionally concise, free from redundant words, and effectively communicates the research focus, with no loss of clarity
	3. Is the title accurately formulated to ensure comprehensibility?	1 point: Poorly formulated with major grammatical mistakes (e.g., incorrect prepositions, verb usage) making it difficult to understand the research's aim	2 points: Poorly formulated with minor grammatical mistakes that slightly hinder understanding of the research's aim	3 points: Moderately comprehensible with occasional grammatical issues that could be improved for clarity	4 points: Well-formulated with minor or no grammatical mistakes, ensuring clear understanding	5 points: Exceptionally formulated with perfect grammar, ensuring complete and immediate comprehensibility

(continued)

(continued)

Section	Evaluating question	Evaluation scale				
		Very unsatisfactory	Satisfactory	Neutral	Satisfactory	Very satisfactory
	4. Are the key concepts and variables (e.g., participants, context, treatments) clearly and specifically included in the title?	1 point: Omits most or all key concepts and variables, making the study's focus unclear	2 points: Includes some key concepts but lacks critical details, such as participants or context	3 points: Includes key concepts and variables but without details, making it difficult to identify the concepts and variables	4 points: Clearly includes key concepts and variables with some details but lacks precision or depth in certain areas	5 points: Excellently incorporates all key concepts and variables with precise descriptions, leaving no ambiguity
	5. Does the title align closely with the research questions/hypotheses?	1 point: Does not reflect the research questions or hypotheses, creating a completely misleading impression of the study	2 points: Partially reflects the research questions or hypotheses but omits key elements that distort the study's focus	3 points: Reflects the research questions or hypotheses with minor omissions or inaccuracies	4 points: Accurately reflects all research questions or hypotheses with no significant omissions or inaccuracies	5 points: Perfectly aligns with the research questions or hypotheses, fully and accurately representing the study's focus
Research questions	6. Can the research questions be addressed scientifically using the existing research methodology?	1 point: Research question is completely unfeasible with existing methodology	2 points: Research question is largely unfeasible due to significant methodological issues	3 points: Feasibility is limited but possible with adjustments	4 points: Research question is feasible with minor refinements	5 points: Research question is entirely feasible and well-supported by methodology
	7. Can the research questions be answered using the available resources (time: 1 year, budget: 100 million VND, personnel: 5 people)?	1 point: All resources are entirely insufficient to answer the questions	2 points: 2 to 3 resources are insufficient, creating major issues	3 points: All resources are moderately sufficient with minor risks	4 points: Resources are sufficient, needing minor adjustments in 1 resource	5 points: Resources are fully sufficient and support the study

(continued)

(continued)

Section	Evaluating question	Evaluation scale				
		Very unsatisfactory	Satisfactory	Neutral	Satisfactory	Very satisfactory
	8. Are the key concepts and variables (e.g., participants, context, treatments) clearly included in the research questions?	1 point: Omits most or all key concepts and variables, making the study's focus unclear	2 points: Includes some key concepts but lacks critical details, such as participants or context	3 points: Includes key concepts and variables but without details, making it difficult to identify the concepts and variables	4 points: Clearly includes key concepts and variables with some details	5 points: Excellently incorporates all key concepts and variables with precise descriptions
	9. Are the research questions accurately formulated to ensure comprehensibility?	1 point: Poorly formulated with major grammatical mistakes (e.g., incorrect prepositions, verb usage) making it difficult to understand the research's aim	2 points: Poorly formulated with minor grammatical mistakes that slightly hinder understanding of the research's aim	3 points: Moderately comprehensible with occasional grammatical issues that could be improved for clarity	4 points: Well-formulated with minor or no grammatical mistakes, ensuring clear understanding	5 points: Exceptionally formulated with perfect grammar, ensuring complete and immediate comprehensibility
	10. Can the keywords and terms in the research questions be precisely defined to enable accurate measurement or identification?	1 point: Keywords and terms are vague and open to multiple interpretations	2 points: Abstract terms are used, making them hard to define or measure	3 points: Keywords and terms are fairly specific but need effort to define	4 points: Minimal ambiguity exists, but some clarification is needed	5 points: Keywords and terms are precise, clear, and easily measurable

(continued)

(continued)

Section	Evaluating question	Evaluation scale				
		Very unsatisfactory	Satisfactory	Neutral	Satisfactory	Very satisfactory
	11. Can the research questions contribute valuable knowledge to the field of teaching, learning or using the English language?	1 point: The research questions fail to address any gap in existing knowledge	2 points: The research questions can provide minimal insight into unresolved issues	3 points: The research questions address a minor gap in existing knowledge or replicate prior work with some new perspective	4 points: The research questions address a significant gap in existing literature and are likely to produce meaningful insights	5 points: The research questions clearly address a critical gap in the field, propose innovative approaches
	The hypotheses are explicitly stated under the HYPOTHESES section: move to question 12 *The hypotheses are NOT explicitly stated: mark N/A for Questions 12 to 16*					
	12. Can the hypotheses be empirically tested through existing research methodologies?	1 point: Hypotheses cannot be empirically tested using current methods	2 points: Hypotheses are difficult to test due to methodological gaps	3 points: Hypotheses are testable with moderate adjustments	4 points: Hypotheses are testable with minor refinements	5 points: Hypotheses are fully testable using existing methodologies
	13. Do the hypotheses indicate their testing methods?	1 point: Hypotheses do not indicate how it can be tested	2 points: Hypotheses suggest several ways for testing but lack indication	3 points: Hypotheses suggest testing methods but lack clarity	4 points: Hypotheses indicate testing methods with minor gaps	5 points: Hypotheses clearly indicate robust and complete testing methods

(continued)

(continued)

Section	Evaluating question	Evaluation scale				
		Very unsatisfactory	Satisfactory	Neutral	Satisfactory	Very satisfactory
	14. Are the key concepts and variables (e.g., participants, context, treatments) clearly included in the research hypotheses?	1 point: Omits most or all key concepts and variables, making the study's focus unclear	2 points: Includes some key concepts but lacks critical details, such as participants or context	3 points: Includes key concepts and variables but without details, making it difficult to identify the concepts and variables	4 points: Clearly includes key concepts and variables with some details	5 points: Excellently incorporates all key concepts and variables with precise descriptions
	15. Can the keywords and terms in the hypotheses be precisely defined to enable accurate measurement or identification?	1 point: Keywords and terms are vague and open to multiple interpretations	2 points: Abstract terms are used, making them hard to define or measure	3 points: Keywords and terms are fairly specific but need effort to define	4 points: Minimal ambiguity exists, but some clarification is needed	5 points: Keywords and terms are precise, clear, and easily measurable
	16. Do the hypotheses contribute valuable knowledge to the field of teaching, learning or using the English language?	1 point: The hypotheses fail to address any gap in existing knowledge	2 points: The hypotheses can provide minimal insight into unresolved issues	3 points: The hypotheses address a minor gap in existing knowledge or replicate prior work with some new perspective	4 points: The hypotheses address a significant gap in existing literature and are likely to produce meaningful insights	5 points: The hypotheses clearly address a critical gap in the field, propose innovative approaches

(continued)

(continued)

Section	Evaluating question	Evaluation scale				
		Very unsatisfactory	Satisfactory	Neutral	Satisfactory	Very satisfactory
Paradigm	17. Does the proposal identify the chosen paradigm (i.e. quantitative, qualitative, mixed-methods)?	1 point: The proposal does not identify the chosen paradigm	2 points: The paradigm is vaguely mentioned but lacks clarity on whether it is quantitative, qualitative, or mixed	3 points: The paradigm is identified but lacks sufficient detail or explanation	4 points: The paradigm is clearly identified with minor gaps in explanation	5 points: The paradigm is explicitly and precisely identified, providing complete clarity and detail
	18. Does the proposal justify the choice of paradigm using relevant literature and citations?	1 point: The proposal provides no justification or supporting literature for the chosen paradigm	2 points: The justification relies on vague or generic statements lacks sufficient citations	3 points: The justification is logical and supported but requires additional literature	4 points: The justification demonstrates strong reasoning and is well-supported, with only minor gaps in citations	5 points: The justification demonstrates strong reasoning and is well-supported with literature
Design	19. Does the proposal clearly identify the chosen research design and its type (i.e., action research, case study, experiment, survey)?	1 point: The research design is not identified	2 points: The research design is vaguely identified with little clarity	3 points: The research design is identified but lacks detail on its type	4 points: The research design is clearly identified with some details	5 points: The research design is explicitly identified with detailed description of types or variations

(continued)

(continued)

Section	Evaluating question	Evaluation scale				
		Very unsatisfactory	Satisfactory	Neutral	Satisfactory	Very satisfactory
	20. Does the proposal explain how the chosen design facilitates answering the research questions/testing hypotheses using relevant literature and citations?	1 point: The proposal does not explain how the design addresses the research questions or hypotheses	2 points: The explanation is weak, with minimal connection to the research questions and insufficient citations	3 points: The explanation connects the design to some research questions/ hypotheses with logical reasoning but limited citations	4 points: The explanation connects the design to all research questions/ hypotheses with clear reasoning	5 points: The explanation logically connects the design to all research questions/ hypotheses with detailed reasoning and supporting citations
	21. Is the design feasible within available resources (time: 1 year, budget: 100 million VND, personnel: 5 people))?	1 point: The design is entirely unfeasible with the available resources	2 points: The design is difficult to implement due to significant resource limitations	3 points: The design is feasible but requires adjustments to align with the available resources	4 points: The design is feasible with minor adjustments needed for 1 resource	5 points: The design is fully feasible and well-aligned with the available resources
Techniques	22. Does the proposal clearly identify the chosen data collection techniques and their type (i.e., interview, questionnaire, observation, documents)?	1 point: The proposal does not identify the chosen data collection techniques	2 points: The techniques are vaguely identified without clarity on type	3 points: The techniques are identified but lack detailed description	4 points: The techniques are identified with some description	5 points: The techniques are explicitly identified with full clarity and detail

(continued)

(continued)

Section	Evaluating question	Evaluation scale				
		Very unsatisfactory	Satisfactory	Neutral	Satisfactory	Very satisfactory
	23. Does the proposal explain how the chosen techniques facilitate answering the research questions/testing hypotheses using relevant literature and citations?	1 point: The proposal does not explain how the techniques facilitate answering the research questions	2 points: The explanation is unreliable, with minimal connection to the research questions and insufficient citations	3 points: The explanation connects the techniques to the research questions/ hypotheses with logical reasoning but limited citations	4 points: The explanation connects the techniques to the research questions/ hypotheses with clear reasoning and adequate citations	5 points: The explanation logically connects the techniques to the research questions/ hypotheses with detailed reasoning and strong citations
	24. Does the proposal explain why the chosen techniques are practical and achievable, considering factors like access to participants, time, and resources?	1 point: The proposal does not explain why the techniques are practical or achievable	2 points: The explanation is limited and fails to consider factors like participants, time, or resources	3 points: The explanation partially addresses practicality but lacks detail	4 points: The explanation clearly describes practicality with minimal gaps	5 points: The explanation comprehensively describes why the techniques are practical and achievable, considering all relevant factors
	25. Do the chosen research techniques effectively gather sufficient data to answer the research questions or test the hypotheses?	1 point: The techniques cannot gather any data to answer all research questions	2 points: The techniques gather some data but are not enough for comprehensive answers or fail to address 1 research question	3 points: The techniques gather enough data but may have some limitations in reliability	4 points: The techniques effectively gather enough data with minor issues	5 points: The techniques fully gather enough reliable data to answer the research questions or test hypotheses

(continued)

(continued)

Section	Evaluating question	Evaluation scale				
		Very unsatisfactory	Satisfactory	Neutral	Satisfactory	Very satisfactory
	26. Are the techniques feasible within available resources (time: 1 year, budget: 100 million VND, personnel: 5 people))?	1 point: The techniques are entirely unfeasible given the available resources	2 points: The techniques are difficult to implement due to significant resource limitations	3 points: The techniques are moderately feasible but require adjustments to align with resources	4 points: The techniques are feasible with minimal adjustments needed	5 points: The techniques are fully feasible and well-aligned with the available resources

Appendix B: Tot Process For Evaluating The Methodological Components

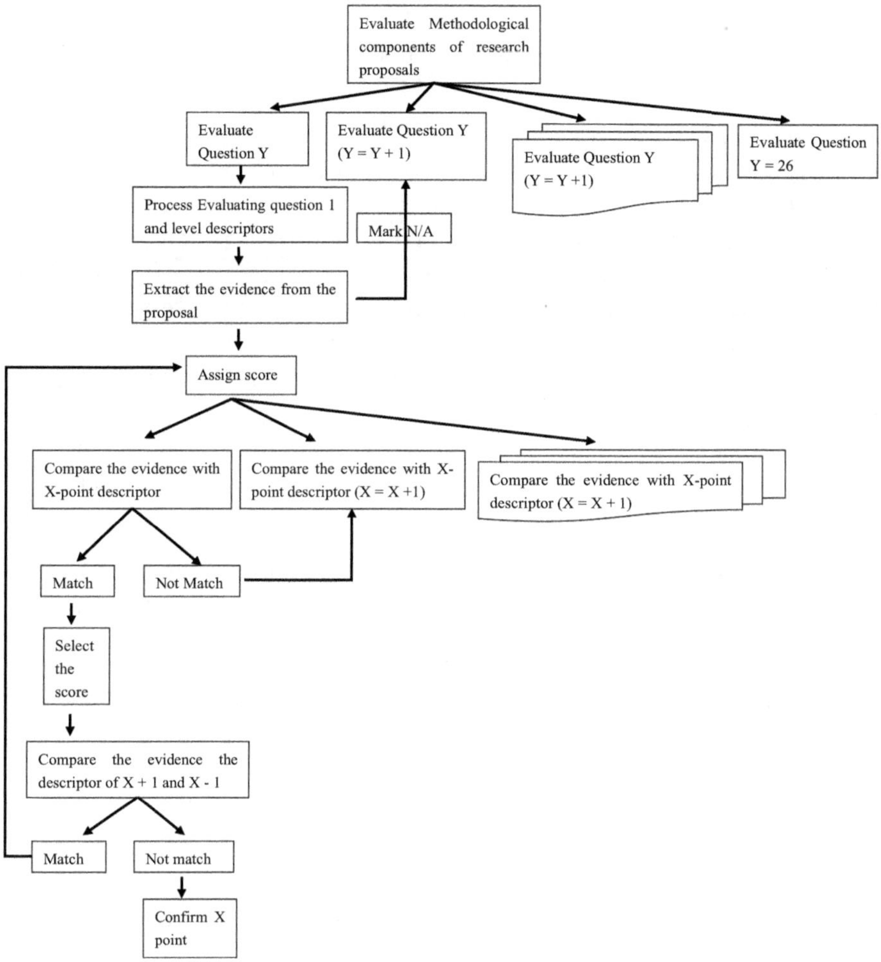

Appendix C: Experiment 1's Weighted Kappa Values

Ratings	Criteria	GPT 1 versus GPT 2		Human versus GPT 1		Human versus GPT 2		K value average of Human and GPT evaluations
		Weighted Kappa[a]	Sig	Weighted Kappa[a]	Sig	Weighted Kappa[a]	Sig	
T1	Ambiguity	0.439	0.001	0.042	0.316	−0.052	0.337	−0.005
T2	Conciseness	0.358	0.005	0.34	0.001	0.219	0.025	0.28
T3	Declarative	.e	.e	.e	.e	.e	.e	.e
T4	Comprehensibility	0.298	0.07	0.181	0.109	0.132	0.248	0.157
T5	Neutrality	.e	.e	.e	.e	.e	.e	.e
T6	Coverage	0.317	0.011	0.484	0	0.23	0.067	0.357
T7	Participants	0.268	0.047	0.297	0.008	0.141	0.212	0.219
T8	Uniqueness	0.294	0.048	0.299	0.011	−0.032	0.783	0.134
T9	Complementarity	.e	.e	.e	.e	.e	.e	.e
T10	Relevance	0.501	0	0.092	0.162	0.054	0.336	0.073
Average T1 to T10		0.354		0.248		0.099		0.173
Q1	Feasibility	0.218	0.025	0.133	0.007	0.067	0.185	0.1
Q2	Practicality	0.17	0.271	0.057	0.198	−0.035	0.314	0.011
Q3	Coverage (participants)	0.424	0.001	0.268	0	0.182	0.005	0.225
Q4	Coverage (research site)	0.768	0	0.348	0	0.38	0	0.364
Q5	Coverage (research phenomenon)	0.14	0.234	0.135	0.039	0.034	0.283	0.085
Q6	Comprehensibility	0.151	0.306	0.126	0.051	0.067	0.193	0.097
Q7	Measurability	0.267	0.024	0.022	0.586	0.049	0.173	0.036
Q8	Significance	0.528	0	0.023	0.383	−0.026	0.525	−0.002
Q9	Ethics	.e	.e	.e	.e	.e	.e	.e
Q10	Alignment	0.403	0.014	0.02	0.694	0.113	0.027	0.067
Average Q1 to Q10		0.341		0.126		0.092		0.109
H1	Feasibility	1	0	0.667	0.134	0.667	0.134	0.667
H2	Resource Constraints	1	0	0.5	0.134	0.5	0.134	0.5
H3	Specificity	1	0	0.25	0.19	0.25	0.19	0.25
H4	Participants	0	0.236	0.063	0.743	0.75	0.089	0.406

(continued)

(continued)

Ratings	Criteria	GPT 1 versus GPT 2		Human versus GPT 1		Human versus GPT 2		K value average of Human and GPT evaluations
		Weighted Kappa[a]	Sig	Weighted Kappa[a]	Sig	Weighted Kappa[a]	Sig	
H5	Research Site	1	0	0.757	0.083	0.757	0.083	0.757
H6	Focus	1	0	0.5	0.134	0.5	0.134	0.5
H7	Clarity	0.4	0.392	−0.5	0.083	−0.154	0.386	−0.327
H8	Measurability	0.667	0.21	0.1	0.386	0.182	0.134	0.141
H9	Ethicality	.e	.e	.e	.e	.e	.e	.e
H10	Alignment	.e	.e	.e	.e	.e	.e	.e
Average H1 to H10		0.758		0.292		0.431		0.362
P1	Identification	0.742	0	0.567	0	0.546	0	0.556
P2	Theoretical justification	0.641	0	0.126	0.047	0.088	0.179	0.107
P3	Effectiveness	0.726	0	0.389	0	0.345	0	0.367
Average P1 to P3		0.703		0.361		0.326		0.344
D1	Identification	0.41	0.001	0.383	0	0.239	0.009	0.311
D2	Theoretical justification	0.42	0	0.208	0.002	0.144	0.016	0.176
D3	Effectiveness	0.431	0	0.215	0.009	0.284	0.002	0.25
Average D1 to D3		0.42		0.269		0.223		0.246
Te1	Identification	0.601	0	0.415	0	0.208	0.075	0.312
Te2	Theoretical justification	0.486	0	0.058	0.127	0.036	0.196	0.047
Te3	Effectiveness	0.252	0.017	0.086	0.133	0.106	0.089	0.096
Average Te1 to Te3		0.446		0.186		0.117		0.152

[a] The estimation of the weighted kappa uses quadratic weights

References

Andrews, R. (2003). *Research questions*. Continuum Research Methods.

Baars, M. J. (2024). *Prompt engineering for beginners: Making A.I.* Work for You. BAARS Media.

Berry, K. J., & Johnston, J. E. (2008). Weighted Kappa for multiple raters. *Perceptual and Motor Skills*, 837–848.

Besta, M., Memedi, F., Zhang, Z., Gerstenberger, R., Piao, G., Blach, N., & Hoefler, T. (2024). *Demystifying chains, trees, and graphs of thoughts.*

Blaxter, L., Hughes, C., & Tight, M. (2010). *How to research* (4th ed.). Open University Press.

Booth, W. C., Colomb, G. G., Williams, J. M., Bizup, J., & FitzGerald, W. T. (2018). Research and writing. In K. L. Turabian (Ed.), *A manual for writers of research papers, theses, and disserations* (p. 199). The University of Chicago Press.

Brown, T. B., Mann, B., Ryder, N., Subbiah, M., Kaplan, J., Dhariwal, P., & Da. (2020). *Language models are few-shot learners.* https://arxiv.org/abs/2005.14165

Checco, A., Bracciale, L., Loreti, P., Pinfield, S., & Bianchi, G. (2021). AI-assisted peer review. In *Humanities and social sciences communications* (vol. 8, pp. 1–11).

Cohen, J. (1968). Weighted kappa: Nominal scale agreement with provision for scaled disagreement or partial credit. *Psychological Bulletin, 40*(4), 213–220.

Creswell, J. W. (2012). *Educational research: Planning, conducting, and evaluating quantitative and qualitative research* (4th ed.). Pearson.

Creswell, J. W. (2014). *Research design: Qualitative, quantitative, and mixed methods approaches.* SAGE Publications.

Doskaliuk, B., Zimba, O., Yessirkepov, M., Klishch, I., & Yatsyshyn, R. (2025). Artificial intelligence in peer review: Enhancing efficiency while preserving integrity. *Journal of Korean Medical Science, 40*(7). https://doi.org/10.3346/jkms.2025.40.e92

Duong, N., Tong, T., & Le, D. (2024). Utilizing ChatGPT in checking academic writing for postgraduate students. *Proceedings of the AsiaCALL International Conference*, 193–203. https://doi.org/10.54855/paic.24614

Duong, T., & Le, T. (2024). Utilizing artificial intelligence in writing feedback: Benefits and challenges for first-year students at Hanoi University of Industry. *Proceedings of the AsiaCALL International*, 238–249.

Esposito, F. (2024). *Programming large language models with azure open AI: Conversational programming and prompt engineering with LLMs.* Microsoft Press.

Fraenkel, J. R., Wallen, N. E., & Hyun, H. H. (2022). *How to design and evaluate research in education* (11th ed.).

Goodfellow, I., Bengio, Y., & Courville, A. (2016). *Deep learning.* The MIT Press.

Hoang T. A., & Vu T. N. (2024). Khám Phá Vai Trò Của Trí Tuệ Nhân Tạo AI—ChatGPT Trong Kỷ Nguyên Chuyển Đổi Số Để Ứng Dụng Vào Giảng Dạy Tiếng Anh (ELT) Tại Đại Học Kinh Tế - Kỹ Thuật Công Nghiệp (UNETI. In *Kỷ Yếu Hội Thảo Khoa Học Quốc Gia: Ngôn Ngữ Học Tính Toán: Những Xu Hướng Mới, Triển Vọng Và Thách Thức* (pp. 31–39).

Hong, R., Pang, X., & Zhang, C. (2024). Advances in reasoning by prompting large language models: A survey. *Cybernetics and Intelligence, 1*, 15.

Kojima, T., Gu, S. S., Reid, M., Matsuo, Y., & Iwasawa, Y. (2023). *Large language models are zero-shot reasoners.* https://arxiv.org/abs/2205.11916

Kousha, K., & Thelwall, M. (2022). *Artificial intelligence technologies to support research assessment: A review.* University of Wolverhampton.

Landis, J. R., & Koch, G. G. (1977). The measurement of observer agreement for categorical data. *Biometrics, 33*(1), 159–174.

Le, T. T. (2024). Evaluating HUFLIT lecturers' perspectives on ChatGPT's capabilities in designing English testing and assessment. *Proceedings of the AsiaCALL International Conference*, 157–181.

Lee, C. J., Sugimoto, C. R., Zhang, G., & Cronin, B. (2013). Bias in peer review. *Journal of the American Society for Information Science and Technology, 1*(64), 2–17.

Liang, W., Zhang, Y., Cao, H., Wang, B., Ding, D., Yang, X., & Zou, J. (2023). *Large language models provide useful feedback on research papers? A large-scale empirical analysis*, vol. 10, p. 3. https://arxiv.org/abs/2310.01783

Lin, J., Song, J., Zhou, Z., Chen, Y., & Shi, X. (2023). Automated scholarly paper review: Concepts, technologies, and challenges. *Information Fusion, 98*, 1–27.
Long, J. (2023). *Large language model guided tree-of-thought.*
Mai, H., & Tran, T. (2024). Examining english-majored students' performance and attitudes towards ChatGPT. *Proceedings of the AsiaCALL International Conference, 6*, 144–156. https://doi.org/10.54855/paic.24611
Nguyen, M. T. (2024). Sự Thích Nghi Của Sinh Viên Ngành Ngôn Ngữ Anh Tại HUFLIT Đối Với Trí Tuệ Nhân Tạo. In *Kỷ Yếu Hội Thảo Khoa Học Quốc Gia 2024* (pp. 445–454).
Nguyen, T. (2024). Sử Dụng Công Cụ Trí Tuệ Nhân Tạo (AI) Trong Việc Giảng Dạy Kỹ Năng Viết Tiếng Anh. In *Kỷ Yếu Hội Thảo Khoa Học Quốc Gia* (pp. 358–369).
Nguyen, T. Y. P., Nguyen, N. T., & Phan, N. K. H. (2025). The challenges of applying ChatGPT in the academic writing of postgraduate students in english major at IUH. *International Journal of AI in Language Education, 2*(1), 20–37. https://doi.org/10.54855/ijaile.25212
Olson, J. M., & Krysiak, R. (2021). Rubrics as tools for effective assessment of student learning and program quality. In T. P. Fudge & S. S. Ferebee (Eds.), *Curriculum development and online instruction for the 21st Century* (pp. 173–200). IGI Global.
OpenAI. (2023, November 6). *Introducing GPTs.* https://openai.com/index/introducing-gpts/
OpenAI. (2024, August). *GPT-4o system card.* https://openai.com/index/gpt-4o-system-card/
Paltridge, B., & Starfield, S. (2020). *Thesis and dissertation writing in a second language a handbook for students and their supervisors* (2nd ed.). Routledge.
Putta, P., Mills, E., Garg, N., Motwani, S., Finn, C., Garg, D., & Rafailov, R. (2024). *Agent Q: Advanced reasoning and learning for autonomous AI agents.* https://arxiv.org/abs/2408.07199
Reynolds, L., & McDonell, K. (2021). *Prompt programming for large language models: Beyond the few-shot paradigm.* https://arxiv.org/abs/2102.07350
Russell, S. J., & Norvig, P. (2021). *Artificial intelligence: A modern approach* (4th ed.). Pearson Education.
Saigon University. (2018). *Chiến lược phát triển Trường Đại học Sài Gòn đến năm 2025 và tầm nhìn.*
Saigon University. (2024). *Giới thiệu.* https://dfl.sgu.edu.vn/gioi-thieu.html
Saigon University. (n.d.). *Brief introduction.* https://en.sgu.edu.vn/
Shadish, W. R., Cook, T. D., & Campbell, D. T. (2002). *Experimental and quasi-experimental designs for generalized causal inference.* Houghton Mifflin.
Shum, K., Diao, S., & Zhang, T. (2024). *Automatic prompt augmentation and selection with chain-of-thought from labeled data.*
Sim, J., & Wright, C. C. (2005). The Kappa Statistic in reliability studies: Use, interpretation, and sample size requirements. *Physical Therapy, 85*(3), 257–268.
Spaapen, J., Dijstelbloem, H., & Wamelink, F. (2007). Evaluating research in context: A method for comprehensive assessment. *Consultative Committee of Sector Councils for Research and Development.*
Syriani, E., David, I., & Kumar, G. (2023). *Assessing the ability of ChatGPT to screen articles for systematic reviews.* https://arxiv.org/abs/2307.06464
Tcherni-Buzzeo, M., & Pyrczak, F. (2024). *Evaluating research in academic journals a practical guide to realistic evaluation* (8th ed.). Routledge.
Thelwall, M. (2024). Can ChatGPT evaluate research quality? *Journal of Data and Information Science, 9*(2), 1–21.
Thelwall, M., & Kurt, Z. (2024). *Research evaluation with ChatGPT: Is it age, country, length, or field biased?* https://arxiv.org/abs/2411.09768
Thomas, R. M. (2003). *Blending qualitative & quantitative research methods in theses and dissertations.* Corwin Press.
Timmerman, B. E., Strickland, D. C., Johnson, R. L., & Payne, J. R. (2011). Development of a 'universal' rubric for assessing students' scientific reasoning skills using scientific writing. *Assessment & Evaluation in Higher Education, 36*(5), 509–547.

Tran, H. N., Le, T. T. N., & Tran, V. B. U. (2025). AI tools in learning academic writing: Benefits and challenges for MA students in the english language studies at the Industrial University of Ho Chi Minh City. *International Journal of AI in Language Education, 2*(1), 74–91. https://doi.org/10.54855/ijaile.25215

Tran, T., & Nguyen, T. (2024). *Evaluating english majors' research proposals using ChatGPT: An experimental study on methodological components at Saigon University.*

UNESCO IELSALC. (2023). ChatGPT and artificial intelligence in higher education: Quick start guide. *United Nations Educational, Scientific and Cultural Organization.*

Vu, P. P., & Le, A. Q. (2024). ChatGPT in language learning: Perspectives from Vietnamese students in Vietnam and the USA. *International Journal of Language Instruction, 3*(2), 59–72. https://doi.org/10.54855/ijli.24325

Wang, X., Wei, J., Schuurmans, D., Le, Q. V., Chi, E. H., Narang, S., & Zhou, D. (2023). *Self-Consistency improves chain of thought reasoning in language models.* ICLR. https://arxiv.org/abs/2203.11171

Wei, J., Wang, X., Schuurmans, D., Bosma, M., Ichter, B., Xia, F., & Zhou, D. (2023). *Chain-of-thought prompting elicits reasoning in large language models.* https://arxiv.org/abs/2201.11903

Yao, S., Yu, D., Zhao, J., Shafran, I., Griffiths, T. L., Cao, Y., & Narasimhan, K. (2023). *Tree of thoughts: Deliberate problem solving with large language models.*

Ye, R., Pang, X., Chai, J., Chen, J., Yin, Z., Xiang, Z., & Chen, S. (2024). *Are we there yet? Revealing the risks of utilizing large language models in scholarly peer review* (preprint). https://arxiv.org/abs/2412.01708

Yenduri, G., Ramalingam, M., Selvi, G.C., Supriya, Y., Srivastava, G., Maddikunta, P. K., & Gadekallu, T. R. (2023). *GPT (Generative Pre-trained Transformer)—A comprehensive review on enabling technologies potential applications, emerging challenges, and future directions.* https://arxiv.org/abs/2305.10435

Zhang, Z., Zhang, A., Li, M., & Smola, A. (2022). *Automatic chain of thought prompting in large language models.*

Phi The Tran currently works as Dean of the Faculty of Foreign Languages at Saigon University and vice President of South Vietnam Teaching English to Speakers of Other Languages (STESOL) under the Association of Vietnam Universities and Colleges (AVU&C). He has been teaching English for 25 years. His research interests are cognitive linguistics, curriculum development, English teaching methods, and the application of technology in education.

Hoang Lan Thi Nguyen is a lecturer in the Department of Foreign Languages at Saigon University, Vietnam. With expertise in TESOL, she instructs a range of English linguistics and education subjects, including research writing. Her research interests are centered on pedagogy acquisition, research writing skills, and the application of technology in education.

Integrating AI Tools in IELTS Writing: A Case Study from Teachers' Perspectives on Personalized Instruction

Nguyen Le Ngoc Anh and Pham Thanh Dieu

Abstract This chapter investigates the integration of artificial intelligence (AI) tools. Specifically, ChatGPT can support personalized instruction in IELTS writing classes. This study investigates student performance and teacher perspectives in a real-world IELTS writing course to address the gap in current research on AI-assisted writing in test preparation contexts. A quasi-experimental design was used in an IELTS writing course at a language center in Can Tho, Vietnam, involving 32 students divided into control and experimental groups. Both groups received the same instruction, but only the experimental group used AI tools to support writing tasks. Pre- and post-test assessments showed that students using AI tools achieved higher improvements, particularly in grammar correction, vocabulary enhancement, and error reduction. Interviews with teachers before and after the course revealed an initial skepticism that shifted to cautious optimism. Teachers recognized the strengths of AI in providing immediate feedback and improving surface-level accuracy but expressed concerns about its limitations in supporting logical coherence and essay development. The findings highlight the importance of teacher mediation and suggest that AI should be used as a supplementary tool, not a replacement for instruction. The chapter concludes by offering practical strategies for ethical and effective integration of AI in writing classrooms, encouraging a balanced approach that combines technological support with human guidance in promoting personalized language learning.

Keywords Integrating AL · IELTS writing · Teachers' perspective

N. Le Ngoc Anh (✉)
Can Tho University, Can Tho, Vietnam
e-mail: vikanhnguyen@gmai.com

P. T. Dieu
Bui Huu Nghia High School, Can Tho, Vietnam

V. P. H. Pham et al. (eds.), *Empowering Educators: Integrating AI Tools for Personalized Language Instruction*, Studies in Computational Intelligence 1228,
https://doi.org/10.1007/978-3-032-01348-4_4

1 Introduction

Artificial intelligence (AI) integration into education has rapidly expanded, particularly in language learning and writing instruction. In recent years, tools such as ChatGPT, Grammarly, and QuillBot have been increasingly explored for their potential to support learners in writing more effectively and independently. These tools offer automated feedback, grammar and vocabulary support, and content suggestions that can enhance students' revision processes. As AI technologies become more advanced and accessible, their use in language classrooms presents opportunities and challenges, especially in high-stakes English language proficiency exams like IELTS.

Writing remains one of the most difficult skills for IELTS test-takers. Students often struggle with grammatical accuracy, vocabulary use, coherence, and task fulfillment—skills that are not easily acquired through rote practice. Traditional classroom methods may not always offer the personalized feedback and revision time needed to master these competencies. AI tools, in this context, offer the potential to fill this gap by providing immediate, individualized responses that allow learners to reflect on their errors and revise their writing in real-time.

Personalized instruction is widely recognized as a crucial factor in language development. However, its implementation can be time-consuming and demanding for instructors, especially in large or exam-focused classes. AI tools may support this approach by adapting to students' individual learning needs and promoting autonomous learning. Previous research, such as that by Nadhifah et al. (2024) and Nazim (2024), has shown that AI can improve learner engagement, support vocabulary growth, and assist in grammar correction. Yet, many of these studies have focused on general language learning rather than specific exam preparation contexts. Furthermore, little is known about how teachers perceive these technologies in their own practice, particularly when it comes to maintaining academic integrity and encouraging deeper thinking.

This chapter responds to these gaps by examining how AI tools can support personalized instruction in IELTS writing and how teachers view the integration of such tools in classroom practice. The study took place at a language center in Can Tho, Vietnam, and followed a quasi-experimental design involving two groups of students with similar writing proficiency levels. While both groups received task-based instruction using the same curriculum and materials, only the experimental group used AI tools throughout the course. The chapter aims to assess student outcomes and how teachers' attitudes toward AI changed before and after the intervention.

This chapter contributes to the growing body of literature on educational technology and language assessment by exploring the practical application of AI in a real-world IELTS course. It provides evidence for how AI can be used ethically and effectively as part of a blended instructional model. The findings offer implications for educators, curriculum designers, and policymakers interested in leveraging AI for language teaching and learning.

2 Literature Review

2.1 *Personalized Instruction*

A central concept in the current study is personalized instruction. Personalized instruction refers to a teaching approach that adapts content, pace, feedback, and support based on students' individual needs, preferences, and learning profiles. Writing instruction may involve offering specific grammar feedback, vocabulary suggestions, or structural advice that meets each learner where they are. Pokrivcakova (2019) emphasizes that personalization in language education can make instruction more effective by allowing students to progress at their own speed and receive feedback that is directly relevant to their individual difficulties. In traditional classrooms, providing this level of tailored support is time-consuming and often unrealistic for teachers handling many students.

Bilad et al. (2023) further explain that AI-powered tools can help implement personalized learning by acting as cognitive tutors, adjusting to learners' performance, and offering real-time, individualized responses. Such technologies enable a shift from a one-size-fits-all model to one where students receive feedback that directly matches their output. This supports autonomy and fosters a deeper understanding of writing mechanics and strategy. When supported by AI, personalized instruction can empower students to identify their own patterns of error, revise more independently, and focus on areas where they need the most support. However, for personalization to be effective, it must be guided by educators who can interpret the feedback, clarify misunderstandings, and provide higher-level insights on writing purpose, audience, and coherence (Umar, 2024).

Despite the potential benefits, implementing personalized instruction through AI requires thoughtful integration. Teachers must be trained to incorporate AI tools effectively and ethically, ensuring that students use them as aids rather than crutches. Personalized instruction supported by AI thus represents a promising yet complex approach to language teaching, particularly in preparing learners for high-stakes exams like IELTS.

3 Understanding AI's Role in IELTS Writing Instruction

3.1 *How AI Tools Assist in Writing Development*

AI tools nowadays are getting more and more important in the education field, especially when it comes to assisting the students in developing the way they write. Such tools are capable of doing things like auto-grading, spotting mistakes, fixing grammar, and improving vocabulary. Besides, they also can give explanations, provide tips for writing, and push students to revise their own written works. Since AI can offer instantly given and personal feedback, it becomes much more useful in IELTS writing teaching. AI supports traditional teaching by letting students improve their writing by themselves. This part discusses how AI makes writing better through auto-grading, grammar and word support, giving explanations, and guides for self-editing, so students can develop more improved writing skills by AI always giving feedback.

3.1.1 Automated Grading and Error Detection

One of the greatest benefits of AI in writing development is its ability to grade written pieces fast, giving back quick responses and organized evaluations. Auto-grading systems using natural language understanding (NLP) algorithms work by looking at student writing and finding where strong parts and weak parts are based on before-made criteria. Pokrivcakova (2019) notes that AI grading helps teachers reduce their workload by giving non-biased assessments. This ensures fairness and lets teachers put more focus on higher-thinking writing skills, like developing arguments and making everything flow better.

Mistake spotting is another very important thing AI tools can do. Programs such as Google Gemini look at student writing and point out many language issues, like grammar wrongs, punctuation missing, and word choice incorrect. Those tools use deep-learn algorithms to spot easy-to-see mistakes and bigger grammar inconsistencies that may make the meaning unclear. Moulieswaran and Kumar (2022) said that AI feedback helps second-language learners a lot by letting them notice patterns in the mistakes they make. Because of this, students fix errors by themselves and get better writing skills with much higher accuracy.

Not only simple mistakes, but AI tools also give deeper responses, putting mistakes in groups by seriousness level and giving reasons for the correction. This way helps students think deeply about learning so they see why they should change something, not just accept fixing. AI checking also sees too many used phrases and similar sentence types, pushing students to make more different and better writing styles. By mixing auto-grading with deep mistake checking, AI tools make writing more correct and make students take a bigger part in making writing better.

According to Nguyen et al. (2025), AI systems used in Vietnamese EFL classrooms have shown strong capability to process and respond to writing submissions with tailored feedback, especially in grammar and spelling. This reduces teacher marking time and provides students with more chances to improve before final submission, especially under exam-focused contexts like IELTS.

3.1.2 Grammar, Structure, and Vocabulary Enhancement

Not only mistake-finding, but AI tools also play a big role in correcting grammar, sentence forming, and word use. Many AI writing tools give real-time grammar fixing suggestions, so students see and fix errors while writing. Those tools mark wrong parts and give reasons for fixing them, strengthening grammar ideas and helping learners keep language rules in mind (Chen, 2024). AI platforms also suggest changes in how sentences are made to make the writing flow better and ideas make more sense so student writing looks more sophisticated and polished.

Word knowledge growth is also a big part of where AI helps. AI language tools look at text and suggest other words, phrase differences, and words that fit the situation best to make student writing richer. Bilad et al. (2023) say learners using AI word suggestion grow their word banks much better than learners who use traditional methods. AI tools also find words that show up too often and give other choices to make writing have more variety and sharpness.

Also, AI tools make text look easier to read by using more natural phrases and improving style. Advanced AI systems check tone and writing type and make changes to match academic, formal, or creative writing needs. By giving strong feedback and point-to-the-problem suggestions, AI helps students craft writing that is more powerful and appropriate for the situation.

AI tools can also make grammar and word learning more fitting for each learner. Not like a normal dictionary or grammar fix tool, AI looks at how a student wrote before and then changes suggestions based on that. This means learners get a response that fits their level and writing style. Over time, seeing this kind of feedback helps students be more confident and write better without needing help all the time. AI is very helpful for IELTS practice and growing language knowledge.

Le and Do (2023) observed that AI-powered feedback supports Vietnamese EFL learners in vocabulary variation and grammatical structures. In their study, participants exposed to AI tools improved their lexical diversity scores, a key element in the IELTS Writing Band Descriptors.

3.1.3 Providing Explanations and Writing Suggestions

AI tools not only fix mistakes; they also explain why change is better and offer writing improvement ideas to help students in their writing. Those explain how helping learners see why a word, phrase, or sentence form is better in a certain place makes them think more about language rules and differences in writing style. Mitra and Banerjee (2022) say that AI feedback makes learning more interactive by letting students think and look at their writing fix instead of just saying yes to changes.

AI writing suggestions include different sentence making, alternative word use, and writing changes to improve quality. Those tools check clarity, shortness, and how easy to understand writing is, helping students arrange their argument and put thoughts in good order. For example, Google Gemini not only fixes grammar wrongs but also tells ways to make writing more interesting and fit for academic work. By seeing unnecessary words and unclear expressions, AI makes sure students write more coherent content.

Tseng and Warschauer (2023) say that AI tools give structured feedback, making writing more logical and strong. This structure helps students see repeating mistake patterns in writing and create plans to improve over time. AI tools also give advice based on student writing level, making sure feedback is useful and understandable. Those adaptive functions help fill space in writing skills by focusing on different areas needing bettering.

AI writing help is very important in growing higher-level writing skills. More than just fixing small mistakes, AI helps improve writing flow, argument strength, and style clarity, helping students move toward advanced writing ability. By incorporating AI feedback into their study habits, students can always improve their writing without depending too much on teachers.

In support, Bui and Le (2023) found that AI explanations promoted metacognitive awareness among students. The ability to compare system-generated suggestions with one's writing process encouraged learners to reflect, revise, and plan more effectively, which is crucial for IELTS Task 2 essay development.

3.1.4 Encouraging Self-Editing and Revision Skills

A big part of writing better is knowing how to check and change writing by oneself. AI tools strengthen this skill by letting students get fast responses and improve each time. As Korenev (2024) says, students using AI for self-fixing are getting better independence in writing because they learn to catch and repair their own writing mistakes before sending them. Being able to do better writing alone not only strengthens language skills but also helps with critical thinking, which is very needed for good communication.

Also, AI edit tools allow students to look at their writing again with structure, clear ideas, and good arguments in mind. Those tools highlight suggestions that make students think about new ways to put their ideas, helping them write more logically sound and convincingly. Umar (2024) says that students who do many rounds of AI-aided self-fixing see much better writing than students who only wait for teacher feedback. By looking closely at AI-given suggestions, students can find ways to make writing better in many ways, from grammar correctness to argument development.

AI edit tools also help self-learning by letting students check different fix choices and pick the best one. This makes them better at looking at writing critically and making them think more about what works best. Over time, students need fewer outside fixes and become more confident in their own writing skills. Because of that, AI tools for editing and revising act as a bridge between teacher fixes and students, allowing them to write better alone, helping both technical skills and creative writing grow.

AI tools play a transformational role in IELTS writing instruction by providing automated grading, error detection, grammar and vocabulary enhancement, detailed explanation, and self-editing support. These technologies do not replace traditional teaching methods but complement them by offering immediate, personalized feedback that fosters improvement in writing. By integrating AI into IELTS writing courses, educators can enhance student learning experiences, promote autonomy, and ensure more effective skill development. However, as with any educational technology, AI effectiveness depends on thoughtful implementation, ensuring that it serves as a supportive tool rather than a complete substitute for teacher guidance.

3.2 *Common Concerns and Misconceptions*

The integration of AI tools in IELTS writing instruction has sparked debate among educators, students, and researchers. While AI offers significant benefits, such as real-time feedback and personalized instruction, concern persists about its role in language education. These concerns revolve around three key areas: the potential for AI to replace teachers, its influence on critical thinking, and the reliability of AI-generated feedback.

3.2.1 The Potential of AI to Replace Teachers

One of the most prevalent concerns regarding AI integration in language education is the fear that it may replace human teachers. As AI technology advances, many educators worry that institutions may begin prioritizing AI-driven instruction as a cost-saving measure, potentially reducing the demand for human educators. Zimotti et al. (2024) highlights that some teachers perceive AI as a threat to their job security, particularly as AI systems become more capable of evaluating writing, providing detailed feedback, and even generating lesson plans tailored to individual students' needs.

However, AI should not be seen as a replacement but rather as a tool that enhances teaching. While AI can streamline various aspects of instruction, it lacks the human connection essential for fostering motivation, empathy, and deeper learning. Nazim (2024) argues that AI lacks the ability to interpret students' emotions, adjust to cultural contexts, and cater to individual learning styles as effectively as human teachers. While AI can efficiently detect grammatical errors and suggest vocabulary improvement, it cannot replace educators' encouragement, critical discussion, and personalized mentorship.

Moreover, AI effectiveness in education depends significantly on human oversight to ensure ethical and contextually appropriate use (Kovalenko & Baranivska, 2024). The role of teachers is evolving rather than diminishing, as they must now focus on guiding students to use AI effectively, interpreting AI-generated feedback critically, and maintaining a balance between automation and human interaction. Rather than displacing teachers, AI can alleviate administrative burdens, allowing educators to dedicate more time to higher-order thinking skills, personalized instruction, and student engagement. When integrated thoughtfully, AI serves as a powerful complement to human instruction, optimizing the learning experience without replacing the essential role of educators.

3.2.2 The Influence of AI on Critical Thinking

Another major concern is the potential for AI tools to hinder students' critical thinking abilities. Some educators fear that over-reliance on AI-generated content may lead students to accept suggestions uncritically, diminishing their ability to analyze and refine their writing independently (Nadhifah et al., 2024). When students use AI extensively for grammar correction, vocabulary suggestion, and content structuring, they may bypass deeper cognitive processes that develop writing proficiency, such as reflection and self-revision.

However, when integrated strategically, AI can serve as a powerful tool to enhance critical thinking rather than suppress it. Tseng and Warschauer (2023) suggest that students should be taught how to engage critically with AI feedback—evaluating recommendations, considering alternative revisions, and making informed decisions about which suggestions to implement. AI tools like Google Gemini can function as interactive writing assistants, prompting students to assess various sentence structures, refine word choices, and experiment with different approaches before finalizing their work. AI encourages a more analytical writing process that fosters independent problem-solving skills when used in this way.

Furthermore, educators play crucial roles in ensuring AI serves as an aid rather than a crutch. Teachers can promote deeper engagement with writing principles by incorporating AI-based assignments that require students to justify revisions and reflect on AI-generated feedback. Encouraging students to compare AI suggestions with traditional grammar rules or peer feedback can further refine their critical thinking ability. As a result, rather than diminishing students' analytical skills, AI has the potential to enhance their ability to think independently, evaluate language use critically, and take a more active role in the writing process when guided effectively.

3.2.3 The Reliability of AI Feedback

The reliability of AI-generated feedback remains a big problem in AI-assisted writing instruction. While AI tools are designed to provide immediate and structured feedback, they are not always correct. Problems such as wrong meaning, not getting the full context, and not being flexible for different writing styles have been reported in studies by Billingsley and Gardner (2024). AI-given advice sometimes makes students make changes that do not really fit or make writing too simple, not really making the overall argument or coherence better. Also, AI often has a hard time getting tone, meaning, and what the audience expects, which is a very important part of good communication.

To fix this issue, teachers need to help students understand and think about AI feedback in a critical way. Nazim (2024) says that teachers should use AI in class as extra help, not as the main grader of student work. When AI feedback is mixed with human feedback, students can find a better way to improve their writing. Teachers should tell students to ask questions about AI suggestions and check them with real academic writing rules and style guides. This can improve students' thinking skills and make them more independent when they make changes in their writing.

Also, AI responses should be added together with teacher explanations and peer reviews to make it work better. As AI tech keeps getting better, teachers must always check how reliable it is so students don't start depending too much on AI to fix their writing. Teaching students how to use AI correctly can help them tell apart good advice from wrong or misleading ones. In the end, AI feedback can be useful for improving writing, but only if it is used smartly with normal teaching methods that support independent thinking and making judgments.

Worrying about AI in IELTS writing is reasonable, but it should be handled by using it in a smart way, not just saying no to it. AI is not here to take the place of teachers but to be a helpful tool that makes learning more personal and fast. While AI may change how people think about writing, good planning and a structured way of using it can make sure it helps thinking skills instead of making them worse. Also, AI feedback can be made better by mixing autosuggestions with teacher checking and student review. By knowing these issues and using AI wisely, teachers can take its good side while avoiding its possible bad effects in IELTS writing teaching.

4 Research Gaps

Although a growing body of research highlights the potential of AI tools in language education, significant gaps remain, particularly regarding their application in structured, exam-oriented writing contexts like IELTS. Many existing studies (e.g., Bilad et al., 2023; Moulieswaran & Kumar, 2022; Pokrivcakova, 2019) focus broadly on how AI enhances grammar correction, vocabulary development, and personalized feedback in academic writing. However, little has been done to examine how these tools specifically support learners in meeting the task requirements, coherence standards, and lexical variety expected in IELTS writing assessments.

A second gap lies in the limited practical research into how AI tools function within real classroom settings. While personalized instruction is often discussed as a benefit of AI (Le & Do, 2023; Umar, 2024), there is a lack of empirical studies exploring how this personalization unfolds in live, teacher-led lessons. Specifically, more evidence is needed on how students interact with AI suggestions, how they revise their drafts over time, and how educators can scaffold AI-supported learning to ensure deeper understanding rather than passive correction.

Moreover, current literature often overlooks the evolving role of teachers when AI is introduced. While studies such as those by Nazim (2024) and Tseng and Warschauer (2023) express concern about AI replacing critical thinking, few explore how teachers' perceptions and instructional strategies shift during and after AI integration. Understanding these shifts is vital for professional development and for informing future training models.

Another pressing issue is the reliability and contextual appropriateness of AI-generated feedback. As Billingsley and Gardner (2024) noted, AI systems may miss rhetorical nuances, misinterpret tone, or suggest stylistic changes that clash with academic expectations. Yet, how teachers mediate these gaps and how their feedback complements AI output is still under-researched.

This study aims to fill these gaps by providing real-world, classroom-based evidence on AI use in IELTS writing. Combining a quasi-experimental design with teacher interviews measures student outcomes and tracks teacher perceptions and strategies changes.

5 Step-By-Step Guide to Integrating AI in IELTS Writing Lessons

The integration of AI tools in IELTS writing lessons requires a structured approach to ensure that students can effectively use these technologies to improve their writing skills while maintaining critical thinking and originality. This section outlines a step-by-step process for incorporating AI tools such as ChatGPT, Grammarly, and QuillBot into IELTS writing instruction, focusing on preparation, introduction, and guided activities that balance AI assistance with traditional learning methods.

5.1 Stage 1: Preparing for AI Integration

5.1.1 Identifying Learning Goals and AI Tool Selection

Knowing a clear learning goal is the first and most important step in putting AI inside an IELTS writing lesson. Teachers must decide exact objectives that match with what students need in writing, whether that means making grammar more accurate, making coherence and cohesion better, or improving how words are used. Making strong learning outcomes helps in choosing the best-suited AI tool that matches teaching methods. Tools like Grammarly give big grammar fixing features, letting the students see and fix sentence structure mistakes better. QuillBot is very good for paraphrasing, letting learners try different sentence forms while keeping meaning. ChatGPT also helps create ideas and supports structuring IELTS writing task responses.

Picking AI tools should be based on what they can do to fit teaching goals, not just how much tech power they have. Billingsley and Gardner (2024) say it is very important to pick AI tools to improve writing skills, not just replace human work. AI tools should be like learning support that makes the student think about their writing, not just auto-fix systems. Teachers must use AI in a way that helps independent learning, making sure students get the skills to think, revise, and make writing better on their own while keeping their own writing voice and originality.

5.1.2 Setting Expectations: Teaching AI Literacy and Responsible Use

Making clear rules for AI knowledge and how to use it right is a very important part of adding AI into IELTS writing learning. It is important that students get a full understanding of AI tools, knowing both what they can do and what they cannot do. Kovalenko and Baranivska (2024) say that AI-made feedback is not always right for context, showing why humans need to check AI suggestions. AI should not be used as a robot replacement for thinking deeply but more as education help that works together with human effort, not instead of it.

To ensure AI is used correctly, teachers must put in place planned lessons that focus on AI rules, academic honesty, and the best way to use AI in learning. Students should be taught how to think about AI feedback, knowing that while these tools are useful, they can sometimes make mistakes or not fully get the meaning of written ideas. Teaching responsible AI use means making students aware of risks when they rely too much on technology. By growing AI knowledge, teachers can help students be smart users of AI, ensuring tech is improving their writing ability instead of weakening it.

5.1.3 Establishing a Balance Between AI Assistance and Manual Effort

Finding the right balance between AI help and manual effort is crucial so that students stay active in their writing and do not just rely on AI correction without thinking. One big problem in using AI for writing teaching is stopping students from being too dependent on AI-made suggestions and not checking their own work. Nadhifah et al. (2024) say that using too much AI can stop students from developing critical thinking skills since they may just accept AI changes without knowing why those changes are made.

To stop this, teachers need to make strict rules that ask students to check and fix AI suggestions by themselves, making them explain why they make certain changes to their writing. This method not only helps with active learning but also makes students better at checking and using feedback in the right way. Also, making a habit of self-fixing can help students grow a feeling of independence in making writing better, helping them have more confidence in how they use language. Using planned activities where students compare AI suggestions with human feedback can also improve their thinking skills. By using AI as a tool for support and not as final authority, teachers can make sure students keep control of their writing while also using benefits from new tech improvements.

5.2 Stage 2: Introducing AI Tools to Students

5.2.1 Demonstrating AI's Strengths and Limitations

Demonstrating AI's strengths and limitations is essential in ensuring that students develop a nuanced understanding of this tool. AI should be seen as a supportive aid rather than an infallible authority. Teachers can illustrate the capability of AI by using real-time demonstrations where AI-generated correction is analyzed, explaining how the tool identifies errors and provides suggestions for improvement. This process allows the student to observe how AI enhances grammar, vocabulary, and structural coherences. However, it is equally important for educators to emphasize the limitations of AI-generated feedback. AI often struggles with understanding contextual appropriateness and produces generic or misleading suggestion that fails to capture the writer's intended meaning (Nazim, 2024).

AI systems lack the ability to discern cultural and situational nuances, which can lead to inaccurateness in word choice, tones, or coherences. Highlighting these shortcomings ensures that students remain critical of AI feedback rather than accepting it uncritically. Encouraging students to compare AI-generated recommendations with their own reasoning and teacher feedback cultivates deeper engagement with the writing process. By integrating discussion on both the benefits and drawbacks of AI, educators can help students become more discerning users, ultimately fostering a balanced approach to AI-assisted learning and independent critical thinking.

5.2.2 Teaching Students How to Use AI for Self-Correction

Teaching students how to properly use AI for self-fixing is very important in helping them learn how to interact critically with technology while improving their writing skills. AI tools help in self-editing by finding mistakes, suggesting different ways to say things, and correcting grammar. However, students must be taught to think deeply about AI feedback instead of agreeing with fixes without questioning.

Teachers have a very important role in showing students how to tell the difference between good AI fixes that make clarity and writing flow better and ones that might accidentally change the meaning of what they are trying to say. Telling students to question AI-made suggestions can strengthen their decision-making ability in writing. When students talk about why some AI changes are good or not good, they can learn more about how language structures work and why stylistic choice is important.

Also, adding thinking-back writing exercises where students explain their reason for accepting or not accepting AI fixes can make learning more active and help with higher-level thinking. Making students take a smart approach to AI-given corrections, letting them keep control over their writing, and making sure they use AI as a tool to help language skills grow instead of as a full automatic error-fixing machine. This kind of balanced way helps both improve writing skills and keep students thinking critically about technology in education.

5.2.3 Structuring AI-Integrated Writing Lessons

Making AI-an AI-included writing lesson requires complete way to make ensure students benefit from AI ideas while still keeping control over their own writing process. A good lesson should have different steps, starting from the draft writing, where students work their ideas and make create say structure by themselves without AI help. This part make ensures they think critically and produce signal work before AI comes in.

The next step is AI-helped revision, where students use AI tools to check their work, find mistakes, and make writing better. But, this part should be done with clear teacher instructions on how to think about AI feedback instead of just saying yes to everything AI suggests. After AI-based revision, teachers should have discussions to talk about AI feedback, making sure students understand why AI makes certain fixes and knowing when human thinking is still needed.

Teachers can show AI's good sides while also pointing out problems, like how AI sometimes does not fully understand the meaning, deeper context, or creativity in writing. The last step is a full review and improvement of the text, where AI-given changes are mixed with teacher feedback and student self-checking. This kind of planned way lets students use AI as a helpful tool while still being fully involved in writing, making them better at creating strong academic text with high quality.

5.3 *Stage 3: AI-Assisted Writing Activities*

5.3.1 First Draft Without AI

The initial phases of the writing process necessitate that students compose their essays without any form of AI assistance. This practice is fundamental in encouraging learners to cultivate independent thought, enhance their fluencies, and fully engage with the conventions of IELTS writing. By drafting without AI support, the student can develop their ability to structure ideas logically, organize arguments effectively, and articulate their thoughts with clarity.

Tseng and Warschauer (2023) underscore the significance of this stage, noting that the absence of AI intervention fosters a deeper cognitive connection to language construction and textual coherences. When students engage with writing in its purest form, they are required to rely on their own grammatical knowledge, lexical range, and critical thinking abilities, all of which are essentials for academic writing. This approach also allows them to explore ideas creatively and become more aware of their strength and weaknesses as writers.

Furthermore, by refraining from AI assistance in the drafting stage, students build essential problem-solving skills that enable them to recognize and correct their own mistakes in later revision. Such an approach fosters greater autonomy in the writing processes, ensures that learners take full responsibility for their development, and engages more critically with the feedback they receive in subsequent phases.

5.3.2 AI-Assisted Self-Editing

After finishing the first drafts, students move to the self-checking phase, where they interact with AI tools to examine their writing more critically. This step requires careful examination of AI-given suggestions about grammar, coherence, and word correctness. Learners should see AI feedback and must actively compare these recommendations with their own thinking to decide which changes improve their writing.

As Moulieswaran and Kumar (2022) note corrections help students understand language structures dee more deeply understand grammar rules better an, and improve their siting style. But, how well AI works in this way depends on how good well students think out AI feedback carefully.

By admitting that all AI-given fixes without questioning can weaken independent thinking and stop self-editing skills from growing. Relying too much on automatic fixing may only make small surface-level improvements while ignoring bigger problems like argument strength, logical flow, and originality. Because of that, teachers must focus on why it is important to check AI suggestions against real academic writing rules. Doing this helps students keep control over their writing and use AI to help, not as a final decision-maker. A balanced way helps students grow independence in writing while also making stronger thinking and reviewing skills that are very important for long-term academic success.

5.3.3 Teacher-Led AI Feedback Review

Teachers play a crucial role in reviewing AI-generated feedback with students by facilitating in-depth evaluations of AI recommendations. This process involves structured discussions where students critically analyze the validity of AI-generated suggestions and assess their alignment with academic writing conventions.

Teachers guide students in distinguishing between helpful AI feedback and misleading or superficial correction, fostering an understanding of nuanced aspects such as coherence, task responses alignment, and contextual appropriateness. By actively engaging in these processes, students are encouraged to justify their editing decisions, reinforce their abilities to assess feedback critically, and make informed revisions.

Additionally, teachers should highlight the limitations of AI tools, particularly their inability to recognize deeper organizational and rhetorical weaknesses within a text. AI-based systems primarily focus on surface-level grammar accuracies but often fail detect logical inconsistencies, argflaws in argument structures, and discrepancies in cultural contexts dressing these oversights in classroom discussions that students develop a more comprehensive understanding of effectiveting.

Umar (2024) underscores the importance of teacher involvement in balancing AI assistance with independent students' efforts and emphasizes that human guidance is essential in developing students' evaluative skills and fostering a more reflective approach to writing. This teacher-led intervention ensures that AI remains a supplementary tool rather than a replacement for critical writing instructions.

5.3.4 Final Revision and Submission

The last steps of AI-helped writing work require students to improve their essays by putting together AI-given feedback with teacher comments. At this time, students must be thinking critically about AI suggestions, picking and using the ones that make clarity, coherence, and grammar more accurate while still keeping their writing original and following IELTS writing band rules.

This step requires deep self-checking, in which students examine whether AI changes really match their original meanings, argument points, and styles. It is very important that students do not just agree with AI-made fixes without thinking but instead check whether the suggestions really improve their writing.

More than just small technical fixes, this part also helps students think deeper by making them review how AI feedback is changing their writing process. Teachers have a big role in pushing students to explain why they accept or not accept AI suggestions, making them create a more aware way of improving writing.

This thinking-back method helps students see clearly their strong writing points and parts needing more improvement, making them take responsibility over how they write. By mixing AI feedback with teacher advice, students join a learning process where technology is used for helping, not for replacing human teaching, keeping a balance between digital help and writing skills growing independently.

Introducing AI into IELTS writing teaching requires smart planning to maximize its benefits while avoiding possible problems. By getting students ready with AI knowledge, showing good ways to use it, and structuring writing work well, teachers can create a place where AI is helping but not replacing human ideas.

The step-by-step approach shown in these guides ensures that students grow independent in writing while using AI as a useful helper. By striking the right balance between tech and traditional learning, AI can be a very strong tool in improving students' writing skills for IELTS success.

6 Case Study: Practical Application of AI in an IELTS Writing Course

6.1 Research Background

The integration of artificial intelligence (AI) into language learning has been a growing area of interest in education research, particularly in assessing its effectiveness in improving students' writing skills. This study was conducted at a language center in Can Tho, Vietnam, where an IELTS writing course was designed to enhance students' writing proficiencies over a three-month period. The course is structured to focus exclusively on writing instruction, emphasizing task-based learning as a key pedagogical approach. Task-based teaching has been widely recognized for its effectiveness in language acquisition, as it encourages learners to engage in meaningful writing activities rather than rote memorization of language structure.

To maintain consistency across instruction, both the control and experimental groups followed the same curriculum using the Mindset for IELTS Level 1 textbook (Cambridge University Press, 2nd edition). This ensured equal content exposure while allowing for comparison between the traditional and AI-supported writing environments. A total of 32 students participated, divided into two comparable groups based on an initial pre-test IELTS Writing score of 4.5. The control group (n = 15) received traditional teacher-led writing instruction, while the experimental group (n = 17) used AI tools, including applications that offered grammar correction, vocabulary support, and idea generation, to assist in the writing process.

The study adopted a mixed-methods research design guided by a comparative instructional framework, which enabled an examination of learning outcomes and pedagogical experiences under two instructional conditions. The framework, adopted from the research of Nguyen et al. (2025), compared AI-assisted instruction with traditional methods by analyzing variations in writing performance, error accuracy, and feedback quality. This comparative lens was not based on an abstract theoretical model but rather on a practical, classroom-oriented comparison intended to inform pedagogical decision-making.

A pre-test and post-test design was applied to measure student writing development. However, in line with reviewer concerns, the pre-/post-test results were limited to measuring student performance only, not teacher perceptions. Adherence to the IELTS Writing Band Descriptors supported the validity and reliability of the writing assessments, and scoring was standardized using established rubric criteria. Nonetheless, future research should include reliability coefficients and inter-rater agreement statistics to further strengthen empirical claims.

Semi-structured interviews were conducted both before and after the teaching intervention to evaluate teachers' perspectives on personalized instruction and AI integration. This qualitative approach was more suitable for capturing nuanced teacher beliefs, evolving attitudes, and pedagogical reflections on AI-assisted instruction. These interviews explored expectations, perceived benefits and limitations, and changes in teaching practice as a result of AI tool usage.

Data analysis was performed using both statistical and qualitative methods. The quantitative component utilized SPSS software to conduct t-tests and ANOVA analyses to determine statistically significant differences in writing scores between groups. For the qualitative data, a thematic analysis was conducted on interview transcripts to identify key themes such as AI usefulness, concerns about over-reliance, and the evolving role of teachers in AI-supported environments.

The study's findings aim to provide valuable insight into the practical applications of AI in IELTS writing instruction. By assessing improvement in student writing performances and documenting teacher experiences, the research seeks to determine whether AI tools could serve as effective supplementary resources in language education. The comparative natures of the study were particularly useful in highlighting AI's strengths and limitations, as well as its potential roles in supporting both learners and educators. This research contributes to ongoing discussions about integrating technology into language learning and provides empirical data on how AI may enhance traditional teaching methodology in IELTS writing courses.

6.2 Answering Research Question 1: "The Effect of Integrating AI Tools on Students' IELTS Writing Performance Through Their Learning Outcomes"

The Descriptive Statistic Test was initially conducted to assess the course performance of students in both groups. Table 1 presents the results of this analysis, revealing notable differences in mean scores between the experimental and control groups. Specifically, the mean course grade score in the experimental group (M_{exp} = 6.21) surpassed that of the control group (M_{con} = 5.06). These findings suggest that students in the experimental group exhibited superior course performance compared to their counterparts in the control group.

Subsequently, an Independent-sample t-test was performed to ascertain the presence of significant differences in academic scores between the control and experimental groups. The analysis yielded a statistically significant result (p = 0.000), as detailed in Table 2. This finding indicates that following the course, students' writing performance in the experimental group surpassed that of the control group, highlighting the efficacy of the integrated AI in enhancing students' academic performance in IELTS writing endeavors.

A descriptive statistical test was conducted to evaluate the component points in students' writing performance in both groups. Table 3 presents the results of this

Table 1 Descriptive statistics of students' course performance within the two groups

	N	Minimum	Maximum	Mean	Std. Deviation
Control group	15	5.0	7.0	5.06	1.668
Experimental group	17	5.5	6.5	6.21	1.648

Table 2 The Independent-sample t-test of students' academic scores between the control group and the experimental group

	t	df	Sig
Students' academic scores	0.134	28	0.000

analysis, revealing notable differences in mean scores between the experimental and control groups across various components. Specifically, the mean score for Task completion in the experimental group ($M_{exp} = 6.71$, SD = 1.748) surpassed that of the control group ($M_{con} = 5.16$, SD = 1.468). Similarly, the Coherence and cohesion mean score in the experimental group ($M_{exp} = 7.24$, SD = 2.008) was higher compared to the control group ($M_{con} = 4.93$, SD = 2.128). For Vocabulary enhancement, the experimental group achieved a higher mean score ($M_{exp} = 5.11$, SD = 1.321) than the control group ($M_{con} = 4.34$, SD = 1.643). In terms of Error correction, the experimental group ($M_{exp} = 8.95$, SD = 1.898) outperformed the control group ($M_{con} = 5.91$, SD = 1.218). These findings suggest that students in the experimental group demonstrated superior performance across all evaluated components of the writing performance, indicating the effectiveness of the integrated AI in teaching.

Subsequently, an Independent-sample t-test was conducted to ascertain the presence of significant differences in the component points of the writing performance between the control and experimental groups. The result, with $p = 0.000 < 0.05$, confirmed that the writing performance in the experimental group surpassed that of the control group. This highlights the efficacy of integrated AI in teaching writing.

Table 3 Descriptive statistics of students' component points in the writing performance within the two groups

		N	Mean	Std. Deviation
Task completion	Control group	28	5.16	1.468
	Experimental group	28	6.71	1.748
Coherence and cohesion	Control group	28	4.93	2.128
	Experimental group	28	7.24	2.008
Vocabulary enhancement	Control group	28	4.34	1.643
	Experimental group	28	5.11	1.321
Error correction	Control group	28	5.91	1.218
	Experimental group	28	8.95	1.898

6.3 Answering Research Question 2: "The Perceptions of Teachers on Integrating AI Tools in Their Teaching"

The way teachers think about AI tools in the classroom changed a lot during the study, showing both problems and good points. Before the course even starts, many teachers feel unsure about bringing AI into their teaching, mostly because they worry it might take the place of normal teaching methods. As one teacher said, a repeating concern was that "AI tools may take away the teacher's role, making students too much depend on technology and not thinking deeply on their own" (T1). Some teachers were afraid that students using AI would skip the learning process, letting the technology do all the work instead of actually engaging with the material themselves.

Even with these early worries, teachers also see how AI tools could be helpful inside the classroom. Many of them understand that AI can be useful for specific writing tasks, like fixing grammar and helping with idea-making, which could save time, so teachers focus more on harder teaching work. One teacher said, "AI could help in small technical parts of writing, so I can use more time guiding students to grow their ideas and improve their essay structures" (T3). This opinion was shared by many, showing that if AI is used in a smart way, it can help students learn instead of making learning weaker.

After the course, teachers' way of seeing AI tools has changed, and many of them are now looking at it more positively for classroom use. Teachers in the experimental group noticed that when AI is used as extra support, it can improve the learning experience. One teacher talked about how AI gives fast feedback: "The AI quickly corrects students' grammar and sentence mistakes, helping them learn faster and improve writing in a short time" (T2). This instant feedback was seen as a big plus of AI, letting students become more independent in learning and reducing teachers' need to always check and fix basic mistakes in writing.

But still, even with these good changes, some problems remain. Some teachers were worried about AI feedback accuracy, especially for harder parts of writing, like tone, logical flow, and strong arguments. One teacher pointed out, "AI is good for fixing grammar, but it still has trouble with difficult writing parts, like making sure ideas flow in logical way" (T3). This problem showed why AI tools should be helping, not replacing, teachers regarding full writing feedback.

Teachers mostly agreed on keeping balance when talking about how AI should be added to teaching. Most say AI should help learning but not completely take over traditional teaching. Teachers suggested that AI tools be used in some parts of the writing process, like first drafts and revision, where they can give quick, small-level feedback, while teachers focus on bigger skills like critical thinking and argument-building. One teacher explained, "AI is really good for helping students clean up their drafts, but it is still the teacher's job to help them with more complex writing skills, like making a strong thesis or making arguments persuasive" (T4).

In general, the results show that teachers see AI as useful when used in the right way along with normal teaching. They agreed that AI can help with some writing tasks but said it must be used carefully so students stay engaged in learning. As one teacher said in the end, "AI has much potential, but we need to use it in a way that helps, not replaces, the human parts of teaching" (T4).

6.4 Discussion

The findings of this study reveal several key strengths and limitations of AI integration in IELTS writing instruction. Statistically significant improvements were observed in students' writing performance in the experimental group who used AI tools, particularly in grammar accuracy and vocabulary use. The mean academic score for this group (M = 6.21) was notably higher than that of the control group (M = 5.06), with t-test results confirming a significant difference ($p = 0.000$). This supports the claim made by Pokrivcakova (2019) and Le and Do (2023) that AI-assisted feedback, particularly when immediate and individualized, contributes to improved linguistic performance and greater learner autonomy.

In line with previous studies (e.g., Moulieswaran & Kumar, 2022), the present research shows that one of AI's most valuable contributions is its ability to provide real-time, surface-level feedback. Students were able to identify and correct grammar and sentence structure errors while writing, leading to more accurate drafts. The experimental group also demonstrated superior performance in error correction (M = 8.95) compared to the control group (M = 5.91). This aligns with Nguyen et al. (2025), who found that EFL students in Vietnam benefited significantly from instant AI-driven corrections, particularly when preparing for high-stakes exams like IELTS.

However, consistent with the findings of Tseng and Warschauer (2023), challenges arose in more complex dimensions of writing, such as logical coherence and argument development. While the experimental group scored higher than the control group in coherence and cohesion (M = 7.24 vs. M = 4.93), interviews with teachers revealed that AI tools often lacked the capacity to provide meaningful feedback on structure and reasoning. Teachers noted that AI-generated suggestions were occasionally generic or contextually inappropriate, leading students to revise in ways that disrupted the logical flow of ideas. This reflects concerns Billingsley and Gardner (2024) raised regarding AI's inability to assess rhetorical nuances or tailor feedback to the writer's intention.

Importantly, teachers' attitudes toward AI tools were not inferred from student performance outcomes but rather gathered directly through pre- and post-interviews. Initially, educators expressed skepticism, fearing that AI might diminish students' critical thinking or foster dependency. These concerns echo earlier critiques by Nazim (2024), who warned that unchecked AI use could undermine students' engagement in higher-order thinking. However, post-interviews revealed that many teachers had revised their views after witnessing how AI could effectively automate repetitive error correction. Several participants acknowledged that AI reduced their workload on mechanical feedback, freeing them to focus more on guiding students in idea development and essay structure.

This shift in perception is consistent with Bui and Le (2023), who suggest that when integrated strategically, AI tools can promote metacognitive reflection among learners and reposition teachers to focus on more complex instructional goals. Nonetheless, teachers emphasized that AI should be used as a supplementary tool during specific phases of the writing process, such as drafting and revising, rather than as a full replacement for teacher feedback. As one participant stated, "AI helps polish the draft, but it's still the teacher who guides students through critical thinking and building a strong argument."

Furthermore, the study highlights that AI feedback alone is insufficient for supporting personalized instruction at higher cognitive levels. While AI can adapt to lexical and grammatical errors based on prior input, it does not always offer differentiated guidance in argument structure, tone, or audience awareness. Teachers remained essential in mediating these gaps, reinforcing Umar's (2024) view that personalized instruction must include human judgment to interpret student needs beyond surface-level errors.

Overall, the findings suggest that when used thoughtfully, AI tools can significantly enhance specific aspects of writing instruction, such as grammatical accuracy and vocabulary diversity. However, they must be embedded within a broader pedagogical framework, including teacher mediation, critical reflection, and context-sensitive instruction. Rather than replacing educators, AI can serve as a valuable support that improves efficiency and allows more time for addressing higher-order writing skills. This aligns with the study's larger implication: for AI to truly support personalized learning in IELTS writing, it must be integrated with care, guided by teacher expertise, and focused on complementing, rather than substituting, the human dimensions of education.

7 Best Practices for Teachers Using AI in IELTS Writing

7.1 Setting Guidelines for Ethical and Effective AI Use

Integrating AI tools into IELTS writing instruction presents opportunities and challenges, making it essential for an educator to establish clear guidelines for their ethical and effective use. The findings from this study indicate that AI tools can be beneficial for improving students' writing skills, particularly in grammar correction and revision. However, without proper regulations, there are risks of students misusing AI by relying on it for content generation rather than learning from its feedback. Teachers must ensure that AI is positioned as a supplementary tool rather than some replacement for the writing processes. Clear guidelines should be set to emphasize that AI is meant to enhance learning rather than complete tasks for students. As Kovalenko and Baranivska (2024) argue, AI should be framed as a tool for developing language proficiencies rather than a shortcut to avoid effort.

Educators should also encourage students to critically assess AI-generated suggestions, ensuring they do not passively accept feedback. This study supports previous research by showing that AI tools provide automated feedback but are not always contextually appropriate. Students need to be trained to recognize when AI-generated recommendations align with IELTS writing criteria and when human judgments are necessary. Ethical AI use in education should focus on fostering a learning mindset where students actively engage with AI feedback rather than relying on it uncritically.

7.2 Avoiding Over-Reliance: Balancing AI with Traditional Instruction

While AI tools offer significant benefits in automating basic corrections, this study highlights the importance of maintaining a balance between AI-assists learning and traditional instructions. One of the key concerns raised by teachers at the beginning of the study was the potential for AI to diminish student engagement in critical thinking. Initially, many teachers fear that students will become passive learners, overly dependent on AI to edit their works rather than develop their own revision skills. However, by the end of the study, the teacher recognized that when used appropriately, AI tools could complement traditional methods by allowing students to focus on higher-order writing skills such as argumentations and coherences.

The statistical analyses of writing performances showed that students in the experimental group performed better than those in the control group, particularly in grammar corrections and task completion. However, students still require teacher interventions to refine essay structures and logical coherences. AI should, therefore, be integrated into the classrooms as a supportive tool rather than some primary instructors. Teachers can incorporate AI at specific stages of the writing process—such as the revision phases—while still emphasizing manual drafting, peer feedback, and teacher-led discussions. By striking these balances, educators can ensure students develop strong writing abilities without overly relying on AI.

7.3 Adapting AI Feedback for Different Student Levels

The effectiveness of AI tools varies depending on students' proficiency levels, making it essential for an educator to adapt AI feedback accordingly. This study demonstrates that while AI-assist learning improves overall writing performances, its impact was most pronounced in error correction and vocabulary enhancements. However, AI-generated feedback does not always align with the specific needs of different learners. Students with lower proficiency levels may benefit from AI's real-time grammatical correction, while more advanced students require more nuance feedback on coherences and argument developments.

Teachers play crucial roles in guiding students on how to interpret AI-generated feedback based on their skill levels. For lower-level students, AI can be particularly useful in reinforcing fundamental grammar rules and sentence structures. In contrast, for higher-level students, teachers should encourage deeper engagement with AI feedback by prompting them to justify and modify AI-generated suggestions rather than automatically accepting them. Teachers can ensure that AI remains an effective and personal learning tool by tailoring AI integration to students' individual learning needs.

7.4 Encouraging Critical Thinking and Personalized Learning with AI

This study's results emphasize that AI should not replace critical thinking but rather serve as a catalyst for deeper engagement with the writing process. AI tools provide immediate feedback, allowing students to identify and correct errors efficiently, but they do not inherently foster analytical skills or creativity. Teachers must actively encourage students to engage with AI-generated feedback in a reflective manner, questioning whether suggested revisions truly improve their writing.

One strategy for achieving this is to incorporate reflective writing exercises, where students must explain why they accept or reject AI suggestions. This approach promotes metacognitive awareness and helps students take greater ownership of their writing. Personal AI-driven learning pathways can also support student development by providing target feedback based on individual performance trends. As highlighted in this study, AI tools have the potential to create more autonomous learners by allowing students to self-correct and track their own progress over time. However, teacher facilitation must guide these autonomies to ensure that students engage meaningfully with the learning processes rather than treating AI as shortcuts.

7.5 Using AI for Formative Assessment and Student Progress Tracking

AI tools can be highly effective for formative assessments, enabling both students and teachers to track progress over time. One of the key advantages observed in the study was that AI provides instant data on students' errors, allowing for more target instruction. Teachers report that AI-assists progress tracking allows them to identify patterns in students' writing and tailor their feedback accordingly. For example, repeated grammatical errors highlighted by AI could be addressed in class discussions or individualized coaching sessions, leading to more efficient teaching interventions.

Furthermore, AI's ability to analyze student performances over multiple assignments offers valuable insights into learning trends. By monitoring AI-generated reports on students' writing developments, the teachers can adjust lesson plans to address common weaknesses while recognizing the areas of improvement. This study aligns with a previous finding by Nazim (2024), who notes that AI-enhances feedback can increase student engagement and motivation when learners see tangible progress in their work. However, the study also suggests that AI-generated assessments should not replace traditional teacher evaluations. AI is best used as a supplementary tool to enhance formative assessments rather than solely to evaluate students' performances.

The findings from this study indicate that AI can play significant roles in enhancing IELTS writing instruction, provided that it is integrated with clear guidelines and teacher mediation. Setting ethical guidelines for AI use ensures that students engage with the technology in a way that supports learning rather than replaces the writing process. Teachers must balance AI-assist learning with traditional instructions to prevent over-reliance and encourage active engagement in writing developments. Adapting AI feedback to different proficiency levels further maximizes its effectiveness and allows students to receive personal support that aligns with their learning needs.

Moreover, AI can serve as a valuable tool for fostering critical thinking and personal learning, particularly when students are encouraged to reflect on their revisions and justify their editing choices. Additionally, AI's roles in formative assessments and student progress tracking can help teachers identify patterns in students' writing and adjust their teaching strategies accordingly. Ultimately, AI should be seen as a complementary resource that enhances, rather than replaces, traditional teaching methods. With thoughtful implementations, AI can significantly contribute to improving writing instruction while maintaining the essential human elements of teaching and learning.

8 Conclusion

This study provides empirical evidence that AI can significantly improve certain aspects of IELTS writing instruction, particularly in grammar correction, vocabulary enhancement, and error identification. Students in the experimental group who received AI-assisted instruction achieved notably higher scores in both overall writing performance and key subskills such as error correction (M = 8.95 vs. M = 5.91) and coherence and cohesion (M = 7.24 vs. M = 4.93). These results suggest that AI tools, when strategically implemented, can support learners in producing more accurate and linguistically polished writing. This aligns with prior findings (e.g., Le & Do, 2023; Nguyen et al., 2025) and reinforces AI's potential as a powerful aid in developing technical writing proficiency.

Teacher interview data further revealed that while AI contributed positively to students' revision processes, it fell short in supporting more complex elements such as logical organization and argument development. Educators observed that AI-generated feedback was sometimes too generic or contextually inappropriate, occasionally leading to structural errors or weaker cohesion. These findings support the view that AI alone cannot fully replace the nuanced feedback and pedagogical insight that teachers provide. Instead, AI should be seen as a complementary tool, useful for automating repetitive tasks, while teachers continue to facilitate deeper learning and guide students in critical thinking and rhetorical development.

A key implication from this research is that AI can enhance personalized learning by offering instant, targeted feedback adapted to individual needs. Students benefited from real-time support and were able to work at their own pace, addressing specific weaknesses, an approach aligned with the principles of adaptive learning. Teachers reported that when used selectively during drafting or revision phases, AI tools allowed them to focus more on higher-order writing instruction, such as thesis development and idea organization.

However, this study also presents several limitations. First, the research was conducted within a single language center in Vietnam, using a small sample of 32 students with similar starting proficiency. The limited context may affect the generalizability of the findings to other educational systems or learner populations. Second, while student performance was measured quantitatively, teacher perspectives were gathered solely through interviews. Future research could benefit from triangulating teacher perceptions with classroom observations or survey data for broader insight. Third, the study focused on a small number of AI tools. Broader evaluations involving different platforms and user interfaces could provide a more comprehensive understanding of how tool design affects learning outcomes.

Based on the study's findings, several best practices can be recommended for teachers. First, AI should be introduced not as a standalone solution but as a support mechanism embedded within the writing process, particularly useful during the drafting, editing, and revising stages. Second, teachers should actively mediate students' interaction with AI feedback by encouraging them to critically evaluate suggestions and compare them with human feedback or writing rubrics. This reflective engagement prevents over-reliance and fosters independent thinking. Third, professional development and collaboration among educators are essential. Supporting teachers with training in AI integration can increase their confidence and pedagogical flexibility, allowing them to adapt technology to their specific classroom contexts.

In conclusion, AI holds substantial promise in supporting IELTS writing instruction, but its success depends on thoughtful integration and teacher involvement. By leveraging AI's strengths in personalization and efficiency while maintaining human oversight and pedagogical guidance, educators can create a balanced instructional environment. Future research should continue to explore how AI can be adapted for different learners, tools, and assessment contexts to ensure its effectiveness as part of a sustainable, learner-centered approach to writing education.

References

Bilad, M. R., Yaqin, L. N., & Zubaidah, S. (2023). Recent progress in the use of artificial intelligence tools in education. *Jurnal Penelitian Dan Pengkajian Ilmu Pendidikan: E-Saintika, 7*(3), 279–315. https://doi.org/10.36312/esaintika.v7i3.1377

Billingsley, F., & Gardner, S. (2024). Utilizing generative AI with second-language users and bilingual students. *Advances in Higher Education and Professional Development*, 109–132. https://doi.org/10.4018/979-8-3693-0487-7.ch005

Cambridge University Press. (2023). *Mindset for IELTS. level 1, student's book with Digital Pack.*

Chen, L. (2024). Research on innovative models of second language teaching in the age of artificial intelligence. *Applied Mathematics and Nonlinear Sciences, 9*(1). https://doi.org/10.2478/amns-2024-0760

Dinh, T. B. H. (2025). Factors affecting ICT integration of EFL teachers at a Vietnamese university. *International Journal of AI in Language Education, 2*(1), 55–73. https://doi.org/10.54855/ijaile.25214

Gkountara, D. N., & Prasad, R. (2022). A review of artificial intelligence in foreign language learning. *2022 25th International Symposium on Wireless Personal Multimedia Communications (WPMC), 18*, 134–139. https://doi.org/10.1109/wpmc55625.2022.10014767

Korenev, A. A. (2024). Strategies of using artificial intelligence for written corrective feedback in language education. *Moscow University Bulletin. Series 19. Linguistics and Intercultural Communication, 27*(2), 68–77. https://doi.org/10.55959/msu-2074-1588-19-27-2-5

Kovalenko, I., & Baranivska, N. (2024). Integrating artificial intelligence in English language teaching: Exploring the potential and challenges of AI tools in enhancing language learning outcomes and personalized education. *European Socio-Legal & Humanitarian Studies*, (1), 86–95. https://doi.org/10.61345/2734-8873.2024.1.9

Mitra, N., & Banerjee, A. (2022). A study on using AI in promoting English language learning. *Lecture Notes in Networks and Systems*, 287–297. https://doi.org/10.1007/978-981-19-4052-1_30

Moulieswaran, N., & Kumar, P. N. S. (2022). Amelioration of google assistant—A review of Artificial Intelligence Stimulated second language learning and teaching. *World Journal of English Language, 13*(1), 86. https://doi.org/10.5430/wjel.v13n1p86

Nadhifah, A. S., Hastin Nursanti Syukur, H. N., Muhammad Ferdy Haryanto, M. F., Roghibatul Luthfiyyah, R. L., & Diana Rahmawati Rozak. (2024). Pre-service English teacher perceptions of AI in writing skills. *Journal of World Englishes and Educational Practices, 6*(2), 26–32. https://doi.org/10.32996/jweep.2024.6.2.3

Nazim, M. (2024). Exploring EFL teachers' insights regarding artificial intelligence driven tools in student-centered writing instructions. *International Journal of English Linguistics, 14*(3), 90. https://doi.org/10.5539/ijel.v14n3p90

Nguyen, T. Y. P., Nguyen, N. T., & Phan, N. K. H. (2025). The challenges of applying ChatGPT in the academic writing of postgraduate students in English major at IUH. *International Journal of AI in Language Education, 2*(1), 20–37. https://doi.org/10.54855/ijaile.25212

Pham, N. N. H. (2025). The use of ChatGPT in EFL students as a learning assistant in their writing skills: A literature review. *International Journal of AI in Language Education, 2*(1), 38–54. https://doi.org/10.54855/ijaile.25213

Pokrivcakova, S. (2019). Preparing teachers for the application of AI-powered technologies in Foreign Language Education. *Journal of Language and Cultural Education, 7*(3), 135–153. https://doi.org/10.2478/jolace-2019-0025

Tseng, W., & Warschauer, M. (2023). Ai-writing tools in education: If you can't beat them, join them. *Journal of China Computer-Assisted Language Learning, 3*(2), 258–262. https://doi.org/10.1515/jccall-2023-0008

Umar, U. (2024). Advancements in English language teaching: Harnessing the power of artificial intelligence. *FLIP Foreign Language Instruction Probe, 3*(1), 29–42. https://doi.org/10.54213/flip.v3i1.402

Zimotti, G., Frances, C., & Whitaker, L. (2024). The future of language education: Teachers' perceptions about the surge of Ai Writing Tools. *Technology in Language Teaching & Learning*, *6*(2), 1–24. https://doi.org/10.29140/tltl.v6n1.1136

Nguyen Le Ngoc Anh is a lecturer at Can Tho University in Viet Nam. Her main research interests are teaching methods and the importance of the library in learning English. She has been an English teacher for more than seven years.

Pham Thanh Dieu is an English teacher in Can Tho City, Vietnam. She currently works at Bui Huu Nghia High School. Her main research interests are teaching methods for learning English. She has been an English teacher for more than three years.

Investigating Vietnamese Undergraduates' Strategies in Using ChatGPT for Writing

Le Trong Nhan Dao

Abstract The rapid advancements in artificial intelligence have facilitated the incorporation of AI models such as ChatGPT into language education, offering learners insightful feedback and support in writing tasks. This study aims to explore learning strategies employed by Vietnamese undergraduates, the obstacles they encounter, their methods for overcoming these hurdles while utilizing ChatGPT to assist with writing English essays, and their perceptions of the effective integration of ChatGPT for writing instruction. With a mixed-methods design, the study involved 61 Vietnamese undergraduates, employing surveys, semi-structured interviews, and simulated writing tasks to collect data. While quantitative data were analyzed descriptively, thematic analysis was applied to qualitative findings to obtain deeper insights into students' experiences with the Chatbot. The results showed that learners mostly employed social, compensation, and memory strategies. Moreover, they often encountered challenges with ChatGPT's content and communication with the Chatbot, which necessitated their attempts to refine prompts and be more critical of ChatGPT's contents. Additionally, in order to appropriately integrate ChatGPT into writing instruction, the participants perceived that more ChatGPT training and teacher support were crucial. These findings provide valuable resources for educators and learners seeking to incorporate AI into language instruction, providing them with insights into learners' preferred strategies for AI-assisted writing, potential difficulties linked with its employment, and viable approaches for utilizing ChatGPT in writing instruction.

Keywords Learning strategies · ChatGPT · Personalized instruction · Challenges · Solutions · Perceptions

L. T. N. Dao (✉)
Faculty of Foreign Languages, Saigon University, Ho Chi Minh City, Vietnam
e-mail: dltnhan@sgu.edu.vn

V. P. H. Pham et al. (eds.), *Empowering Educators: Integrating AI Tools for Personalized Language Instruction*, Studies in Computational Intelligence 1228,
https://doi.org/10.1007/978-3-032-01348-4_5

1 Introduction

1.1 AI in Language Education

The technological advancement of modern society has led to the invention of artificial intelligence, whose application has been manifested in the form of AI (artificial intelligence) models, such as ChatGPT, one of the most inventive man-made tools. ChatGPT is an AI model that can respond to users' inquiries with remarkable speed and customization owing to its access to a huge trained database and the Internet. These advantages make ChatGPT a valuable tool in many disciplines, including language education.

With the increasing popularity of ChatGPT in language instruction, the AI model has often been leveraged to enhance the writing skills of second language learners at various proficiency levels in many educational institutions all over the globe. In terms of its usage in writing, ChatGPT is known to be a helpful assistant that provides not only immediate feedback and error corrections but also revisions so that the overall quality of the writing can be enhanced.

1.2 Language Education in Vietnam

The most common foreign language being learned by students of all ages in Vietnam is English, which is believed to open doors to more career opportunities for those who master the language. As technological tools grow in Vietnam, educators have been exploring ways to incorporate them into English instruction (Dinh, 2025), and learners' attitudes towards the use of these technologies were often positive (Ho, 2024). In recent years, the world has witnessed significant advancements in AI technology and acknowledged its potential across various fields, including language learning. Vietnamese educators, under similar influence, have started to explore the application of AI in language instruction, such as vocabulary acquisition (Ngo, 2024) and academic writing (Nguyen et al., 2025; Tran et al., 2025). AI tools, particularly ChatGPT, have been found to be beneficial for enhancing students' writing ability and serving as valuable assistants for educators (Nguyen et al., 2025; Pham & Cao, 2025; Tran et al., 2025). Nevertheless, the employment of AI in language education, particularly writing skills in the Vietnamese context at the tertiary level, remains rather modest, and English writing continues to be a challenge for Vietnamese undergraduates. For instance, students may often encounter problems with using lexical and grammatical resources and issues pertaining to paragraphing and maintaining coherency, all of which hinder their development of English writing proficiency. Therefore, with its capacity for personalization, AI could serve as an invaluable tool to meet the varied demands of Vietnamese second language learners.

1.3 Significance of the Study

The constant developments of AI have made this technology becoming more common in language classrooms, allowing for more personalized learning. With technological aids, particularly AI-powered tools, learners might be able to address their particular needs and enhance their writing skills, such as identifying recurring mistakes, forming an outline, collaborating to understand a problem, acquiring feedback on writing styles, or simply obtaining ideas for a topic. Moreover, the utilization of AI is also beneficial from educators' perspectives. Acquiring insights into how students use the Chatbot can provide teachers with useful knowledge for better integration of AI for personalizing instruction, such as obtaining knowledge regarding problems faced by students to inform teachers' instructions and create more tailored and diverse approaches suitable to individual needs. However, despite its promising impacts, a thorough understanding of AI usage among Vietnamese undergraduates remains relatively limited, making the prospect of integrating this technology and reaping its benefits a daunting task. Additionally, there is a gap of knowledge concerning how students utilize ChatGPT for academic writing, as while studies have been conducted on the benefits of AI tools (Guo et al., 2024; Pratama & Hastuti, 2024; Wei, 2023), little is known about particular strategies students employ when interacting with them, specifically in the Vietnamese context, as well as the difficulties they encounter, their adaptive solutions, and how AI can be integrated.

To fill this gap in the literature about the use of AI in language education in Vietnam, this study examines the types of writing strategies employed by Vietnamese undergraduates, the obstacles they encounter, their solutions, and their perceptions of integrating ChatGPT for personalized language learning. Specifically, in the context of the present study, writing strategies referred to the diverse approaches employed by learners, as classified by Oxford's (1990) framework of Language Learning Strategies (LLS), and measured using descriptive statistics, when utilizing ChatGPT for English writing. The difficulties were characterized as obstacles faced by learners throughout their process of leveraging AI for writing assistance. These ChatGPT-related challenges were thematically analyzed and presented as percentages. Solutions were defined as strategies utilized by learners to address challenges encountered while using ChatGPT for writing support, whereas perceived integrational approaches, on the other hand, referred to students' suggestions for incorporating ChatGPT into language instruction. These qualitative data were obtained by analyzing students' responses thematically and calculating their frequency and percentage. By shedding light on these aspects, the findings of this study would add more knowledge to the existing literature on AI-assisted language education and offer practical recommendations for personalized integration of artificial intelligence models, specifically ChatGPT, into language instruction.

2 Literature Review

2.1 Language Learning Strategies

The term 'strategy', as Oxford (1990) mentioned, refers to conscious planning and direct managing of steps and actions toward a goal or objective. Thus, by extending it to the realm of education, particularly language learning, Oxford (1990) described Language Learning Strategies (LLS) as a range of actions utilized by learners to facilitate effective language acquisition, which can be categorized into six dimensions: cognitive, metacognitive, compensation, memory, social, and affective strategies. This implies that different learners may have different preferred sets of actions toward learning a language, as pupils have different backgrounds, proficiency levels, and motivations, in order to help them address their linguistic tasks in a manner that is most comfortable and effective for them. Teachers will undoubtedly benefit from understanding how students implement each strategy when writing an English essay through the assistance of AI, as it will provide them with a critical framework of reference regarding the direction in which they should integrate specific strategies into their instruction. Memory strategies enable learners to encode linguistic items and establish meaningful connections among them. This can be achieved by correlating them with similar linguistic objects and concepts, setting them in context, employing visual and auditorial cues, systematic review, or physical and mechanical responses (Oxford, 1990). Cognitive strategies involve thinking and other mental tasks. Learners manipulate or modify language items to understand them. These strategies involve practicing, receiving, sending, analyzing, reasoning, and structuring (Oxford, 1990). Compensation strategies, as described by Oxford (1990), primarily focus on utilizing the power of guessing to figure out the meanings of language items, whether through linguistic cues, such as adjacent words, or non-linguistic ones, such as the contextual setting in which the word appears. These strategies are also observable when learners attempt to overcome linguistic constraints to convey ideas in daily usage through various methods, including paraphrasing, reverting to body language and gestures, or employing the first language. Metacognitive strategies refer to how learners monitor and manage their learning process through planning, organizing, selecting, and self-evaluating (Oxford, 1990). These strategies can be understood as conscious reminders employed by learners to regulate and guide their learning process. In writing, metacognitive strategies are demonstrated when learners have finished writing and returned to proofread their work to assess its coherence, grammatical accuracy, and other criteria. Affective strategies emphasize the enhancement of one's emotions, attitudes, motivations, and values, as these aspects can influence language learning (Oxford, 1990). These strategies manifest when learners seek to boost their confidence through motivational speeches or engage in entertaining activities to alleviate their anxiety. Lastly, Social strategies entail using social communication, including clarification or correction, collaboration with friends, and becoming aware of others' cultural influences, thoughts, and emotions to enhance their language learning (Oxford, 1990).

2.2 Studies on Writing Strategies with Strategy Inventory for Language Learning

Oxford's Strategy Inventory for Language Learning (SILL), developed in 1990, has been extensively utilized to investigate language learning strategies. This comprehensive tool allows educators and academics alike to analyze how students approach language learning, such as participating in planning or asking for help from others. However, the amount of literature on SILL's application to writing remains limited. Further investigation into learners' LLS in writing would benefit both teachers and researchers. McMullen (2009) examined Saudi Arabian male and female EFL students' LLS and how their majors affected them. The researcher employed SILL and found that both genders mainly utilized social strategies. Additionally, while science students preferred metacognitive techniques, management information system students favored social strategies. Moreover, McMullen (2009) noted enhancement in organization, coherence, and writing mechanics, which may be linked to metacognitive and compensation strategies. Interestingly, these findings seemed to share some similarities with that of Taheri et al. (2020), who conducted a study on Iranian EFL learners utilizing SILL and revealed that low-achievers often employed social strategies, whilst high-achievers prioritized compensation strategies. Furthermore, the use of memory and compensatory strategies were highly correlated with writing. In the Thai context, Pongsukvajchakul (2021) also investigated learners' LLS for English writing. The author found that social and memory strategies were dominant, similar to earlier studies (McMullen, 2009; Taheri et al., 2020). It seems that the utilization of AI was not the focus of previous literature on writing strategies. Thus, further studies on their usage are crucial, as new strategies may arise due to the AI's profound knowledge and ability to handle language tasks. Educators can adjust and design lessons by identifying frequently utilized strategies by learners.

2.3 AI Uses in Language Learning

Among the typical uses of AI, the ability to deliver constructive feedback has often been found to be valuable. Using a mixed-methods approach with pre-and post-test procedures, Rad et al. (2023) used generative AI to assess whether it might increase students' writing feedback literacy, and the researchers found that the experimental group witnessed a significant enhancement. Their findings matched those of Guo et al. (2024), who also observed that AI greatly improved students' peer feedback and their writing skills after conducting pre-and post-tests.

AI use has also boosted learning motivation and engagement. Yuan and Liu (2025) found that Chinese EFL learners were much more motivated, engaged, and contented with learning when AI was utilized, while the group without AI experienced marginal change. These findings aligned with earlier studies, as Wei (2023) found that undergraduates showed better L2 motivation, self-learning regulation, and improved English learning outcomes under AI-mediated instruction. Guo and Li (2024) also studied how student-created generative chatbots might improve writing. The findings indicated that the chatbots were developed to meet each student's demands and obstacles. Furthermore, the students reported having more confidence and motivation from customized instruction and guidance, resulting in a generally more positive attitude about writing.

In the Vietnamese context, Pham and Cao (2025) systematically reviewed past studies on the use of ChatGPT in English teaching and learning in Vietnam. The researchers examined 12 studies across several journals and concluded that there were both positive and negative contributions. According to the researchers, ChatGPT could create personalized learning environments, assist teachers in providing feedback and grading, developing language skills, and the tool could be combined with traditional teaching methods. However, issues related to over-reliance, academic dishonesty, inconsistency, reliability, lack of training, and ethical and privacy concerns were also found. Regarding personalized language learning, generative AI models' advantages, such as customized constructive feedback, motivation, language acquisition, and engagement, are crucial for establishing individualized learning experiences and improving students' writing. Pham and Cao (2025) mentioned that AI tools, particularly ChatGPT, held a prominent role in establishing a personalized learning environment in Vietnamese EFL classrooms, as ChatGPT could tailor its feedback and support to meet diverse learners' needs. Thus, personalized instruction with ChatGPT at the core in the writing context may involve AI-integrated instructional approaches centralized around establishing a tailored learning environment to address learners' specific needs. This includes designing customized writing tasks or guiding students to utilize AI to enhance their writing in particular ways that align with their preferred learning strategies, depending on the aspects of writing they seek to refine.

It is imperative that educators and researchers understand how students use AI chatbots like ChatGPT to utilize their potential. Examining strategies employed by learners when using ChatGPT can yield significant insights for the appropriate incorporation of AI in language education, ensuring that students not only improve their writing abilities but also cultivate autonomy and confidence in their learning journey.

2.4 *Writing Difficulties of Learners and Solutions*

Ananda et al. (2024) adopted a qualitative design, using semi-structured interviews to investigate writing problems faced by EFL learners when writing an argumentative essay and their strategies to overcome them. The authors discovered that students tended to encounter issues relating to developing arguments and source integration, such as finding supporting evidence and citations. The participants chose to approach more information sources, utilizing technology and more reviewing. With a similar research design, Alsariera and Yunus (2023) aimed to examine problems affecting learners' writing coherency. The authors found that the issue with limited lexical resources was the main contributor hindering learners' coherence in writing. Both studies attempted to propose solutions to address writing challenges faced by learners, such as the use of modern technology in writing instruction, teacher training, employment of modern teaching methods, providing personalized feedback, and improving curricula (Alsariera & Yunus, 2023; Ananda et al., 2024).

However, considering the rapid growth of AI use in education, some of these problems may become irrelevant, as, for instance, a student can effortlessly demand the intelligent bot to provide appropriate words needed for the context. A thorough understanding of how students employ artificial intelligence is imperative to identify novel problems associated with writing so that more viable approaches to writing instruction can be incorporated into the classroom.

2.5 *Integration of ChatGPT in Writing Instruction*

Meniado et al. (2024) studied the experiences and perceptions of Vietnamese and Thai EFL learners regarding the use of ChatGPT for L2 writing. The researchers followed a mixed-methods design and incorporated surveys and interviews as their research instruments. Their results indicated that although there was a slight difference in how two groups of learners perceived ChatGPT effectiveness, the overarching attitude was positive. The findings also pointed out that the primary uses of ChatGPT involved generating ideas, organization, refinement, clarification, and editing. Similarly, in the Vietnamese context, it was found that ideas development, enhanced language use, and finding references were among the most prevalent benefits for Vietnamese postgraduates (Tran et al., 2025). However, Pham (2025) also reported similar benefits of using ChatGPT as a writing assistant. However, the researcher stressed that AI tools should be used with caution due to challenges such as possible inaccuracies and privacy problems. From the teacher's perspective, results were rather similar (Nguyen, 2023), showing that EFL teachers also held favorable views towards ChatGPT; however, participants voiced their problems regarding the over-reliance on the Chatbot and unfair assessment.

Moreover, applications of using ChatGPT to enhance learners' overall writing skills have often been observed, with mostly favorable results leaning towards the Chatbot (Al-Sofi, 2024; Mahapatra, 2024). In the study by Pratama and Hastuti (2024), the authors found that the intervention of AI tools significantly impacted their participants' writing skills. In addition, the students also viewed the tool favorably, as they perceived AI to positively affect their learning outcomes. Furthermore, Guo and Wang (2024) pointed out how feedback by ChatGPT could be supplementary to teachers, as while the teachers were found to often have the tendency to focus on language and content-related issues, the AI provided informative feedback on organizational problems in addition to the content and language. Concerns regarding the comprehensibility of AI were also identified, as they tended to be lengthy, containing unnecessary content, as well as lacking awareness of the local context, similar to other findings (Silalahi, 2025; Song & Song, 2023), and ethical problems, such as plagiarism, fairness in assessment, academic integrity, or dependency, were also raised (Alkamel & Alwagieh, 2024; Nguyen, 2023; Nguyen et al., 2025; Tsai et al., 2024).

Therefore, understanding students' learning strategies for large language models, particularly ChatGPT, in writing tasks, addressing concerns regarding the use of artificial intelligence chatbots, acquiring insights into how students resolve these challenges, and how they believe ChatGPT should be integrated into writing instruction are essential for the effective integration of AI for personalized language instruction.

2.6 Research Questions

To provide more knowledge to the existing literature, the present study aims to bridge the aforementioned gaps by seeking to address the following research questions:

(1) What writing strategies are employed by Vietnamese undergraduates while using ChatGPT for writing?
(2) What difficulties do Vietnamese undergraduates face while using ChatGPT for writing?
(3) How do Vietnamese undergraduates overcome their difficulties?
(4) How do Vietnamese undergraduates perceive strategies for integrating ChatGPT in writing instruction?

3 Methodology

3.1 Research Design

The current study followed a mixed-methods design, with the questionnaire adapted from Taheri et al. (2020), which was based on SILL by Oxford (1990), allowing precise categorical classifications of how learners approach writing with the assistance of ChatGPT (McMullen, 2009; Pongsukvajchakul, 2021; Taheri et al., 2020). The author believed that solely relying on either qualitative or quantitative data was inadequate for the proper integration of ChatGPT into language instruction, as more nuanced perspectives were essential for a thorough understanding (Meniado et al., 2024; Pratama & Hastuti, 2024). The qualitative data, including in-depth insights into challenges faced by students while utilizing ChatGPT, strategies to overcome them, strengths of ChatGPT, and students' viewpoints on essential measures for its integration in educational settings, were supported and augmented by quantitative data featuring a statistical representation of the strategies employed by learners when leveraging artificial intelligence, particularly ChatGPT while writing. This yielded a comprehensive understanding of English learners' usage of the intelligent Chatbot, establishing a vital basis for the future integration of artificial intelligence in L2 instruction.

3.2 *Participants*

The participants of this study were Vietnamese undergraduates of the Foreign Language faculty of a university in Vietnam, and they were all familiar with English and knowledgeable to an extent. 61 students, all above eighteen, agreed to respond to the questionnaire, and 14 took part in the interview phase. These participants were conveniently selected as there were few available classes when the author collected data for the study. The author was given permission by another lecturer to access their classes' students, and the students were all briefed of the purpose as well as informed of the confidentiality and the voluntary nature of the research, so those who joined the study gave consent of their own will.

3.3 *Instruments*

3.3.1 Questionnaire

The questionnaire employed in the current study was adapted and developed based on the one in Taheri et al. (2020), which was based on SILL of Oxford (1990), specifically the one for learners whose first language was not English. The questionnaire encompassed 35 five-point Likert scale items: (1) Never or almost never true; (2) Usually not true; (3) Somewhat true; (4) Usually true; (5) Almost or almost always true, and 3 open-ended questions were added to gather students' perspectives on difficulties and advantages of ChatGPT, and suggestions to employ ChatGPT effectively in teaching. The author took rigorous steps to refine the instrument and ensure it produces extensive insights into students' strategies for writing with ChatGPT. The author adapted the items and made adjustments where necessary in order to make the questionnaire relevant and suitable for the current context, as SILL was designed to examine how learners generally learn language instead of concentrating on one particular aspect, such as writing. For instance, an item related to physically acting out a new language item or writing down feelings in a diary was omitted as it was not appropriate for the AI-assisted writing context. The adaptation also focused on maintaining alignment with the concept of each language strategy following Oxford's (1990) framework, namely, memory, cognitive, compensation, metacognitive, affective, and social strategies to ensure the validity of the items. Moreover, to further enhance the clarity and language of the instrument, ChatGPT was utilized to assist with the adaptation process, rephrasing and editing questionnaire items to better align with the present study's focus while retaining the core concept of each strategy (Lew et al., 2024; Kurt Pehlivanoğlu et al., 2024). The author then reviewed and assessed all suggestions thoroughly and modified them as needed to improve relevancy and appropriateness. To ensure internal consistency, the author calculated Cronbach's Alpha, which yielded a value of 0.91 ($\alpha = 0.91$), indicating the reliability of the current instrument.

3.3.2 Semi-structured Interviews

To further investigate and gain deeper insights, semi-structured interviews were conducted with 14 students. Six key questions targeted the overall experience, strategies, challenges, solutions, impact of ChatGPT on their writing skills, and recommendations for integrating ChatGPT in writing skills instruction. Each interview session lasted between five and twelve minutes, was carried out in Vietnamese to acquire the most accurate responses possible, and was audio-recorded with the consent of the interviewee.

3.3.3 Simulated Writing Tasks

To encourage the authentic use of ChatGPT, the author assigned the participants two writing tasks and instructed them to utilize ChatGPT 3.5, the free version, to assist them during the writing process. The tasks included an argumentative essay and a problem–solution essay to encourage the students to implement a variety of strategies and interactions with ChatGPT.

3.4 Data Collection and Analysis

The researcher obtained consent from a colleague to perform the study with their students. Essential details regarding the study, including its objectives, procedures, and potential risks, which there were none, were communicated to the students. Participants were also informed of any ethical considerations. Following a briefing on the fundamentals, a total of 61 participants gave their consent to participate in the study. No personally identifiable information was collected. The process comprised two stages: the initial stage included simulated writing activities, while the subsequent one involved the distribution of the questionnaire and the implementation of interviews. Initially, participants engaged in two simulated writing tasks in English, with clear instructions to guarantee comprehension, intended to promote the utilization of ChatGPT and the application of diverse writing strategies. The students were given 3–6 days to complete the set of writing tasks. During the second phase, participants were instructed to complete a questionnaire distributed through Google Forms for convenience. Semi-structured interviews were subsequently conducted online via Zalo, a calling app, to meet the interviewees' availability and restricted schedules. The interviews were in Vietnamese to remove any potential linguistic barriers and encourage interviewees to articulate themselves confidently and without hesitation. All interview responses were transcribed and translated into English. The quantitative data were analyzed using SPSS, employing descriptive statistics to identify common strategies participants used while writing with ChatGPT. For the qualitative data, thematic analysis was applied to uncover recurring themes related to the writing strategies, common uses, difficulties, solutions, strengths, and recommendations for integration. Qualitative data were also translated to English prior to analysis. By combining quantitative and qualitative approaches, the study ensured a thorough understanding of the study objectives.

4 Result

4.1 Strategies Used While Utilizing ChatGPT for Writing

Based on Table 1, undergraduates tended to employ social strategies (M = 3.75, SD = 0.63). The second highest category was compensation (M = 3.53, SD = 0.65), which was noticeably smaller than the most dominant strategy. Other statistics revealed that while memory (M = 3.47, SD = 0.80) was the third frequently employed strategy, metacognitive (M = 3.46, SD = 0.62) was almost as prominent as memory. The smallest categories included cognitive (M = 3.35, SD = 0.60) and affective (M = 3.21, SD = 0.74).

Table 2 displays the percentages and means of the most frequently employed strategy, social. Additionally, compensation and memory are illustrated due to their rather high usage.

Considering social strategies, participants usually preferred asking for clarification or explanation (78.8%). Additionally, the majority of students appeared to have at least usually collaborated with the AI to tackle problems that arose during the writing process at 67.3%. When it comes to treating the AI like a writing assistant and learning about relevant cultural aspects, it seems that these strategies did not receive sufficient attention from students; however, while the former usage remained

Table 1 Writing strategies with mean score

	N	Mean	SD	Minimum	Maximum
Social	61	3.75	0.63	2.0	5.0
Compensation	61	3.53	0.65	1.6	4.8
Memory	61	3.47	0.80	1.5	5.0
Metacognitive	61	3.46	0.62	2.2	4.7
Cognitive	61	3.35	0.60	1.3	4.8
Affective	61	3.21	0.74	1.0	5.0
Overall	61	3.45	0.53	1.9	4.5

Table 2 Social strategies

Item	Mean	Never or almost never true (%)	Usually not true (%)	Somewhat true (%)	Usually true (%)	Always or almost always true (%)
When I didn't understand a suggestion or explanation from ChatGPT, I asked it to clarify or explain again	4.12	1.7	1.7	18.1	41	37.8
I treated ChatGPT like a writing assistant and asked for its feedback	3.78	3.3	3.3	27.9	44.3	21.4
I collaborated with ChatGPT to solve specific questions or challenges during the writing process	3.82	0	5.0	27.9	47.6	19.7
I used ChatGPT to learn about cultural aspects relevant to my writing topic	3.30	8.2	14.8	31.2	31.2	14.8

relatively considerable at 65.7%, only 46% reported to have usually or always used the latter (Table 2).

Illustration of Table 3 elucidated that most participants usually or always tended to make up for their lack of linguistic knowledge by asking ChatGPT to provide synonyms or alternatives, with 64.1% of the respondents reporting to have employed them. The strategy involving asking ChatGPT to help make ideas clearly communicated was quite as significant, as up to 64% of respondents decided to use them while writing with ChatGPT. In the third place, making guesses based on contexts did not seem to garner much attention from students, but it remained quite noticeable at 55.8%, compared to asking ChatGPT for help with constructing sentences and trying to understand the overall meaning, which only accounted for 50.9% and 47.6% respectively.

Table 4 provided usage of memory strategies, with the highest category being using examples created by ChatGPT for memorization and comprehension, at 67.3%. A significant number of students, 60.8%, reported to have usually or always asked ChatGPT to provide definitions and examples. Over half of the participants, 59.1% and 57.5%, respectively, asked ChatGPT to provide contextual aids and establish associations with existing knowledge for memory aids.

Table 5 showed that in terms of metacognitive strategies, more than two-thirds of the students took advantage of ChatGPT's feedback to be aware of their errors in writing (72.2%), noticeably more than seeking advice based on their current needs (59.1%) and exploring ways to employ the Chatbot for writing (57.4%). Additionally, roughly half of the students utilized ChatGPT for outlining (50.9%).

With regard to cognitive strategies (Table 6), the most common approach was to skim through ChatGPT's suggestions, choosing only to read the necessary parts

Table 3 Compensation strategies

Item	Mean	Never or almost never true (%)	Usually not true (%)	Somewhat true (%)	Usually true (%)	Always or almost always true (%)
When I didn't understand a word or sentence pattern suggested by ChatGPT, I guessed its meaning based on the context	3.48	5.0	13.2	26.3	41.0	14.8
I focused on the overall meaning of ChatGPT's suggestions instead of looking up every unfamiliar word	3.43	0	19.7	32.8	32.8	14.8
When I couldn't think of an exact word, I asked ChatGPT to generate synonyms or alternative phrases	3.56	8.2	9.9	18.1	46	18.1
When I face difficulties expressing my ideas clearly, I use ChatGPT to provide alternative ways of saying them	3.79	3.3	3.3	29.6	39.4	24.6
I asked ChatGPT for help when I have to construct complex sentences that I cannot complete on my own	3.37	9.9	6.6	32.8	39.4	11.5

(70.6%). This was closely followed by using ChatGPT to summarize ideas (67.3%). Other uses generally hovered around the 50% mark, except for the usage pertaining to analysing structures and breaking down patterns, which was at 34.5% and 36.2%, respectively.

Regarding affective strategies, about 51% of the participants employed ChatGPT for emotional reliefs, while other strategies received little attention by most of the students (Table 7).

Additionally, interview data shed light on what aspects of students' writing had been improved by employing the aforementioned writing strategies (Table 8).

Evidently, participants reported on improvement in vocabulary and grammar the most, citing how it helped to make their vocabulary more academic *(S5, Interview)*, and how it raised the accuracy of their word usage as well as grammar *(S4, Interview)*. Enhancement in idea generation and organization were also mentioned, as some had a diverse range of ideas they could cover *(S1, Interview)* and some felt their ideas sounded more academic *(S11, Interview)*.

Table 4 Memory strategies

Item	Mean	Never or almost never true (%)	Usually not true (%)	Somewhat true (%)	Usually true (%)	Always or almost always true (%)
I used ChatGPT to connect new vocabulary or ideas with concepts I already knew	3.58	1.7	8.2	32.8	46	11.5
I asked ChatGPT to create examples to help me understand and remember new vocabulary or grammar	3.74	3.3	9.9	19.7	44.3	23
I asked ChatGPT to suggest scenarios or contexts where vocabulary or grammar could be applied to help me understand and remember them	3.50	8.2	8.2	24.6	44.3	14.8
I asked ChatGPT to give definitions and explanations for new words or grammar	3.61	9.9	11.5	18.1	29.6	31.2
I reviewed vocabulary and phrases suggested by ChatGPT regularly to reinforce my learning	3.25	8.2	19.7	29.6	24.6	18.1
I asked ChatGPT to create memorable patterns or examples to help me remember new vocabulary or grammar	3.17	9.9	14.8	31.2	37.8	6.6

4.1.1 Difficulties Faced While Using ChatGPT for Writing

Thematic analysis of the survey's open-ended responses revealed that more than half of the difficulties were related to content, such as obstacles related to the quality and relevance of generated responses and ideas, and communication issues, which pertained to challenges linked to interaction with ChatGPT, such as how smooth or difficult it was to get the message across.

Table 9 illustrates the difficulties experienced by students, expressed in terms of the total number of instances and percentage for each theme, as they used ChatGPT for writing. It was found that the most commonly reported issues were related to the contents of ChatGPT responses, with 39.5% having experienced these difficulties: *"...while it provides well-written responses, sometimes the ideas are too general and require further refinement to fit the context" (S10), "Sometimes the answer lacks the depth, spontaneity, or contextual precision we need "(S11), "The lack of deep content" (S48).* Secondly, challenges linked to communicating with the GPT chatbot

Table 5 Metacognitive strategies

Item	Mean	Never or almost never true (%)	Usually not true (%)	Somewhat true (%)	Usually true (%)	Always or almost always true (%)
I tried to explore as many ways to use ChatGPT in writing as possible	3.63	1.7	8.2	32.8	41.0	16.4
I used ChatGPT's feedback to identify errors and improve my writing	3.91	3.3	8.2	16.4	39.4	32.8
I asked ChatGPT for advice on how to improve specific aspects of my writing	3.55	5.0	13.2	23.0	41.0	18.1
I used ChatGPT to create an outline for my writing	3.38	8.2	11.5	29.6	36.1	14.8
I asked ChatGPT to help me set specific goals for my writing	3.00	14.8	19.7	26.3	29.6	9.9
I reflected on how I used ChatGPT during the writing process	3.28	3.3	11.5	41.0	42.7	1.7

were reported at 26.8%: *"ChatGPT might occasionally misunderstand the user's intent or fail to maintain continuity in longer texts" (S3)*, *"Sometimes, ChatGPT doesn't understand my requirements so I have to simplify it for ChatGPT "(S8)*, *"How to write an effective prompt" (S18)*. Lastly, linguistic and technical issues were observed in 17 instances, such as *"ChatGPT often uses a lot of high-level/ complex words" (S32)*, while fearing that ChatGPT would negatively affect them in some ways was mentioned 7 times, such as *"I depend on too much ChatGPT so I'm very lazy to create new ideas and develop the sentences." (S12)*.

Interview findings of students' personal usage of the Chatbot and corresponding difficulties that they encountered were illustrated in Table 10. The responses were translated into English, coded according to their usage, and matched with the appropriate themes previously identified. A total of 9 uses were identified: vocabulary (10), idea brainstorming (7), paraphrasing (6), error correction (6), outlining and organizing (6), grammar (2), evaluation (2), clarification (2), and quoting (2). Most of the challenges are related to content (10), language, and technical issues (7).

4.1.2 Strategies Used to Overcome Difficulties

To address the aforementioned issues, students tended to opt for various strategies to overcome them, which were classified into four separate themes (Table 11).

Table 6 Cognitive strategies

Item	Mean	Never or almost never true (%)	Usually not true (%)	Somewhat true (%)	Usually true (%)	Always or almost always true (%)
I used ChatGPT to create sentences using new vocabulary or grammar structures multiple times	3.33	5.0	19.7	26.3	36.1	13.2
I used ChatGPT to help me write sentences naturally following the style of native speakers	3.51	6.6	11.5	24.6	39.4	18.1
I asked ChatGPT to create sentences using words I already knew in different contexts	3.22	11.5	19.7	18.1	37.8	13.2
I applied new sentence patterns and vocabulary suggested by ChatGPT in my writing	3.53	1.7	9.9	34.5	42.7	11.5
I skimmed through ChatGPT's suggestions and selected only the parts relevant to my writing	3.89	1.7	6.6	21.4	42.7	27.9
I asked ChatGPT to suggest English words similar to words in Vietnamese	2.89	19.7	21.4	18.1	32.8	8.2
I analyzed sentence structures created by ChatGPT to understand their rules	2.96	8.2	26.3	31.2	31.2	3.3
I used ChatGPT to break down phrases or sentence patterns into parts to help me understand	3.04	11.5	16.4	36.1	29.6	6.6
I asked ChatGPT to revise my sentences or paragraphs	3.41	8.2	16.4	18.1	41.0	16.4
I used ChatGPT to summarize and condense ideas in my writing	3.73	5.0	8.2	19.7	44.3	23.0

Table 7 Affective strategies

Item	Mean	Never or almost never true (%)	Usually not true (%)	Somewhat true (%)	Usually true (%)	Always or almost always true (%)
I used ChatGPT to help me feel less anxious or worried when I felt stuck during the writing process	3.38	6.6	13.2	29.6	37.8	13.2
I used ChatGPT to encourage myself to keep writing even when I was afraid of making mistakes	3.14	14.8	8.2	37.8	27.9	11.5
I used ChatGPT's positive feedback to feel more confident about my writing skills	3.33	9.9	8.2	32.8	37.8	11.5
I noticed when I felt tense or anxious while using ChatGPT to assist my writing	2.99	13.2	26.3	21.4	27.9	11.5

Table 8 Frequency of areas of improvement in writing with ChatGPT assistance

Theme	Frequency
Vocabulary	11
Grammar and sentence structure	7
Idea	5
Organizing and outlining	4
Coherence and cohesion	3
Paraphrasing	1

Table 9 Difficulties experienced by students while using ChatGPT for writing

Theme	Difficulties	Percentage (%)
Contents	28	39.5
Communication	19	26.8
Language and technical issues	17	24
Ethical concerns	7	9.9
Total	71	100

With regard to prompt refinement, it was the largest, with 66.7% of strategies falling into this category. Some interviewed participants mentioned as follows: *Divide follow-up prompts into smaller chunks so ChatGPT can understand (S1, interview); to make prompt more specific (S2); Write more specific prompt with clear instructions*

Table 10 Comparisons of students' uses of ChatGPT and their difficulties

Student	Uses of ChatGPT	Difficulties
1	Paraphrasing, rewriting, vocabulary, evaluation	Contents lacking details, ineffective prompts
2	Idea brainstorming, vocabulary, paraphrasing	Ineffective prompts, lengthy contents
3	Idea brainstorming, outlining and organizing	Incomplete contents, trouble with communicating with ChatGPT
4	Error correction, vocabulary	Contents lacking diversity, conclusion, summary, overusing nouns
5	Idea brainstorming, clarification, outlining and organizing, paraphrasing, vocabulary, error correction	Contents did not meet given criteria, did not tackle main points, repeating words, reduced independent thoughts
6	Outlining and organizing, paraphrasing, grammar, clarification	Ineffective prompts, irrelevant contents
7	Idea brainstorming, paraphrasing, error correction	Making ChatGPT sound human
8	Outlining and organizing, evaluation, error correction	Incorrect and unnecessary information
9	Vocabulary, idea brainstorming	Unnecessary information, ChatGPT delayed responses under heavy loads
10	Error correction, vocabulary	Contents lacking logic and depth
11	Grammar, idea brainstorming, vocabulary, error correction	Irrelevant and incomplete contents
12	Vocabulary, outlining and organizing, paraphrasing, quoting	Making ChatGPT sound human
13	Idea brainstorming, vocabulary	ChatGPT's use of overly formal vocabulary
14	Outlining and organizing, vocabulary, quoting	Cannot use the photo-capturing function

(S3, interview); Make it clear what ChatGPT needs to do so it can understand (S4, interview); Clarify prompts by making them more specific (S8, interview).

The theme related to using ChatGPT critically, at around 20%, included students' opinions, such as *using it as a supporting tool without total dependency. Use external sources and think critically while using (S5, interview); Consult external sources to complement ChatGPT (S10, interview); Write daily to reduce dependency on ChatGPT (S12, interview).* Regarding the third theme, only one was mentioned: *Instruct ChatGPT to write like a human (S7, interview).* Similarly, the last theme had one case as it was related to *ChatGPT's "photo-capturing function" (S14, interview).*

Table 11 Frequency and percentage of students' solutions for different writing challenges with ChatGPT

Theme	Frequency	Example	Writing strategies	Percentage (%)
Prompt refinement	10	*"Add more specific follow-up prompts to make sure ChatGPT understand", "Write more specific prompts with clear instruction"*	Social	66.7
Critical use of ChatGPT	3	*"Use it as a supporting tool, without total dependency. Use external sources and think critically while using", 'Consult external sources to complement ChatGPT"*	Cognitive, social, metacognitive	20
Human-style adaptation	1	*"Instruct ChatGPT to write like a human"*	Metacognitive	6.7
Technical adaptation	1	*"Manually type the prompt when the photo-capturing function is unavailable."*	Compensation	6.7

4.1.3 Students' Perceptions of Integrating ChatGPT for Personalized Writing Instruction

Useful Features of ChatGPT

Qualitative thematic analysis of survey open-ended responses revealed several areas where each student believed ChatGPT to be most beneficial, providing insights into how teachers could tailor instruction to supplement ChatGPT's strengths (Table 12). After grouping small and relevant themes, a total of 8 categories were identified. Some students mentioned, for instance, *"ChatGPT gives me a lot of good ideas for my writing. Besides, the feedback from ChatGPT also helps me improve my writing skills." (Idea generation & feedback and refinement, S8); "GPT chat online is very fast and reasonable, I always use it when I write my essay" (Speed and convenience, S5); "It can write in various tones and formats, from formal essays to casual blogs or creative stories." (Writing flexibility, S3).*

Integration Strategies

Both the survey answers and interview results were thematically analyzed and combined in Table 13 to offer a complete picture of key recommendation areas that arose from the data. Two major themes were ChatGPT training and providing modelling and guidance for its use. Responses such as *"I'm not sure about this*

Table 12 Distribution of students' perceptions of ChatGPT's strengths

Theme	Frequency
Idea generation	21
Language enhancement	20
Information and example provision	18
Speed and convenience	13
Language correction	12
Writing processes	11
Feedback and refinement	11
Writing flexibility	5

Table 13 Students' perceptions of approaches for ChatGPT integration

Theme	Frequency
ChatGPT training	30
Modeling and guidance for ChatGPT writing support	29
Promoting balanced usage	22
Refining ChatGPT answers	12
Encouraging autonomy	10
Giving assignments and activities	9

issue" were not counted as they did not suggest any particular way to integrate AI into instruction, and thus, they could not be transformed into actionable measures.

ChatGPT training: This theme revolved around teaching students to craft clear and specific prompts in order to interact better with ChatGPT, pointing out strengths and limitations, and educating them about Chatbot so effective instructions could be made to better communicate and understand ChatGPT. Both survey answers and interview responses primarily stressed the focus on the importance of knowing how to write effective prompts for ChatGPT. They believed that teachers could help them refine and adjust their prompts to communicate with ChatGPT more effectively. Example: *"Teachers can support students by guiding them on how to create effective prompts, such as providing clear and specific instructions to ChatGPT" (S23, Survey); "Teachers can guide students on how to write good prompt, and instruct students on an effective procedure to use ChatGPT" (S13, Interview).*

Modeling and guidance for ChatGPT writing support: This involved the utilization of ChatGPT by teachers to facilitate the improvement of learners' writing skills through ChatGPT, including various aspects of writing such as grammar, vocabulary, sentence organization, outlining, or generating ideas. Example: *"I think teachers can guide their students to learn how to build sentence structure, paragraph structure as well as writing from ChatGPT." (S8, Survey); "Teachers can also use ChatGPT to find examples for highly advanced vocabulary to help students with comprehension" (S10, Interview).*

5 Discussion

The present study aimed to investigate the types of strategies used by Vietnamese undergraduates when utilizing ChatGPT for writing. In this section, significant findings were presented and discussed. Knowing how learners use ChatGPT, identifying their challenges and methods of resolution, and obtaining their feedback on the implementation of ChatGPT in learning are, in my view, vital constituents for attaining a thorough understanding of ChatGPT's potential and fundamental to its integration for personalized language instruction.

5.1 Writing Strategies Employed

Social strategies emerged as the most significant, with participants actively engaging with ChatGPT as an interactive assistant, always prepared to help with their personal needs. This showcases the nature of employing artificial intelligence in a learning context, reflecting its capability to respond and provide content directly related to the inquiry of the one who asks it as if it were an actual individual. In the case of this current study, students usually tended to collaborate with ChatGPT to solve their own problems and ask the intelligent Chatbot to explain or clarify their requests. One student said, *"It can answer most of my questions, assist me to complete the writing tasks quickly but ensure it's reasonably accurate." (S22, Survey)*. This finding seems to align with Pongsukvajchakul (2021), who also found that Thai EFL learners tended to employ social strategies the most, more than other writing strategies. Although the study of Pongsukvajchakul (2021) did not involve AI, the similar use of learning strategies is interesting. A possible explanation could be that participants in the present study were still freshmen, similar to most of those in Pongsukvajchakul's (2021) study, and thus, they were more likely to seek help from those with more experience and expertise to develop their writing skills.

Nevertheless, the current study's findings were similar to Taheri et al. (2020) in terms of the common uses of compensation and memory strategies. The utilization of compensation strategies seemed practical and understandable from the student's point of view. Since ChatGPT possesses a huge repertoire of language knowledge, it could supply students with plenty of words appropriate for the context or alternative phrases to help with expressing ideas, as one student stressed the strength of ChatGPT: *"It can give me vocabulary, check my grammar and guide me how to paraphrase for becoming a better task" (S26, Survey)*. The prominence of memory strategies in the present study was not expected, as it was anticipated that students would rather use ChatGPT's generated responses than try to understand and remember new vocabulary or grammar. However, this was not the case, as the participants seemed to have used examples created by ChatGPT to aid the memorization and comprehension of linguistic items. This could be because of the desire to boost their range of vocabulary and grammar, as ChatGPT could provide extensive explanation and learners could interact with ChatGPT to sort out any knowledge gaps. Moreover, the preference for these strategies may have led to the improvement in student's use of vocabulary and grammar, as shared by most interviewees: *"It improves my vocabulary and grammar, making them more academic…" (S5, Interview); "Improve my vocabulary and grammar accuracy" (S14, Interview).* These findings were consistent with those measuring the impact of AI on learners' writing skills (Mahapatra, 2024; Pratama & Hastuti, 2024; Song & Song, 2023).

From the perspective of learners, ChatGPT seems to be a study companion with exceptional English language proficiency, capable of responding to questions and offering personalized, useful alternatives. The interactive and adaptive characteristics of ChatGPT serve as a valuable asset for students, who often have different challenges and goals in writing, as the AI provides sufficient time for them to make inquiries and then collaborates with them to resolve these concerns. Furthermore, ChatGPT might provide students with immediate context-specific explanations, feedback, and support for their writing tasks unlike textbooks or other materials. These findings certainly highlighted ChatGPT's potential to be integrated for personalized instruction, enabling students to tailor their interactions to satisfy their unique learning needs.

5.2 Difficulties Faced While Using ChatGPT

Nearly two-fifths of participants had issues with AI-generated responses. ChatGPT's contents were occasionally too vague, irrelevant, or lacking detail. One student described the experience as follows: *"One challenge I faced was ensuring that the content generated by ChatGPT matched the specific tone or structure I needed. While it provides well-written responses, sometimes the ideas are too general and require further refinement to fit the context…" (S10, Survey).* These results were consistent with prior studies (Guo & Wang, 2024; Silalahi, 2025) that also found AI models' flaws. This shows a constant problem with ChatGPT, which seems to lack some grasp of the user's needs, requiring follow-up instructions to sort it out with the AI. However, the student might also be a factor, since the Chatbot can only act on the instructions it receives. On the other hand, a human teacher can interpret vague questions and diagnose students' needs more precisely based on their past contact and experience. Thus, if teachers guide students on what areas to focus on, the AI might provide more precise and relevant content. ChatGPT communication was another key challenge for participants, with over a quarter of students facing this hurdle. One expressed their experience as follows: *"Sometimes, ChatGPT doesn't understand my requirements so I have to simplify it for ChatGPT." (S8, Survey).* This limitation of ChatGPT, or AI in general, was consistent with those of other investigations (Guo & Wang, 2024; Silalahi, 2025). This issue shows a clear communication barrier between ChatGPT and its users, as the AI misinterprets the student. When students make unclear or broad requests, the AI may become confused. ChatGPT can give tailored explanations, yet unclear instructions and students' limited language skills may affect its accuracy. This suggests that teachers should guide students in creating focused, unambiguous prompts that express their aims to ChatGPT to improve communication with the Chatbot.

Post-interview analysis reaffirmed these findings. The problems seemed linked, with one capable of influencing the other. Students who used ChatGPT for brainstorming or lexical choices generally encountered issues with the AI's output quality and relevancy. Notably, those who complained about ChatGPT's responses had trouble making good prompts. This shows that various challenges related to the depth or length of ChatGPT-generated content may arise from a lack of clarity from user instructions, as ChatGPT can only generate information dependent on the commands and context provided to it. These trends imply that it is imperative to help students create prompts, select information, and organize ideas to understand ChatGPT's contents. If these difficulties were left unattended, a personalized learning experience would be affected and its effects on students would be diminished. Unless teachers intervene and offer their support, ChatGPT, despite its immense knowledge, remains constrained by the inquiries of students.

5.3 Strategies to Overcome Difficulties

An analysis of interview responses revealed that the strategy employed by most students to overcome this setback was related to social strategies. The strategy refers to how learners interact and collaborate to reach their goals (Oxford, 1990). In the context of this study, it seems that learners have adopted these strategies and viewed ChatGPT as a 'social partner' with whom they could exchange ideas in order to remove misunderstanding and eventually reach the desired outcome. These exchanges of interactions, in light of the present study, manifested as acts of refining prompts. Problems with ChatGPT's generated contents often involved a lack of details, missing information, or the relevance of its answer. As previously discussed, these issues partly stemmed from a lack of directives and clarity of users' inquiries. For instance, participants shared that they had to *"Give follow-up prompts to make ChatGPT clarify or rewrite responses until it is appropriate for personal needs" (S11, Interview)* or *"Write more specific prompts with clear instruction" (S3, Interview)*. This emphasis on refining prompts in order to acquire meaningful responses from ChatGPT was consistent with past studies (Al-Sofi, 2024; Xiao & Zhi, 2023). These adaptations from learners were understandable since the quality of ChatGPT's responses largely depends on how well the instruction was given, as identified in the previous section. More detailed inputs would certainly lead to more tailored outputs by ChatGPT. To exemplify this, one could not expect a broad question to yield answers with small details catering to personal preferences. By revising and making follow-up prompts, learners allow ChatGPT opportunities to assess its current understanding of their needs so it can respond appropriately with an updated perspective. With the conversational nature of AI, learners can always ask it to clarify or expand on certain parts in order to reach a sense of mutual understanding between both parties, similar to how they interact with others in real life. Moreover, a number of interviewed participants (20%) opted to adopt a more critical use of ChatGPT in order to solve their problems with the Chatbot, such as using it as a complementary tool, employing critical thinking while using, or simply practicing writing daily to reduce dependency on ChatGPT. Utilizing inputs from other sources would help add more depth to ChatGPT's responses, and carefully evaluating the AI's answers would allow students to select only details relevant to their needs. Nevertheless, students' strong preferences for social strategies to overcome difficulties with using ChatGPT implied that students' personalized learning experience with ChatGPT could be further enhanced if they received proper guidance on refining prompts and giving instructions to AI, which can then generate more focused and relevant responses tailored to individuals' needs. This again supports the potential of integrating AI into instruction, with teachers as a vital factor.

5.4 Recommendations for Integrating ChatGPT

After having gathered necessary information on how learners use ChatGPT for writing, this section will present and discuss their perceptions on the integration of AI along with what students perceive as useful to them. Based on these findings, further recommendations will be made to suggest viable approaches for educators to incorporate ChatGPT into instruction and enhance students' personalized learning experience.

The most popular opinion concerning how teachers could integrate ChatGPT was ChatGPT training, which involved teaching students about writing prompts, strengths, and limitations of ChatGPT, as well as any information necessary for the effective use of the Chatbot. Considering how students tended to mostly employ social strategies while using ChatGPT for writing and faced major issues related to AI-generated content, it is only plausible that the majority of them desired more training provided by the teacher to use the Chatbot, and helping them to do so might greatly boost the positive impact of ChatGPT for students' personalized learning. This finding is similar to previous studies (Alenezi et al., 2023; Al-Sofi, 2024), which also called for training to facilitate effective usage. Certainly, teacher guidance would allow students to craft better prompts with clear instructions so that the AI could produce responses precisely tailored to their needs. Moreover, teachers could educate students about ChatGPT's capabilities so that they are aware of its shortcomings and can prepare appropriate compensatory measures. There is an implication that teachers should be knowledgeable in ChatGPT to some extent before incorporating it into their instruction so they can assist learners with crafting prompts specific to their needs. Moreover, as previously identified in the study, idea generation, language enhancement, information, and example provision were found to be the major strengths of ChatGPT. This indicates that training sessions should revolve around these aspects for optimal efficiency, such as crafting prompts specifically for brainstorming ideas or making instructional commands to request a list of vocabulary with style and usage depending on the student's desire. Alternatively, ChatGPT's least favored feature lay in its inflexibility in writing. The present study's findings suggest that this phenomenon might also be attributed to students' lack of clear instructions, as the Chatbot's extensive linguistic knowledge should have enabled it to compose in various tones.

Regarding the second popular approach, a considerable number of students believed that teachers could help students personalize their learning, especially their writing, through ChatGPT by providing guidance and modeling using ChatGPT for writing support. The positive impact of AI on developing students' language skills has often been demonstrated in previous studies (Guo & Li, 2024; Liu et al., 2024; Yener & Selcuk, 2024), as artificial intelligence models often possess a vast amount of knowledge regarding the English language, resulting in learners' improved use of language skills. In a similar vein, ChatGPT is capable of producing highly complex sentences in English with advanced lexical items. However, one student stated that teachers should *"guide their students to learn how to build sentence structure, paragraph structure as well as writing from ChatGPT" (S8, Survey).* Although ChatGPT is highly proficient in linguistic knowledge, in order to harness its full potential and turn them into chunks of usable knowledge that students can learn, it is better used with the guidance of a teacher (Alenezi et al., 2023), as some students may feel overwhelmed by the responses generated by the AI, considering how learners often reported issues with ChatGPT's contents either lacking depths or containing irrelevant details, as well as difficulty with making effective prompts. This implies that by modeling how ChatGPT could be used to supplement those strategies, students' overall personalized learning experience would be substantially enhanced. Furthermore, a portion of students felt teachers should instruct them on the responsible and balanced usage of ChatGPT. The majority of participants shared a similar notion that students should use it as a reference source rather than having the AI do all the work, as it can lead to significant long-term consequences, including diminished independent thinking skills, as well as a loss in one's creativity and personal touch in writing (Alkamel & Alwagieh, 2024; Al-Sofi, 2024; Nguyen, 2023). Thus, this implies that teachers should maintain a balanced use of ChatGPT in teaching and not make it mandatory, as some pupils may prefer to think on their own and only depend on the AI when necessary.

6 Conclusion

6.1 Major Findings and Recommendations

This study aimed to investigate the types of learning strategies employed by Vietnamese undergraduates when they employed ChatGPT for writing. Moreover, difficulties with using ChatGPT, solutions to overcome them, and students' perceptions regarding how ChatGPT could be integrated into personalized learning were examined. The current study demonstrated that social strategies were the most prevalent, followed by compensation and memory strategies. With those preferences, learners generally had problems with the quality and relevancy of ChatGPT-generated content and difficulty with interacting and delivering instructions to the Chatbot. To overcome these issues, students often used adaptive strategies, such as engaging in conversations with ChatGPT and working with it to refine prompts and ask follow-up questions to clarify or elaborate on their points, emphasizing the social interactive aspects of their strategies. Some students took a more cognitive approach to ChatGPT's issues by critically assessing the AI's answers and consulting trustworthy sources or experts. Moreover, teachers should provide students with extensive knowledge of ChatGPT, as they often interact with the Chatbot to solve problems and customize content.

Additionally, students thought that teachers' modeling of uses of ChatGPT for writing support, such as understanding grammar or improving sentence structure, would benefit their writing skills. Hence, to improve students' individualized learning with ChatGPT in writing instruction, teachers should thoroughly understand ChatGPT's functionalities and how to write effective prompts. Furthermore, modeling how to use ChatGPT to improve different areas of writing should also be clearly illustrated.

6.2 Implications

Overall, the findings indicate the presence of social interactions that occur during the students' employment of ChatGPT to aid their writing. In the present study, social strategies were the most prominent, reflected by students' tendency to actively communicate with ChatGPT to resolve particular needs, such as clarifying questions, asking for feedback, or collaborating to work through difficulties. In a broader sense, this implication may align with Vygotsky's ideas about Zone of Proximal Development (Shabani et al., 2010; Vygotsky, 1978), which essentially advocates for knowledge learners can gain via interaction with others, possibly more knowledgeable beings, as the AI tool appeared to have performed functions similar to an experienced partner, offering advice and correction in order to guide learners to gradually polish their writing. Thus, several pedagogical implications could be drawn from this. First, training students to use ChatGPT effectively is necessary, especially in making prompts. Second, teachers should employ teaching methods that favor cooperation and peer interactivity when integrating AI. Since ChatGPT could provide immediate responses tailored to individual needs, learners should be encouraged to actively engage in communication with the Chatbot and interact with their peers, as the information given by ChatGPT may occasionally lack precision, thus making use of its personalized benefits while mitigating its shortcomings. Moreover, educators may need to establish guidelines for evaluating AI contents, as it was discovered that there may be inaccuracies, and develop suitable assessment methods for courses that integrate ChatGPT into instruction.

6.3 Limitations and Suggestions for Future Research

Although the study contributes knowledge to the use of ChatGPT by Vietnamese undergraduates and how it might be incorporated into instruction to facilitate personalized learning, it has several limitations. First, the sample size was rather modest, with only 61 students in their first year, thus limiting its generalizability to a wider context. Second, findings in the study were gathered from the perspective of students. Additional inputs from teachers would have added more insights. Third, the learning strategies used by students were only investigated via two writing tasks. It might be possible that studies with larger scales and longer implementation periods might yield distinct findings. Future research could be conducted on a larger sample size with students of varied backgrounds and levels of proficiency. Additionally, the participants could be expanded to include teachers or experts with ChatGPT and more writing tasks could be implemented to delve deeper into the learning strategies used by students.

References

Alenezi, M. A. K., Mohamed, A. M., & Shaaban, T. S. (2023). Revolutionizing EFL special education: How ChatGPT is transforming the way teachers approach language learning. *Innoeduca International Journal of Technology and Educational Innovation, 9*(2), 5–23. https://doi.org/10.24310/innoeduca.2023.v9i2.16774

Alkamel, M. A. A., & Alwagieh, N. A. S. (2024). Utilizing an adaptable artificial intelligence writing tool (ChatGPT) to enhance academic writing skills among Yemeni university EFL students. *Social Sciences & Humanities Open, 10*, Article 101095. https://doi.org/10.1016/j.ssaho.2024.101095

Alsariera, A. H., & Yunus, K. (2023). Issues and challenges in the use of coherence among Jordanian EFL students in writing academic essays. *Journal of Nusantara Studies (JONUS), 8*(2), 141–156. https://doi.org/10.24200/jonus.vol8iss2pp141-156

Al-Sofi, B. B. M. A. (2024). Artificial intelligence-powered tools and academic writing: To use or not to use ChatGPT. *Saudi Journal of Language Studies, 4*(3), 145–161. https://doi.org/10.1108/sjls-06-2024-0029

Ananda, C. R., Mardiah, R., & Fajaryani, N. (2024). Writing argumentative essays: Jambi EFL students' challenges and strategies. *IJELTAL (Indonesian Journal of English Language Teaching and Applied Linguistics), 9*(2), 339–357. https://doi.org/10.21093/ijeltal.v9i2.1722

Dinh, T. B. H. (2025). Factors affecting ICT integration of EFL teachers at a Vietnamese university. *International Journal of AI in Language Education, 2*(1), 55–73. https://doi.org/10.54855/ijaile.25214

Guo, K., & Li, D. (2024). Understanding EFL students' use of self-made AI chatbots as personalized writing assistance tools: A mixed methods study. *System, 124*, Article 103362. https://doi.org/10.1016/j.system.2024.103362

Guo, K., Pan, M., Li, Y., & Lai, C. (2024). Effects of an AI-supported approach to peer feedback on university EFL students' feedback quality and writing ability. *The Internet and Higher Education, 63*, Article 100962. https://doi.org/10.1016/j.iheduc.2024.100962

Guo, K., & Wang, D. (2024). To resist it or to embrace it? Examining ChatGPT's potential to support teacher feedback in EFL writing. *Education and Information Technologies, 29*(7), 8435–8463. https://doi.org/10.1007/s10639-023-12146-0

Ho, P. X. P. (2024). Using ChatGPT in English language learning: A study on I.T. students' attitudes, habits, and perceptions. *International Journal of TESOL & Education, 4*(1), 55–68. https://doi.org/10.54855/ijte.24414

Kurt Pehlivanoğlu, M., Gobosho, R. T., Syakura, M. A., Shanmuganathan, V., & de-la-Fuente-Valentín, L. (2024). Comparative analysis of paraphrasing performance of ChatGPT, GPT-3, and T5 language models using a new ChatGPT generated dataset: ParaGPT. *Expert Systems, 41*(11), Article e13699. https://doi.org/10.1111/exsy.13699

Lew, R., Ptasznik, B., & Wolfer, S. (2024). The effectiveness of ChatGPT as a lexical tool for English, compared with a bilingual dictionary and a monolingual learner's dictionary. *Humanities and Social Sciences Communications, 11*(1), Article 1324. https://doi.org/10.1057/s41599-024-03775-y

Liu, Z. M., Hwang, G. J., Chen, C. Q., Chen, X. D., & Ye, X. D. (2024). Integrating large language models into EFL writing instruction: Effects on performance, self-regulated learning strategies, and motivation. *Computer Assisted Language Learning*, 1–25. https://doi.org/10.1080/09588221.2024.2389923

Mahapatra, S. (2024). Impact of ChatGPT on ESL students' academic writing skills: A mixed methods intervention study. *Smart Learning Environments, 11*(1), Article 9. https://doi.org/10.1186/s40561-024-00295-9

McMullen, M. G. (2009). Using language learning strategies to improve the writing skills of Saudi EFL students: Will it really work? *System, 37*(3), 418–433. https://doi.org/10.1016/j.system.2009.05.001

Meniado, J. C., Huyen, D. T. T., Panyadilokpong, N., & Lertkomolwit, P. (2024). Using ChatGPT for second language writing: Experiences and perceptions of EFL learners in Thailand and Vietnam. *Computers and Education Artificial Intelligence, 7*, Article 100313. https://doi.org/10.1016/j.caeai.2024.100313

Ngo, K. T. (2024). The use of ChatGPT for vocabulary acquisition: A literature review. *International Journal of AI in Language Education, 1*(2), 1–17. https://doi.org/10.54855/ijaile.24121

Nguyen, T. T. H. (2023). EFL teachers' perspectives toward the use of ChatGPT in writing classes: A case study at Van Lang University. *International Journal of Language Instruction, 2*(3), 1–47. https://doi.org/10.54855/ijli.23231

Nguyen, T. Y. P., Nguyen, N. T., & Phan, N. K. H. (2025). The challenges of applying ChatGPT in the academic writing of postgraduate students in english major at IUH. *International Journal of AI in Language Education, 2*(1), 20–37. https://doi.org/10.54855/ijaile.25212

Oxford, R. L. (1990). *Language learning strategies: What every teacher should know*. Heinle and Heinle Publishers.

Pham, M. T., & Cao, T. X. T. (2025). The practice of ChatGPT in English teaching and learning in Vietnam: A systematic review. *International Journal of TESOL & Education, 5*(1), 50–70. https://doi.org/10.54855/ijte.25513

Pham, N. N. H. (2025). The use of ChatGPT in EFL students as a learning assistant in their writing skills: A literature review. *International Journal of AI in Language Education, 2*(1), 38–54. https://doi.org/10.54855/ijaile.25213

Pongsukvajchakul, P. (2021). Language learning strategies used in English writing by Thai undergraduate students. *Shanlax International Journal of Education, 9*(2), 54–59. https://doi.org/10.34293/education.v9i2.3626

Pratama, R. M. D., & Hastuti, D. P. (2024). The use of artificial intelligence to improve EFL students' writing skills. *English Learning Innovation, 5*(1), 13–25. https://doi.org/10.22219/englie.v5i1.30212

Rad, H. S., Alipour, R., & Jafarpour, A. (2023). Using artificial intelligence to foster students' writing feedback literacy, engagement, and outcome: A case of Wordtune application. *Interactive Learning Environments, 32*(9), 5020–5040. https://doi.org/10.1080/10494820.2023.2208170

Shabani, K., Khatib, M., & Ebadi, S. (2010). Vygotsky's zone of proximal development: Instructional implications and teachers' professional development. *English Language Teaching, 3*(4), 237–248. https://doi.org/10.5539/elt.v3n4p237

Silalahi, R. M. (2025). Indonesian university students' perceptions of ChatGPT for English essay writing. *Polyglot Jurnal Ilmiah, 21*(1), 1–35. https://doi.org/10.19166/pji.v21i1.8896

Song, C., & Song, Y. (2023). Enhancing academic writing skills and motivation: assessing the efficacy of ChatGPT in AI-assisted language learning for EFL students. *Frontiers in Psychology, 14*, Article 1260843.https://doi.org/10.3389/fpsyg.2023.1260843

Taheri, H., Sadighi, F., Bagheri, M. S., & Bavali, M. (2020). Investigating the relationship between Iranian EFL learners' use of language learning strategies and foreign language skills achievement. *Cogent Arts & Humanities, 7*(1), Article 1710944. https://doi.org/10.1080/23311983.2019.1710944

Tran, H. N., Le, T. T. N., & Tran, V. B. U. (2025). AI tools in learning academic writing: Benefits and challenges for MA students in the English language studies at the Industrial University of Ho Chi Minh City. *International Journal of AI in Language Education, 2*(1), 74–91. https://doi.org/10.54855/ijaile.25215

Tsai, C. Y., Lin, Y. T., & Brown, I. K. (2024). Impacts of ChatGPT-assisted writing for EFL English majors: Feasibility and challenges. *Education and Information Technologies, 29*(17), 22427–22445. https://doi.org/10.1007/s10639-024-12722-y

Vygotsky, L. S. (1978). *Mind in society: The development of higher psychological processes* (M. Cole, V. John-Steiner, S. Scribner, & E. Souberman, Eds.). Harvard University Press.

Wei, L. (2023). Artificial intelligence in language instruction: impact on English learning achievement, L2 motivation, and self-regulated learning. *Frontiers in Psychology, 14*, Article 1261955.https://doi.org/10.3389/fpsyg.2023.1261955

Xiao, Y., & Zhi, Y. (2023). An exploratory study of EFL learners' use of ChatGPT for language learning tasks: Experience and perceptions. *Languages, 8*(3), Article 212. https://doi.org/10.3390/languages8030212

Yener, B., & Selcuk, H. (2024). AI-Assisted strategies for enhancing present perfect tense proficiency in university preparatory students. *The Literacy Trek, 10*(3), 339–361. https://doi.org/10.47216/literacytrek.1556837

Yuan, L., & Liu, X. (2025). The effect of artificial intelligence tools on EFL learners' engagement, enjoyment, and motivation. *Computers in Human Behavior, 162*, Article 108474. https://doi.org/10.1016/j.chb.2024.108474

Le Trong Nhan Dao is a lecturer at Saigon University, Vietnam, where he teaches courses on English skills, cross-cultural communications, and the cultures of English-speaking countries. He has a Master's degree in Linguistics with TESOL conferred by Benedictine University, USA. His research interests include the development of learners' productive skills, student motivations, and cultural effects on learning.

Human-AI Collaboration in Vietnamese Students' Argumentative Writing: A Mixed-Methods Study

Truong Bach Le and Bao Kham

Abstract This study explores the integration of the Academic Writing Assistant (AWA), an AI-powered chatbot, in a tertiary-level English as a Foreign Language (EFL) course focused on argumentative writing. Ninety-five third-year students participated in the study, which employed a mixed-methods design comprising questionnaires, reflective journals, and interviews to examine learners' cognitive, affective, and behavioral engagement. Findings reveal that AWA supported students in organizing ideas, revising drafts, and meeting deadlines. The immediacy and clarity of AI-generated feedback were particularly valued, while concerns about adaptability, data privacy, and reliability were noted. The chatbot contributed to enhanced writing confidence, autonomy, and critical thinking, especially when implemented within ethically guided, instructor-mediated frameworks. The study emphasizes the need for pedagogically sound and ethically responsible approaches to AI-assisted writing instruction in higher education.

Keywords Chatbot-assisted writing · Human-AI collaboration · Argumentative writing · Academic integrity · Higher education

1 Introduction

Artificial intelligence (AI) has increasingly influenced education, particularly in academic writing. Among AI-powered tools, chatbots have emerged as prominent writing assistants, facilitating various stages of the writing process, including idea generation, structuring, editing, and revision. The integration of chatbots into educational settings aligns with the broader shift toward AI-enhanced learning, which seeks to optimize student engagement, writing efficiency, and critical thinking skills.

T. B. Le (✉) · B. Kham
University of Foreign Languages and International Studies, Hue University, Hue City, Vietnam
e-mail: tbachle@hueuni.edu.vn

B. Kham
e-mail: baokham@hueuni.edu.vn

V. P. H. Pham et al. (eds.), *Empowering Educators: Integrating AI Tools for Personalized Language Instruction*, Studies in Computational Intelligence 1228,
https://doi.org/10.1007/978-3-032-01348-4_6

However, while these tools offer promising benefits, their role in fostering independent writing skills, academic integrity, and human-AI collaboration remains an area of debate (Barrett & Pack, 2023; Zou & Huang, 2023).

Existing research has primarily focused on students' perceptions of AI-generated writing assistance, highlighting its effectiveness in grammar correction, coherence improvement, and structural organization (Özçelik & Ekşi, 2024). Some studies have explored the pedagogical applications of AI in writing instruction, emphasizing its potential to support personalized learning (Li et al., 2024). Research has also demonstrated that chatbot-assisted writing can improve students' efficiency in generating ideas and structuring arguments, particularly in argumentative essay writing (Guo et al., 2023). However, despite these contributions, there remains a significant gap in understanding chatbot-assisted writing within a structured framework that captures the complexity of human-AI collaboration. Most studies adopt general perceptions and outcome-based measures without applying theoretical models that systematically analyze the interactions between students and AI tools.

A major methodological gap in the literature is the lack of studies employing the Human-AI Collaboration (HAIC) framework in language education. The HAIC framework provides a structured approach to examining how students and AI interact, distribute tasks, and engage in collaborative decision-making (Fragiadakis et al., 2024). While this framework has been applied in fields such as healthcare and business, its use in language education, particularly in chatbot-assisted writing, is minimal. Studies have shown that AI chatbots can enhance collaborative learning by assisting with structural coherence and revision processes (Črček & Patekar, 2023), yet there is limited research that explores how students interact with chatbots beyond efficiency and grammatical corrections. The lack of structured human-AI interaction models in education limits insights into the dynamics of trust, adaptability, and mutual learning between students and AI systems (Mason, 2024). Additionally, current research often focuses on short-term improvements in writing rather than the long-term cognitive engagement and writing autonomy that AI-assisted tools may cultivate (Zou & Huang, 2023).

Another critical methodological gap is the limited application of mixed methods research design in chatbot-assisted writing studies. While quantitative approaches provide measurable insights into writing improvement, they often fail to capture the subjective and experiential dimensions of human-AI collaboration, such as students' confidence, adaptability, and perceived value of chatbot feedback (Fragiadakis et al., 2024). Conversely, qualitative research explores these nuanced experiences but may lack the generalizability of quantitative data. A mixed-methods approach is essential for obtaining a comprehensive understanding of chatbot-assisted writing, integrating both objective measures of writing development and subjective student experiences (Guo et al., 2023). However, current studies rarely employ this approach, leading to fragmented insights that do not fully reflect the pedagogical implications of chatbot-assisted learning (Özçelik & Ekşi, 2024).

To address these gaps, this study seeks to: (1) assess the utility of AI-driven chatbots in facilitating argumentative essay composition, particularly in refining text organization, delivering constructive feedback, and enhancing students' capacity to construct coherent arguments; and (2) explore the influence of chatbot-assisted writing on students' progression and autonomy, examining how learners interpret and apply AI-generated suggestions, regulate their reliance on chatbot assistance, and cultivate critical engagement with automated feedback. By employing the HAIC framework and integrating a mixed-methods approach, this research provides a systematic evaluation of how AI writing tools contribute both to the technical refinement of academic writing and the development of independent, self-regulated writers.

2 Literature Review

2.1 The Role of Chatbots in Writing Instruction

The integration of artificial intelligence (AI) into writing instruction has gained significant attention, with AI-powered tools such as chatbots emerging as key writing assistants (Mahapatra, 2024; Polakova & Ivenz, 2024). These tools facilitate various stages of the writing process, including idea generation, structuring, editing, and revision (Barrett & Pack, 2023; Zou & Huang, 2023). Chatbots enhance writing efficiency, provide immediate feedback, and improve structural coherence, making them attractive tools for students. However, concerns persist regarding their impact on independent writing skills, critical thinking, and academic integrity (Mason, 2024).

Empirical evidence confirms that chatbots markedly improve specific writing outcomes, though questions remain about feedback depth. Chatbot-assisted writing significantly enhances grammatical accuracy, coherence, and logical organization (Özçelik & Ekşi, 2024). Guo et al. (2023) found that chatbots improve students' ability to construct well-structured arguments, particularly in academic and argumentative writing. However, while chatbots provide efficiency and accessibility, they often lack the nuanced understanding and contextual adaptability of human instructors, raising concerns about the depth and specificity of AI-generated feedback (Zou & Huang, 2023).

Despite these advantages, existing research largely focuses on performance metrics and student perceptions while neglecting structured theoretical frameworks that assess the complexity of human-AI collaboration in writing (Fragiadakis et al., 2024). Additionally, chatbot-generated feedback is often generic, lacking personalization, making it less effective in refining students' writing styles (Barrett & Pack, 2023).

2.2 Limitations of AI Feedback, Trust, and Ethical Concerns in Chatbot-Assisted Writing

One of the primary challenges in chatbot-assisted writing is the limited adaptability of AI feedback. They struggle with context-sensitive evaluation, particularly in complex argumentation and rhetorical development (Zou & Huang, 2023). Barrett and Pack (2023) found that students frequently misinterpret chatbot-generated feedback, leading to over-reliance on AI rather than the development of independent writing skills.

Another critical issue is trust and confidence in chatbot feedback. While some students find chatbot suggestions helpful, others question their reliability, especially when AI-generated responses lack depth and specificity (Guo et al., 2023). Research suggests that students who lack confidence in AI feedback tend to double-check AI-generated suggestions with human instructors or peer reviewers, reinforcing the necessity of hybrid AI-human collaboration in writing instruction (Mason, 2024).

Beyond pedagogical concerns, chatbot-assisted writing raises ethical challenges, particularly regarding academic integrity and plagiarism. As AI-generated text becomes more prevalent in student writing, concerns arise about student dependency on AI for content generation (Stahl & Eke, 2024). The discussion findings reinforce this concern, as some students unintentionally integrate AI-generated content without critically evaluating its accuracy. Institutions must develop clear policies on AI usage in academic writing, ensuring that AI supports student learning rather than replacing critical thinking and independent authorship. Ethical considerations also include transparency in AI-generated content and the need for students to develop AI literacy to engage critically with chatbot-generated suggestions.

2.3 Previous Studies: Situating the Research Gap

While the potential of chatbots in writing instruction has been acknowledged in recent studies, a closer examination of the methodologies and theoretical grounding of these works reveals a number of persistent research gaps. This subsection reviews selected studies to situate the current investigation more precisely within the landscape of chatbot-assisted academic writing, particularly focusing on argumentative essay writing in EFL contexts.

Barrett and Pack (2023) conducted a study that explored both student and teacher perceptions of generative AI in writing. Although they provided valuable insights into the usability and utility of AI tools, the study was limited to surface-level observations and did not incorporate a structured framework to analyze the nature of human-AI collaboration. Similarly, while Črček and Patekar (2023) reported increased efficiency in drafting and editing among students using ChatGPT, their study focused predominantly on usability rather than pedagogical development, offering limited insight into how AI tools influence deeper writing processes such as argumentation or critical reasoning.

Guo et al. (2023) approached the issue from an activity theory perspective, exploring EFL students' engagement with chatbot-assisted argumentative writing. Their findings indicated that chatbots improved text structure and logical progression. However, the authors' adoption of activity theory did not fully address the intricacies of task delegation, trust dynamics, and continuous learning—areas central to human-AI collaboration.

Other studies, such as that by Özçelik and Ekşi (2024), highlighted improvements in grammar and lexical accuracy but relied heavily on outcome-based metrics and learner perceptions. These investigations rarely employed mixed methods to triangulate data, which may lead to an oversimplified understanding of students' interactions with AI tools. Polakova and Ivenz (2024), for instance, focused on the effects of ChatGPT feedback on student writing development but did not consider how students regulate their reliance on AI feedback or how chatbot usage evolves over time—a key area of interest in the present study.

Importantly, while Fragiadakis et al. (2024) proposed a comprehensive HAIC framework applicable to a variety of disciplines, there has been limited application of this model in educational contexts. Their review emphasized the need for methodological rigor and proposed evaluation criteria such as trust, adaptability, and decision-making. Yet, studies that systematically integrate these criteria into AI-assisted writing research remain scarce. Moreover, the issue of over-reliance and academic integrity is still underexplored. While Mason (2024) and Stahl and Eke (2024) have raised concerns about ethical dilemmas associated with AI use in student writing, empirical research that systematically examines these issues from the students' lived experiences is still scarce.

In summary, existing studies have contributed foundational insights into the role of AI in writing instruction but are often marked by one or more of the following limitations: (a) lack of theoretical grounding in human-AI collaboration frameworks, (b) absence of mixed-methods design, (c) superficial engagement with student autonomy and metacognition, and (d) inadequate attention to ethical and contextual complexities. This study aims to bridge these gaps by integrating the HAIC framework with a mixed-methods approach and focusing on both cognitive and ethical dimensions of chatbot-assisted writing in a Vietnamese EFL context.

2.4 Evaluating Human-AI Collaboration in Writing Instruction

The Human-AI Collaboration (HAIC) framework provides a structured approach to analyzing how students interact with AI in writing tasks (Fragiadakis et al., 2024). While AI is frequently used in healthcare and business, its integration into language education remains underexplored, particularly regarding task allocation and revision strategies.

Fragiadakis et al. (2024) emphasize that AI-assisted writing should be evaluated through a mixed-methods approach that captures both quantitative and qualitative dimensions. Effective AI assessment should integrate:

- Task performance metrics to measure writing efficiency and coherence improvements.
- Interaction quality assessments to evaluate student engagement with AI-generated feedback.
- Ethical considerations ensuring AI-generated content aligns with academic integrity policies.
- Adaptability measures to determine how well AI tools personalize feedback and accommodate individual writing styles.

By applying this framework, AI's role in enhancing student learning and writing skill development can be assessed systematically, ensuring alignment with pedagogical objectives and ethical considerations.

2.5 *Modes of Human-AI Collaboration in Writing*

Fragiadakis et al. (2024) identify three primary modes of Human-AI Collaboration: Human-Centric, AI-Centric, and Symbiotic Collaboration, each differing in human control, AI autonomy, and shared decision-making.

- Human-Centric mode: Humans retain primary control over decision-making, using AI as a support tool rather than a replacement. This approach aligns with scaffolded AI interaction, where AI assists in grammar correction and structural feedback but does not replace higher-order thinking and argument development (Huang & Rust, 2022).
- Symbiotic mode: This model fosters mutual collaboration, where humans and AI work interactively to enhance writing. Research suggests that AI-assisted creative writing benefits most from two-way engagement, strengthening argumentation skills and self-regulated learning (Li et al., 2024).
- AI-Centric mode: AI assumes primary decision-making roles, automating tasks like syntax refinement and paragraph organization (Barrett & Pack, 2023). However, excessive reliance on AI reduces metacognitive engagement, potentially hindering students' ability to develop independent writing skills (Mason, 2024).

In summary, the HAIC evaluation framework proposed by Fragiadakis et al. (2024) provides a structured model to assess AI's role in writing instruction as shown in Table 1. By applying this framework, AI-assisted writing can be evaluated in a structured manner, ensuring that AI technologies support student learning outcomes while maintaining ethical and pedagogical integrity.

Table 1 Categories and subcategories of HAIC framework

Category	Subcategory	Metrics
Goals	Individual goals	Learning curve, prediction accuracy, teaching efficiency
	Collective goals	Overall system accuracy, objective fulfillment rate
Interaction	Communication methods	Ease of use, clarity of communication
	Feedback mechanisms	Frequency of feedback, feedback quality, feedback impact
	Adaptability	Strategy adaptation effectiveness, adaptability score
	Trust and safety	Trust score, safety incidents, error reduction rate, confidence
Task allocation	Complementarity	Query efficiency, expertise utilization
	Flexibility	Adaptability score, dynamic task allocation
	Efficiency	Model improvement rate, learning curve, resource utilization
	Responsiveness	Response time, real-time performance
	Collaborative decision making	Impact of corrections, decision effectiveness
	Continuous learning	Model improvement rate, learning curve, knowledge retention
	Mutual support	Error reduction rate, confidence, task completion time
	Robustness	Adversarial robustness, system reliability

3 Research Methodology

3.1 Context and Participants

This study was conducted at a university specializing in foreign language education, where the integration of artificial intelligence tools into pedagogical practices remains contingent upon individual lecturers' levels of enthusiasm, digital literacy, and awareness. While institutional leadership actively encourages faculty members to incorporate AI into their teaching methodologies, this advocacy has not been accompanied by formalized policies, structured training initiatives, or standardized guidelines. Consequently, AI adoption across the institution remains highly inconsistent, with implementation varying significantly based on instructors' expertise and willingness to engage with AI-driven pedagogical tools.

The study's participants comprised full-time third-year undergraduate students majoring in English or English Language Teaching (ELT). A total of 95 students participated in the study, among whom 11 were selected for semi-structured interviews, and 23 maintained reflective writing journals to provide in-depth qualitative insights into their experiences. These students were enrolled in Writing 5, the most advanced argumentative essay writing module, which focuses on two primary essay genres: "for and against" and "opinion" essays. The course spanned a 15-week semester and was the only module where students were formally permitted to utilize ChatGPT as a supplementary tool for essay development. All these students studied with the one and the same writing instructor, so they received the same instruction and materials, the same training by the instructor with the same guidelines. These will help guarantee participant homogeneity.

During the initial weeks of the course, all participants received structured training on how to interact effectively with the chatbot "Academic Writing Assistant" (AWA). This training was based on two instructional documents: the *Technical Guidance* and the *Guideline on Essay Writing*. Students were taught to use the chatbot selectively at key stages—such as brainstorming, outlining, and receiving structural and lexical feedback—while being instructed to write and revise their drafts independently. The training emphasized prompt design strategies, including specificity, clarity, and ethical usage. The *Guideline on Essay Writing* further reinforced appropriate chatbot engagement by mapping out which writing stages merited AI support and which required independent student input. Through these comprehensive instructions, the study ensured that student-chatbot interactions were guided, consistent, and aligned with academic integrity standards.

To ensure the ethical use of the chatbot *Academic Writing Assistant* during the intervention, the researcher provided students with clear guidance based on institutional integrity policies and internal course documents. Specifically, the *Technical Guidance* document instructed students to use the chatbot ethically by writing their own content, avoiding copy-pasting of generated texts, and disclosing AI assistance when required. This guidance was explicitly framed as the sixth item in the list of recommended practices for using chatbot prompts effectively. Additionally, as described previously, the *Guideline on Essay Writing* outlined appropriate moments for chatbot engagement while emphasizing that drafting and revisions based on peer or bot feedback should be done independently. By integrating these two instructional documents into the course design, the researcher ensured that students received structured support for responsible AI use, thereby reducing the risk of plagiarism and promoting academic integrity throughout the writing process.

In addition to utilizing the chatbot, students engaged in a variety of collaborative learning activities facilitated through the Moodle-based Learning Management System (LMS), a platform with which they were already familiar. The primary LMS-based activity involved structured peer feedback. Students were grouped and tasked with providing feedback on their peers' initial drafts via the Wiki function, where comments were posted in designated comment boxes. After revising their essays based on this feedback, they submitted their revised drafts to the Workshop box, where they were assigned peer reviewers outside their original groups for a second round of feedback. Finally, upon completion of their final drafts, students submitted their work to the Assignment box, where it was formally assessed by the instructor, who provided additional feedback. Through this structured process, students had access to multiple sources of feedback, including that of their peers, their instructor, and the AI-based writing assistant, facilitating a multi-dimensional approach to academic writing development.

3.2 Research Design

This study employs a mixed-methods research design, integrating both quantitative and qualitative approaches. The quantitative component was implemented through structured questionnaires, while the qualitative data were obtained from students' reflective journals and semi-structured focus group interviews. The rationale for adopting a mixed-methods approach is twofold.

First, qualitative and quantitative methodologies possess distinct limitations, particularly in the context of examining human-AI collaboration. As Fragiadakis et al. (2024) assert, while quantitative metrics provide objective measures of performance, they often fail to encapsulate the nuanced dynamics of human-AI interaction, including factors such as trust, satisfaction, and ethical considerations. Conversely, qualitative methods offer rich insights into subjective experiences but lack the statistical generalizability afforded by quantitative approaches. In this study, the quantitative component primarily captures students' perceptions across 12 subcategories of human-AI interaction, including adaptability, feedback mechanisms, trust, and efficiency. The qualitative component explores deeper dimensions of user experience, such as confidence, awareness, perceived impact, challenges, and concerns.

Second, the adoption of a mixed-methods design addresses existing methodological fragmentation while enhancing the generalizability and robustness of findings. It enables a comprehensive evaluation of human-AI collaboration, ensuring that both the objective performance of AI systems and the subjective experiences of users are systematically analyzed (Polakova & Ivenz, 2024).

In summary, the mixed-methods approach within the Human-AI collaboration framework ensures both objective performance of the whole system but also the subjective experiences in a comprehensive way.

3.3 Data Collection

The study employed three primary data collection instruments: questionnaires, reflective journals, and focus group interviews.

3.3.1 Questionnaire Design and Alignment with the HAIC Framework

The questionnaire was meticulously designed to assess the effectiveness of the Academic Writing Chatbot within the framework of Human-AI Collaboration (HAIC). This framework encompasses three primary categories—Goals, Interaction, and Task Allocation—which structure the evaluation of AI-human collaboration in academic writing.

The Goals category evaluates the chatbot's contribution to individual learning outcomes, such as writing accuracy and efficiency, as well as collective goals, which assess the chatbot's role in facilitating collaborative writing processes. The Interaction category examines communication effectiveness, adaptability, feedback mechanisms, and trust. Specifically, the questionnaire assesses the chatbot's clarity, responsiveness, and ability to tailor feedback based on student input. The Task Allocation category investigates how responsibilities are distributed between the chatbot and students, ensuring that the chatbot functions as a complementary tool rather than a replacement for critical thinking and independent writing.

The alignment between the questionnaire and the HAIC framework ensures that all essential aspects of AI-human collaboration in academic writing are systematically measured. The structured approach captures learning outcomes, adaptability, user trust, communication effectiveness, and task efficiency, making the questionnaire a valid and reliable tool for evaluating AI integration in academic writing instruction. Appendix 1 presents the direct mapping of questionnaire items to the HAIC framework, demonstrating the comprehensive nature of the assessment.

This structured alignment of questionnaire items with the HAIC framework ensures that the chatbot's role in supporting academic writing is evaluated from multiple perspectives, covering both technical performance and user experience. The inclusion of diverse subcategories guarantees a holistic assessment of the chatbot's effectiveness in enhancing student writing skills.

3.3.2 Reflective Journals

Student journals were employed to document evolving experiences with the chatbot, capturing reflections on its perceived benefits, limitations, and overall impact on writing development. Journal entries were collected at two critical junctures: mid-semester and end-of-semester.

At mid-semester, students provided their initial impressions, expectations, and concerns regarding chatbot-assisted writing. This phase facilitated an understanding of how students engaged with AI in the early stages of the writing process, including brainstorming, structuring arguments, and revising drafts. The end-of-semester journal entries allowed students to reflect on changes in their writing skills, confidence, and independence. Additionally, they assessed the chatbot's role in fostering critical thinking and whether its utility persisted throughout the course. The comparative analysis between traditional feedback (peer and instructor) and chatbot-assisted writing was also explored. This structured approach enabled a longitudinal examination of students' perceptions of AI-assisted writing.

3.3.3 Focus Group Interviews

Semi-structured focus group interviews were conducted to gain in-depth qualitative insights into students' experiences with the chatbot. Each focus group comprised four to six participants, facilitating interactive discussions while ensuring diverse perspectives.

The interview content focused on five thematic dimensions: usefulness, usage practices, perceived value, impact, and challenges. Participants discussed how the chatbot assisted in idea generation, essay organization, linguistic accuracy, and feedback interpretation. They also compared chatbot-based feedback with instructor-led feedback and assessed whether AI contributed to their writing development or introduced new challenges. Specific difficulties, such as over-reliance, ambiguous feedback, and limitations in addressing complex writing nuances, were examined. Interviews were conducted via Zoom, recorded, transcribed, and analyzed systematically.

These interviews were conducted at the conclusion of the semester, approximately one week after the questionnaires was administered. The interval between the interviews and the questionnaires was timed carefully to prevent participants from forgetting certain details or reinterpreting experiences, affecting the accuracy and specificity of their responses (Flick, 2018). The interval between questionnaires and interviews also gave participants adequate time to reflect and to provide richer and more detailed and potentially more critical perspectives (Kvale & Brinkmann, 2015).

To guard against "groupthink"—the tendency to conform to group opinions, a potential problem of focus group interviews, several strategies were applied. First, group size was kept small enough (4–6 participants) to reduce conformity pressure (Morgan, 2019). Second, moderator facilitation was used to encourage diverse opinions or alternative viewpoints (Krueger & Casey, 2015). Third, structured interview guides used probing questions that encouraged alternative perspectives (Liamputtong, 2011). Finally, employing journals as triangulation would lessen the influence of groupthink (Creswell & Creswell, 2018).

3.4 Data Analysis

3.4.1 Quantitative Data Analysis (Questionnaires)

A combination of descriptive and inferential statistical methods was employed to analyze questionnaire data. Descriptive statistics, including means and standard deviations, were used to summarize overall trends in participants' responses. To assess the reliability of the questionnaire, Cronbach's alpha was calculated for each survey component, with values above 0.70 considered acceptable for internal consistency ($\alpha = 0.93$). A reliability analysis was conducted by computing inter-item correlations, ensuring that each survey dimension demonstrated a high level of coherence before proceeding with further statistical tests.

For comparative analysis, a one-way ANOVA was performed to determine whether significant differences existed among the measured categories. Post-hoc pairwise comparisons were conducted using the Tukey HSD test to identify specific subgroup differences when ANOVA results indicated statistical significance. Additionally, effect sizes were calculated using Cohen's d to determine the practical significance of observed differences. Pearson correlation analysis was employed to examine the strength and direction of relationships between key factors, particularly investigating whether interactions between chatbot feedback mechanisms and user engagement influenced writing efficiency. The correlation matrix was reviewed to ensure no multicollinearity issues before conducting further regression or predictive modeling if needed.

3.4.2 Qualitative Data Analysis (Journals and Interviews)

Thematic analysis was conducted to analyze qualitative data from journals and interviews. Six overarching themes emerged:

1. Improvement in Writing Skills—Increased clarity and organization in writing.
2. Dependency on Chatbot—Gradual shift from reliance to independent writing.
3. Challenges with Complex Tasks—Difficulty in addressing nuanced writing elements.
4. Skill Development Beyond Grammar—Enhanced critical thinking and argumentation.
5. Overall Effectiveness—The chatbot as a useful yet limited writing aid.
6. Future AI Integration—Potential for AI refinement in academic writing instruction.

Interview transcripts corroborated these findings, revealing that students perceived the chatbot as beneficial for brainstorming and linguistic accuracy but less effective in refining arguments and structuring complex essays. Trust issues and the need for personalized AI feedback were recurrent concerns.

The integration of mixed-methods research in this study provides a holistic assessment of AI's role in academic writing. The quantitative findings highlight the chatbot's effectiveness in task allocation and goal achievement, whereas qualitative insights underscore evolving student perceptions, emphasizing both benefits and areas for improvement. Notably, while the chatbot is perceived as an effective supplementary tool, its limitations in addressing trust, adaptability, and feedback precision necessitate further refinement.

4 Findings and Discussion

This section presents the study's findings and discussion on student perceptions and experiences regarding AI-powered chatbots in argumentative essay writing. It explores three key themes—goal achievement, interaction, and task allocation—analyzing how chatbots support writing development, enhance efficiency, and shape students' self-reliance. Drawing on questionnaire data, journal reflections, and interviews, the findings highlight both the benefits, such as improved structure and clarity, and the challenges, including feedback interpretation and trust concerns. The discussion contextualizes these insights within existing literature, examining the chatbot's role in writing improvement and ethical implications, while also identifying areas for enhanced adaptability and personalization.

4.1 Findings

4.1.1 Chatbot Effectiveness in Supporting Argumentative Essay Writing

This subsection presents the findings from an analysis of student perceptions and practices regarding the use of an AI-powered chatbot for argumentative essay writing. The findings are categorized into three primary themes—Goals, Interaction, and Task Allocation—reflecting key aspects of the chatbot's performance. The analysis employs descriptive statistics, analysis of variance (ANOVA), and pairwise mean comparison to assess user experiences and identify strengths and areas for improvement.

Goal Achievement and Writing Support

The chatbot's role in facilitating students' academic writing goals was evaluated across multiple dimensions, including collaboration, skill development, and feedback integration. The findings in Table 2 indicate a generally positive perception, with all mean scores exceeding 3.9 on a 5-point scale, reinforcing the chatbot's role as a valuable academic writing aid. The overall mean rating for the Goals component was 4.09, making it the highest-rated category among the three primary components assessed.

Table 2 Goals category means and standard deviations

Statements	M	SD
1. The chatbot effectively assists in enhancing my accuracy in writing structured "for and against" and "opinion" essays	4.15	0.96
2. The chatbot's suggestions have helped me achieve my writing objectives in the unit	4.07	0.89
3. I find that the chatbot efficiently guides my learning without requiring extensive additional resources or time	4.09	0.81
4. The chatbot and I work well together to improve the overall quality of my essay drafts	4.16	0.84
5. The chatbot's feedback and my edits work in tandem to meet the objectives of the writing unit	3.96	0.80
6. Using the chatbot has contributed to a noticeable improvement in my essay writing performance overall	4.13	0.75
Overall goals category	4.09	0.84

Among the evaluated subcategories, the highest-rated item was "The chatbot and I work well together to improve the overall quality of my essay drafts" (M = 4.16, SD = 0.84), suggesting that students perceive the chatbot as an effective co-creator in refining their academic writing. Similarly, "The chatbot effectively assists in enhancing my writing skills" received a mean score of 4.15, further affirming its contribution to students' academic development. These findings suggest that users value the chatbot's ability to provide structured guidance that aligns with their learning objectives.

The journal and interview findings support these results, as multiple participants reported that the chatbot helped them with structuring essays and improving clarity. One journal entry stated:

> The chatbot's structure suggestions helped me divide essays logically.

Similarly, an interview participant emphasized:

> Thanks to the chatbot, the structure of my essay is clearer.

While the overall perception of the chatbot's role in goal achievement was positive, some aspects of feedback integration were rated slightly lower. The item "The chatbot's feedback and my edits work in tandem to meet the objectives of the writing unit" had the lowest mean score within this component (M = 3.96, SD = 0.80), indicating that some students experienced difficulties in incorporating chatbot-generated suggestions into their revisions. The lowest-rated item, aligns with interview findings, where participants expressed challenges in interpreting chatbot feedback:

> The chatbot's feedback is sometimes unclear and hard to understand.

Additionally, journal reflections highlighted that the chatbot's responses were sometimes too generic or lacked depth, making it necessary for students to supplement its feedback with additional sources:

Table 3 Goals category: ANOVA results

F-statistic	*p*-value
0.71	0.61

When feedback isn't suitable, I usually double-check with other sources.

As can be seen from Table 3, the statistical analysis of variance (ANOVA) conducted on the subcomponents of the Goals category revealed no significant differences ($p > 0.05$), suggesting a relatively uniform perception of the chatbot's effectiveness in supporting academic writing goals. However, pairwise comparisons in Table 4 indicate that Collaboration was rated slightly higher than Feedback Integration, suggesting that while students appreciate the chatbot's collaborative aspects, they may require more refined support in applying its feedback effectively.

Overall, the findings suggest that the chatbot is particularly effective in collaborative writing and skill development, reinforcing its role as a structured writing assistant. The chatbot's ability to provide revision support and guidance was highly rated, aligning with results from the Interaction category analysis, which also emphasized chatbot-assisted revision as a significant strength. However, the relatively lower rating for feedback integration suggests a need for more contextualized and adaptive feedback mechanisms, ensuring that users can effectively apply chatbot-generated suggestions to their writing. The absence of significant statistical differences among subcomponents reinforces that users perceive goal achievement as a cohesive experience, but the slight disparity between collaboration and feedback integration highlights areas where refinement could enhance user engagement and writing effectiveness. These results underscore the chatbot's effectiveness in goal-oriented academic writing support while indicating that further improvements in feedback integration could enhance its role as a comprehensive writing assistant.

Interaction and User Engagement

As evident from Table 5, the chatbot's interaction effectiveness was assessed across multiple dimensions, including feedback mechanisms, communication methods, adaptability, and trust and safety. The findings indicate moderately positive perceptions, with an overall mean score of 3.94 (SD = 0.46). While the chatbot was generally

Table 4 Goals category correlation matrix

	1. Q 1	2. Q 2	3. Q 3	4. Q 4	5. Q 5	6. Q 6
1. Q 1	1.00	0.39	0.24	0.38	0.35	0.37
2. Q 2	0.39	1.00	0.01	0.35	0.12	0.24
3. Q 3	0.24	0.01	1.00	0.22	0.30	0.43
4. Q 4	0.38	0.35	0.22	1.00	0.29	0.39
5. Q 5	0.35	0.12	0.30	0.29	1.00	0.47
6. Q 6	0.37	0.24	0.43	0.39	0.47	1.00

rated favorably, notable variation across subcomponents suggests that some aspects of interaction require further refinement to improve user experience and engagement.

Among the four assessed subcategories, Feedback Mechanism received the highest rating (M = 4.07, SD = 0.72), suggesting that users found the chatbot's feedback relevant, specific, and easy to understand. However, the low rating for item 5 in the previous category indicated wide variability in students' reaction to this subcategory. The Communication Methods subcategory was rated slightly lower (M = 3.94, SD = 0.77), with chatbot response clarity receiving the highest individual score (M = 4.02), indicating that users generally found chatbot responses

Table 5 Interaction category means and standard deviation

Subcategory	Statements	M	SD
Communication methods	7. The chatbot's responses are clear and easy to understand	3.97	0.79
	8. The chatbot's suggestions are relevant and understandable for my writing tasks	4.02	0.74
	9. I feel that the way the chatbot communicates its feedback aligns with my needs for essay writing	3.84	0.79
	Overall subcategory	3.94	0.77
Feedback mechanism	10. I find it easy to give feedback to the chatbot (e.g., when its suggestions aren't useful)	3.99	0.75
	11. The chatbot seems to adapt its suggestions based on my previous responses or feedback	4.02	0.82
	12. The chatbot's feedback is specific and relevant to my writing, improving my drafts as a result	4.20	0.58
	Overall subcategory	4.07	0.72
Adaptability	13. The chatbot adjusts its guidance based on my individual writing style and needs	3.85	0.82
	14. The chatbot adapts its feedback to different sections of the essay, such as introductions, body paragraphs, and conclusions	4.07	0.67
	15. I feel that the chatbot's guidance changes over time in response to my progress in the unit	3.85	0.82
	Overall subcategory	3.91	0.75
Truth and safety	16. I trust the chatbot's suggestions for improving my essay structure and content	3.91	0.69
	17. I feel confident in the chatbot's recommendations to help me produce accurate and effective essays	3.87	0.72
	18. I feel safe using the chatbot, knowing that my work and personal data are secure	3.79	0.81
	Overall subcategory	3.86	0.74

understandable. These findings suggest that structured feedback delivery and clear communication were key strengths of chatbot interaction.

The journal and interview data corroborate these findings, highlighting that students value the chatbot's structured feedback and clear communication. One journal entry mentioned:

> Grammar improved through specific corrections, and vocabulary expanded with academic terms.

Similarly, an interview participant confirmed:

> I write faster and make fewer mistakes thanks to the chatbot.

Conversely, Trust and Safety received the lowest rating (M = 3.86, SD = 0.74), with the item "I feel safe using the chatbot, knowing that my work and personal data are secure" receiving the lowest individual score (M = 3.79). This suggests ongoing concerns regarding privacy, security, and response reliability. The Adaptability subcategory (M = 3.91, SD = 0.75) was also rated lower than feedback and communication, indicating that while the chatbot demonstrates some capacity for adapting to user needs, it may not consistently tailor responses to individual writing styles or progress.

Journal reflections aligned with this, as some students expressed uncertainty about the chatbot's feedback consistency and data security:

> I feel safe using the chatbot, but sometimes I question if its suggestions are always right.

An interview participant also noted:

> When feedback isn't suitable, I usually double-check with other sources.

A one-way ANOVA test ($p = 0.07$) as shown in Table 6 confirmed no statistically significant differences among subcategories, although the result approached significance. Post-hoc pairwise comparisons in Table 7 revealed a significant difference between Feedback Mechanism and Trust and Safety ($p = 0.01$), with feedback rated significantly higher. In contrast, differences between Communication Methods, Adaptability, and Trust and Safety were not statistically significant ($p > 0.05$), suggesting that users experienced similar levels of satisfaction with these components.

The findings indicate that users highly value the chatbot's ability to provide structured feedback and clear responses, which aligns with the Goal Achievement and Writing Support findings, where feedback delivery was also rated positively. However, adaptability and trust in the chatbot remain key concerns, particularly regarding its ability to personalize responses and ensure security in data handling.

Table 6 Interaction category ANOVA results

F-statistic	*p*-value
2.29	0.07

Table 7 Interaction subcategory pairwise T-test results

Comparison	T-statistic	*p*-value
Communication methods versus feedback mechanism	− 1.49	0.13
Communication methods versus adaptability	0.40	0.68
Communication methods versus trust and safety	1.01	0.31
Feedback mechanism versus adaptability	1.94	0.05
Feedback mechanism versus trust and safety	2.59	0.01
Adaptability versus trust and safety	0.62	0.53

The significant difference between feedback effectiveness and trust in safety underscores a key gap between users' appreciation of feedback quality and their confidence in the system's reliability.

Overall, the chatbot is perceived as a competent feedback provider with clear communication, yet its ability to adapt and ensure user security remains a limitation. The absence of significant differences among adaptability, communication, and trust suggests that these aspects are viewed as interconnected, with improvements in adaptability potentially enhancing user trust. These results reinforce that while the chatbot effectively facilitates writing interaction, addressing privacy concerns and refining its adaptability could significantly enhance user engagement and confidence in its recommendations.

Task Allocation and Writing Process Efficiency

The task allocation category as indicated in Table 8 was assessed based on multiple subcategories, including Responsiveness, Efficiency, Flexibility, Complementarity, Collaborative Decision-Making, Continuous Learning, Mutual Support, and Robustness. The findings suggest that users generally perceive the chatbot as an effective tool for writing support, with some dimensions receiving particularly high ratings while others indicate areas for improvement.

Responsiveness received the highest overall rating (M = 4.21, SD = 0.75), highlighting the chatbot's ability to provide quick and timely feedback. Users appreciated its responsiveness in addressing writing needs, particularly for time-sensitive tasks such as meeting deadlines and revising essays efficiently.

Journal reflections and interviews support these findings, with students acknowledging the time-saving advantages of chatbots. One journal participant observed:

> Chatbot helps me think more thoroughly during brainstorming and provides specific ideas for drafting.

Similarly, an interviewee confirmed:

> The chatbot reduces the time it takes me to complete my essays.

Similarly, Collaborative Decision-Making (M = 4.12, SD = 0.77) was rated favorably, indicating that users found the chatbot valuable in helping them make structural and content-related decisions. These findings suggest that the chatbot plays

Table 8 Task allocation means and standard deviations

Subcategory	Statements	M	SD
Complementarity	19. The chatbot's analytical abilities complement my critical thinking and creativity in essay writing	3.79	0.81
	20. The chatbot handles tasks I find difficult (e.g., organization or style), allowing me to focus on content	3.98	0.82
	21. I feel that I can rely on the chatbot to assist me with challenging parts of essay writing	3.98	0.74
	Overall subcategory	3.91	0.79
Flexibility	22. The chatbot adjusts its role depending on the part of the essay I am working on	4.19	0.69
	23. I find that the chatbot's support is flexible, adapting to my writing process as needed	3.85	0.74
	24. The chatbot can shift between providing general guidance and specific feedback, depending on my requirements	3.98	0.77
	Overall subcategory	4.0	0.7
Efficiency	25. The chatbot reduces the time it takes me to complete and refine my essays	3.97	0.83
	26. I feel that the chatbot uses resources efficiently, giving valuable suggestions without overwhelming me with information	4.21	0.78
	27. The chatbot streamlines my writing process, making it easier to complete my essays within deadlines	3.84	0.85
	Overall subcategory	4.0	0.82
Responsiveness	28. The chatbot responds quickly to my inputs and requests for guidance	4.20	0.81
	29. The chatbot provides feedback in a timely manner, allowing me to make revisions effectively	4.21	0.70
	30. The chatbot is responsive to time-sensitive tasks, such as preparing essays for upcoming deadlines	4.23	0.75
	Overall subcategory	4.21	0.75
Collaborative decision making	31. The chatbot's suggestions help me make better decisions about structure and content in my essays	4.18	0.80
	32. I feel that my input is valued by the chatbot, as it integrates my edits and preferences into its guidance	4.08	0.77

(continued)

Table 8 (continued)

Subcategory	Statements	M	SD
	33. The chatbot supports me in evaluating different perspectives, especially in "for and against" essays	4.11	0.74
	Overall subcategory	4.12	0.77
Continuous learning	34. I notice that the chatbot remembers my past work and offers more relevant guidance as I progress	415	0.73
	35. The chatbot's feedback becomes increasingly tailored to my specific writing strengths and weaknesses over time	3.94	0.85
	36. The chatbot's ability to "learn" from my input enhances my writing experience and essay quality	3.86	0.81
	Overall subcategory	3.90	0.7
Mutual support	37. I feel supported by the chatbot in areas where I need assistance, like grammar and coherence	3.93	0.73
	38. I am able to support the chatbot by providing feedback, which it uses to improve its assistance	4.22	0.72
	39. The chatbot's support allows me to build on my writing skills and improve independently	4.08	0.65
	Overall subcategory	4.0	0.7
Robustness	40. The chatbot provides consistent and reliable feedback across different types of essays	4.08	0.74
	41. I trust the chatbot to perform reliably without frequent errors or disruptions	4.01	0.72
	42. The chatbot can handle a variety of writing tasks (e.g., grammar, structure, argumentation) with consistent quality	3.71	0.92
	Overall subcategory	3.9	0.7

an active role in guiding users through the writing process, supporting them in refining their arguments and ensuring coherent organization.

Efficiency (M = 4.01, SD = 0.82) and Flexibility (M = 4.01, SD = 0.73) were also rated positively, indicating that users perceive the chatbot as an effective tool for streamlining the writing process and adapting to different writing tasks. However, the standard deviations suggest some variation in user experiences, with some respondents finding the chatbot highly efficient while others feel it does not consistently optimize their workflow. While the chatbot is adaptable to different writing phases, some users may find that it lacks the ability to adjust fully to their specific writing styles.

Despite these strengths, Continuous Learning (M = 3.98, SD = 0.80), Complementarity (M = 3.91, SD = 0.79), and Robustness (M = 3.93, SD = 0.74) received lower ratings, suggesting that these aspects require further improvement. Users reported inconsistent experiences with the chatbot's ability to retain past interactions and provide increasingly tailored feedback over time.

Complementarity was one of the lowest-rated aspects, suggesting that while the chatbot assists with technical elements of writing, it does not always align seamlessly with users' creative and analytical processes. Additionally, Robustness was the lowest-rated subcategory, indicating that some users found the chatbot inconsistent in performance across different types of writing tasks. While it provides reliable support in some instances, its effectiveness may fluctuate depending on the complexity of the writing task or the level of assistance required.

The findings suggest that the chatbot is highly valued for its ability to provide timely feedback and assist in decision-making, reinforcing its role as a supportive writing assistant. However, areas such as learning adaptability, personalization, and reliability require further refinement. Future improvements should focus on enhancing adaptive learning mechanisms, ensuring the chatbot better remembers user preferences, and improving stability in performance across different writing tasks. Addressing these areas will help create a more personalized and reliable user experience, further strengthening the chatbot's effectiveness in writing assistance.

The ANOVA and pairwise t-test results from Tables 9 and 10 provide insights into how users perceive the different subcategories of task allocation and whether meaningful differences exist in their evaluations. The ANOVA test ($F = 0.66$, $p = 0.70$) found no statistically significant differences among subcategory means, indicating that users rated the chatbot's performance consistently across various aspects of task allocation. However, pairwise comparisons reveal nuanced distinctions between specific subcategories.

The only statistically significant difference was found between Complementarity and Responsiveness ($p = 0.03$), suggesting that users perceive a clear gap between the chatbot's ability to complement their writing style and its ability to provide quick feedback. This indicates that while Responsiveness is highly valued, the chatbot may not always align effectively with users' cognitive and creative writing approaches. Another notable finding is that Responsiveness versus Efficiency ($p = 0.06$) approached significance, indicating that while users appreciate fast feedback, they may not always find it helpful in improving overall efficiency.

Most other pairwise comparisons did not yield significant differences ($p > 0.05$), meaning that users generally rated the chatbot's performance consistently across different task allocation dimensions. Subcategories such as Flexibility, Mutual

Table 9 Task allocation category ANOVA results

F-statistic	*p*-value
0.66	0.70

Table 10 Task allocation category pairwise T-test results

Comparison	T-statistic	*p*-value
Complementarity versus flexibility	– 0.52	0.62
Complementarity versus efficiency	– 0.14	0.89
Complementarity versus responsiveness	– 2.44	0.03
Complementarity versus collaborative decision making	– 1.36	0.21
Complementarity versus continuous learning	– 0.99	0.34
Complementarity versus mutual support	– 1.20	0.27
Complementarity versus robustness	– 0.31	0.76
Flexibility versus efficiency	0.40	0.69
Flexibility versus responsiveness	– 1.75	0.10
Flexibility versus collaborative decision making	– 0.87	0.40
Flexibility versus continuous learning	– 0.46	0.66
Flexibility versus mutual support	– 0.68	0.50
Flexibility versus robustness	0.18	0.86
Efficiency versus responsiveness	– 1.98	0.06
Efficiency versus collaborative decision making	– 1.17	0.27
Efficiency versus continuous learning	– 0.77	0.45
Efficiency versus mutual support	– 1.00	0.33
Efficiency versus robustness	– 0.24	0.81
Responsiveness versus collaborative decision making	0.80	0.44
Responsiveness versus continuous learning	1.22	0.26
Responsiveness versus mutual support	1.00	0.33
Responsiveness versus robustness	1.63	0.13
Collaborative decision making versus continuous learning	0.42	0.68
Collaborative decision making versus mutual support	0.17	0.87
Collaborative decision making versus robustness	0.81	0.44
Continuous learning versus mutual support	– 0.26	0.80
Continuous learning versus robustness	0.38	0.71
Mutual support versus robustness	0.61	0.55

Support, Continuous Learning, and Robustness showed no significant differences, reinforcing that users view these areas as relatively similar in effectiveness.

Overall, while users perceive the chatbot as broadly effective across all subcategories, the significant gap between Complementarity and Responsiveness suggests that further refinements are needed in how the chatbot integrates with user-specific writing styles. Additionally, the near-significant difference between Responsiveness and Efficiency indicates that speed alone is not sufficient—users expect more meaningful and structured feedback to enhance efficiency. Future improvements should focus on strengthening adaptive learning, refining personalized assistance, and enhancing consistency in performance across writing tasks.

4.1.2 Comparative Analysis of Categories and Interpretation

The mean scores from Table 11 reveal that users slightly favored Goals (M = 4.09, SD = 0.84) over Task Allocation (M = 4.01, SD = 0.75) and Interaction (M = 3.94, SD = 0.94). This suggests that users perceive the chatbot as most effective in helping them achieve writing goals, followed by supporting task allocation, while interaction quality received the lowest rating. The standard deviations indicate that interaction had the highest variability, implying inconsistencies in user experiences regarding chatbot engagement and communication.

To evaluate the chatbot's comparative performance across the three categories—Goals, Interaction, and Task Allocation—a one-way ANOVA test (F = 0.86, p = 0.42) was conducted. The results in Table 12 indicate no statistically significant differences among these categories, suggesting that users rated the chatbot's effectiveness consistently across all dimensions. While no significant statistical variations were detected, the mean ratings and pairwise comparisons provide additional insights into user preferences.

Pairwise t-tests from Table 13 further reinforce the ANOVA findings, as all comparisons yielded p-values greater than 0.05, confirming no statistically significant differences between any two categories. Specifically, Goals versus Interaction (t = 0.92, p = 0.36), Goals versus Task Allocation (t = 0.42, p = 0.67), and Interaction versus Task Allocation (t = − 0.57, p = 0.56) suggest that users perceive the chatbot's effectiveness as relatively similar across all three dimensions.

Despite the statistical similarities, small variations in mean ratings suggest slight but meaningful trends in user preferences. Users slightly preferred Goals over Interaction, suggesting that they found the chatbot more effective in assisting with goal achievement than in fostering meaningful engagement. Similarly, Task Allocation was rated slightly higher than Interaction, indicating that while users value the chatbot's role in organizing and managing writing tasks, interaction quality remains an area requiring improvement.

Table 11 Means and standard deviations of goals, interaction and task allocation

Category	Mean	Standard deviation (SD)
Goals	4.09	0.84
Interaction	3.94	0.94
Task allocation	4.01	0.75

Table 12 ANOVA results for goals, interaction, and task allocation

F-statistic	p-value
0.86	0.42

Table 13 Categories pairwise T-test results

Comparison	T-statistic	p-value
Goals versus interaction	0.92	0.36
Goals versus task allocation	0.42	0.67
Interaction versus task allocation	− 0.57	0.56

These findings suggest that users prioritize the chatbot's ability to support goal achievement and task management over its interactive capabilities. While the chatbot effectively assists in structuring writing and distributing tasks efficiently, improving engagement features—such as adaptability, personalization, and user trust—could enhance overall user experience.

Overall, the chatbot performs consistently across all three categories, reinforcing its role as a valuable writing support tool. However, interaction and engagement remain areas for further refinement, as users may require more dynamic, personalized, and responsive interactions to maximize the chatbot's effectiveness. Future improvements should focus on enhancing adaptive learning, refining chatbot interaction strategies, and ensuring greater system reliability, creating a more holistic and user-centered writing support experience.

4.1.3 Impacts of AI-Assisted Chatbot on Students' Writing Development and Independence

While the questionnaire findings provided a structured evaluation of chatbot-assisted writing, the journal reflections and interview data offer additional qualitative insights that deepen our understanding of students' evolving experiences, concerns, and expectations. These findings highlight aspects that were not fully captured in the structured questionnaire responses, providing a more nuanced perspective on chatbot usage in academic writing.

Evolving Dependency and Self-Regulation in Writing

A key theme that emerged from both journal and interview findings was students' initial reliance on the chatbot, followed by a gradual shift toward independent writing. Many participants reported that, at the start, they heavily depended on the chatbot for idea generation, grammar correction, and structuring their essays. Some journal participants reflected:

> Initially, I heavily relied on the chatbot for structuring my essay and grammar corrections, but over time, I started writing more independently.
>
> At first, I was very worried about relying too much on the chatbot. However… I learned to balance between using the tool and putting in my own effort.
>
> After using it for about 3–4 weeks, I no longer asked the chatbot to create outlines… My ideas and perspectives are now more clearly expressed.

Similarly, an interview participant shared:

> At first, I needed the chatbot for almost everything. But now, I only use it for feedback and editing.

This evolution suggests that while students benefit from chatbot support, they also develop self-regulation strategies over time, shifting from passive AI reliance to strategic and selective use.

Challenges in Contextual Understanding and Adaptability

A recurring limitation mentioned in journal reflections was the chatbot's difficulty in adapting to complex writing contexts. While students appreciated its grammar and structure-related feedback, they found that the chatbot struggled with nuanced, discipline-specific writing tasks. One journal entry highlighted:

> The chatbot is great for organizing ideas, but when I need deeper analysis or a specific academic tone, its responses feel too generic.

Interview participants echoed this sentiment, noting that the chatbot often failed to account for contextual variations in writing:

> I use the chatbot mainly for general feedback, but when writing more advanced essays, I have to ignore some of its suggestions because they don't fit the academic context.

This indicates that while chatbots are useful for foundational writing support, they currently lack adaptability for complex, discipline-specific writing tasks, which require deeper contextual understanding.

Perceptions of Trust, Accuracy, and Ethical Concerns

Another significant theme that emerged was students' skepticism regarding the chatbot's accuracy and trustworthiness. Some students expressed concerns that AI-generated feedback was inconsistent, requiring additional verification from external sources. One journal participant remarked:

> I appreciate the chatbot's feedback, but I always double-check its suggestions with my instructor or online sources.

Similarly, interview participants mentioned concerns about academic integrity, particularly the risk of over-reliance on AI-generated content:

> If students just copy what the chatbot suggests without thinking critically, it could lead to unintentional plagiarism.

These findings suggest that while students recognize the value of AI in writing, they also acknowledge its limitations and the ethical implications of chatbot-assisted writing. This aligns with concerns raised in educational discussions about AI's role in academic integrity and the need for institutional guidelines on responsible AI use.

The Need for Personalized and Adaptive AI Feedback

While chatbots provide structured assistance, students expressed a strong desire for more personalized feedback that aligns with their individual writing styles and progress over time. One journal participant stated:

> It would be great if the chatbot could remember my past work and suggest improvements based on my personal writing strengths and weaknesses.

An interviewee similarly suggested:

> If the chatbot adapted its feedback based on my previous essays, it would be much more useful in the long run.

These reflections highlight the need for adaptive AI models that evolve alongside students' writing development, rather than offering static and generalized feedback.

Combining AI with Human Feedback for Optimal Learning

Both journal and interview findings underscored the importance of balancing AI support with human feedback. Students recognized that while chatbots enhance efficiency, they cannot replace the depth of feedback provided by instructors and peers. One journal participant noted:

> The chatbot is helpful, but I still need feedback from my professor to refine my arguments.

An interview participant similarly concluded:

> I think AI should be a supplement, not a replacement. The best approach is combining chatbot feedback with teacher guidance.

This suggests that chatbots function best as a collaborative tool, rather than a standalone writing assistant. The findings support hybrid learning models, where AI complements human instruction to create a more holistic academic writing experience.

Overall, these additional insights from journal and interview findings provide a richer understanding of students' interactions with chatbot-assisted writing beyond the questionnaire data. While chatbots offer efficiency, structural support, and language refinement, they also present challenges related to contextual adaptability, trustworthiness, and ethical concerns. Students emphasized the importance of self-regulated learning, with many transitioning from high chatbot reliance to strategic and selective use. Furthermore, there is a clear demand for personalized AI feedback, as well as the need to integrate AI assistance with human feedback to optimize learning outcomes. Moving forward, improving AI adaptability, ethical usage policies, and hybrid learning approaches will be critical in enhancing the role of chatbots in academic writing.

4.2 Discussion

The findings from the interviews, journal reflections, and questionnaire responses highlight both the affordances and challenges associated with chatbot-assisted writing. While students acknowledge the chatbot's utility in enhancing writing organization, efficiency, and self-reliance, concerns regarding over-dependence, contextual misalignment, and academic integrity persist. These findings align with and diverge from existing literature on AI-assisted writing tools.

4.2.1 Alignment with Theoretical Frameworks

The discussion of chatbot-assisted writing can be framed through the Human-AI Collaboration (HAIC) Framework (Fragiadakis et al., 2024), which categorizes interactions between humans and AI systems into three modes: AI-centric, Human-centric, and Symbiotic. This framework provides a structured approach to understanding how students engage with chatbots in academic writing and the extent to which AI functions as a supportive tool or an autonomous agent.

AI-Centric Mode: Automation and Writing Assistance

In AI-centric collaboration, AI takes the lead in decision-making and execution, minimizing human intervention. The journal findings indicate that some students rely heavily on chatbots for idea generation, grammar correction, and structural organization. This aligns with studies demonstrating that AI tools can automate repetitive tasks in writing, such as sentence structuring and word choice refinement (Barrett & Pack, 2023). However, prior research warns that an AI-centric approach risks reducing metacognitive engagement, leading to passive content consumption rather than active writing development (Mason, 2024). Additionally, recent studies on chatbot-assisted writing highlight the limitations of AI-generated feedback, particularly in handling complex argumentation and contextual depth (Zou & Huang, 2023).

Human-Centric Mode: AI as a Writing Support Tool

In contrast, the human-centric mode positions AI as an augmentative tool, where students retain full control over the writing process while leveraging AI-generated feedback. The findings suggest that many students use chatbots primarily for pre-writing (brainstorming) and post-writing (editing and revision). This reflects previous research emphasizing scaffolded AI interaction, wherein AI assists but does not replace critical thinking in writing. Studies on AI-assisted language learning (Özçelik & Ekşi, 2024) highlight that chatbots enhance students' awareness of sentence structure, coherence, and lexical choices without undermining their creativity.

However, the journal findings also reveal gaps in AI adaptability, particularly in handling complex argumentation and individualized feedback. This supports prior studies indicating that AI tools struggle with contextual depth and argument development, which remain reliant on human critical analysis (Zou & Huang, 2023). To maximize the benefits of a human-centric AI model, educators must emphasize metacognitive strategies that train students to critically assess chatbot-generated content rather than uncritically adopting it.

Symbiotic Mode: Interactive and Adaptive Writing Collaboration

The symbiotic mode represents an optimal balance where humans and AI interact dynamically, each enhancing the other's strengths. The interview findings indicate that while students recognize AI's efficiency, they also value peer and instructor feedback for deeper learning. This aligns with Human-AI symbiosis principles, where iterative learning cycles between human input and AI feedback refine writing skills over time (Fragiadakis et al., 2024).

The questionnaire data suggests a strong correlation between interaction quality and task efficiency, meaning that improving chatbot adaptability and trust mechanisms could foster more dynamic collaboration. Prior research highlights that integrating AI-driven feedback with human intervention yields the most effective learning outcomes (Tschandl et al., 2020). This approach mirrors findings in AI-assisted creative writing, where students benefit most from interactive engagement rather than passive reliance (Li et al., 2024).

Implications for Writing Instruction

The HAIC framework suggests that chatbot-assisted writing should be strategically integrated to balance efficiency with cognitive engagement. The findings support a hybrid instructional model, wherein:

- AI is used selectively for grammar refinement, idea structuring, and brainstorming (Human-centric).
- Students retain agency over argumentation and critical revisions to ensure depth and originality (Symbiotic).
- Educators scaffold AI literacy, ensuring that students engage critically with AI-generated content rather than defaulting to automation (AI-Centric risks).

By positioning AI as a collaborative writing assistant rather than a replacement for cognitive effort, students can develop more autonomous writing skills while still leveraging the efficiency of AI feedback loops.

4.2.2 The Use of Mixed Methods

One notable finding from the qualitative data was students' struggle to interpret chatbot feedback, even when the quantitative results indicated overall satisfaction with chatbot-assisted learning. This underscores the importance of using mixed methods to uncover discrepancies that may not be evident through a single research approach. Additionally, qualitative responses highlighted students' evolving relationship with AI tools—initial reliance on chatbot suggestions transitioning toward a more independent writing process—which was less apparent in the quantitative results alone.

The present study's findings align with and expand upon existing research on chatbot-assisted writing. Prior studies, such as those by Zou and Huang (2023) and Guo et al. (2023), have highlighted the effectiveness of AI chatbots in improving structural organization and grammatical accuracy in student writing. Like these studies, our findings confirm that students perceive chatbots as useful tools for refining essay coherence and clarity. However, this study extends previous research by emphasizing students' challenges in fully integrating chatbot feedback into their writing process, an issue less frequently addressed in existing literature.

Studies such as those by Zou and Huang (2023) and Guo et al. (2023) support the present study's findings by demonstrating that chatbots can enhance structural organization and coherence in writing. However, unlike the study, which highlights student difficulties in interpreting chatbot-generated feedback, prior research has often assumed that chatbot assistance is seamlessly integrated into students' writing processes. Similarly, Fragiadakis et al. (2024) emphasize the need for structured frameworks in human-AI collaboration, aligning with the present findings that chatbot guidance is often perceived as rigid and less adaptable to students' individual writing styles.

Conversely, findings from Barrett and Pack (2023) challenge some of the conclusions drawn in this study. While the study suggests that students progressively transition from chatbot dependence to independent writing, Barrett and Pack (2023) report sustained reliance on chatbot-generated content without significant improvement in writing autonomy. Furthermore, Mason (2024) raises concerns regarding trust in AI-generated content, a theme also evident in this study, although Mason's study indicates a stronger preference for human feedback over chatbot assistance.

The use of mixed methods in this study also has several implications for future research and pedagogical practices. First, it highlights the importance of integrating both quantitative and qualitative insights to develop a more nuanced understanding of AI-assisted writing. This approach can inform educators on how to tailor instructional strategies that address both measurable learning outcomes and student experiences. Second, the findings suggest that chatbot feedback mechanisms should be designed to be more adaptable to individual learner needs, an insight that could guide future AI development. Finally, employing mixed methods can serve as a model for future research exploring human-AI collaboration in education, ensuring that studies capture both the efficiency of AI tools and their impact on students' cognitive engagement and trust.

By integrating quantitative analysis with qualitative inquiry, this study presents a comprehensive picture of chatbot-assisted writing, reinforcing the necessity of mixed-methods research in evaluating AI's role in education.

4.2.3 Enhancement of Writing Skills and Process

The interview and journal findings indicate that students perceive chatbot assistance as beneficial for brainstorming, structuring, and refining their writing. These perceptions are consistent with previous research that identifies AI chatbots as effective scaffolds for pre-writing and revision phases in second language writing instruction (Zou & Huang, 2023). Moreover, chatbot feedback appears to help students refine grammar and vocabulary, corroborating findings by Özçelik and Ekşi (2024), who highlight the role of AI in improving formal register knowledge in academic writing.

However, the data suggest that while chatbots facilitate surface-level improvements, they fall short in enhancing deeper analytical skills. This limitation echoes concerns raised by Guo et al. (2023), who found that chatbots lack the nuanced contextual awareness needed to support complex argumentative writing. Similarly, doctoral students in Zou and Huang's (2023) study expressed skepticism about AI-generated content's originality and depth, noting that reliance on chatbots might compromise critical thinking.

4.2.4 Efficiency, Task Management, and Long-Term Writing Autonomy

Students reported in their journals that chatbots significantly reduced the time required for idea generation and drafting, supporting findings from previous studies. This efficiency aligns with research by Campbell and Cox (2024), who argue that chatbots streamline the research writing process by automating structuring and citation management. The ability of AI to provide immediate feedback was also noted as a key advantage, reinforcing previous findings that chatbots enable iterative learning by offering real-time revisions (Guo et al., 2023).

However, despite these benefits, dependency on chatbots for routine writing tasks raises concerns about students' long-term writing development. The gradual shift from reliance to selective use observed in the study mirrors trends reported in previous research, where students initially depended on chatbots but later integrated AI selectively to enhance their writing without diminishing their own agency (Jacob et al., 2023).

The present study affirms that AI-assisted learning, particularly via chatbot tools, cultivates long-term writing autonomy by enabling learners to strategically balance technological assistance with independent ideation. This is aligned with Jacob et al. (2023), who found that second language writers effectively collaborated with ChatGPT while preserving authorial voice and agency throughout the writing process. Similarly, Zou and Huang (2023) reported that doctoral students viewed ChatGPT as a self-learning partner that aided writing across multiple stages, reinforcing the current finding that chatbot usage fosters strategic independence and cognitive growths. Contrastingly, Bašić et al. (2024) observed no performance gains in essay scores for students using ChatGPT, suggesting that uncritical reliance on AI tools may hinder development if not paired with metacognitive awareness. Additionally, Herbold et al. (2024) noted that while AI-generated essays scored higher on structural features, they lacked human-like epistemic markers, implying that over-reliance may stifle critical engagement. Despite these concerns, the trajectory seen in this study—where learners transition from dependence to deliberate integration and transfer of AI-mediated skills—demonstrates a maturation process also echoed by Li et al. (2024), who found that students gradually applied AI-derived strategies across academic genres. Thus, the current findings reinforce the long-term pedagogical value of AI when implemented with learner agency, while simultaneously cautioning against passive consumption of AI output.

4.2.5 Challenges: Dependency, Academic Integrity and Ethical Concerns

A key challenge emerging from the findings is the increasing dependency on chatbots for writing tasks. Many students reported extensive use of AI for idea generation and content refinement, raising concerns that their writing autonomy and critical thinking skills may be compromised. This aligns with prior research suggesting that prolonged reliance on AI tools can hinder higher-order thinking and independent problem-solving (Mason, 2024). As AI becomes an integral part of academic writing, students may struggle to transition away from chatbot assistance, leading to diminished creativity and intellectual engagement.

Academic integrity remains a major concern in AI-assisted writing, as some students adopt chatbot-generated content uncritically, raising ethical issues for both students and educators. Existing studies caution that AI-generated text can appear coherent while being factually inaccurate, contributing to misinformation and academic dishonesty (Črček & Patekar, 2023). Furthermore, many students lack awareness of the ethical implications of using AI-generated content without proper attribution, which has been a recurring issue in academic discussions (Bašić et al., 2024). The absence of clear institutional policies on AI-assisted writing exacerbates these risks, highlighting the need for structured guidelines and academic interventions to ensure responsible AI use.

Ethical dilemmas surrounding chatbot-assisted writing also extend to questions of accountability and bias. The opaque nature of AI decision-making raises concerns about misinformation, further complicating its ethical use in education (Stahl & Eke, 2024). To address these risks, researchers emphasize the importance of AI literacy training, equipping students with the skills to critically assess and ethically engage with AI tools (Kumar & Sangwan, 2024). Additionally, educators must play a proactive role in defining responsible AI use, ensuring that students balance AI assistance with authentic intellectual contributions (Herbold et al., 2024). Institutions must develop explicit ethical frameworks that not only preserve academic integrity but also foster informed, independent engagement with AI in writing.

4.2.6 Recommendations for Educators

Given the benefits and limitations outlined in the findings, the following recommendations are proposed for educators seeking to integrate chatbot-assisted writing effectively into their curricula. These recommendations focus on fostering critical AI literacy, encouraging strategic usage, establishing ethical guidelines, and balancing AI with human feedback to optimize student learning outcomes while mitigating potential risks associated with chatbot reliance.

Educators should incorporate AI literacy training to help students critically engage with chatbot-generated content. This includes evaluating coherence, logical reasoning, and factual accuracy to ensure that AI-assisted writing maintains academic integrity and intellectual depth (Barrett & Pack, 2023). Classroom activities could involve comparative analysis of AI-generated versus human-written texts, allowing students to identify strengths, weaknesses, and potential biases in chatbot responses. Encouraging students to critically assess chatbot feedback before integrating it into their writing will promote analytical thinking and independent decision-making.

Students should be guided to use chatbots strategically rather than relying on them for full-text generation. Chatbots can be highly effective for brainstorming, outlining, structuring arguments, and refining drafts, but over-dependence on AI-generated content may hinder the development of independent writing skills. To support this, educators can implement scaffolded writing exercises where students progressively reduce their reliance on AI assistance while increasing their autonomy in writing. This approach ensures that students develop confidence in their abilities while leveraging AI as a complementary tool rather than a primary writing source.

To prevent misuse and over-reliance on AI in academic writing, institutions should establish clear ethical guidelines that promote academic integrity, responsible AI usage, and transparency. These policies should emphasize that while chatbots can support revision and brainstorming, they should not replace original student work. Just as students must properly cite external sources, they should acknowledge AI-generated content when applicable. Additionally, educators must define clear boundaries between ethical AI assistance and academic misconduct, ensuring students use AI tools as learning aids rather than as substitutes for independent thought. Addressing concerns about AI-generated plagiarism and excessive reliance, institutions should provide guidance on distinguishing appropriate chatbot use from unethical writing practices, fostering a balanced and responsible integration of AI in education.

To ensure a well-rounded writing development process, chatbot feedback should be supplemented with human input from peers and instructors (Guo et al., 2023). While AI-generated feedback is often immediate and structured, it lacks the depth and contextual awareness that human reviewers provide. Assignments should encourage students to engage in reflective writing exercises, where they analyze chatbot suggestions, document their revision process, and assess the effectiveness of AI-generated feedback. Such activities foster critical engagement with AI assistance, ensuring that students develop metacognitive skills rather than passively accepting chatbot-generated revisions (Bilal et al., 2023).

By integrating these recommendations, educators can create a balanced and responsible approach to AI-assisted writing instruction, leveraging chatbot benefits while safeguarding against academic and cognitive risks. A structured pedagogical approach that incorporates critical AI literacy, selective chatbot usage, ethical policies, and balanced feedback mechanisms will enhance students' writing skills while fostering independent critical thinking and academic integrity.

5 Conclusion

The findings of this study highlight the significant role of chatbot-assisted writing in enhancing students' engagement, efficiency, and structural organization in argumentative essay writing. The chatbot was perceived as an effective tool for idea generation, grammar refinement, and coherence improvement, aligning with previous studies emphasizing its role in supporting language learners. However, while students valued the chatbot's immediate feedback and ability to streamline the writing process, concerns emerged regarding its adaptability, trustworthiness, and depth in handling complex argumentation. These limitations suggest that while AI-powered writing tools can support academic writing, they should not replace human critical engagement or instructor feedback.

The application of the Human-AI Collaboration (HAIC) framework in this study provided a structured analysis of chatbot-student interaction, task allocation, and feedback mechanisms, addressing a critical gap in AI-assisted writing research. The chatbot functioned effectively as a collaborative assistant, helping students manage various aspects of essay composition. However, interaction findings revealed that while students generally found chatbot-generated feedback useful, they faced challenges in interpreting and applying its suggestions to refine deeper analytical skills. This reinforces the need for AI tools to offer more adaptive, context-aware guidance to better support students in developing higher-order writing competencies.

The use of a mixed-methods research design in this study allowed for a comprehensive understanding of chatbot-assisted writing by integrating quantitative measures of chatbot efficacy with qualitative insights into students' perceptions and experiences. While quantitative data confirmed the chatbot's contribution to improving structural and linguistic aspects of writing, qualitative findings revealed concerns about over-reliance, trust in AI-generated content, and the chatbot's limitations in facilitating deeper cognitive engagement. The combination of these methods provided a holistic view of the chatbot's role, bridging the gap between objective writing improvements and students' subjective experiences of AI interaction.

These findings have important pedagogical and technological implications. Educators should integrate chatbot-assisted writing within a structured instructional approach, ensuring that AI tools serve as enhancements rather than replacements for student learning. AI chatbots should be introduced as scaffolded support mechanisms, complementing teacher feedback and promoting critical engagement with AI-generated content rather than passive acceptance. Additionally, institutions should develop explicit guidelines for AI usage in academic writing, addressing concerns about academic integrity, transparency in AI-generated content, and ethical considerations.

From a technological perspective, AI developers should work toward enhancing chatbot adaptability by improving personalized feedback mechanisms and refining AI's ability to engage in deeper, context-aware writing support. Future chatbot iterations should incorporate dynamic learning models that evolve with user interactions, ensuring that AI tools can better align with students' unique writing styles and analytical needs. Furthermore, chatbot training should extend beyond surface-level linguistic corrections, incorporating argumentative reasoning, logical structuring, and source evaluation to provide a more robust writing support system.

Despite its contributions, this study has several limitations. While the HAIC framework provided a structured lens for analyzing chatbot-student interactions, the study focused primarily on students' perceptions and experiences. Future research should incorporate more direct measures of writing improvement, such as comparative analysis of AI-assisted and non-AI-assisted writing outcomes over a longer period. The study was conducted within a single institution specializing in foreign language education, which may limit the generalizability of the findings to broader academic contexts. Future studies should explore chatbot-assisted writing across different educational settings and linguistic backgrounds to determine how AI adapts to varying pedagogical needs.

The rapid evolution of AI technologies presents a challenge in maintaining up-to-date assessments of chatbot efficacy. As AI systems continue to develop, future research should adopt longitudinal approaches to track how students' writing skills evolve with sustained chatbot use, particularly regarding cognitive independence and metacognitive awareness. While the mixed-methods design allowed for a holistic exploration of chatbot-assisted writing, there is a need for more in-depth qualitative investigations into how students navigate chatbot feedback, revise their work, and develop self-regulated writing strategies.

Overall, the study underscores the importance of balancing AI assistance with human oversight to optimize the benefits of chatbot-assisted writing. While AI-powered chatbots can effectively support students in structuring and refining their essays, they must be integrated with pedagogical strategies that encourage critical thinking, self-regulated learning, and responsible AI use. Future research should explore ways to enhance chatbot adaptability, improve personalized feedback mechanisms, and develop institutional guidelines for ethical AI use in writing instruction. By further refining AI's role within academic writing, educators can ensure that these tools serve as valuable supplements rather than substitutes for student learning, ultimately fostering both writing proficiency and cognitive independence.

Appendices

Appendix 1: Mapping Questionnaire Items to (Sub)categories of the Human-AI Collaboration Framework

Category	Subcategory	Description	Corresponding questionnaire items	Justification
Goals	Individual goals	AI and human objectives for collaboration success	Q1, Q2, Q3	Measures chatbot's role in personal learning, writing accuracy, and efficiency
	Collective goals	Shared AI-human objectives aimed at system-wide optimization	Q4, Q5, Q6	Assesses chatbot's impact on overall writing improvement and goal achievement
Interaction	Communication methods	Effectiveness and clarity of AI-human communication	Q7, Q8, Q9	Examines clarity, relevance, and user-friendliness of chatbot responses
	Feedback mechanisms	AI's ability to adjust based on user feedback	Q10, Q11, Q12	Evaluates chatbot's ability to incorporate user feedback into learning
	Adaptability	AI's capacity to modify guidance based on human input	Q13, Q14, Q15	Determines whether chatbot adapts guidance based on student progress
	Trust and safety	The degree of trust and security perceived by users	Q16, Q17, Q18	Measures user confidence in chatbot suggestions and data security
Task allocation	Complementarity	AI supplements human skills rather than replacing them	Q19, Q20, Q21	Ensures chatbot supports rather than replaces critical thinking
	Flexibility	AI dynamically shifts roles based on task requirements	Q22, Q23, Q24	Examines chatbot's ability to adapt to different writing stages
	Efficiency	AI improves task completion speed	Q25, Q26, Q27	Assesses whether chatbot speeds up writing and revision processes
	Responsiveness	AI reacts quickly to human input	Q28, Q29, Q30	Measures chatbot's promptness in responding to student needs
	Collaborative decision making	AI assists in structuring and refining content	Q31, Q32, Q33	Evaluates chatbot's assistance in structuring and refining essays

(continued)

(continued)

Category	Subcategory	Description	Corresponding questionnaire items	Justification
	Continuous learning	AI refines suggestions based on past interactions	Q34, Q35, Q36	Examines chatbot's ability to improve guidance over time
	Mutual support	AI helps users, and users refine AI through feedback	Q37, Q38, Q39	Determines chatbot's effectiveness in mutual learning and feedback integration
	Robustness	AI performs consistently across writing tasks	Q40, Q41, Q42	Ensures chatbot provides consistent support across different writing tasks

Appendix 2: Academic Writing Chatbot Questionnaire

Instructions: Please rate each statement based on your experience with the Academic Writing Chatbot in the writing unit. Use the following scale:

1. Strongly Disagree
2. Disagree
3. Neutral
4. Agree
5. Strongly Agree.

Goals

1. The chatbot effectively assists in enhancing my accuracy in writing structured "for and against" and "opinion" essays.
2. The chatbot's suggestions have helped me achieve my writing objectives in the unit.
3. I find that the chatbot efficiently guides my learning without requiring extensive additional resources or time.
4. The chatbot and I work well together to improve the overall quality of my essay drafts.
5. The chatbot's feedback and my edits work in tandem to meet the objectives of the writing unit.
6. Using the chatbot has contributed to a noticeable improvement in my essay writing performance overall.

Interaction

Communication Methods

7. The chatbot's responses are clear and easy to understand.
8. The chatbot's suggestions are relevant and understandable for my writing tasks.
9. I feel that the way the chatbot communicates its feedback aligns with my needs for essay writing.

Feedback Mechanisms

10. I find it easy to give feedback to the chatbot (e.g., when its suggestions aren't useful).
11. The chatbot seems to adapt its suggestions based on my previous responses or feedback.
12. The chatbot's feedback is specific and relevant to my writing, improving my drafts as a result.

Adaptability

13. The chatbot adjusts its guidance based on my individual writing style and needs.
14. The chatbot adapts its feedback to different sections of the essay, such as introductions, body paragraphs, and conclusions.
15. I feel that the chatbot's guidance changes over time in response to my progress in the unit.

Trust and Safety

16. I trust the chatbot's suggestions for improving my essay structure and content.
17. I feel confident in the chatbot's recommendations to help me produce accurate and effective essays.
18. I feel safe using the chatbot, knowing that my work and personal data are secure.

Task Allocation

Complementarity

19. The chatbot's analytical abilities complement my critical thinking and creativity in essay writing.
20. The chatbot handles tasks I find difficult (e.g., organization or style), allowing me to focus on content.
21. I feel that I can rely on the chatbot to assist me with challenging parts of essay writing.

Flexibility

22. The chatbot adjusts its role depending on the part of the essay I am working on.
23. I find that the chatbot's support is flexible, adapting to my writing process as needed.
24. The chatbot can shift between providing general guidance and specific feedback, depending on my requirements.

Efficiency

25. The chatbot reduces the time it takes me to complete and refine my essays.
26. I feel that the chatbot uses resources efficiently, giving valuable suggestions without overwhelming me with information.
27. The chatbot streamlines my writing process, making it easier to complete my essays within deadlines.

Responsiveness

28. The chatbot responds quickly to my inputs and requests for guidance.
29. The chatbot provides feedback in a timely manner, allowing me to make revisions effectively.
30. The chatbot is responsive to time-sensitive tasks, such as preparing essays for upcoming deadlines.

Collaborative Decision Making

31. The chatbot's suggestions help me make better decisions about structure and content in my essays.
32. I feel that my input is valued by the chatbot, as it integrates my edits and preferences into its guidance.
33. The chatbot supports me in evaluating different perspectives, especially in "for and against" essays.

Continuous Learning

34. I notice that the chatbot remembers my past work and offers more relevant guidance as I progress.
35. The chatbot's feedback becomes increasingly tailored to my specific writing strengths and weaknesses over time.
36. The chatbot's ability to "learn" from my input enhances my writing experience and essay quality.

Mutual Support

37. I feel supported by the chatbot in areas where I need assistance, like grammar and coherence.
38. I am able to support the chatbot by providing feedback, which it uses to improve its assistance.
39. The chatbot's support allows me to build on my writing skills and improve independently.

Robustness

40. The chatbot provides consistent and reliable feedback across different types of essays.
41. I trust the chatbot to perform reliably without frequent errors or disruptions.
42. The chatbot can handle a variety of writing tasks (e.g., grammar, structure, argumentation) with consistent quality.

Thank you for completing this questionnaire. Your responses will help us evaluate and improve the Academic Writing Chatbot's effectiveness in supporting essay writing in this unit.

Appendix 3: Interview Questions: Exploring Students' Perceptions and Practices When Using "Academic Writing Assistant"

Perceptions of Chatbot Usefulness

1. How has the chatbot supported you in generating ideas and organizing your essay?

   Can you share a specific example where the chatbot was especially helpful or unhelpful?

Practices When Using the Chatbot

2. How do you usually use the chatbot when writing an essay? At which stage of the writing process do you find it most or least helpful?
3. After receiving feedback from the chatbot, how do you decide to revise your writing? Can you provide an example of how you applied its feedback?

Perceptions of Chatbot Value

4. In what ways do you feel the chatbot has improved your writing skills? Do you think it helps you write more effectively or efficiently?
5. How does the feedback from the chatbot compare to that from your teacher or peers? Which do you find more valuable, and why?

Impact of the Chatbot

6. Has using the chatbot improved the overall quality of your essays? Can you describe how it has influenced your writing process over time?
7. Do you feel more confident in writing after using the chatbot? How has it affected your confidence in structuring and revising your writing?

Difficulties in Using the Chatbot

8. Have you encountered any challenges or difficulties in understanding or applying the chatbot's feedback? How do you usually handle these issues?
9. Have you ever felt that you rely too much on the chatbot for certain aspects of your writing? How do you balance using it with developing your own writing ability?

Open Question

10. Do you have any suggestions for improving the chatbot so that it better supports your essay writing process?

Appendix 4: Journal Writing Guidance 1

Please describe your thoughts and experiences while writing three for-and-against essays with the support of the Academic Writing Assistant by responding in detail to the following questions:

1. *Initial Impressions*
    - What were your thoughts when you first started using the Academic Writing Assistant?
    - How did you feel about the idea of using a chatbot to support academic writing?
2. *Usage Experience*
    - Describe how you typically interact with the chatbot. What specific features do you use most often (e.g., grammar checking, topic suggestions, structural guidance)?
    - Can you provide specific examples of tasks or assignments for which you used the chatbot? How did it support you in those cases?
3. *Impact on the Writing Process*
    - In what ways has the chatbot affected your writing process? Consider aspects such as brainstorming, drafting, revising, and editing.
    - Have you noticed any changes in your writing style or quality since you started using the chatbot? If yes, please elaborate.
4. *Learning Outcomes*
    - What new skills or knowledge have you gained from using the Academic Writing Assistant? How do you believe these will benefit your future writing efforts?
    - Reflect on any challenges you faced while using the chatbot. How did you overcome these challenges, and what did you learn from the experience?
5. *Comparative Analysis*
    - How does your experience with the Academic Writing Assistant compare with more traditional methods of seeking writing help (e.g., peer feedback, consulting instructors)?
    - Do you see the chatbot as a supplement or a replacement for human feedback? Why?
6. *Personal Reflection*
    - How has your confidence in your writing ability changed since you started using the chatbot?
    - Which aspect of the chatbot do you find most beneficial, and are there any features you believe could be improved?
7. *Future Use and Recommendations*

- How do you plan to continue using the Academic Writing Assistant in your future writing assignments?
- What recommendations would you give to other students who are considering using a chatbot to support their academic writing?

Appendix 5: Journal Writing Guidance 2

Here are suggested questions for university students to reflect on their experience with the chatbot in the second half of the writing unit, which focuses on essay writing. These questions aim to explore the changes in their perceptions and use of the chatbot after completing the entire unit:

1. *How has your confidence in writing evolved by the end of the unit?*
    - Have you noticed any improvements in structuring, organizing, or expressing your ideas more clearly?
    - Has your reliance on the chatbot changed over time, and how do you now view your independent writing abilities?
2. *In what ways did the chatbot continue to influence your essay writing during the second half of the unit?*
    - Did you use it for different types of essays, and if so, how did it help with new essay formats?
    - How did its role in tasks such as generating ideas, structuring essays, and refining grammar evolve?
3. *Did you experience any new challenges when using the chatbot for the second half of the unit?*
    - Were there any instances where the chatbot's feedback felt more or less relevant as your writing tasks became more complex?
4. *Have your concerns about over-reliance on the chatbot shifted as you progressed through the unit?*
    - Do you feel more capable of balancing chatbot assistance with your own critical thinking and writing efforts?
5. *Looking back on the entire unit, how would you assess the overall effectiveness of the chatbot in helping you improve your essay writing skills?*
    - What specific skills (e.g., grammar, vocabulary, essay structure) do you feel have improved the most?
6. *Based on your experience with the chatbot, would you approach future writing tasks differently?*

- How do you plan to integrate what you've learned about using the chatbot into future writing assignments beyond this unit?

References

Barrett, A., & Pack, A. (2023). Not quite eye to A.I.: Student and teacher perspectives on the use of generative artificial intelligence in the writing process. *International Journal of Educational Technology in Higher Education, 20*(59). https://doi.org/10.1186/s41239-023-00427-0

Bašić, Ž., Banovac, A., Kružić, I., & Jerković, I. (2024). *Better by You, better than Me? ChatGPT-3 as writing assistance in students' essays.* University Department of Forensic Sciences, University of Split. Retrieved from [University of Split Repository]

Bilal, H. A., Faiz, R., Asghar, I., & Safdar, A. (2023). Optimizing ChatGPT as a writing aid for EFL learners: Balancing assistance and skill development in writing proficiency. *Linguistic Forum - A Journal of Linguistics, 5*(3), 24–37. https://doi.org/10.53057/linfo/2023.5.3.3

Campbell, L. O., & Cox, T. D. (2024). Utilizing generative AI in higher education teaching and learning. *Journal of the Scholarship of Teaching and Learning, 24*(4), 162–173.

Črček N., & Patekar J. (2023). Writing with AI: University students' use of ChatGPT. *Journal of Language and Education, 9*(4), 128–138. https://doi.org/10.17323/jle.2023.17379

Creswell, J. W., & Creswell, J. D. (2018). *Research design: Qualitative, quantitative, and mixed methods approaches* (5th ed.). Sage.

Flick, U. (2018). *An introduction to qualitative research* (6th ed.). Sage.

Fragiadakis, G., Diou, C., Kousiouris, G., & Nikolaidou, M. (2024). Evaluating human-AI collaboration: A review and methodological framework. *arXiv preprint*. https://doi.org/10.48550/arXiv.2407.19098

Guo, K., Li, Y., Li, Y., & Chu, S. K. (2023). Understanding EFL students' chatbot-assisted argumentative writing: An activity theory perspective. *Education and Information Technology, 29*, 1–20.

Herbold, S., Hautli-Janisz, A., Heuer, U., Kikteva, Z., & Trautsch, A. (2024). *AI, write an essay for me: A large-scale comparison of human-written versus ChatGPT-generated essays.* Faculty of Computer Science and Mathematics, University of Passau. Retrieved from [University of Passau Repository]

Huang, M.-H., & Rust, R. T. (2022). A framework for collaborative artificial intelligence in marketing. *Journal of Retailing, 98*(2), 209–223. https://doi.org/10.1016/j.jretai.2021.12.003

Jacob, S. R., Tare, T., & Warschauer, M. (2023). Emergent AI-assisted discourse: a case study of a second language writer authoring with ChatGPT. arXiv:2310.10903. https://doi.org/10.48550/arXiv.2310.10903

Krueger, R. A., & Casey, M. A. (2015). *Focus groups: A practical guide for applied research* (5th ed.). Sage.

Kumar, A., & Sangwan, S. R. (2024). Conceptualizing AI literacy: Educational and policy initiatives for a future-ready society. *International Journal of All Research Education and Scientific Methods (IJARESM), 12*(4), 1543–1551. Available at: www.ijaresm.com

Kvale, S., & Brinkmann, S. (2015). *Interviews: Learning the craft of qualitative research interviewing* (3rd ed.). Sage.

Li, X., Yang, Z., Zhang, W., & Yang, Z. (2024). ChatGPT and teacher human-machine collaboration for personalized teaching—Taking poetry writing teaching as an example. *IEEE International Conference on Educational and Information Technology (ICEIT)*, 1–12. https://doi.org/10.1109/ICEIT61397.2024.10540814

Liamputtong, P. (2011). *Focus group methodology: Principles and practice.* Sage. https://doi.org/10.4135/9781473957657

Mahapatra, S. (2024). Impact of ChatGPT on ESL students' academic writing skills: A mixed methods intervention study. *Smart Learning Environments, 11*(9). https://doi.org/10.1186/s40561-024-00295-9

Mason, S. R. (2024). *Perceptions of ACSI secondary school administrators and teachers concerning the use of generative AI chatbots to support struggling writers*. Doctoral dissertation, Columbia International University. https://doi.org/10.13140/RG.2.2.22206.61764

Morgan, D. L. (2019). *Basic and advanced focus groups*. Sage.

Özçelik, N. P., & Ekşi, G. Y. (2024). Cultivating writing skills: The role of ChatGPT as a learning assistant—A case study. *Smart Learning Environments, 11*(10). https://doi.org/10.1186/s40561-024-00296-8

Polakova, P., & Ivenz, P. (2024). The impact of ChatGPT feedback on the development of EFL students' writing skills. *Cogent Education, 11*(1), 2410101. https://doi.org/10.1080/2331186X.2024.2410101

Stahl, B. C., & Eke, D. (2024). The ethics of ChatGPT—Exploring the ethical issues of an emerging technology. *International Journal of Information Management, 74*, Article 102700. https://doi.org/10.1016/j.ijinfomgt.2023.102700

Tschandl, P., Rinner, C., Apalla, Z., Argenziano, G., Codella, N., Halpern, A., Janda, M., Lallas, A., Longo, C., Malvehy, J., Paoli, J., Puig, S., Rosendahl, C., Soyer, H. P., Zalaudek, I., & Kittler, H. (2020). Human-computer collaboration for skin cancer recognition. *Nature Medicine, 26*(8), 1229–1234. https://doi.org/10.1038/s41591-020-0942-0

Zou, M., & Huang, L. (2023). The impact of ChatGPT on L2 writing and expected responses: Voice from doctoral students. *Education and Information Technologies, 29*, 13201–13219. https://doi.org/10.1007/s10639-023-12397-x

Dr. Le Bach Truong, DEd (University of Melbourne) is a senior lecturer at the Faculty of English, University of Foreign Languages and International Studies, Hue University, Vietnam. His primary academic interests include language education, computer-assisted language learning (CALL), discourse analysis, translation, and sociolinguistics.

Dr. Bao Kham is a distinguished scholar and researcher specializing in English language education, curriculum development, and applied linguistics. He holds a Doctor of Education in Education from La Trobe University, Australia, and an M.A. in Instruction and Curriculum Studies from the University of Sydney, Australia. His work has significantly contributed to language teaching methodologies, digital learning, and teacher education in Vietnam. He served as Vice Rector and Rector of the University of Foreign Languages, Hue University (now the University of Foreign Languages and International Studies, Hue University).

EFL Teachers' Identity Tensions and Transformation in AI-Driven Teaching in China: A Dialogical Approach

Chao Du, Yongjing Peng, Norhakimah Khaiessa binti Ahmad, and Ahmad Halimah binti Jamil

Abstract The spread of artificial intelligence (AI) in tertiary education has remarkably influenced language teachers' professional identity construction. However, little is known about the identity tensions EFL teachers experience during this shift. This study is built on a dialogical approach to identity and discusses the role of inner tensions in making sense of one's AI-driven identity tensions. We used a qualitative case study design to collect data from narrative frames and interviews with ten EFL teachers. Thematic data analysis revealed that EFL teachers experienced three identity tensions. They include conflicting I-positions due to challenged beliefs and traditional values, new I-positions in teacher-student power relationships and pedagogical practices as well as constrained I-positions arising from students' inadequate AI-digital literacy, technical limitations of AI-driven tools and contextual factors. While managing tensions in the teacher-AI-student triadic dynamic, participants' Intelligent-TPACK, evolving conceptions of AI-driven teaching and adjustment in pedagogical decision-making and action-taking were highlighted to strengthen their AI-driven identity and professional development. Implications are provided for teacher educators, university administrators and policy makers to help EFL teachers better construct AI-driven identity.

Keywords EFL teachers · AI-driven teaching · Identity tensions · I-position · Intelligent-TPACK

C. Du · N. K. binti Ahmad · A. H. binti Jamil
Faculty of Educational Studies, Universiti Putra Malaysia, Serdang Selangor, Malaysia
e-mail: norhakimah@upm.edu.my

A. H. binti Jamil
e-mail: halimah.jamil@upm.edu.my

Y. Peng (✉)
Henan Sport University, Henan, China
e-mail: Pennypeng1666@gmail.com

V. P. H. Pham et al. (eds.), *Empowering Educators: Integrating AI Tools for Personalized Language Instruction*, Studies in Computational Intelligence 1228,
https://doi.org/10.1007/978-3-032-01348-4_7

1 Introduction

Artificial Intelligence (AI) is shaping the wider education context (Loftus & Madden, 2020), especially in language education. The capacity of AI to "process data and information in a way that resembles intelligent behavior" (UNESCO, 2020, p. 10) has led people to utilize AI-driven tools to develop the system of education, tutoring and learning (Huang et al., 2023; Zhai et al., 2021). The most used AI-driven tool in education is language learning (Lu & Lin, 2024). These tools offer learners positive experiences that alleviate their foreign language learning anxiety (Al-Raimi et al., 2024), provide immediate feedback crucial for successful language acquisition (Klimova et al., 2023) and enhance their language learning autonomy (Huynh, 2024). Therefore, more and more attention has been paid to the role of AI in language education, including (1) students' AI-driven learning effectiveness and AI education in the curriculum (e.g., Goulart et al., 2024; Yuan & Liu, 2025); and (2) teachers' AI-related perceptions and pedagogical practice (e.g., Dakakni & Safa, 2023; Liu & Xiao, 2025). It can be inferred that one of the emerging trends that have been explored is the integration of AI in teachers' pedagogical practice and students' AI education (Brandão et al., 2024; Kwihangana, 2024). Boulay (2016) argues that AI is an effective classroom assistant to facilitate personalized learning, more research should focus on English teaching with AI-driven tools.

The integration of AI-driven tools in language teaching reveals many challenges, which highlight the agent role of teachers. These challenges include: (1) ethical issues, including students' plagiarism (Dakakni & Safa, 2023); (2) students' diminished creativity (Lesia Viktorivna et al., 2022) and wrong input due to limited "fact-check" ability (Kohnke et al., 2023, p. 545); (3) teachers' limited technical proficiency to lean and apply AI in pedagogical practice (Liu & Xiao, 2025). All the challenges cause tensions in teachers' identity, the center of the language teaching–learning process (Beauchamp & Thomas, 2009). As teachers need to negotiate and interrelate their multiple I-positions to strive for a sense of coherence and continuity (Akkerman & Meijer, 2011) in dealing with the challenge of new pedagogical positions and responsibility (Ren & Pan, 2024; Zhai et al., 2021). Of crucial importance is attention to teacher identity tensions, as it significantly influences their willingness and readiness to adopt AI in teaching (Lan, 2024) and resilience to deal with these challenges in the AI era (Zhou et al., 2024). Only by understanding teachers' identity tensions and their strategies to thrive in such tensions can we help them better construct their AI-driven identities to facilitate students' personalized learning and serve educational goals.

Limited research has been conducted on the influence of AI on language teachers' professional development (Zhai et al., 2021) and identity construction (Kwihangana, 2024). Exceptions include studies exploring university EFL teachers' identity insecurity in AI-driven teaching from the sociocultural perspective (Ren & Pan, 2024) and English-medium instruction tertiary teachers' identity transformation with more confidence by using AI-driven tools (Tsou et al., 2024). These studies emphasized the contextual and dynamic nature of identity, overlooking teachers' self-dialog among multiple positions. The dialogical approach of teacher identity provides a framework to understand the tensions and uncertainties that teachers experience in the AI era for its focus on their negotiation of conflicts among multiple positions and voices (Akkerman & Meijer, 2011). Hence, research on language teachers' AI-driven identity tensions and transformation from a dialogical approach is essential for better understanding this topic.

The Chinese government has made efforts to promote the use of AI in universities (Knox, 2020) and AI has become a key term in English as a foreign language (EFL) teaching (Zhou et al., 2024). However, AI-driven EFL teaching is constrained by teachers' ineffective integration of teaching methods with language intelligence technologies (Hu & Wang, 2021), limited AI-related skills and less concern about ethical implications (Yuan, 2024). All these real-world issues manifest the necessity to investigate Chinese university EFL teacher identity tensions and transformation in the AI era, offering insights into the application of AI within the broader educational ecosystem. Against this backdrop, we will focus on the voices and experiences of Chinese university EFL teachers' identity tensions to better understand their AI-driven identity transformation by answering the following research question:

What identity tensions do university EFL teachers experience in the era of AI?

2 Literature Review

2.1 A Dialogical Approach to Identity Tensions in the Era of AI

A dialogical conceptualization of teacher identity is a useful analytical framework for studying teachers' identity tensions. This framework sees identity from multiplicity-unity, discontinuity-continuity and social-individual dimensions (Akkerman & Meijer, 2011). Firstly, the multiplicity of identity means multiple I-positions, which are considered as the voiced position, driven by one's intention. One will experience identity negotiation when moving from one position to another. Notably, these multiple I-positions may exist in conflicts because of conflicting views, beliefs and perceptions. However, these multiple I-positions are always in a dialogical relationship of inter-subjective exchange and temporary dominance. Secondly, the continuity nature of identity can motivate the individual to create a dialogical space between different I-positions and maintain a consistent and coherent sense of self. Meanwhile, identity is not static but a fluid and dynamic process, reflecting its discontinuous nature. Such nature is reflected not only in identity change but also in the process of evoking specific aspects of the self in particular situations. It is noteworthy that this discontinuity nature does not deny the continuity of identity. It means an individual's continuity through narratives to present one's intentions and actions consistently, maintained by routinized personal behavior as well as cultural and historical mediation. Thirdly, identity is social, indicating the motivating role of interaction with others (individuals and communities) on one's actions and development in a certain direction. It does not mean the individual is utterly subordinated to the social environment, the individual nature of identity will motivate one's autonomy to develop new I-positions by appropriating the communities' discourse as their own and introducing new voices into the communities.

The three dimensions of the dialogue approach facilitate understanding teachers' identity tensions and identity complexity. The educational landscape has been increasingly changed by the force of AI (Loftus & Madden, 2020), which possibly leads to teachers' identity tensions, as identity is socially constructed (Beijaard et al., 2004). These identity tensions can be analyzed from teachers' self-dialogue in striving to maintain a coherent and consistent sense of self when they are struggling to pursue identity unity in diverse I-positions, dealing with identity change to keep identity continuity, and highlighting identity autonomy to overcome constraints from social subordination. From the perspective of a dialogical approach, we reviewed the literature and found that teachers experience identity tensions when using AI-driven tools due to challenged beliefs and knowledge base, changing identities and constrained identities.

2.2 *Identity Tensions from Challenged Beliefs and Knowledge Base*

Teachers experience identity tensions in their conflicting positions from challenged traditional pedagogical beliefs and knowledge base. The application of AI-driven tools challenged teachers' original teaching methods and responsibility by facilitating personalized learning for students through instant feedback (Nguyen, 2024). For example, tertiary EFL teachers experienced identity tensions from weakened authority and new AI-enhanced responsibilities to negotiate their identity between traditional teaching methodologies and the innovative demands of AI-enhanced environments (Zhou et al., 2024). This study emphasized the role of emotional resilience in turning adversity into an advantage in dealing with identity tensions (Yang et al., 2022) and the influence of pedagogical content knowledge on teachers' identity development (Barahona & Toledo-Sandoval, 2022). Similarly, university ESL teachers' positive attitude towards AI training in monitoring students and guiding them to use AI properly to achieve personalized learning, revealed teachers' need to enrich their intelligent knowledge base of ethics and awareness to develop students' digital literacy (Dakakni & Safa, 2023). It is obvious that language teachers need to reconsider their pedagogical beliefs and enrich their AI-related knowledge to better survive in the AI era.

Scholars have paid attention to teachers' knowledge base with technology and digital literacy. The previous study has explored the vital role of teachers' technological, pedagogical and content knowledge (TPACK) in alleviating university English language teachers' identity tensions from the pressures of online teaching during global crisis time (Golzar et al., 2023). With the development of AI, Celik (2023) added the ethical component in teachers' TPACK, emphasizing the necessity of teachers to evolve their knowledge base in the AI era. Specifically, the Intelligent-TPACK with consideration of ethics means teachers' professional knowledge of selecting and applying suitable AI-driven tools to perform a teaching strategy to accomplish teaching goals with the ethical assessment of the tools. The ethical assessment criteria includes transparency (understanding the decision-making process and rationale behind AI tools), fairness (the absence of algorithmic bias and promotes equity among students), accountability (the responsibility of AI developers and designers) and inclusiveness (accessibility for all learners). Other scholars also emphasized the contributing role of teachers' digital literacy competence on their identity (Karataş & Yüce, 2024; Zhang et al., 2024). With the development of AI, Lee and Park (2024) developed AI-digital literacy. It involves technical proficiency in using AI tools, critical evaluation of AI responses, communication skills with AI, creative application for enhancing innovation, and ethical competence to address legal or ethical issues. In sum, teachers need to develop their emotional resilience, enrich their Intelligent-TPACK and develop their AI-digital literacy to better deal with AI-driven identity tensions and pursue identity unity.

2.3 *Identity Tensions from Changing Identities*

The fluid nature of identity means that teachers may encounter identity tensions when their identity is changing in practice. For instance, English-medium instruction university teachers experienced identity transformation while changing their teaching approach from teacher-oriented to student-oriented teaching with the convenience of AI-assisted personalized learning (Tsou et al., 2024). They have changed their roles in helping students to become confident in critical thinking, adopting a more interactive and student-centered approach and being co-learners with AI when doing research. This study also emphasized the importance of monitoring students' learning and improving students' AI-digital literacy in the AI era, including avoiding students' misuse of AI-driven tools. Such identity tensions are more pronounced among EFL/ESL teachers. They have used AI-driven tools to streamline content discovery, prepare teaching and assessment materials, enhance linguistic accuracy and demonstrate AI-driven tools to students (see Dakakni & Safa, 2023; Liu & Xiao, 2025; Zaim et al., 2024). These teachers also faced challenges such as meeting curriculum requirements, maintaining pedagogical quality, limited digital literacy and a lack of awareness regarding AI security. It highlights the importance of developing teachers' critical thinking, creativity and ethical awareness in using AI-driven tools (Firat, 2023). Notably, AI-driven tools can facilitate personalized language learning for students, while teachers must shift their position from knowledge transmission to organizing knowledge based on students' external position (Zhai et al., 2021).

2.4 Identity Tensions from Constrained Identities

The social nature of identity motivates individuals to act and develop in a certain direction, leading to identity tensions when teachers' autonomy is constrained in the community (Akkerman & Meijer, 2011). For example, Chinese university teachers experienced professional identity tensions in AI-enhanced training. Such tensions came from teachers' constrained autonomous positions in pursuing unique teaching styles, maintaining personal interactions over-reliance on technology, and the desire to preserve traditional in-person learning and moral guidance while using AI tools (Lan, 2024). It emphasized teachers' autonomous positions in adding new content to the AI-driven teaching community (Akkerman & Meijer, 2011) and their irreplaceable roles in teacher-student interaction. Such autonomous positions were also reflected in teachers' critical roles in curriculum design, lesson planning and assessment (Fassbender, 2024; Zhai et al., 2021) as well as their expertise in understanding student needs, providing feedback, fostering a supportive learning community and nurturing students' digital literacy (Kostka & Toncelli, 2023). Notably, teachers' autonomous positions rely on community support, including organizational support and training as well as regional connectivity and peer support (Lu & Lin, 2024). The literature shows that teachers without proper community support struggle to apply effective teaching approaches (Mustafa et al., 2024) and construct their professional identity (Lan, 2024). In sum, teachers' AI-driven identity can be better understood through micro- and macro-analysis of their I-positions in response to others in the socio-cultural environment.

3 Methodology

To understand Chinese EFL teachers' identity tensions when using AI-driven tools in teaching, we employed a qualitative case study approach. Because this approach emphasizes "an in-depth description and analysis of a bounded system" (Merriam, 2009, p. 40), allowing us to capture and interpret each participant's identity tensions in the bounded real-life context.

3.1 Research Context and Participants

We selected EFL teachers in tertiary education for the frequent application of AI-driven tools in their teaching (Knox, 2020). The public non-elite universities were chosen for their representativeness of higher education in China, reflecting the average situation of the phenomenon of interest (Patton, 2002). English in the university is a compulsory course for students in China. College English is a compulsory course for non-English major students and the students majoring in English have more specialized English courses, such as American literature, academic writing and business English. For better job opportunities or further education, non-English major students usually take the College English Test (CET) and English major students are required to take the Test for English Majors (TEM).

Considering the "particularistic" characteristic of the qualitative case study (Merriam, 2009, p. 43), the purposeful sampling method and snowball sampling method were applied to better address our research question. The participants were chosen based on three criteria to obtain rich data: (1) Obtaining education qualification certificates; (2) Working as full-time EFL teachers in a non-elite university; and (3) Having teaching experiences with AI-driven tools. We first identified five participants, who then recommended other EFL teachers who met the selection criteria. While the second author was collecting data, the first author conducted a preliminary analysis. When we received data from the 10th participant, we found that no new codes were emerging. Therefore, a total of 10 participants were included in this study, whose demographic information is provided in Table 1.

Table 1 Participants' demographic information

Name	Gender	Age	Degree	Major	Teaching experience	Teaching subject	Title
T1	Female	41	Master	English language and literature	15 years	College English	Lecture
T2	Female	50	Master	English linguistics	27 years	Academic writing	Associate professor
T3	Female	43	Master	Applied linguistics	22 years	College English	Associate professor
T4	Female	44	Master	Translation	10 years	College English	Teaching Assistant
T5	Female	40	Ph.D. candidate	English	14 years	American literature	Lecture
T6	Female	36	Ph.D. candidate	Business English	8 years	Business English	Lecture
T7	Female	35	Master	English	7 years	College English	Lecture
T8	Female	44	Doctor	TESL	20 years	Oral English	Associate professor
T9	Female	40	Ph.D. candidate	TESL	9 years	Integrated English	Associate professor
T10	Female	36	Doctor	Comparative education	12 years	College English	Associate professor

3.2 Positionality Statement and Ethical Matters

As qualitative researchers, all four authors share their pertinent identities as language teachers and researchers. Especially the second author, as a Chinese university EFL teacher, offers an "insider's perspective" (Merriam, 2009, p. 14). This positionality enabled the researcher to better understand the participants' context, resulting in interviews that were more in-depth and context-specific (Yang et al., 2021). Simultaneously, the diverse teaching experiences and occupational backgrounds of the four authors played a significant role in reducing bias during data interpretation (Trent, 2017). We also employed member checking of the findings with participants to reduce the bias. In sum, member checking, a thick description of the findings, and a detailed account of the data collection and analysis procedures ensured the trustworthiness of this study (Lincoln & Guba, 1985). The permission from the universities was obtained before beginning to collect the data. The participants were assured that their names and the names of their universities would remain confidential and used solely for research purposes. The participants were briefed on the data collection process, and after understanding the expectations, they signed consent forms and could withdraw at any time.

3.3 Data Collection

We used narrative frames and detailed interviews for data collection methods. A narrative frame is "a written story template consisting of a series of incomplete sentences and blank spaces of varying lengths" to better understand participants' experiences of AI-driven tools in teaching and their reflections on these experiences (Barkhuizen, 2011, p. 402). This self-reflective writing with the designed narrative structure can help us obtain the information to answer the research question. We followed Barkhuizen's (2014) design and administration of narrative frames to contextualize narrative frames (Appendix A), based on the dialogical conceptualization of teacher identity. After getting the permission of the participants, the second author sent the narrative frames to them via email. Meanwhile, to avoid the potential to de-personalize the participants' experience in the narrative frameworks, the second author also conducted detailed interviews face to face (20–30 min). Such detailed interviews facilitated to expand on the points participants had made in their narrative frames and ask them to reflect on their experiences.

3.4 Data Analysis

The narrative frames and the interview transcripts were imported into ATLAS.ti. 25 and analyzed independently and then collaboratively with the thematic analysis (Braun & Clarke, 2023). The first author coded the data iteratively to identify repeating segments that may challenge participants' I-positions (e.g., value, beliefs, students' unethical engagement) and then grouped these repeating segments to form code clusters (e.g., challenged knowledge base, students' inadequate AI-digital literacy). Other authors assisted with data analysis and review of the manuscript. Specifically, during the data analysis process, we had discussions online every week to negotiate and decide on the initial codes and code clusters in the data and collectively reached the themes presented in this study, as shown in Table 2.

4 Findings

Our findings indicate that the application and advancement of AI in the field of education have fundamentally transformed the traditional teacher-student dyadic interaction model, leading to a new triadic interaction framework involving teacher-AI-student dynamics in language teaching. Within this AI-driven triadic interactive context, teachers face challenges to their established pedagogical beliefs and traditional values. Moreover, the integration of AI necessitates a redefinition of teachers'

Table 2 Data analysis process

Themes	Clusters	Codes (frequency)
Conflicting I-positions	Challenged pedagogical beliefs	Students' competence-based and student-centered teaching (17); Teacher-centred teaching (11); Irreplaceable role of teachers in teaching (24); Value of English teaching (11); Positive attitude (10); Continued learning of Intelligent-TPACK (15)
	Challenged value of English teaching	
New I-positions	Teacher-student power shift	Lesson design (29); Assessment (12); Naturing students' AI digital literacy (15); Open emotional vulnerability (7); Weakened authority (12); Intelligent-TPACK; (23); Critical and creative thinking (2)
	AI-driven pedagogical decision-making and action-taking	
Constrained I-positions	Macro socio-cultural and micro institutional contexts	Lack of education policy support (2); Lack of school administrative support (18); Students' resistant engagement (9); Students' uncritical engagement (7); Students' unethical engagement (10); Accuracy and reliability issues (8); Data dependency and lack of creativity (6); Limited Intelligent-TPACK (16); Reflection (2); emotional experiences (15); Socio-cultural factors (10)
	Students' inadequate AI-digital literacy	
	Technical limitations of AI-driven tools	

I-positions within their pedagogical practice and the teacher-student power relationship. However, in the process of repositioning themselves, participants' autonomy was constrained by students' underdeveloped digital literacy, technical limitations of AI-driven tools and contextual conditions. Overall, the participants experienced identity tensions arising from conflicting I-positions, new I-positions and constrained I-positions, and they employed various strategies to navigate these tensions.

4.1 Identity Tensions from Conflicting I-positions

The multiple nature of identity means teachers may encounter identity tensions from their conflicting multiple I-positions, including challenged pedagogical beliefs and traditional values. When they described their identity in traditional EFL teaching, they all mentioned the teacher-centered role of knowledge transmission, such as the role as the knowledge disseminator (T1, T5, T4, T6, T10, T9, T8) and as the monitor of students' knowledge learning (T2, T3, T7). Their I-positions in knowledge transmission and monitoring reflected their knowledge-centered pedagogical beliefs. However, it appeared that this pedagogical belief was challenged by competence-centered beliefs when they were asked about the influence of AI on EFL teaching during the interviews. Specifically, participants preferred to assign learning tasks to improve students' competence, including filming a short video in English (T1), following steps of AI to organize materials in academic writing (T2) and discussing the content provided by AI in groups to enhance critical thinking skills (T3, T5). Students' smooth channels of knowledge acquisition made teachers adopt student-centered pedagogical beliefs. For example, participants argued that they were not the knowledge transmitters but more aware of helping students better understand the world and improve their adaptability in the AI era (T4, T7, T10, T9, T6). It can be inferred that participants were experiencing I-position negotiation to more competence-centered and student-centered pedagogical beliefs.

Facing such challenges, all participants expressed their efforts in enhancing their intelligent-TPACK, including integrating AI into English language teaching (T1, T3, T4, T7, T8), developing prompt engineering skills (T2, T6, T9), adopting AI-assisted learning strategies (T4, T5) and improving research competence (T10, T3) to stay current. It suggests that participants' AI-driven I-positions were gradually constructed based on their continued learning in Intelligent-TPACK, which provided them with standards or criteria to guide them in AI-driven teaching. It also highlights the importance of participants' cognitive competence, including their learning abilities in alleviating their identity tensions.

Notably, although all the participants held a positive attitude towards AI in facilitating their academic research and reducing their workload, some of them also argued the challenged traditional value of EFL teaching. For example, the participants thought that the listening, speaking, reading, and writing skills of English majors were challenged by the powerful translation capabilities of AI (T1, T3, T4, T10). T10 was not sure about university EFL teachers' future, depending on "the extent of AI development, as well as the demand for and regulatory requirements of EFL teachers in higher education". T3 even thought that "English teachers without critical thinking would be replaced by AI". Facing these tensions, most participants revealed their internal dialogue that they believed although English majors and English teachers were facing challenges, they could not be replaced. This was because teachers' role in providing emotional support (T4, T5, T6, T8, T7), in-person communication with students (T2, T3, T4, T5, T6, T8, T7), motivating students' learning (T1), monitoring students' progress (T1, T2, T8, T9), and provision of systematic learning and practice guidance (T9) could not be replaced by AI. It can be inferred that the challenged value of EFL teaching caused tensions in participants' traditional I-positions and they dealt with such tensions through their internal dialogue based on their irreplaceable role in teacher-student interaction.

4.2 *Identity Tensions from New I-positions*

Identity is fluid in a dynamic process with changes in thoughts, moods and behaviors. The participants experienced tensions when responding to students' use of AI-driven tools in EFL learning, including new I-positions in teacher-student power relationships and their pedagogical decision-making and action-taking. When the participants wrote about their negative emotional experiences within the narrative framework or responded to whether their authority was influenced by AI, some participants acknowledged experiencing such concerns. T1's example is relatively representative:

> In my classes, students with poor listening skills use AI to translate my words. They may notice occasional imprecise pronunciation or incorrect word choices...When they face difficulties, they turn to AI for answers, often finding them more comprehensive than my explanations, which may lead them to question my professional competence.

As shown in the excerpt, T1's identity tensions came from her challenged professional competence in response to students' use of AI-driven tools in class. Similarly, T3 shared her visiting scholar experience that teachers' professional competence was questioned to provide accurate knowledge when students could acquire knowledge more quickly using AI-driven tools. T2 described her colleagues' experience that their limited Intelligent-TPACK and AI-driven teaching experience made them vulnerable in evaluating a graduate student's research topic on AI-assisted translation. Similar concerns were also reflected in participants' limited feedback perspectives on students' writing (T4, T2), lack of Intelligent-TPACK to monitor students' learning (T1, T2, T4, T3, T5) and deficient demonstrating skills of AI-driven tools (T9). All the excerpts reflected participants' re-interpretation of past teacher-student power relationships in the AI era. More specifically, students' use of AI tools had disrupted the traditional teacher-student binary interaction. In the triadic teacher-AI-student interaction, participants were no longer the main source of knowledge. Students with

AI-driven tools had more power to evaluate and question the participants, weakening their authority.

Facing such an evaluated and challenged position, T1 and T4 showed their open emotional vulnerability, termed as showing confidence to risk opening themselves to emotionally stressful situations (Lasky, 2005). For instance:

> T4: Teachers are human too, so mistakes are inevitable. When students point them out, there is no need to feel embarrassed. Instead, discussing the issue together and reaching the correct conclusion can be a valuable learning process for both teachers and students.
>
> T1: English is not our native language, it's normal to make some mistakes! Just harness human creativity to give AI some prompts to better support AI-assisted teaching.

The experts illustrated participants' openness to admit their shortcomings compared with AI-driven tools and their confidence to navigate such tensions through creativity in teacher-AI-student interaction. It also reflected participants' strategies to adjust their pedagogy. It suggests that participants' emotional competence, such as open emotional vulnerability can facilitate them better adapt and survive in the AI era.

Additionally, participants also experienced new I-positions through their adjustment in pedagogical decision-making and action-taking, including lesson design, assessment and nurturing students' AI-digital literacy. For example, all the participants mentioned their use of AI-driven tools in searching for sources to design their lessons, including interdisciplinary knowledge and background information (T1, T2, T9), supplementary materials for textbook content (T3, T4, T6, T5, T8, T1), personalized materials based on student interest and needs (T4, T6, T7, T10). It can be inferred that AI-driven tools reduced participants' workload and avoided over-reliance on textbooks, allowing them to focus more on students' learning backgrounds, interests and needs during the lesson design process. Notably, some participants mentioned factors that ensure the personalization of resources based on students' needs, including teachers' teaching experience (T2, T3), critical thinking and creativity (T2, T3) and familiarity with students (T4, T7). It suggests that AI's powerful information-gathering capabilities evoke specific aspects of participants' I-position in searching, selecting, and organizing resources during their lesson design phase, reflecting their Intelligent-TPACK to obtain adaptive feedback.

Furthermore, participants' new I-position was also reflected in the assessment process with AI-driven tools, especially for providing feedback on students' writing. T1 and T2 stated that using AI tools to assess students' writing compensates for teachers' limited writing proficiency and energy with large classroom sizes. T1 also emphasized the benefits of using AI-driven tools for students' personalized learning in writing by "correcting students' grammatical errors and enhancing the logical coherence of their articles". Both teachers provided students with the assessment criteria as prompts and asked them to submit their essays with AI-generated feedback. This implies that AI-driven tools make the assessment process more transparent and actively involve students in the assessment process. During such teacher-AI-student assessment processes, participants' I-positions changed as well, for example,

> T1: Teachers can have more energy to summarize and reflect on students' problems in writing by reviewing AI's feedback and addressing these issues in a targeted manner.
>
> T2: I always select five students to ask them to analyze the AI-generated feedback on their own, helping them reflect on their errors and make progress.

The excerpts illustrated that the teacher-AI-student ternary assessment process evoked participants' monitoring and reflective aspects of their I-positions in assessment. It suggests that AI-driven tools in assessment facilitate teachers to have more energy in providing formative assessment and nurturing students' AI-digital literacy. In addition to promoting students' reflection with AI-driven tools in writing, participants also nurtured students' AI-digital literacy in technical proficiency based on their own Intelligent-TPACK. For example, participants would demonstrate how to input prompts in identifying research areas (T2), engage in self-directed learning to search for information and better understand key concepts in class (T4, T6, T7, T5, T3, T8, T10) as well as improve academic writing (T9, T1, T2) with AI-driven tools. It can be concluded that participants evoked their new I-positions in developing students' AI-digital literacy, including students' technical proficiency, communication proficiency and creative application.

4.3 Identity Tensions from Constrained I-positions

The social nature of identity means others shape one's I-positions, but individuals retain the autonomy and agency to influence the community as well. Tensions arise when their autonomy is constrained. In this study, the participants' I-positions were constrained because of students' inadequate digital literacy, technical limitations of AI-driven tools and limited community support. Specifically, students' unethical, uncritical and resistant engagement constrain participants' I-positions in AI-driven teaching. For example, the participants felt angry or frustrated when their students used AI-driven tools to generate a paper for submission (T1, T2, T4, T5, T10) and to generate answers for online exams (T3, T5). They experienced negative emotions because students' unethical engagement with AI-driven tools violated their intentions in using AI for teaching:

> T1: Students did not use the prompts I taught them to enhance their writing but instead resorted to plagiarism. Even in the final exam, despite having the same topic, they still struggled to write.
>
> T5: I organize online exams to use AI in assessing students' learning outcomes, but some students use AI to search for answers during the exam.

The excerpts illustrated participants' awareness of students' unethical use of AI-driven tools. However, when asked about the strategies, all of them expressed "helplessness" but had to develop their critical thinking to judge or rely more on students' self-discipline. T3 even decided to switch back to paper-and-pencil exams. Some other participants also expressed their anxiety about students' learning effectiveness because some of them over-relied on AI to generate answers instead of thinking independently (T5, T2, T3, T10). It suggests that participants needed to adjust their pedagogy to better monitor students' AI-driven learning. They also need to develop students' AI-digital literacy with ethical education, especially their ethical competence. However, none of the participants mentioned the ethical assessment of AI-driven tools, influencing their awareness to develop students' AI-digital literacy in critical evaluation to evaluate the accuracy and reliability of AI-driven tool's responses.

Some participants highlighted the influence of students' positive engagement in their AI-driven identity construction:

> T8: I am more willing to continue exploring ways to integrate AI into teaching when students cooperate and actively engage within this process, such as using AI-driven tools I recommended for practicing their oral English.

The expert showed the influence of students' engagement on teachers' motivation to integrate AI in teaching. Such influence was also reflected in participants' negative emotions from students' low engagement, especially for those students who were struggling academically (T2, T4, T6). It can be explained that students, as significant others, played a significant role in the development of teachers' I-positions by introducing ways of thinking and acting. So, developing students' AI-digital literacy is an important task for participants.

Furthermore, participants' AI-driven identities were also constrained by the technical limitations of AI-driven tools, reflecting their limited Intelligent-Technology pedagogical knowledge. For example, T6 described her worst moment:

> …when I discovered that the personalized recommendations provided by AI tools did not meet the real needs of some students, or were disconnected from real-world contexts, causing students confusion.

The excerpt illustrated T6's students' "confusion" when T6 failed to use AI-driven tools to facilitate students' personalized learning. It can be inferred that in the triadic teacher-AI-student EFL learning process, teachers play a crucial role in filtering and selecting suitable information, thereby enhancing students' personalized learning. This process placed higher demands on participants' Intelligent-TPACK to obtain adaptive feedback from AI-based tools for teaching and learning. Other participants also expressed their worst moments regarding the technical limitations of AI-driven tools. For example:

> T7: …I searched materials related to art for visual arts students, but the AI-recommended resources did not meet their needs and caused more confusion. This experience made me feel helpless and anxious because I was worried that the AI's suggestions were not accurate enough, which could affect students' enthusiasm for learning and their professional development.
>
> T8: …I felt frustrated when I realized that the materials I obtained from AI were not suitable for students' oral English learning. Perhaps there was an issue with my prompts. For example, when I wanted oral expressions as examples for my students, I instead received some written expressions.

As shown in the excerpts, participants' negative emotional experiences as the indicator reflected their identity tensions caused by overgeneralization, inaccuracy and superficiality of AI tools based on its database. It also reflected teachers' limited Intelligent-TPACK to provide proper learning resources for students' personalized learning. Facing such tensions, T8 and T9 both mentioned their strategies to reflect on and adjust their prompts to get resources suitable for students and the requirements of the course. These excerpts illustrated the influence of participants' reflections on dealing with AI-driven identity tensions.

Notably, the enhancement of such Intelligent-TPACK is contingent upon robust community support and teachers' ongoing professional learning, influenced by the micro institutional and macro socio-cultural contexts. For example, when the participants described their first learned about AI-driven tools, they mentioned school AI-related training (T1, T4, T5, T6), academic lectures (T3, T7, T9), self-learning (T2, T5, T8, T10) and learning from colleagues (T4, T5, T6, T8). It can be explained that others' voices become a part of participants' thinking and reasoning, dialogically contributing to participants' self-definition. However, some participants complained about the limited community support which constrained their autonomy in AI-driven teaching, including school administrative support and education policy support. Specifically, English, as a marginalized subject, was not regarded as a key support program by the school, therefore, equipment investment in AI for the English discipline remains limited, including AI-powered educational platforms (T5, T8) and limited access to AI-driven tools (T10). Some other participants argued that the school has invested funds in building intelligent classrooms, however, due to insufficient follow-up training, frontline teachers benefited little, resulting in a low adoption rate (T1, T3, T2). T2 and T3 even expressed their anger to the school administrators, as the suggestions they submitted to the school leadership for facilitating AI-integrated teaching were all rejected, including offering AI-integrated courses and purchasing AI systems to support teaching. T3 also mentioned another factor:

> Both the school and teachers do not prioritize teaching, the "publish or perish" pressure diverts teachers' attention away from integrating AI into teaching.

Participants' self-narrative demonstrated the institutional constraints on their autonomy to integrate AI in EFL teaching and introduce new voices into the communities. It suggests that only if the school community offers opportunities to hear participants' voices and support the development of their AI-driven I-positions, can the participants contribute to the developmental potential of communities in AI-driven teaching innovation. Furthermore, some participants expressed the constraints of the education policy, including the lack of AI-oriented curriculum guidance (T2) and AI-oriented professional development direction for college EFL teachers (T10). It can be explained by the informant role of the community to motivate participants to develop further in a certain direction. In sum, the participants experienced identity tensions due to their constrained autonomy in the integration of AI in EFL teaching, which, in turn, also influenced the development of the community in the AI era.

5 Discussion

In this study, we investigated the identity tensions of ten university EFL teachers through dialogic engagement in their AI-driven teaching. We drew on the dialogical conceptualization of teacher identity and found that their identity tensions came from conflicting I-positions, new I-positions and constrained I-positions, in a teacher-AI-student triadic interaction model. Based on the findings, we propose a conceptual framework for university EFL teachers' AI-driven identity, as illustrated in Fig. 1.

Firstly, as shown in the left circle, participants' Intelligent-TPACK, as the knowledge base, is the standard or criteria to guide their AI-driven teaching and identity transformation. Our finding resonated with Dakakni and Safa (2023), who also reported that university ESL teachers displayed a general lack of awareness regarding the impact of AI on national security. However, the participants in our study showed insufficient knowledge of AI ethics due to their insufficient knowledge of AI ethics, making none of them assess AI-driven tools in teaching. Furthermore, this knowledge base is crucial for participants to navigate challenges in AI-driven teaching, such as searching for proper resources to meet students' needs (Firat, 2023). Participants' inadequate Intelligent-TPACK in using prompts effectively was similar

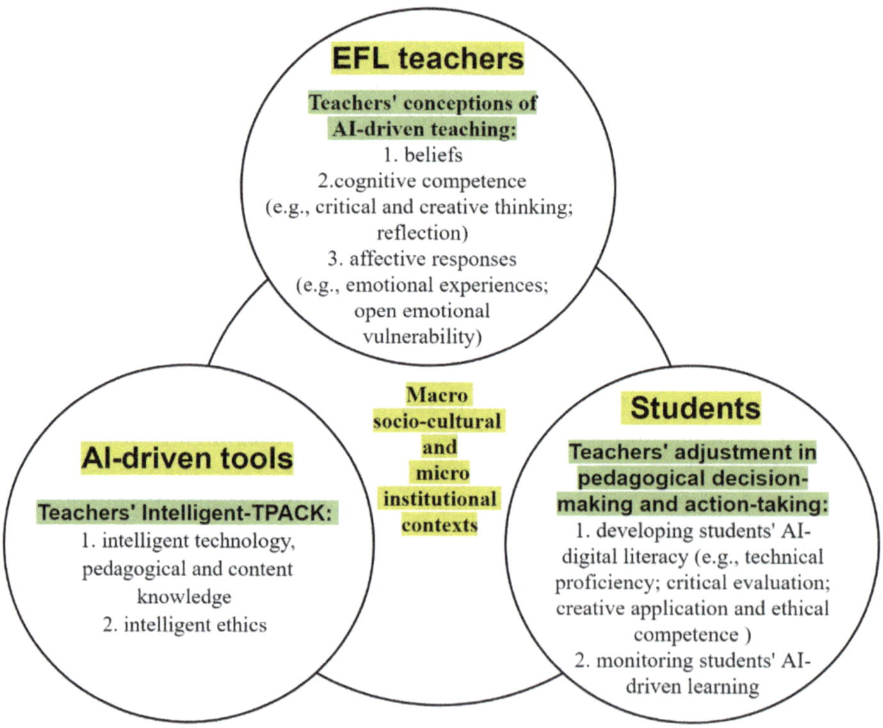

Fig. 1 University EFL teachers' AI-driven identity

to the difficulties faced by Chinese university EFL teachers who struggled with poor-quality prompts that hindered the elicitation of adaptive outputs (Liu & Xiao, 2025). Notably, we found that participants' Intelligent-TPACK was not static, but evolving and dynamic with their continued learning, aligning with university EFL teachers' strategies to continue learning and enrich the AI-related knowledge base (Zhou et al., 2024). It can be inferred that our participants, like other Chinese university EFL teachers, are active learners in developing an AI-driven identity, but further training in Intelligent-TPACK with ethical consideration is needed.

Second, participants need to evolve their conceptions of AI-driven teaching to better survive in the AI era, as shown in the middle circle of the conceptual framework. These conceptions indicate their understanding of the nature and purposes of integrating AI in EFL teaching, reflecting their beliefs, cognitive competence and affective responses. Specifically, participants encountered identity tensions from conflicting pedagogical beliefs between knowledge-centered to more competency-centered and student-centered pedagogical beliefs and new positions in teacher-student power relationships. The findings were similar to English-medium instruction university teachers' adoption of a more interactive and student-centered approach in AI-driven teaching (Tsou et al., 2024). Meanwhile, participants' strategies support the significant role of EFL teachers' cognitive competence in dealing with such tensions. It includes improving university teachers' critical and creative thinking in using and evaluating their generated content in course design (Firat, 2023) and reflection to better understand students' needs and offering supportive feedback (Kostka & Toncelli, 2023). In addition to cognitive competence, our findings also highlighted participants' affective responses toward their AI-driven identity tensions. Specifically, our study emphasized the indicator role of emotional experiences on participants' identity tensions caused by overgeneralization, inaccuracy and superficiality of AI tools and their weakened authority. Dealing with such tensions, different from university EFL teachers' emotional resilience to promote adaptability (Zhou et al., 2024), participants revealed their open emotional vulnerability (Lasky, 2005), to admit their shortcomings and emphasize their irreplaceable roles in creativity and emotional interaction with students. This process highlights the interconnection between participants' emotional responses and their AI-driven identity tensions.

Third, participants need to adjust their pedagogical decision-making and action-taking to better deal with students' inadequate AI-digital literacy. Participants' new teaching responsibility in nurturing students' AI digital literacy in technical proficiency, communication proficiency and creative application through demonstration was similar to Lebanese university teachers' demonstration to assist students in writing their essays with AI-driven tools (Dakakni & Safa, 2023). However, our study is distinct in unpacking the inadequate education to develop students' AI-digital literacy in critical evaluation to evaluate the accuracy and reliability of AI-driven tool's responses (Lee & Park, 2024). It may be because of participants' insufficient Intelligent-TPACK about how to improve students' digital literacy in critical evaluation. Furthermore, our study supports the urgent challenges teachers face in monitoring students' misuse of AI-driven tools (Dakakni & Safa, 2023; Liu & Yushchik, 2024). It means more knowledge should be supplemented into Intelligent-TPACK to develop students' AI-digital literacy, including developing students' critical thinking in the proper use of AI-driven tools.

Additionally, the influence of the macro socio-cultural and micro institutional context on participants' AI-driven identity tensions and transformation cannot be overlooked. The findings are similar to the factors on the use of AI-driven tools in education, including the need for organizational support in providing infrastructure (Lu & Lin, 2024). In addition to these constraints, our study also highlights the influence of the Chinese socio-cultural context on participants' AI-driven identity tensions. This influence included teachers' low motivation to integrate AI in teaching because of the "publish or perish" pressure, marginalized status of English subjects as well as ambiguous AI-oriented curriculum guidance and professional development direction for university EFL teachers. Attention needs to be paid to this aspect to help teachers better construct their AI-driven identity.

6 Conclusion and Implication

This study explored ten university EFL teachers' AI-driven identity tensions in the teacher-AI-student triadic model. Such a triadic model is influenced by the macro socio-cultural and micro institutional contexts. Based on this model, we summarized three implications to help university EFL teachers better deal with AI-driven identity tensions and facilitate their identity transformation in the AI era: (1) Teacher educators need to add AI-TPACK in pre-service and in-service teachers' training to enrich their knowledge base, especially the knowledge of intelligent ethics and improving students' AI-digital literacy. Attention also needs to be paid to evolving teachers' conceptions of AI-driving teaching, including developing teachers' cognitive and affective competence to better deal with tensions in the AI era; (2) Policymakers should add requirements and standards for cultivating students' digital literacy in the English curriculum guidelines, including students' critical and creative thinking of evaluating the digital content. They should also provide clear directions for EFL teachers' AI-driven teaching. (3) School administrators should provide self-dialogue space and autonomy for individual teachers to add new voices in the development of AI-driven teaching in the community and provide support to teachers' innovation in AI-driven teaching practice, including regional connectivity and peer support environments.

The study is not without limitations. The data in similar research should be interpreted with caution, as we conducted this study over only one semester with ten university EFL teachers in a Chinese context. Examining AI-driven identity tensions among K-12 EFL teachers would provide valuable insights, particularly considering the unique physical and mental characteristics of young learners. Additionally, the focus was restricted to teachers' AI-driven tensions, future research should include teachers' AI-driven identity construction by considering the relationships between teachers' AI-TPACK and students' AI-digital literacy to better understand language teacher identity transformation in the AI era.

Appendix

Narrative Frame

Dear teachers,

We are researching university EFL teachers' identity tensions with the use of AI-driven tools to facilitate students' personalized learning. We want to know what tensions you experienced and how you deal with them. Please fill in the lines below with examples and details and if you think something should be added, write it at the end.

Name【】Age【】 Degree【】Teaching experiences【 years】Major【】subject【】

As a traditional EFL teacher, my role involves_________________________because I need to____. For example, being a _________means_______________________________________.

____

I first learned about AI-driven tools when_______________________________. I used them primarily to____in teaching because it can ____. For example,____.

Using AI-driven tools makes me play different roles as a teacher, such as_________________. For example, I need to be a________when I____.

I remember that the worst moment I encountered while using AI-driven tools was when I____. This experience made me feel _______, because______________________________

____.

Therefore, I tried to solve the problem by_______________________________to better thrive in the AI era. Looking back, I realized that to better handle similar challenges, I would need support from______________________________. Because____. For example, ____.

In the future, while using AI-driven tools, I hope to become the kind of teacher who____.For example, ____.

Please write about other highly sensitive moments you have experienced in your teaching with the use of AI-driven tools to facilitate students' personalized learning.

References

Akkerman, S. F., & Meijer, P. C. (2011). A dialogical approach to conceptualizing teacher identity. *Teaching and teacher education*, *27*. https://doi.org/10.1016/j.tate.2010.08.013

Al-Raimi, M., Mudhsh, B. A., Muqaibal, M. H., & Al-Yafaei, Y. (2024). To what extent has Artificial Intelligence impacted EFL teaching and learning? A systematic review. *JURNAL ARBITRER*, *11*(3), 399–412. https://doi.org/10.25077/ar.11.3.399-412.2024

Barahona, M., & Toledo-Sandoval, F. (2022). Exploring Chilean EFL student teachers' development of teacher identity through perezhivanie [Article]. *Journal of Language, Identity and Education.* https://doi.org/10.1080/15348458.2022.2075875

Barkhuizen, G. (2011). Home tutor cognitions and the nature of tutor—learner relationships. In P. Benson & H. Reinders (Eds.), *Beyond the language classroom* (pp. 161–174). Palgrave. https://doi.org/10.1057/9780230306790_13

Barkhuizen, G. (2014). Revisiting narrative frames: An instrument for investigating language teaching and learning. *System, 47*, 12–27. https://doi.org/10.1016/j.system.2014.09.014

Beauchamp, C., & Thomas, L. (2009). Understanding teacher identity: An overview of issues in the literature and implications for teacher education. *Cambridge Journal of Education, 39*(2), 175–189. https://doi.org/10.1080/03057640902902252

Beijaard, D., Meijer, P. C., & Verloop, N. (2004). Reconsidering research on teachers' professional identity. *Teaching and Teacher Education, 20*(2), 107–128. https://doi.org/10.1016/j.tate.2003.07.001

Boulay, B. D. (2016). Artificial intelligence as an effective classroom assistant. *IEEE Intelligent Systems, 31*(6), 76–81. https://doi.org/10.1109/MIS.2016.93

Brandão, A., Pedro, L., & Zagalo, N. (2024). Teacher professional development for a future with generative artificial intelligence–an integrative literature review. *Digital Education Review, 45*, 151–157. https://doi.org/10.1344/der.2024.45.151-157

Braun, V., & Clarke, V. (2023). Thematic analysis. In F. Maggino (Ed.), *Encyclopedia of quality of life and well-being research* (pp. 7187–7193). Springer International Publishing. https://doi.org/10.1007/978-3-031-17299-1_3470

Celik, I. (2023). Towards Intelligent-TPACK: An empirical study on teachers' professional knowledge to ethically integrate artificial intelligence (AI)-based tools into education. *Computers in Human Behavior, 138*, Article 107468. https://doi.org/10.1016/j.chb.2022.107468

Dakakni, D., & Safa, N. (2023). Artificial intelligence in the L2 classroom: Implications and challenges on ethics and equity in higher education: A 21st century Pandora's box. *Computers and Education: Artificial Intelligence, 5*, Article 100179. https://doi.org/10.1016/j.caeai.2023.100179

Fassbender, W. J. (2024). "I can almost recognize its voice": AI and its impact on ethical teacher-centaur labor. *English Teaching: Practice & Critique, 23*(1), 104–117. https://doi.org/10.1108/ETPC-08-2023-0101

Firat, M. (2023). What ChatGPT means for universities: Perceptions of scholars and students. *Journal of Applied Learning and Teaching, 6*(1), 57–63. https://doi.org/10.37074/jalt.2023.6.1.22

Golzar, J., Sarwarzada, T., & Miri, M. A. (2023). Coping with teacher professional identity tensions: Using TPACK during global crisis time. *Journal of Language, Identity & Education*, 1–19. https://doi.org/10.1080/15348458.2023.2281952

Goulart, L., Matte, M. L., Mendoza, A., Alvarado, L., & Veloso, I. (2024). AI or student writing? Analyzing the situational and linguistic characteristics of undergraduate student writing and AI-generated assignments. *Journal of Second Language Writing, 66*, Article 101160. https://doi.org/10.1016/j.jslw.2024.101160

Huang, X., Zou, D., Cheng, G., Chen, X., & Xie, H. (2023). Trends, research issues and applications of artificial intelligence in language education. *Educational Technology & Society*, *26*(1), 112–131. https://doi.org/10.30191/ETS.202301_26(1).0009

Huynh, Q. Q. (2024). A literature review on EFL students' integration of Al-based tools in English learning and the perceived impact on autonomy. *International Journal of AI in Language Education, 1*(2), 30–51. https://doi.org/10.54855/ijaile.24123

Karataş, F., & Yüce, E. (2024). AI and the future of teaching: Preservice teachers' reflections on the use of artificial intelligence in open and distributed learning. *International Review of Research in Open and Distributed Learning*, *25*(3), 304–325. https://doi.org/10.19173/irrodl.v25i3.7785

Klimova, B., Pikhart, M., Polakova, P., Cerna, M., Yayilgan, S. Y., & Shaikh, S. (2023). A systematic review on the use of emerging technologies in teaching English as an applied language at the university level. *Systems, 11*(1).

Knox, J. (2020). Artificial intelligence and education in China. *Learning, Media and Technology, 45*(3), 298–311. https://doi.org/10.1080/17439884.2020.1754236

Kohnke, L., Moorhouse, B. L., & Zou, D. (2023). ChatGPT for language teaching and learning. *RELC Journal, 54*(2), 537–550. https://doi.org/10.1177/00336882231162868

Kostka, I., & Toncelli, R. (2023). Exploring applications of ChatGPT to English language teaching: Opportunities, challenges, and recommendations. *TESL-EJ, 27*(3), n3. https://doi.org/10.55593/ej.27107int

Kwihangana, F. (2024). Teacher positioning in educational ICT policies: Implications for digital teacher identity development in under-resourced contexts. *Journal of Education Policy*, 1–24. https://doi.org/10.1080/02680939.2024.2386309

Lan, Y. (2024). Through tensions to identity-based motivations: Exploring teacher professional identity in artificial intelligence-enhanced teacher training. *Teaching and Teacher Education, 151*, Article 104736. https://doi.org/10.1016/j.tate.2024.104736

Lasky, S. (2005). A sociocultural approach to understanding teacher identity, agency and professional vulnerability in a context of secondary school reform. *Teaching and Teacher Education, 21*(8), 899–916. https://doi.org/10.1016/j.tate.2005.06.003

Lee, S., & Park, G. (2024). Development and validation of ChatGPT literacy scale. *Current Psychology, 43*(21), 18992–19004. https://doi.org/10.1007/s12144-024-05723-0

Lesia Viktorivna, K., Andrii Oleksandrovych, V., Iryna Oleksandrivna, K., & Nadia Oleksandrivna, K. (2022). Artificial intelligence in language learning: What are we afraid of. *Arab World English Journal*. https://doi.org/10.24093/awej/call8.18

Lincoln, Y. S., & Guba, E. G. (1985). *Naturalistic inquiry*. Sage.

Liu, X., & Xiao, Y. (2025). Chinese university teachers' engagement with generative AI in different stages of foreign language teaching: A qualitative enquiry through the prism of ADDIE. *Education and Information Technologies, 30*(1), 485–508. https://doi.org/10.1007/s10639-024-13117-9

Liu, Z., & Yushchik, E. (2024). Exploring the prospects of using artificial intelligence in education. *Cogent Education, 11*(1), 2353464. https://doi.org/10.1080/2331186X.2024.2353464

Loftus, M., & Madden, M. G. (2020). A pedagogy of data and Artificial Intelligence for student subjectification. *Teaching in Higher Education, 25*(4), 456–475. https://doi.org/10.1080/13562517.2020.1748593

Lu, W., & Lin, C. (2024). Meta-Analysis of influencing factors on the use of artificial intelligence in education. *The Asia-Pacific Education Researcher*. https://doi.org/10.1007/s40299-024-00883-w

Merriam, S. B. (2009). *Qualitative research: A guide to design and implementation*. Jossey-Bass.

Mustafa, M. Y., Tlili, A., Lampropoulos, G., Huang, R., Jandrić, P., Zhao, J., Salha, S., Xu, L., Panda, S., Kinshuk, López-Pernas, S., & Saqr, M. (2024). A systematic review of literature reviews on artificial intelligence in education (AIED): A roadmap to a future research agenda. *Smart Learning Environments, 11*(1), 59. https://doi.org/10.1186/s40561-024-00350-5

Nguyen, H. A. (2024). Harnessing AI-based tools for enhancing English speaking proficiency: Impacts, challenges, and long-term engagement. *International Journal of AI in Language Education, 1*(2), 18–29. https://doi.org/10.54855/ijaile.24122

Patton, M. Q. (2002). *Qualitative research & evaluation methods*. Sage.

Ren, B., & Pan, X. (2024). Understanding EFL teacher identity and identity tensions in a Chinese university context. *International Journal of Applied Linguistics* (n/a). https://doi.org/10.1111/ijal.12622

Trent, J. (2017). Discourse, agency and teacher attrition: Exploring stories to leave by amongst former early career English language teachers in Hong Kong. *Research Papers in Education, 32*(1), 84–105. https://doi.org/10.1080/02671522.2016.1144215

Tsou, W., Lin, A. M. Y., & Chen, F. (2024). Co-journeying with ChatGPT in tertiary education: Identity transformation of EMI teachers in Taiwan. *Language, Culture and Curriculum, 37*(4), 529–543. https://doi.org/10.1080/07908318.2024.2362326

UNESCO. (2020). *AI in education: Change at the speed of learning*. Retrieved from: ite.unesco.org/wp-content/uploads/2020/11/StevenDugganAI-in-Education2020.pdf

Yang, S., Shu, D., & Yin, H. (2021). 'Frustration drives me to grow': Unraveling EFL teachers' emotional trajectory interacting with identity development. *Teaching and Teacher Education, 105*, Article 103420. https://doi.org/10.1016/j.tate.2021.103420

Yang, S., Shu, D., & Yin, H. (2022). "Teaching, my passion; publishing, my pain": Unpacking academics' professional identity tensions through the lens of emotional resilience. *Higher Education, 84*(2), 235–254. https://doi.org/10.1007/s10734-021-00765-w

Yuan, L. (2024). Where does AI-driven education, in the Chinese context and beyond, go next? *International Journal of Artificial Intelligence in Education, 34*(1), 31–41. https://doi.org/10.1007/s40593-023-00341-6

Yuan, L., & Liu, X. (2025). The effect of artificial intelligence tools on EFL learners' engagement, enjoyment, and motivation. *Computers in Human Behavior, 162*, Article 108474. https://doi.org/10.1016/j.chb.2024.108474

Zaim, M., Arsyad, S., Waluyo, B., Ardi, H., Al Hafizh, M., Zakiyah, M., Syafitri, W., Nusi, A., & Hardiah, M. (2024). AI-powered EFL pedagogy: Integrating generative AI into university teaching preparation through UTAUT and activity theory. *Computers and Education: Artificial Intelligence, 7*, Article 100335. https://doi.org/10.1016/j.caeai.2024.100335

Zhai, X., Chu, X., Chai, C. S., Jong, M. S. Y., Istenic, A., Spector, M., Liu, J.-B., Yuan, J., & Li, Y. (2021). A review of artificial intelligence (AI) in education from 2010 to 2020. *Complexity, 2021*(1), 8812542. https://doi.org/10.1155/2021/8812542

Zhang, S., Mingyue Gu, M., Sun, W., & Jin, T. (2024). Digital literacy competence, digital literacy practices and teacher identity among pre-service teachers. *Journal of Education for Teaching, 50*(3), 464–478. https://doi.org/10.1080/02607476.2023.2283426

Zhou, Q., Hashim, H., & Sulaiman, N. A. (2024). Digital echoes: Crafting Chinese EFL teacher identity in the era of AI-enhanced instruction—A qualitative exploration. *Forum for Linguistic Studies, 6*(5), 32–50. https://doi.org/10.30564/fls.v6i5.6864

AI-Powered Tools in Lesson Planning Process: Voices from EFL Novice Teachers

Nguyen Truong Sa, Hoang Ngoc Quynh Nhu, Vo Nhat Sinh, and Doan Minh Hue

Abstract It is common that novice teachers, lacking experience and guidance, often struggle in designing effective lesson plans. However, with the assistance of Artificial Technology (AI) tools, they can now compensate for their weaknesses. The impetus of this study was to unpack how novice EFL teachers could leverage these tools to create lesson plans. Data was collected through a questionnaire designed to seek aptitude and readiness in incorporating AI to prepare lesson plans from forty novice teachers. Furthermore, interviews focused on their lesson planning were conducted to assess whether the outcome was satisfying. The results revealed a common agreement among them on AI's appreciable usefulness in streamlining lesson planning. These tools support the creation of drills, images, and activities and visual aid templates based on teachers' original ideas. However, teachers still need to adapt AI-suggested materials to fit learning styles and students' varied competencies and reconsolidate the plan to make a hybrid and personalized final one. The recommendations focus on the teachers' aspiration for continuous self-advancement of AI literacy, yet they should employ AI-offered content cautiously to ensure students' accuracy and suitability.

Keywords AI-power tools · Lesson planning · Novice teachers · Lesson design

N. T. Sa (✉) · H. N. Q. Nhu · V. N. Sinh · D. M. Hue
Industrial University of Ho Chi Minh City, Ho Chi Minh City, Vietnam
e-mail: nguyentruongsa@iuh.edu.vn

H. N. Q. Nhu
e-mail: hoangngocquynhnhu@iuh.edu.vn

V. N. Sinh
e-mail: vonhatsinh@iuh.edu.vn

D. M. Hue
e-mail: doanminhhue@iuh.edu.vn

V. P. H. Pham et al. (eds.), *Empowering Educators: Integrating AI Tools for Personalized Language Instruction*, Studies in Computational Intelligence 1228,
https://doi.org/10.1007/978-3-032-01348-4_8

1 Introduction

1.1 Rationale

Lesson planning is crucial to teaching as a well-planned lesson enables the teacher, especially the novice ones, to predict solutions for possible class issues, increasing his/her confidence, professionalism, and the lesson's appeal. Along with the development of technology in the field of English language teaching (ELT), Artificial Intelligence (AI) is emerging as a highly potential tool that may support not only the effectiveness of lesson planning but also the gathering and preparation of teaching aids as well as materials. Previous studies have revealed the benefits AI-powered tools can yield to EFL teachers' lesson planning, such as the work done by Van den Berg and Plessis (2023), which indicated that models like ChatGPT have the capacity to supply materials and assist mechanisms, such as lesson plans, to teachers. Not only that, Kehoe (2023) discussed in his study on Generative Tools for Enhanced Lesson Planning that through the detailed objectives and requirements keyed in by teachers, such AI applications can generate efficient lesson plans and subject plans, supporting the teaching practitioners in an evidently critical task. Being aware of the prospects, this study seeks to investigate the approaches that novice English as a foreign language (EFL) teachers can take advantage of the benefits of the available AI-powered tools to enhance the quality of lesson planning for their teaching practice.

In our research work, we aimed to obtain reports from novice teachers about the current manners they were adopting AI-powered tools in their lesson planning, their insights on the benefits and drawbacks of making use of these tools, and what they expected as actions to be taken to ensure that the technologies would offer a positive impact. Accordingly, suggestions from the teachers were collected and analyzed to see what they expected to make the best use of AI-power tools for planning their lessons.

1.2 Research Objectives

The ultimate goal of this study was to suggest possible strategies to use AI-powered tools to help with lesson planning for novice teachers. To fulfill that, our first research objective was to identify how novice EFL teachers are using AI-powered tools in lesson planning. Secondly, we intended to examine the self-evaluated effects of these tools on their lesson planning. Lastly, we would consider their recommendations of what should be done to enhance their effectiveness in lesson planning with AI assistance.

1.3 Research Questions

Based on the aforementioned research objectives, the research questions to be addressed in this study were:

- How are novice EFL teachers employing AI-powered tools in their lesson planning?
- What are the perceived effects that AI-powered tools are having on the process?
- What are the teachers' recommendations for the employment of AI-powered tools in lesson planning?

2 Literature Review

2.1 Lesson Planning and Novice Teachers

Enow and Goodwyn (2018) defined lesson planning as "the design of learning for groups of students". Lesson planning is of paramount significance in teaching as it provides a structured framework that outlines educational objectives, teaching methods, and assessment strategies, serving as a roadmap for teachers to follow (Van den Berg & Du Plessis, 2023). To be more specific, it specifies what students are expected to learn and how the teaching and learning process will be organized (Moundridou et al., 2024). However, this is a demanding and time-consuming duty as in order to develop detailed and effective lesson plans, teachers must equip themselves with pedagogical skills, critical thinking, and adaptability. Higton et al. (2017) underscore that non-teaching tasks, such as lesson planning, require teachers' time and effort.

According to Enow and Goodwyn (2018), lesson planning may be characterized as "very visible" for novices but "invisible" for expert teachers as it closely relates to experimental improvisation that draws on deeply internalized cases and situations of previously successful learning designs. Meanwhile, novice teachers are those who are newly qualified and have zero to less than 5 years of experience in their profession (Makoa & Segalo, 2021), someone who is entering a new teaching culture and practice, and they teach the students for the first time (Septiani et al., 2019). At the novice stage of the career, from the argument of Mutton et al. (2011), the teachers are still experimenting with theoretical knowledge. Shulman (2013) and Gitomer and Zisk (2015) added that novice teachers still continue to consolidate and experiment with subject content knowledge with different dimensions of pedagogical knowledge. Enow and Goodwyn (2018) noted that this process tends to be rather mechanistic and inflexible. Therefore, lesson planning is particularly vital, and poor planning or deviation from the plan is extremely threatening to the teaching. However, According to Ab Aziz et al. (2019), many novice teachers failed to prepare lesson plans due to being burdened with school non-teaching tasks. Besides, time-consuming is another issue emphasized in studies such as Akcan (2016), Saad and Dawson (2018) and Faqe

Abdulla (2024). It is common for them to feel overwhelmed with a high volume of lesson plans that they have to prepare before classes, leading to inadequate and ineffective lesson plans. Hence, a new technology to confront these issues is crucial in supporting novice teachers specifically with lesson planning (Fathil et al., 2021).

In short, lesson planning has been found to be a crucial but challenging task for novices; these causes may lead to their need for assistance when preparing for their teaching. When support from more experienced teachers are not always available, AI appears to be a 24 hours per day partner for novice teachers to engage with.

2.2 AI to Support Lesson Planning

AI is defined as a subfield of computer science focused on understanding human thought processes and replicating their effects through information systems (Hashem et al., 2024; Wang et al., 2024). AI-powered tools (or AI tools for short) are the AI that is not only utilized to analyze students' performance, engagement, and challenges, personalize their learning pathways, but also reduce the burden on teachers by streamlining their lesson planning and automating their administrative tasks (Kehoe, 2023; Van den Berg & Du Plessis, 2023; Nguyen et al., 2025; Pham & Cao, 2025). Kehoe (2023) points out that Chat GPT enables rapid content generation and quickly develops lesson plans. Additionally, ChatGPT or Google Bard enhances resource accessibility by providing a variety of educational references to plan a lesson. With the assistance of ChatGPT, a teacher can gauge prompts with specificity, variability, and drawbacks in lesson plan development (Dornburg & Davin, 2024). The results of Dornburg and Davin (2024) indicated that ChatGPT can increase the detailedness of instructions, reduce output variance, and generate a number of useful suggestions. Teachers can also submit their lesson plans for quality and effectiveness feedback (Van den Berg & Du Plessis, 2023). However, it is essential for teachers to critically evaluate the generated content for accuracy and relevance. In a recent study by Pahmi and Syafwin (2022), AI's features incorporated in Capcut and Canva can significantly enhance instructional planning. With Capcut, teachers can make instructional videos that are engaging and easily understandable for students. Additionally, Capcut's audio caption function automatically generates captions for video by recognizing spoken words and transcribing them into text. This is especially useful for both teachers and students. Meanwhile, Canva allows teachers to design a variety of educational resources, from images and posters to lesson plans, presentations, and student handouts, using Magic Write and Magic Design features. In Dornburg and Davin's (2024) study, 10 teachers were requested to use the Argumate chatbot to create lesson plans for teaching argumentative writing. Upon completion, the findings depicted that there were a variety of options teachers could select to plan with the employment of the chatbot. Also, in 2024, Kacso and Huszti found that the chatbot MagicSchool could study individual student data on learning styles, strengths, and weaknesses and support personalized learning. It was also found that this technology offered automated content creation. It could teach the provided objectives and supply teachers with abundant interactive activities, quizzes, and worksheets suited to varied proficiency levels.

So far, researchers have been paying close attention to teachers and educators, especially the arts and more experienced ones', use of powerful tools in lesson planning and development. Given the earlier discussed challenges of novices, it is significant to study more deeply their strategies for adopting powerful tools when developing a lesson plan and their perceptions of the effectiveness of such employment.

3 Research Design

Mixed-method research was employed to investigate the current issues of lesson planning and the effectiveness of using AI technology to support novice teachers' work. Both quantitative and qualitative data were collected and analyzed to increase the reliability of the study.

The study involved 40 novice Vietnamese teachers of English with less than 3 years of experience in teaching English. 34 of the participants were ages ranging from 23 to 25; 6 of them were a little bit older (30–35 years old), but they were also new to English teaching. At the time of the current study, all participants are working at private and public schools teaching Children English, General English, exam preparation, and English for Basic Communication courses in Ho Chi Minh City, Vietnam.

Two research tools—questionnaires and semi-structured interviews—were exploited to answer the research questions. After crafting a questionnaire based on key issues discussed in the literature, the researchers revised and validated the tool by piloting it with some novice teachers and asking for comments from 2 experts in educational research. The finalized version consists of 15 open and closed questions with 3 parts.

- Part 1: Six questions about participants' background information, such as teaching experience (time, learners' age, teaching programs), lesson habits, and lesson planning strategies.
- Part 2: The part is entitled Popular AI tools being employed by the participants.
- Part 3: This section consists of feedback on the positive and negative effects of AI tools and suggestions on how to best use these tools in lesson planning.

The questionnaire was then sent out to novice teachers of English from different schools in Ho Chi Minh City and 40 responses were submitted. While scanning the feedback, the researchers randomly chose 5 respondents who gave informative and/or interesting responses from the questionnaire to invite to join in-depth interviews. Afterward, semi-structured interviews were held to get in-depth information from the participants about the benefits and challenges when using AI tools in lesson planning. The participants were interviewed individually in order to ensure their responses were objective and independent. The collected quantitative data were then counted and analyzed using Microsoft Excel, and the interview data was read and investigated using a content analysis strategy in qualitative research.

4 Findings and Discussion

4.1 How Novice EFL Teachers Are Employing AI-Powered Tools for Lesson-Planning

In checking whether the participants were spending many attempts on lesson planning, the results showed that the majority of them (52.5%) devoted sufficient time and effort in the selection and utilization of various content from sources for their lessons. 17.5% of the participants said they struggled structuring the lesson and selecting contents to use and teach. Interestingly, the remaining 30% admitted that they depended excessively on the teachers' book guidance rather than investing more time in instructional planning. The findings suggest that most beginner teachers do make much effort to search for and apply suitable teaching materials for their teaching. This finding aligns with the arguments of Akcan (2016), Higton et al. (2017), and Saad and Dawson (2018), highlighting that lesson planning requires a significant amount of time and effort from novice teachers.

When asking for the popular challenges faced when planning lessons, the most chosen difficulties were "lacking creative ideas and engaging activities" (65%), adapting teaching materials (50%), "time constraint" (47.5%), and "limited resources" (40%). This echoes the challenges put forward in Akcan (2016) and Faqe Abdulla's (2024) findings, which found that it takes time for novice teachers to produce lesson plans as they have difficulty in selecting, structuring appropriate activities, and adapting instructional materials to meet classroom dynamics and students' diverse levels. Similarly, Emiliasari (2019) reported that learning resources and time allocation are noteworthy causes of impediment to designing a lesson plan. Therefore, according to a response that was widely agreed upon by the participants, "employing AI becomes our best solution to deal with such constraints."

As shown in Fig. 1, from a total of 40 responses to the suggested and given names of AI tools, it was transparent that the novice teachers were aware of and made good use of AI-powered tools in their lesson planning. The respondents employed various tools, namely ChatGPT, Midjourney, Google Bard, SlidesAI, CapCut, Canva, Dalle 2, and Grammarly. ChatGPT, Canva, and Grammarly, which have distinct functions, stand out as the most prominent choices. In the interviews, some other AI tools mentioned and also recommended by some teachers were Apple Siri, Google Assistant, Gamma, Gemini, Magic School, Natural Reader, POE, Vennage, and Eduaide. The most frequently chosen AI among them were Google Assistant, Canva, ChatGPT, and Grammarly.

For the purposes of employing AI, Fig. 2 shows that the most popular reported purposes were generating examples (72.5%) and generating ideas for classroom

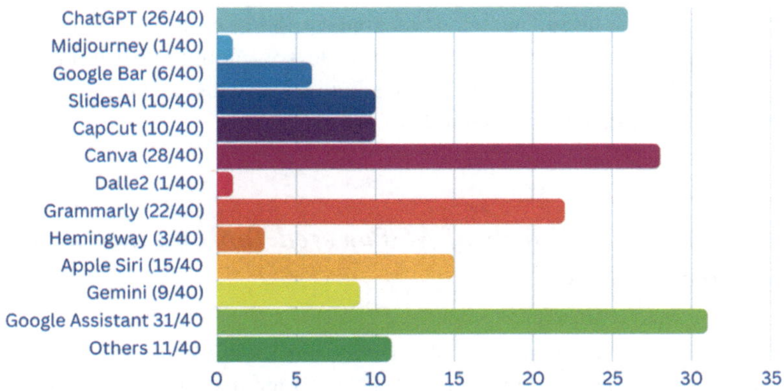

Fig. 1 AI-powered tools employed by the novice teachers for lesson planning

activities and games (67.5%). This purpose is closely followed by media item creation such as making movement for objects and illustrations (62.5%), creating images, PowerPoint slides, videos, and flashcards (55%), substitutes (50%), and sketching lesson plans from textbook content (47.5%). Meanwhile, personalizing and differentiating learning activities and creating lesson plans from scratch came only with 35% and 17.5% respectively. A small number of the teachers employed AI tools for sounding/voicing and other purposes. It can be inferred from the data that AI was used to support the teachers' creation of the lesson content and activity design more than replacing the teachers' role in forming general objectives and developing main procedures for the lessons.

In the interviews, the participants also confirmed the employment of AI tools and gave more specifics on the teaching/learning activities that AI tools can help. Accordingly, the most common choices among the teachers were creating flashcards, pictures, or videos, assisting with error correction, generating teaching aids, giving examples and supplements, designing quizzes and games, creating sample texts, developing drills, infographics, and diagrams, and giving prompts. The teachers noted that "AI almost can support in a variety of teaching goals and contexts," whether

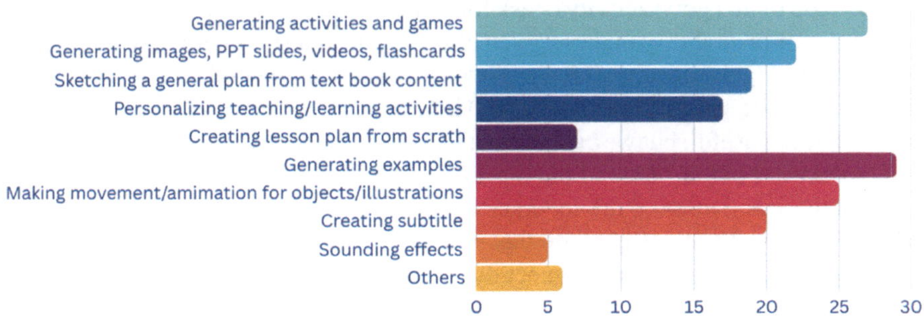

Fig. 2 Popular purposes of employing AI for lesson planning

they prepared to teach linguistic items (vocabulary and/or grammar), language macro skills, test preparation, or simply organizing fee lessons/activities in children English hours. They added, "As AI is a tool, any teacher can adopt as a 'productive' assistant for any teaching approach and method."

4.2 *The Perceived Effects of AI-Powered Tools on the Lesson Planning Process*

Figure 3 illustrates the advantages of AI-powered tools for novice teachers when planning lessons. Most of the teachers (31/40) reported that they always got different support and resources from different tools. Although any of their first plans always had a tailored look as it was a combination of different activities and visual aids created by the teachers and different AI tools, the rich resources made them "feel pleased and the lesson would be more unique." However, they would need some more time to reconsolidate the first-crafted plans. In the interviews, some teachers even claimed that they reallocated each activity's time slot. Similarly, with the support of AI tools, the layout and template were not aligned with the typical requirements of their schools and institutions. Therefore, in most cases, the final plans were a hybrid result developed by both AI and humans. Ultimately, their lesson plans became extremely unique and personalized. Next, more than half of them found the suggested activities or games were interesting and relevant to be employed, and there was no need for more adaptation. Such activities, as admitted, had created a funny and positive mood in their lessons. 18 out of 40 teachers (45%) believed that AI tools are also really supportive in proofreading, making the lesson plan error-free in terms of grammar and word use, and helping their English more standard. Interestingly, some other effects in the questionnaire received very much lower evaluations from the teachers. For example, the number of teachers who thought that AI tools were able to identify learners' common backgrounds and references and accordingly generate relevant teaching and learning materials was 30% (12 teachers). Only 22.5% of them believed that they could learn something and improve their creativity from the AI-created activities. They claimed, "If I had more time to prepare the lesson, I might also develop of that good activity or ask for some good advices from teachers". As the percentage of favorability in these given effects in the questionnaire was not too high when explaining this result, all 5 interviewees stated that they felt unsure about their confidence in the activities generated by AI. As stated by interviewee No. 5, "we have to use, they are useful, but we cannot trust their results and use the activities or games with no more revision." One of the biggest concerns shared among the interviewees was that these activities could not create a plan to meet different learning styles and needs. This insight seems to share the argument of Boughaddou and Chorfi (2024) that AI technology often fails to meet different learners' needs.

Interestingly, as shown in Fig. 4, the planning process would become even more time-consuming if the quality of their prompts was not clear and well-oriented

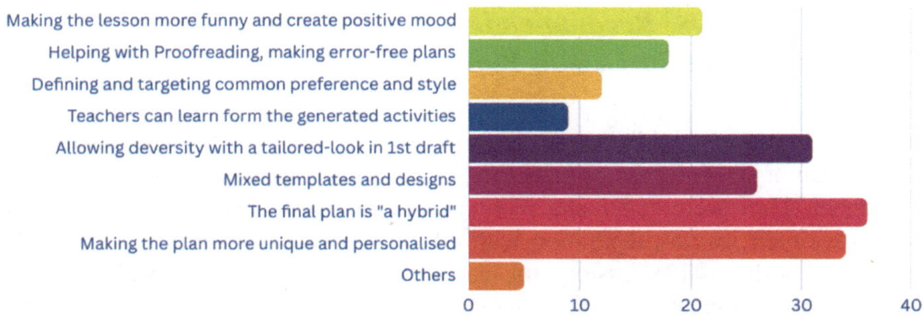

Fig. 3 Some positive effects of AI tools on lesson plans and planning process

enough. This idea was shared among 27 out of 40 teachers. Some of them admitted that useless and/or need-further-revision plans may also come from their own skills of handling and giving prompts to the AI tools. It will take more time than looking for games or images from Google if they do not master the tool usage and give detailed and exact prompts. Then, AI might also be troublesome for AI-novice teachers. Other negative issues of AI that were admitted and reported by teachers were killing teacher creativity development and AI over-reliance. These kinds of possible negative effects were once noted by Hastomo et al. (2024), who found that most teachers claimed that AI tools made them lazier and totally dependent. It is also noticeable that 35% of participants expressed concern that AI-based supplementary visuals occasionally fail to meet expected standards, and finally 22.5% shared that classroom activities suggested by AI are sometimes unsuitable or awkward to students that they refuse to participate. Some of them stated that the illustrations sometimes contained irrelevant items and content that may distract the students. The data revealed in this part is again comparable to that from the work of Boughaddou and Chorfi (2024), which found that the use of AI-powered tools may occasionally fail to satisfy diverse learners' needs and impede teachers' involvement in lesson planning and teaching. Water-marked and too many distracting items in the products created by AI tools were sometimes problematic to the teacher.

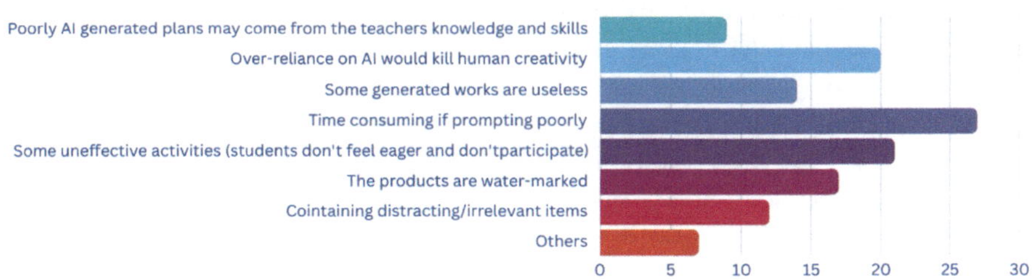

Fig. 4 Reported negative effects of AI tools and AI-generated lesson plans

4.3 *The Teachers' Recommendations on AI-Powered Employment for Lesson Planning*

Believing that AI is a highly beneficial tool when used carefully, the teachers recommended that organizations formulate their AI policies to guide implementation and investment. They were eager and willing to be involved deeper in learning how to improve their lesson preparation with AI. A significant portion of them (57%) approved that discussion sessions for teachers to share experiences and strategies would do them wonders. Regular hands-on training, supported by 55% of novice teachers, is crucial to build confidence and competence in utilizing AI. One key point suggested by teachers is that training courses should not only teach effective AI utilization but also address potential risks and the fact that AI can replace teachers in the near future. Many of them proposed schools equip classrooms with adequate facilities as they believed that it would encourage them to use technology and AI more in their teaching. Half of the participants recommended that "schools should subsidize the finance for the subscription of certain AI tools to allow teachers to use all of their functions," enabling teachers to exploit the tools' full potential.

Figure 5 shows a comparison of different ways teachers should consider harnessing their AI-powered tools to streamline their lesson planning. The majority, 87.5% of the participants, emphasized the importance of "carefully checking the suitability level of AI-based ideas and materials before planning and applying them in their lessons" and attached great importance to ensuring the validity and quality of the content recommended. A considerable number of respondents (85%) indicated that "Teachers should combine the suggestions of AI with their own teaching ideas," and the necessity of teachers' involvement in making an engaging and relevant lesson was recognized. Interestingly, only 42.5% (17 of the respondents) agreed with the suggestions to "self-practice and enhance self-familiarity with AI. "In explaining this, the responses were that they needed to be officially trained first as AI training was not one of their modules at teacher training schools; none of their workplaces provided such training either. Finally, only 14 educators think they should actively seek help and discuss with others on using AI for lesson planning suggests teachers' preference toward figuring out AI tools on their own rather than relying on external help or discussions. Meanwhile, 17 believed that the teacher should care about students' feedback and demand AI-created materials.

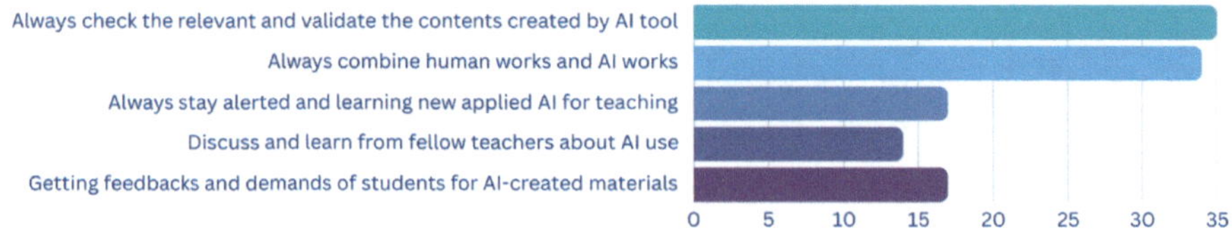

Fig. 5 Recommendations on the novice teachers

5 Conclusion

This study has explored educators' perspectives, particularly novice teachers, on how they utilize AI-powered tools to streamline the lesson planning process. The findings revealed valuable insights into how these teachers make use of AI tools, namely the purposes for which they typically employ them, the AI tools they are likely to lean on, perceived benefits and drawbacks, and their recommendations for better employment. Teachers highlighted the platforms' capabilities to generate games and create visual teaching materials that support engaging and interactive lessons based on teachers' ideas and prompts. These features allow teachers to create diverse resources tailored to different learner needs and make their lessons become hybrid and more personalized. Moreover, they consistently verify the suitability of AI-generated products as they are yet certain of AI's accuracy and capabilities. However, some teachers show concerns about over-reliance on AI tools, the need for digital literacy, and the financial burden of subscription fees required to access full functionality. The findings suggest that educational institutions should offer hands-on training courses on effective AI utilization as well as some potential risks of overreliance on AI tools to optimize their usefulness.

The current study could not evaluate the effectiveness of AI-made lesson plans by observing how the teachers teach their classes; this evaluation will provide a further perspective on the implementation step of the plans. Moreover, future research could examine the long-term impact of these tools on teaching quality and explore strategies for overcoming challenges. Further studies may also focus on the rapid evolution of AI tools and the challenges this poses for teachers. Examining whether the rapid development of AI hinders or enhances their teaching practices would provide valuable insights for sustainable AI integration in education.

References

Ab Aziz, A. A., Swanto, S., & Azhar, S. B. H. J. (2019). Coping with stress: Exploring the lived experiences of English teachers who persist in Malaysian rural schools. *Indonesian Journal of Applied Linguistics, 8*(3), 506–514.

Akcan, S. (2016). Novice non-native English teachers' reflections on their teacher education programmes and their first years of teaching. *Issues in Teachers' Professional Development, 18(1),* 55–70. https://doi.org/10.15446/profile.v18n1.48608

Boughaddou, H., & Chorfi, K. I. (2024). Exploring middle school English teachers' and inspectors perceptions of using AI tools as lesson planning resources in the city of Tiaret (Doctoral dissertation, Ibn Khaldoun University of Tiaret).

Dornburg, A., & Davin, K. J. (2024). ChatGPT in foreign language lesson plan creation: Trends, variability, and historical biases. *ReCALL, 1*–16.

Emiliasari, R. N. (2019). Lesson planning in EFL classroom: A case study in lesson plan preparation and implementation. *Wiralodra English Journal (WEJ), 3*(2), 367–375.

Enow, L., & Goodwyn, A. (2018). The invisible plan: How English teachers develop their expertise and the special place of adapting the skills of lesson planning. *English in Education, 52*(2), 120–134. https://doi.org/10.1080/04250494.2018.1438119

Faqe Abdulla, B. I. (2024). Analyzing the structure and effectiveness of lesson plans for pre-service English language teachers. *International Journal of English Learning and Applied Linguistics (IJELAL), 4*(2), 143–162.

Fathil, F. M., Ziden, A. A., & Osman, S. Z. M. (2021). Lesson planning practices and lesson planning system design preferences among novice ESL teachers. *Journal of Educational Research & Indigenous Studies, 3*(1), 170–184.

Gitomer, D. H., & Zisk, R. C. (2015). Knowing what teachers know. *Review of Research in Education, 39*, 1–53.

Hastomo, T., Mandasari, B., & Widiati, U. (2024). Scrutinizing Indonesian pre-service teachers' technological knowledge in utilizing AI-powered tools. *Journal of Education and Learning (EduLearn), 18(4),* 1572–1581. https://doi.org/10.11591/edulearn.v18i4.21644

Hashem, R., Ali, N., El Zein, F., Fidalgo, P., & Abu Khurma, O. (2024). AI to the rescue: Exploring the potential of ChatGPT as a teacher ally for workload relief and burnout prevention. *Research and Practice in Technology Enhanced Learning, 19,* 023. https://doi.org/10.58459/rptel.2024.19023

Higton, J., Leonardi, S., Richards, N., Choudhury, A., Sofroniou, N., & Owen, D. (2017). *Teacher workload survey 2016: Research report.* Department for Education. https://warwick.ac.uk/fac/soc/ier/people/dowen/publications/tws_2016_final_research_report_feb_2017.pdf

Kehoe, F. (2023). Leveraging generative AI tools for enhanced lesson planning in initial teacher education at post primary. *Irish Journal of Technology Enhanced Learning, 7*(2), 172–182.

Makoa, M. M., & Segalo, L. J. (2021). Novice teachers' experiences of challenges of their professional development. *International Journal of Innovation, Creativity and Change, 15*(10), 930–942.

Moundridou, M., Matzakos, N., & Doukakis, S. (2024). Generative AI tools as educators' assistants: Designing and implementing inquiry-based lesson plans. *Computers and Education: Artificial Intelligence, 7,* Article 100277. https://doi.org/10.1016/j.caeai.2024.100277

Mutton, T., Hagger, H., & Burn, K. (2011). Learning to plan, planning to learn: The developing expertise of beginning teachers. *Teachers and Teaching, 17*, 399–416.

Nguyen, T. Y. P., Nguyen, N. T., & Phan, N. K. H. (2025). The challenges of applying ChatGPT in the academic writing of postgraduate students in English Major at IUH. *International Journal of AI in Language Education, 2*(1), 20–27. https://doi.org/10.54855/ijaile.25212

Pahmi, L. D., & Syafwin, M. (2022). Using the Capcut Application as a learning media. *Journal International Inspire Education Technology, 1*(1), 40–51.

Pham, M. T., & Cao, T. X. T. (2025). The practice of ChatGPT in English teaching and learning in Vietnam: A systematic review. *International Journal of TESOL & Education, 5*(1), 50–70. https://doi.org/10.54855/ijte.25513

Saad, A., & Dawson, C. (2018). Requirement elicitation techniques for an improved case-based lesson planning system. *Journal of Systems and Information Technology, 20*(1), 19–32. https://doi.org/10.1108/JSIT-12-2016-0080

Septiani, A., Emiliasari, R. N., & Rofi'i, A. (2019). The novice English teachers' experience: Practices and challenges. *Academic Journal PERSPECTIVE: Language, Education and Literature, 7(2),* 45–54. https://doi.org/10.33603/perspective.v7i2.2708

Shulman, L. (2013). Those who understand: Knowledge growth in teaching. *Journal of Education - Boston University School of Education, 193*, 1–12.

Van den Berg, G., & Du Plessis, E. (2023). ChatGPT and generative AI: Possibilities for its contribution to lesson planning, critical thinking and openness in teacher education. *Education Sciences, 13*(10), 998.

Wang, S., Wang, F., Zhu, Z., Wang, J., Tran, T., & Du, Z. (2024). Artificial intelligence in education: A systematic literature review. *Expert Systems with Applications, 252*, Article 124167.

AI-Enhanced Language Learning Skills and Practices

Teachers' Perspectives on Employing Diffit for AI-Assisted EFL Reading Tasks

Thi Luong Nguyen and Hai Linh Nguyen

Abstract The incorporation of AI in education has revolutionised teaching practices by providing tools to reduce workload and enhance task diversity. In Vietnam, the utilisation of AI in language education is capturing educators' attention and offering significant potential to innovate task creation. Among these tools, Diffit stands out as a particularly user-friendly and efficient option for teachers to automatically create reading quizzes. However, little research has been conducted to explore teachers' perspectives on its benefits and challenges in practical use. This study investigates the attitudes of 18 EFL teachers at a university in Hanoi towards utilizing Diffit in their reading lessons. The study employed a mixed-methods approach, including pre and post intervention online surveys to examine shifts in teacher's perceptions and semi-structured interviews with 8 teachers to gather deeper insights. The findings indicated that teachers generally hold positive attitudes towards Diffit in generating reading quizzes, while also highlighting some challenges in its implication. This paper offers practical implications for exploiting AI-driven tools, especially Diffit to improve teaching effectiveness.

Keywords AI · ESL/EFL teaching · Diffit · Reading quizzes · Teacher perspectives

1 Introduction

AI in Education has become one of the important innovations that help faculty in improving efficiency, making lessons personalized, and decreasing the burden of work on instructors. On the applications of intelligence learning in language education, the following has manifested the capability of showing grip on some of

T. L. Nguyen (✉) · H. L. Nguyen
FPT University, Hanoi, Vietnam
e-mail: luongnt22@fpt.edu.vn

H. L. Nguyen
e-mail: linhnh80@fpt.edu.vn

V. P. H. Pham et al. (eds.), *Empowering Educators: Integrating AI Tools for Personalized Language Instruction*, Studies in Computational Intelligence 1228,
https://doi.org/10.1007/978-3-032-01348-4_9

the challenges are as follows; AI can help in automating tedious tasks like lesson plan preparing, questions setting and developing suitable course content (Russell & Norvig, 2016; Shin, 2018). These tools allow the teachers to concentrate on higher order teaching methodologies without compromising the quality of the support learners receive. As highlighted by Liang et al. (2021), the ability of AI is in the fact that it can tailor learning activities for every learner, which in turn supports exemplary students' performance. Furthermore, Siyam et al. (2022) emphasized the role of AI in empowering teachers with innovative teaching methodologies, creating dynamic and engaging learning environments.

In Vietnam, the increasing need for English competency has put great pressure on the educational system to provide top-notch instruction suited to different student demands. Lately, this situation has sparked a growing interest among teachers who are keen on trying out AI tools like ChatGPT and other AI platforms to make the language learning process more engaging. These tools are gradually finding their place in EFL classrooms as teachers have discovered how they can shake up traditional teaching and give their students a real boost. Recent studies, for example, suggest that teachers' utilization of the tools not only helps students learn more and better but also sharpens their language skills with the lessons tailored to their needs, which thereby takes some pressure off teachers (Hieu & Thao, 2024; Pham et al., 2024).

While some educators are concerned about AI's possible limits on creativity, others argue that AI technology may stimulate creative engagement and critical thinking among students (Pham & Le, 2024). According to Hieu and Thao (2024), this integration enables the teachers to embrace technological influences in their practice thus bringing about professional change. Given that technology plays a paramount role in contemporary educational processes, the integration of AI is approved and adopted by educators of EFL settings. For instance, Duong et al. (2024) and Nguyen et al., (2024a, 2024b) have highlighted the effective application of AI tools, such as The Language Hub System, in vocational education, which demonstrates their ability to enhance both student engagement and teaching efficiency. As educators actively seek to incorporate AI tools into their curricula, they focus on optimizing learning experiences through innovative language instruction and personalized learning approaches (Pham et al., 2024). Besides, the application of AI, that is revolutionizing normal instructional techniques and changing teaching abilities, forces teachers to change their roles and instructional methods to reflect these innovations (Pham & Le, 2024).

However, while these advances allow teachers to gain increased access to valuable informational resources, there is a dearth of knowledge concerning how these technologies are viewed by teachers, as well as how they are incorporated into the classroom curriculum. It is, therefore, important to note that to make the effective usage of AI tools in learning achievable teachers should be understood. Teachers' attitudes, as well as the challenges they face, play a pivotal role in determining the effectiveness of AI adoption in classrooms (Kaplan-Rakowski & Grotewold, 2023). Since technology is ubiquitously present in classrooms nowadays, it has become necessary to investigate these opinions to define how the gap between technology possibilities and classroom applications can be eliminated.

Of these AI tools, Diffit, is designed to auto-generate reading quizzes. With its user-friendly interface and ability to create tasks tailored to different proficiency levels, Diffit has emerged as a valuable resource for EFL educators. It fulfills an important demand for individualized teaching and assists teachers in facilitating comprehensible and functional reading assignments. Nevertheless, it is agreed that while Diffit holds great promise and shows a great potential for practical application in the context of teaching, the available knowledge regarding its implementation into teaching practices remains quite scarce. Through examining the opinions of EFL teachers from a university in Hanoi about the implementation of Diffit into the context of reading lessons, the study provides implications for beneficial integration of AI-based technologies into language learning context. Ultimately, it contributes to the accumulating literature on AI in education and offers guidance regarding the application of AI in EFL instruction.

2 Literature Review

2.1 AI in EFL Education

The integration of AI technologies in EFL learning has come to be the revolution in techniques of teaching offer as well as meaning in learning experiences. Scholars such as Konar (2018) argue that AI has transformed teaching as a result of implementing a flexible, statistical, and customized approach to instruction in addressing a range of the learner's needs. This corresponds to the study by Katsarou et al. (2023) focused on intelligent and automated instructional technologies such as intelligent tutoring systems and chatbots in the context of L2 academic vocabulary and found that such technologies may help facilitate enhanced language competence, motivation and the students' interest.

AI technologies have a critical engagement in structuring specific learning paths, efficient differentiation to the learners, and the multiple problems of low language proficiency. Russell and Norvig (2016) have identified that EFL learners get into certain difficulties with complicated linguistic features and different ability levels; However, AI enables solutions for the speedy accomplishment through qualitative presentation. The advanced technologies such as natural language processing (NLP) applied in the Grammarly, Duolingo, Rosetta Stone type of tools offer evidence based real time feedback on grammar, vocabulary, and pronunciation (Deng & Yu, 2023). These platforms have been a success in teaching specific aspects of language for example writing and the use of vocabulary. These claims are corroborated by studies of Song and Song (2023) and Wang et al. (2023) that showed the benefits of both AI-assisted instruction on writing quality motivation and overall language skills as a result from the provided feedback and direction. Furthermore, in the study by Hoang et al. (2023), chatbots and virtual agents are also described as enhancing real-life conversational practice, which, in turn, enhances the speaking and comprehension skills in real-life situations.

The automation of learning task creation represents another significant advantage of AI. Some of the studies brought into light how tools such as GPT-3 reduces time and effort from teachers in developing reading comprehension quizzes that it assists in. For instance, Lelkes et al. (2021) and Khan et al. (2021) argue that such tools can produce good quality questions, right solutions, as well as reasonable wrong options; this feature makes such quizzes invaluable in EFL context given that quizzes can offer critical practice in this language proficiency area. Previous models for generating quizzes were rule-based only but, as Dijkstra et al., (2022) explain, neural and transformer-based methods have enhanced the difficulty and precision of such questions. Such platforms like Quillionz or EduQuiz are actual examples of such developments, performing the actions of tasks creating, thus freeing more time for open, non-traditional, effective teaching in classes (Nguyen et al., 2024a, 2024b). Moreover, AI has been shown to boost learner engagement and motivation by incorporating gamified activities, multimedia modules, and simulations.

Concerns about the accuracy of AI-generated content also persist. Errors in grammar, cultural appropriateness, and alignment with pedagogical goals can detract from the effectiveness of AI tools. Salameh (2024) highlights such issues, particularly in the context of generating meaningful distractors for comprehension tasks.

2.2 *Teaching Reading Skills in EFL Classrooms*

When it comes to EFL education, reading skills are crucial for language acquisition because of their framework for students' total language ability. Mastering reading skills not only enhances students' comprehension, vocabulary, and grammar, but also offers students chances to be exposed to culture, which are essential elements of second language learning. Nowadays, teaching reading skills in EFL classrooms requires a combination of various strategies and methods to improve students' comprehension, engagement and also their overall reading proficiency. To date, several studies have investigated multiple effective approaches to enhance these skills. For example, Sanjaya et al. (2014) report that teachers often combine multiple methods to teach reading skills, such as the Grammar Translation Method, Direct Method, and Communicative Language Teaching (CLT), which can help address the varied needs of EFL learners. Besides, one study by Lestari (2017) examines the critical reading development in EFL lessons. It claimed that teaching critical reading is essential because students are exposed to a vast amount of reading material, which encourages students to analyze and evaluate texts, enhancing their comprehension and analytical skills. Unlike Lestari, Hermagustiana (2017) argues that integrating vocabulary teaching into reading lessons is crucial for improving comprehension, in which teachers employ various strategies like explicit and implicit vocabulary instruction to enhance students' understanding of texts and their vocabulary retention. Another reading teaching strategy is examined by Pornita et al. (2023) who shows that the reciprocal teaching strategy including steps like predicting, questioning, clarifying and summarizing has proven effective in improving students' reading skills as it increases student participation and enhances comprehension.

In recent years, AI has stepped in to improve teachers' reading teaching process. AI-driven tools, namely adaptive learning platforms and intelligent tutoring systems, are often used to provide personalized learning experiences to meet each student's needs. He (2024) and De Kumang et al. (2024) claim that AI can significantly boost students' reading comprehension by adapting content to match their proficiency level, on top of which real-time feedback is also provided to increase students' engagement and enable their efficient learning. Such tools are particularly beneficial for students with distinct needs, since they bring flexible and easy-to-access learning experiences (Jafarian & Kramer, 2025). Thanks to AI's ability to create personalized and captivating content, teachers can fire up students' excitement for reading, which in turn lifts their academic results.

2.3 Teachers' Perceptions of AI Integration in EFL Education

EFL teachers have noticed a large number of benefits from utilizing AI tools, particularly in terms of lowering workloads for them and increasing their effective teaching methods. For instance, recent research by Zhou and Hou (2025) concludes that AI applications are helpful in automating the creation of teaching materials, handling grading, and promoting students' classroom engagement. Likewise, recent analysis of Hazaymeh et al. (2024) claim that AI tools are beneficial for teachers to tailor their instruction and modify their methods as necessary thanks to the tools' data-driven insights into student performance. Additionally, AI tools have proven themselves that they can step up the quality of students' writing by offering immediate and constructive feedback on content and structure. Widiati et al. (2023), for example, point that AI writing assistants can help students better organize their ideas and coherence of their work which are essential for their language development.

Although AI has many promising benefits in EFL education, it is obviously associated with some challenges which teachers need to tackle. One of the key obstacles is the lack of proper technical support and professional training, which according to Zhou and Hou (2025) holds back AI tools' effectiveness. Commenting on this, they argue that many teachers express a need for more comprehensive training to tap into the full potential of the technology in their teaching practices. Moreover, in a recent study, Özkan et al. (2024) express concerns regarding students' misuse of them for cheating and plagiarism because students may dishonestly exploit AI tools in their assignments. In the same vein, a study by Parviz (2024) involves another concern about AI's impact on students' mental development, including their emotional growth and critical thinking skills. The research indicates teachers worry

Table 1 EFL teachers' perceptions of AI-assisted reading tasks from some recent research

Study	Sample size	AI tool	Acceptance rate of AI suggestions	Perceived benefits	Perceived limitations
Xin (2024)	3 teachers	ChatPDF	10–62.5%	Prompt text modification, task design, pedagogical insights	Inability to interpret multimodal elements, occasional unreliable answers
Nguyen et al., (2024a, 2024b)	48 teachers	Quillionz	Undefined	Positive views on AI-generated quizzes, potential for enhancing student learning experiences	Need for more effective implementation strategies
Hazaymeh et al. (2024)	46 instructors	Various AI apps	Undefined	Personalized feedback, adaptive learning, increased engagement	Challenges in implementation, need for professional training

that students' being dependent on AI may negatively influence their ability to think critically and creatively.

The successful blending of AI into EFL lessons depends on several factors like the support and resources provided by institutions. If teachers receive access to technical help and good training, they are more likely to integrate AI tools effectively into their teaching routines (Pratama et al., 2024; Zhou et al., 2024). Also, teachers' personal attitudes towards technology play a critical role. For instance, the more teachers welcome new technologies, the more readily they embrace AI tools. Those, on the other hand, with doubting opinions may take a more careful approach to applying it into their classrooms (Zhou et al., 2024) (Table 1).

2.4 *Diffit and Task Automation*

Recently, EFL teachers have shown considerable interest in AI tools for its ability in task automation. To illustrate this, a mixed-method study by Nguyen et al., (2024a, 2024b) describes that Quillionz enables teachers to create questions from text passages they provide, which saves time and enhances the variety and precision of assessment questions. In other words, teachers appreciate these automating tools for their ability to produce personalized and customizable learning materials that match each student's distinct requirements. Among these tools, Diffit stands out thanks to its specially designed ability to generate reading comprehension quizzes. Diffit makes the quiz creation process simpler when compared to traditional methods which often require teachers a great amount of time and effort. Furthermore, Diffit's pre-made questions are catered to reading passages to ensure that they effectively meet learning goals and significantly reduce the workload on teachers.

One of the key features of Diffit is its capability to generate reading quizzes from the texts provided by educators. The tool analyzes reading material and creates different question types such as multiple-choice questions, true/false statements, and fill-in-the-blank exercises. These quizzes can be tailored to focus on learning outcomes, such as comprehension of key ideas, vocabulary acquisition, and aptitude for making inferences. Additionally, according to the official website, Diffit adjusts to the language proficiency levels of students with a view to guaranteeing that quizzes are both accessible and appropriately challenging. This automation not only saves time but also contributes to consistency of quality and diversity of assessment materials among different classes (Fig. 1).

There is a significant research gap regarding Diffit's practical application into EFL education despite its noticeable advantages. While some studies have examined the potential of AI-driven tools like Quillionz for creating reading tasks, limited research has been conducted to specifically focus on Diffit's use in reading lessons, which is a significantly necessary topic because understanding how Diffit is used can provide vital insights of the tool's effectiveness and usability. Moreover, there is a lack of exploration into how AI tools like Diffit affect teachers' task design process, particularly in terms of changes in teaching methodology and teachers' perceptions of how AI influences their task creation choices.

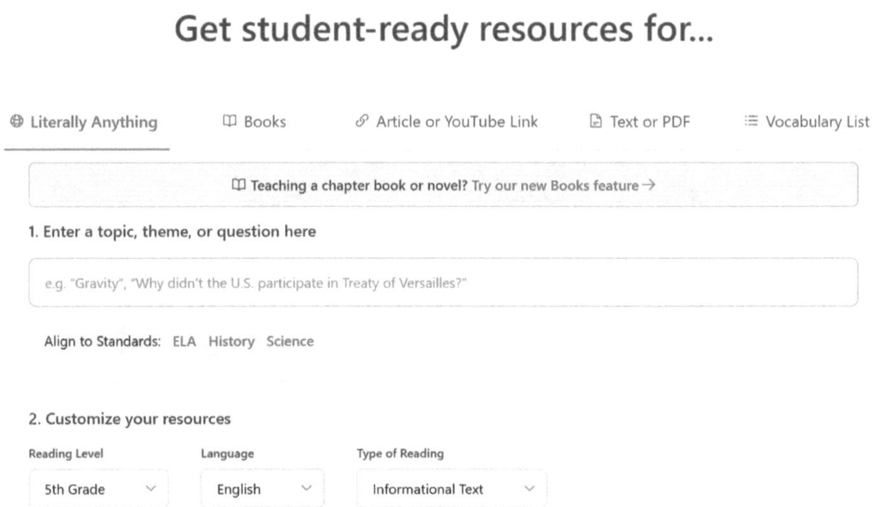

Fig. 1 Diffit's interface on the official website

2.5 Theoretical Framework

When it comes to technology adoption, the Technology Acceptance Model (TAM) is widely recognized as one of the most used frameworks to examine the decision to adopt any tools. This framework indicates that two key elements, including the usefulness and the ease of use, can influence both the initial adoption and continued use of the tools. In this study, the researchers apply the TAM framework to investigate teachers' perceptions of using Diffit to simplify and improve English reading lessons. Additionally, the research also examined whether teachers find Diffit easy to use and how its ease of use can affect teachers' ongoing adoption of the tool in their classrooms (Fig. 2).

The Unified Theory of Acceptance and Use of Technology (UTAUT) (Davis et al., 1989) is another well-known model utilized to examine technology use behavior. The UTAUT model is based on four key constructs, including performance expectancy, effort expectancy, social influence, and the external elements—facilitating conditions such as resources, assistance, and training to explain individual behavioral intention to use a system, which in turn affects their actual usage behavior. In this study, the use of UTAUT enables a more in-depth examination of how teachers' behavioral intentions to use Diffit are influenced not only by the tool's perceived benefits (such as task automation and time savings), but also by the presence of facilitating conditions such as adequate training and institutional support (Fig. 3).

In this study, the authors utilized the combination of TAM and UTAUT to examine teachers' perceptions of Diffit effectively.

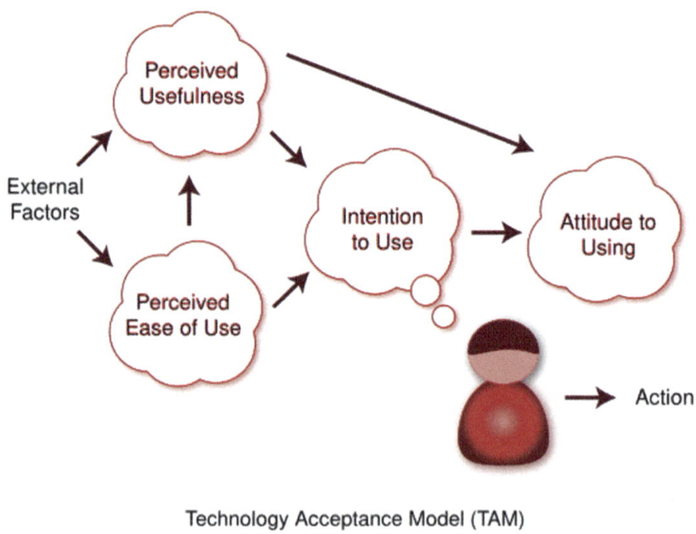

Fig. 2 TAM version 1

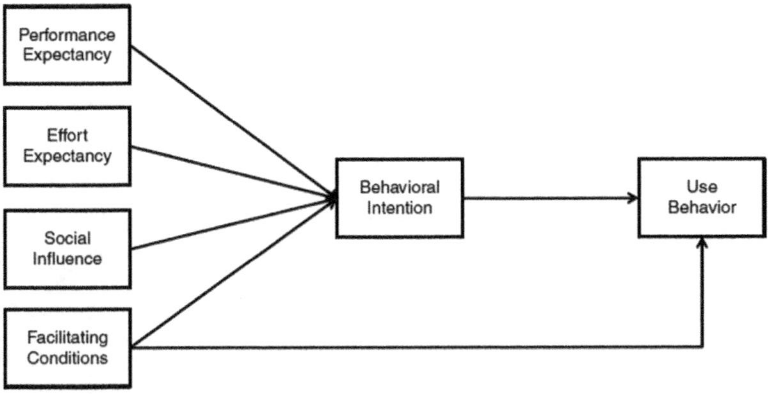

Fig. 3 The UTAUT model

2.6 Research Question

The aim of the study is to investigate teachers' attitudes toward using Diffit to automatically generate English reading quizzes, focusing on both its benefits and challenges as well as its impact on their teaching practices. Thus, to fulfill the aim, the authors seek to answer the following research question:

> What are the perceptions of English teachers at vocational colleges towards the effectiveness of Diffit in generating reading comprehension quizzes for non-English major students?

3 Methodology

3.1 Participants and Sampling

The research was conducted at a university in Hanoi, Vietnam, which puts a strong emphasis on integrating innovative technology into education. This university offers a diverse range of academic programs to prepare students for future careers, such as information technology, software development, multimedia communications, graphic design, languages, digital marketing and so on. At this university, students participate in a six-semester English language program as an integral part of the curriculum. This English course is designed to specifically enhance students' English proficiency for both academic and professional purposes within a globalized context. The program integrates My English Lab, an online platform developed by Pearson Education, to facilitate students' learning efficiency through various interactive exercises, online assignments, and assessments, and personalized feedback. In this study, the students of participating teachers were at Level 2 (Pre-intermediate) and followed the Top Notch 2 curriculum, which focuses on communication in daily conversations and building a strong foundation for more advanced skills. Classes are conducted in

Table 2 Demographic information of the participants (N = 18)

Variable	Number	Percentage
Gender		
Female	17	94.4
Male	1	5.6
Years of teaching experience		
Less than 2 years	2	11
2–5 years	8	44
6–10 years	6	33
More than 11 years	2	12
Academic qualifications		
Master's degrees	14	75
Doctorate degrees	4	25

a blended learning environment, where students are required to bring their laptops to English classes for active participation in both online and offline components of the course.

There were 18 teachers responsible for teaching English for English level 2 students involved in this research. They are young and enthusiastic teachers aged between 25 and 30, including 17 females and male. Furthermore, all participants held advanced academic qualifications, with 75% holding master's degrees (75%) and 25% holding doctorate degrees. The teachers also brought diverse teaching experience, with 11% having less than 2 years of experience, 44% had 2–5 years, 33% had 6–10 years, and 12% with more than 11 years of teaching experience. Subsequently, 8 teachers were randomly selected to participate in semi-structured interviews to gain deeper insights into their perceptions and experiences with the integration of Diffit in their teaching practices. To ensure confidentiality, the names of interviewed teachers were kept anonymous and referred to as T1 through T8 (Table 2).

3.2 Data Collection and Analysis

Two instruments were employed in this survey: pre and post intervention online surveys (via Google forms) and semi-structured interviews to collect comprehensive data. The survey questionnaires were developed based on the relevant literature and research conducted by Eichler (2024) and Moura and Carvalho (2024), who examined the teachers' perceptions of using AI in tools in the language classrooms. In this study, the surveys were modified to meet the research's objective and focus on using Diffit to automatically generate reading quizzes.

The pre-intervention survey was distributed to 18 participants online, aiming to investigate teachers' perception and experience in using AI in their instructional methods, as well as their expectations and willingness to adopt Diffit in their English reading lessons. The survey comprised three sections with 13 questions in total. There were four questions in the first section which were designed to gather participants' demographic information, such as age, gender, years of experience and their academic qualifications. The second section comprised six questions that ranged from Likert-scale to open-ended formats to explore teachers' perceptions and experience with AI, including the first three items assessed participants' familiarity with AI tools, the frequency of using AI tools in their teaching practices, and specific tools they had utilized. Questions four through six explored the application of AI tools in their English classes and challenges teachers have encountered when using them. Teachers who have not used AI for reading tasks were allowed to skip the corresponding question. The third section featured three questions to assess teachers' familiarity, expectations and their willingness to integrate Diffit, an AI-driven platform, into their reading lessons during a five-week intervention program.

To ensure teachers were adequately prepared to use Diffit, the researchers conducted a 30-min online training session via Google Meet. During the session, teachers were introduced to the Diffit platform and its key features, including how to create and customize quizzes. A live demonstration was provided to show how to generate reading quizzes and adjust settings. This training aimed to ensure that teachers were confident and well-prepared to use Diffit in their lessons. Following the five-week intervention, the researchers conducted a post- intervention online survey to gather feedback from all 18 participants. The purpose of the second survey was to examine teachers' experiences and attitudes towards the effectiveness and impact of Diffit on their teaching practices and students' engagement during reading lessons. There were three main sections with a total of 11 questions. Specifically, the first section (items 1–5) collected teachers' general feedback on Diffit through Likert-scale questions (ranging from strongly disagree to strongly agree), along with another option to assess their overall impression, as well as benefits they gained from this platform. The second section (five items) aimed to identify main challenges teachers face while using this platform. This section also included an open-ended chance for teachers to share additional challenges not listed in the provided options. The final section explored teachers' reflections on the intervention and their willingness to continue using Diffit in the future. After the post- survey, the research invited eight teachers to participate in semi-structured interviews to gain teachers' deeper insights into their experiences in using Diffit. The interview consisted of four questions and lasted about 5 min for each teacher to further explore their personal experience, providing specific benefits and drawbacks they encountered while using this platform over a period of five weeks. According to Mackey and Gass (2005), interviews facilitate participants in expressing their experiences and perspectives in their own words. This method provided an in-depth exploration of teachers' thoughts and emotions about incorporating AI tools into reading lessons.

For data analysis, both qualitative and quantitative methods were utilized. Quantitative data from the survey were analyzed through descriptive statistics to identify teachers' experiences in incorporating AI in language teaching, as well as evaluate the significant changes in participants' perspectives and experiences before and after using Diffit in five weeks. The data were presented in tables and figures to provide a clear visual representation of the results. Regarding the qualitative data, responses from open-ended questions in pre and post intervention surveys and semi-structured interviews were recorded and transcribed thoroughly. Additionally, the researchers employed thematic analysis based on Braun and Clarke's (2006) approach to identify main ideas, and group them into themes to explore common experiences and perspectives from the participants. By combining results from both surveys and interviews, the analysis ensured a more comprehensive and reliable understanding of how Diffit was used and its impact on teaching. This approach offered meaningful insights into the integration of AI into language education.

4 Findings and Discussion

4.1 Teachers' Initial Perceptions of Using AI Tools for English Reading Lessons

When asked whether they use AI for their English reading lessons, all 18 surveyed teachers affirmed that they do, highlighting the growing significance of AI in EFL education and reflecting an expanding familiarity with AI tools among teachers. This result highlights an increasing trend in incorporating AI in their instructional methods, which was also found in recent research (Arvin et al., 2023; Taufikin et al., 2024).

As shown in Table 3, all 18 surveyed teachers affirmed their use of AI tools in English reading lessons which highlight the growing importance of AI in EFL education. Chat GPT was the most widely used tool, with 17 teachers (94.40%) incorporating it into their reading lessons. Additionally, approximately 84% of respondents reported using Copilot and Gemini for designing reading materials and tasks. Quizizz followed closely, with 13 teachers (72.20%) using it to create interactive quizzes that promote student engagement. Surprisingly, tools such as Quillionz and QuestionWell were used by only 3 teachers (16.70%), while Deepseek, Jungle AI, and Blackbox AI were used by 2 teachers (11.10%). This indicates that the teachers are highly adept at integrating technology into their instructional practices, particularly in enhancing reading lessons. These findings align with previous studies that emphasize the significant role of AI tools in enhancing teaching effectiveness and personalizing students' learning experiences (Chien et al., 2021; Park & Doo, 2024; Vaidya, 2024). Furthermore, as noted by researchers, gamified learning platforms like Quizizz contribute to increased student engagement and comprehension, which further supports the positive impact of AI in education (Wang et al., 2024; Liu et al., 2024; Nguyen et al., 2024a, 2024b).

Table 3 AI tools used by surveyed teachers

AI tools	Number of teachers using it	Percentage (%)
Chat GPT	17	94.40
Copilot	15	83.30
Gemini	15	83.30
Quizizz	13	72.20
Quillionz	3	16.70
Deepseek	2	11.10
Jungle AI	2	11.10
QuestionWell	3	16.70
Blackbox AI	2	11.10

4.2 Teachers' Perceptions Towards Major Benefits of AI Tools

Figure 4 displays the key benefits teachers expect AI tools to bring to their English reading lessons. The results demonstrate an extremely positive attitude towards the advantages of AI tools among teachers. As can be seen in the chart, saving time emerged as the most significant benefit with almost all respondents emphasizing the importance of AI tools in saving time for their teaching. This finding aligns with Feng (2023), who noted that AI tools can significantly reduce teachers' administrative workload, allowing them more time to focus on direct student interaction and content delivery. Regarding the benefit of providing personalized learning experiences, a large proportion of respondents (75%) believe that AI tools help facilitate customized learning to enhance student outcomes. This supports previous studies, which found that AI platforms can tailor content to individual students' needs, thus enhancing learning outcomes (Zhang & Dong, 2024; Wang et al., 2025). Moreover, 65% of teachers affirmed that AI platforms can help foster student participation and interaction, reflecting the significant role of technology in creating a more dynamic, student-centered reading classroom. This finding is consistent with research by Sangarsu (2023), who observed that AI-driven platforms can help create more interactive and student-centered classrooms, particularly in language learning contexts. Task diversity ranks fourth on the list with 55% of respondents noting that AI tools help diversify learning activities, thereby facilitating teaching by offering varied and engaging learning experiences.

In the open-ended section, several additional benefits of AI were revealed. Teachers mentioned that AI tools offer valuable online teaching resources and promote collaboration among educators across different institutions by enabling the sharing of reading materials and lesson plans. Some teachers also emphasized AI's potential to support differentiated instruction, as AI can automatically adjust task difficulty based on individual student performance. This capability allows teachers to address a wide range of abilities within the same classroom. These findings align with studies on AI application in language teaching, which emphasize that AI can generate a wide range of learning tasks, from gamified exercises in face-to-face

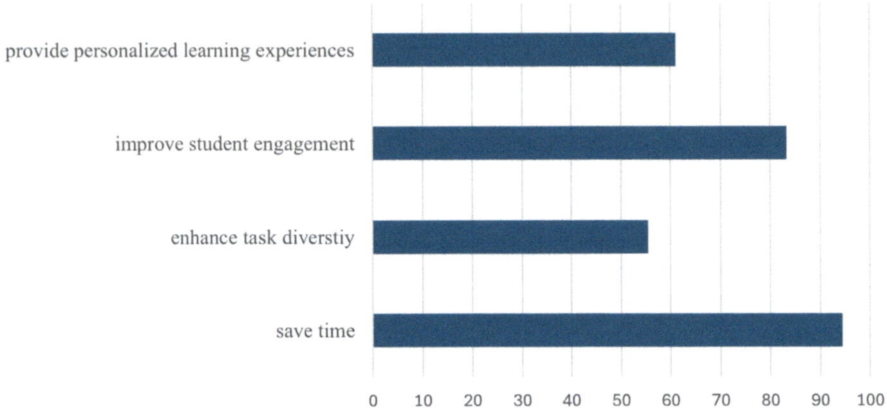

Fig. 4 Benefits of using AI tools in English reading lessons

classes to virtual learning environments. These tasks cater to diverse learning styles and interests, helping to increase student motivation and engagement (Aslam et al., 2024; Daghestani et al., 2020).

4.3 Teachers' Perceptions Towards Main Challenges When Using AI Tools

Figure 5 highlights the primary challenges faced by teachers in adopting AI tools in their teaching practices. Clearly shown in the above chart, the most common problem, identified by 77.8% of teachers, was limited accessibility and resources. It means that a considerable proportion of surveyed teachers encounter challenges in obtaining the necessary technology and resources required to incorporate AI effectively in their reading instruction. This finding is consistent with research by Alisoy (2025) who indicated that resource constraints have been persistent issues in education. Additionally, 40% of respondents reported having difficulty integrating AI with existing teaching practices. This finding aligns with Saravanakumar et al. (2023), who identified that many teachers face challenges when attempting to integrate AI into their established pedagogical frameworks. Interestingly, only 22 and 16% of participants considered lack of training or guidance and technology difficulties as big challenges, respectively, which implies that teachers generally feel confident in their technical skills when using AI tools. This is contrary to that of Familoni and Onyebuchi (2024) who found that technical barriers remain a significant obstacle to the smooth functioning of AI tools in educational contexts.

In the "other" section of the survey, teachers reported several difficulties they encountered when using AI tools. One of the main concerns, highlighted by some teachers, was the lack of sufficient technical support and troubleshooting assistance,

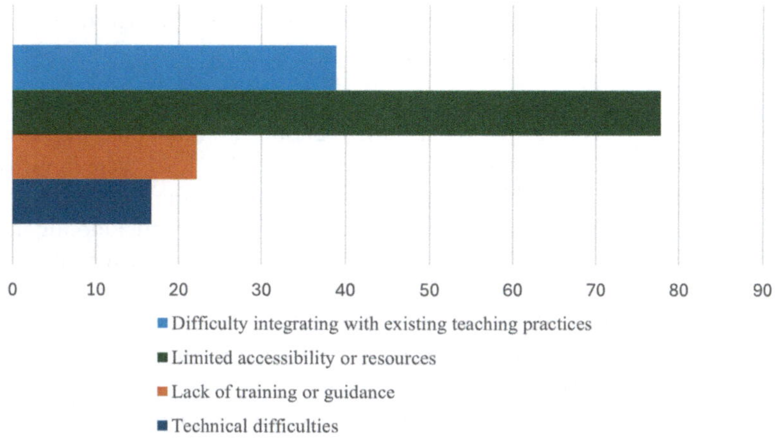

Fig. 5 Teachers' main challenges when using AI in their reading lessons

making it difficult for them to resolve technical issues promptly. This finding indicates a gap in the available support infrastructure for teachers, which can hinder the smooth integration of AI in their teaching practices. This is consistent with Šumak et al. (2024), who noted that educators often face challenges in incorporating technology into classrooms without adequate technical support. Additionally, some teachers noted that certain students struggled with adapting to AI-based tasks, especially those less familiar with technology. This challenge reflects a broader issue of digital literacy, with varying levels of student comfort and proficiency with technology. This finding emphasizes the importance of not only providing AI tools but also investing in increasing students' digital literacy. As Alisoy (2025) pointed out, improving students' digital skills is essential for them to fully benefit from AI-enhanced learning experiences. Another emerging concern from teachers was the over-reliance on technology, which they feared could reduce the human connection and interaction between teachers and students, especially in reading lessons. Teachers also reported difficulties in balancing AI integration with traditional teaching methods. This finding aligns with Saravanakumar et al. (2023), who highlighted the need for a harmonious balance between using AI to enhance learning and maintaining essential human interaction in the classroom. These concerns further support the idea that AI tools should complement, rather than replace, traditional pedagogical methods (Harry & Sayudin, 2023). Previous studies, such as those by Alenezi et al. (2023), emphasize the need for a balanced approach where AI is used alongside traditional teaching methods to maximize its benefits.

4.4 *Teachers' Perceptions Towards Using Diffit for Reading Lessons Before the Intervention*

As shown in Fig. 6, before the 5-week intervention, a sustainable proportion of teachers (78.6%) had not heard of Diffit before, while only 21.4% were familiar with this AI platform. This result highlights a significant gap in the awareness of Diffit among teachers, which could spark their interest in exploring and adopting this tool in their English lessons. The fact that nearly 21.4% of teachers had heard of Diffit prior to the study emphasize a growing interest in AI-assisted learning tools within educational communities. Recent studies also underscore the trend in AI adoption in classrooms to reduce teachers' workload and enhance the learning experience (Saravanakumar et al., 2023) (Fig. 7).

When asked whether Diffit helps save time, 27.8% of participants agreed that Diffit would help save time in preparing reading quizzes, while 33.3% remained neutral and nearly 40% disagreed with the statement. Regarding the personalization of quizzes based on students' levels, a significant number of teachers expressed doubt. More than half of respondents disagreed with the statement, while 22% remained uncertain or agreed with it. In terms of increasing student engagement with reading tasks, nearly 30% of teachers were unsure, and surprisingly 45% of surveyed teachers did not believe that this AI platform could enhance student interest in reading tasks. However, about 30% viewed this benefit positively. Regarding Diffit's ability to improve quiz quality, responses were varied, with 40% disagreeing and only 11% agreeing. There was still an uncertainty among teachers, with nearly 30% feeling unsure whether Diffit could improve quiz quality. Similarly, many teachers remained doubtful about Diffit's potential to reduce their workload. Specifically, 40% of respondents were uncertain and 16.7% disagreed, while 27.8% believe that Diffit is an effective platform to reduce their workload in reading lessons. Despite some hesitations about the effectiveness of Diffit, there was a positive trend in teachers' willingness to adopt Diffit in reading lessons, with a striking 84% agreed. Only a small percentage of teachers were neutral or uninterested in using this tool for their lessons.

Fig. 6 Teachers' Awareness of Diffit before the study

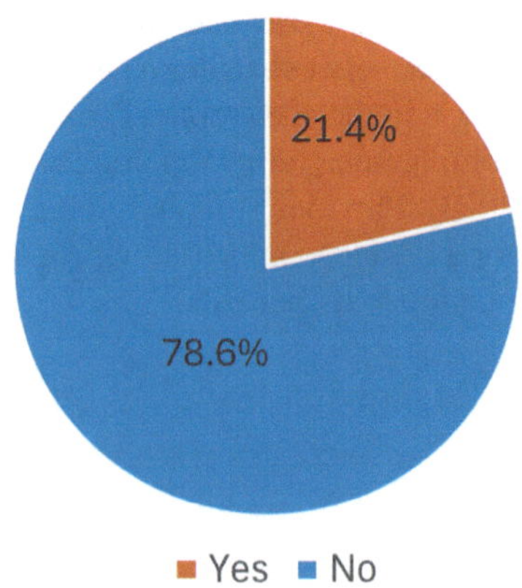

	I think Diffit will save me time in preparing reading quizzes.	I think Diffit will provide personalized quizzes based on students' levels.	I think Diffit will increase student engagement with reading tasks.	I think Diffit will improve the quality of reading comprehension quizzes.	I think Diffit will reduce my workload significantly in reading lessons.	I am willing to use Diffit to generate reading comprehension quizzes
■ Strongly Agree	11.1%	5.6%	11.1%	11.1%	5.6%	27.8%
■ Agree	16.7%	16.7%	16.7%	22.2%	22.2%	55.6%
■ Neutral	33.3%	22.2%	27.8%	27.8%	38.9%	5.6%
■ Disagree	22.2%	27.8%	27.8%	22.2%	16.7%	11.1%
■ Strongly Disagree	16.7%	27.8%	16.7%	16.7%	16.7%	0.0%

Fig. 7 Teachers' perceptions of Diffit before the intervention

To conclude, data from pre-survey express a positive attitude towards Diffit application into English lessons among surveyed teachers. These results further support the ideas of Uygun (2024) who indicated that teachers recognize the potential benefits of AI but remain uncertain about its practical application while they tend to trust AI's generated content after experiencing its positive results. Although there are some initial doubts about Diffit's potential to save time, personalize quizzes and reduce workload, teachers still express their willingness to try integrating this tool in their reading lessons. Recent studies conducted by Özer-Altınkaya and Yetkin (2025), and Saravanakumar et al. (2023) concluded the same results about the readiness and excitement of teachers to experiment with AI tools, which emphasizes teachers' recognition and belief in the significantly potential values of AI integration into their English teaching process.

5 Teachers' Perceptions Towards Using Diffit for Reading Lessons After the Intervention

After the five-week integration of Diffit to create reading quizzes, teachers were asked to provide their perceptions and feedback on experiencing the tool via the post-intervention survey and semi-structured interviews. The results from the survey, as presented in Fig. 8, illustrate a generally positive reception of Diffit by the participating teachers.

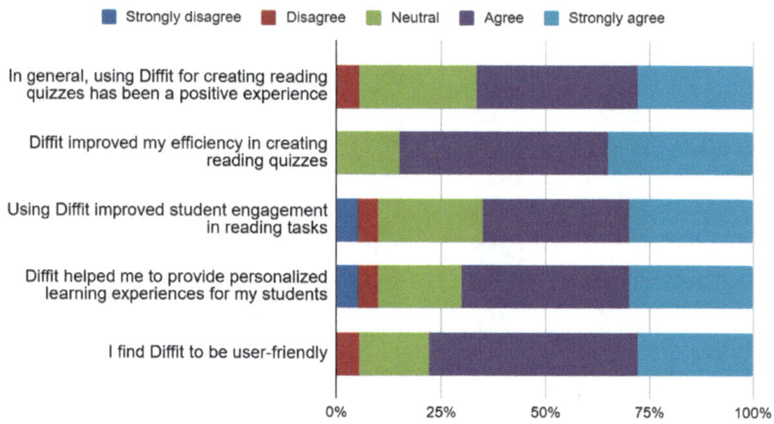

Fig. 8 Teachers' perceptions after five-week utilization of Diffit

As can be seen from the data in Fig. 8, an overwhelming majority of teachers (almost 67%) reported that using Diffit for creating reading quizzes was a positive experience. Specifically, about 28% strongly agreed, and 39% agreed that the tool enhanced their teaching experience. No teachers, surprisingly, expressed strong disagreement with the tool's effectiveness, and only a small percentage (less than 6%) disagreed. These findings suggest that, in general, Diffit was well-received by teachers, who found it to be a beneficial addition to their teaching practices for reading lessons, which is consistent with previous studies that highlighted the importance of AI tools in enhancing teaching effectiveness (Kundi, 2024).

Similarly, in terms of improving efficiency, the results were also promising. According to the figure above, a great number of participants (approximately 95%) either agreed or strongly agreed that Diffit improved their efficiency in creating reading quizzes. The data is noteworthy since one of the key benefits of AI in education is the ability to automate teachers' routine tasks, such as quiz creation, which thereby allows them to have more time to focus on other aspects of instruction. This finding supports earlier studies of Aryanti and Santos (2024) and Abiola et al. (2024) that suggest AI integration can significantly reduce teachers' administrative burdens.

Regarding student engagement, the majority of those who responded to this item (nearly 40% agreeing and 33% strongly agreeing) indicated that Diffit improved student engagement in reading tasks. As shown in Fig. 8, this outcome is particularly significant as fostering student engagement is a critical challenge in language education. Interestingly, while the majority found that Diffit positively influenced student participation, a small percentage of teachers remained neutral or disagreed, which points out that the tool's impact might vary depending on classroom dynamics or individual teacher preferences. This divergence is an important point for further exploration, as it raises questions about how different teaching contexts may influence the effectiveness of AI tools (Saravanakumar et al., 2023). Another key aspect of Diffit's effectiveness was its ability to support personalized learning. Most of those surveyed (particularly 44.5% in strong agreement and 33.33% in agreement) claimed that Diffit assisted them to provide more personalized learning experiences for their students. This result aligns with the current educational emphasis on personalized learning where tools like Diffit allow teachers to tailor tasks to students' individual proficiency levels. Previous research conducted by Ruslim and Khalid (2024) has found similar results that AI systems can help to generate differentiated instruction in order to meet students' diverse learning needs.

Furthermore, teachers also claimed Diffit to be a user-friendly platform. As shown in Fig. 8, a significant number of respondents (80%) found the tool easy to use, particularly with the proportion of 50% and 27.78% in strong agreement and agreement, respectively. This is a vital factor in the adoption of any new technology, in which user-friendliness is often a barrier to the successful integration of AI tools into classrooms (Zhou & Hou, 2025). The positive feedback suggests that Diffit is accessible to teachers with varying levels of technological proficiency, which is crucial for widespread adoption in diverse educational settings. These results are consistent with those from the semi-structured interviews, where the majority of teachers also expressed positive feedback about Diffit's effectiveness in creating reading quizzes. "Diffit has made quiz creation so much easier and faster", one informant commented, which supports the reported improvement in teachers' efficiency. Findings from interviews further support the benefit of Diffit in generating a wide range of question types such as multiple-choice, short-answer, and open-ended prompts from various resources including books, texts, pdf files, and even youtube links. One significant benefit of Diffit mentioned by almost all interviewed teachers was the complementary templates for students to practice, which help enhance student engagement and interaction.

Figure 9 presents main challenges that teachers encountered while using Diffit in five weeks. One interesting finding was that even though teachers considered Diffit a user-friendly platform, 40% of them reported having technical difficulties. This result was also reflected in the interview section with some teachers mentioning that they faced occasional glitches when generating reading questions from youtube links or book chapters. Additionally, a third of respondents considered lack of training or guidance a prominent challenge, which highlights the significance of technical support and detailed guidance. In the interview section, many teachers also required additional training or clearer guidance to utilise Diffit effectively. As mentioned in the literature review, providing sufficient training and support for teachers when implementing a new technology is crucial (Wang et al., 2024; Zhou et al., 2024). Only a small portion of teachers (16.7%) reported having difficulty integrating Diffit with existing teaching practices and customizing quizzes to specific learning objectives. Similarly, when interviewed, teachers expressed their confidence in using Diffit to automatically generate and customize their quizzes to fit their goals. These results show that most teachers easily get used to Diffit and find it simple to create and modify reading quizzes using this AI platform.

Data from Fig. 10 further support the positive attitude towards the effectiveness of Diffit. When asked if teachers had any problems related to the quality of questions generated by Diffit, a significant majority of teachers (83.3%) claimed that they

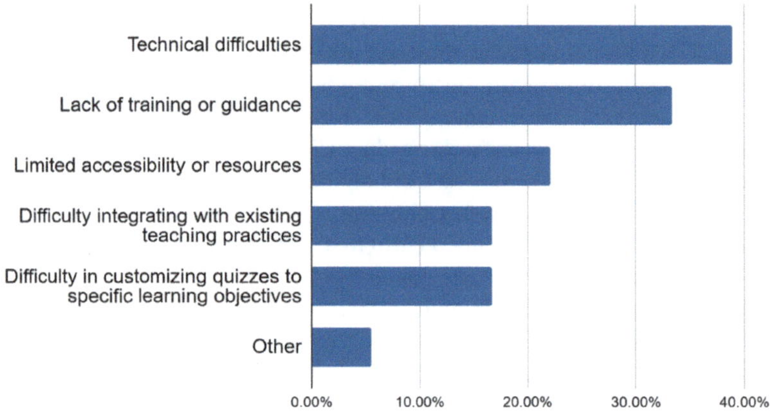

Fig. 9 Challenges while using Diffit

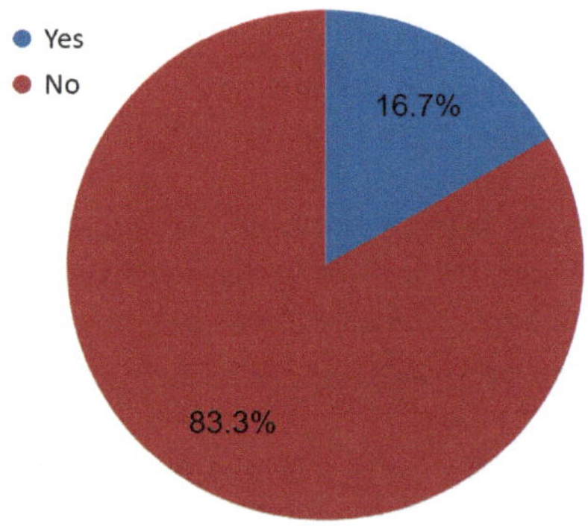

Fig. 10 Teachers' opinion about the accuracy or relevance of the reading quizzes generated by Diffit

did not encounter any. This finding suggests that this tool generally produces high-quality quizzes that align with the reading materials and learning objectives. This also accords with our interview findings since teachers mentioned that the quizzes created by Diffit are mostly accurate and relevant to the text, which saves them a lot of time in preparing questions. This result is positive and promising as in some relevant research, a lot of teachers express their uncertainty about the quality of AI-generated questions (Nguyen et al., 2024a, 2024b; Arvin et al., 2023; Hazaymeh et al., 2024).

5.1 Teachers' Recommendations

In addition to benefits and challenges, teachers also proposed some key recommendations to improve Diffit. Half of interviewed teachers emphasized the need for greater personalization (T1, T6, T7, and T8), particularly the ability to adjust quiz difficulty based on individual student performance rather than just proficiency levels. This result is in line with that of previous study, indicating that AI tools should be flexible and responsive to diverse learning needs (Su et al., 2024). Additionally, T2 and T3 suggested that the website should provide clearer guidance for first-time users, such as tutorial pop-up guides because there are a large number of users who may be less familiar with technology. T3 specifically suggested, "It would be great if the web contains a tutorial video pop up on the main interface, so users can easily know what to do". Teachers also expressed an interest in collaborative features which allow them to share quiz templates to foster a community of learning and collaboration. Furthermore, some teachers recommended that the web provide a tracking section for teachers to assign homework and monitor student working progress. Moreover, teachers proposed adding features such as quiz export options Google Forms or integration with interactive platforms like Quizzizz or Kahoot. Some also noted that it would be better to replace grade levels (from kindergarten to 11th Grade+) by proficiency levels (e.g., A1 to C2) to easily generate appropriate questions. Overall, these recommendations emphasize teachers' desire for an AI tool which is user-friendly and capable of providing detailed insights into student performance while also promoting collaboration with others.

6 Conclusion

In conclusion, our study emphasizes the significant shift in teachers' perspectives of utilizing Diffit—an AI platform for enhancing reading tasks before and after a 5-week integration. Results from mixed-method approach, combining quantitative pre and post surveys, and qualitative interviews, effectively reflect teachers' positive attitudes towards Diffit's potential to reduce workload, generate various types of question from different sources (e.g., book chapters, pdf, texts and YouTube links), provide interactive templates for students to practice, and promote student engagement in reading lessons. While the integration of AI tools can significantly enhance teaching strategies and student interaction, challenges such as web support for first-time users, technical difficulties while using the web, and concerns about the quality of questions were also noted. Findings from interviews also highlight teachers' recommendations, including the addition of tutorial and collaborative features, quiz export options to Google Form or online interactive games to further improve this AI platform.

Although our results are promising, the study has limitations due to its small sample size, short duration, and merely focus on reading comprehension, which might not fully capture the long-term impact or effectiveness of Diffit. Therefore, further research is encouraged to explore the broader application of Diffit in diverse educational contexts and investigate students' experiences when using this platform. Moreover, research which compares Diffit with other AI tools to evaluate its strengths and weaknesses is also recommended.

References

Abiola, O. A, Shukurat, E., & Chiekezie, N. (2024). Integrating AI and technology in educational administration: Improving efficiency and educational quality. *Open Access Research Journal of Science and Technology, 11*(2), 116–127. https://doi.org/10.53022/oarjst.2024.11.2.0102

Alenezi, M. A. K., Mohamed, A. M., & Shaaban, T. S. (2023). Revolutionizing EFL special education: How ChatGPT is transforming the way teachers approach language learning. *Innoeduca International Journal of Technology and Educational Innovation, 9*, 5–23. https://doi.org/10.24310/innoeduca.2023.v9i2.16774

Alisoy, H. (2025). The impact of AI-powered personalized learning on ESL student outcomes. *EuroGlobal Journal of Linguistics and Language Education, 2*(2), 89–98. https://doi.org/10.69760/egjlle.2500187

Arvin, N., Hoseinabady, M., Bayat, B., & Zahmatkesh, E. (2023). Teacher experiences with AI-based educational tools. *AI and Tech in Behavioral and Social Sciences.* https://doi.org/10.61838/kman.aitech.1.2.5

Aryanti, R. A., & Santosa, M. H. (2024). A systematic review on artificial intelligence applications for enhancing EFL students' pronunciation skill. *The Art of Teaching English as a Foreign Language, 5*, 102–113. https://doi.org/10.36663/tatefl.v5i1.718

Aslam, S., Safina, Faisal, O., & Kamal, H. (2024). Analyzing AI's role in promoting diversity and inclusivity within educational systems, addressing different learning styles and needs. *Review of Applied Management and Social Sciences.* https://doi.org/10.47067/ramss.v7i4.446

Braun, V., & Clarke, V. (2006). Using thematic analysis in psychology. *Qualitative Research in Psychology, 3*(2), 77–101. https://doi.org/10.1191/1478088706QP063OA

Chien, C. L., Chang, H. H., & Wu, Y. T. (2021). The effects of artificial intelligence on teaching and learning: A review. *Educational Technology & Society, 24*(1), 1–12. https://www.jstor.org/stable/26976667

Daghestani, L. F., Ibrahim, L. F., Al-Towirgi, R. S., & Salman, H. A. (2020). Adapting gamified learning systems using educational data mining techniques. *Computer Applications in Engineering Education, 28*(3), 568–589. https://doi.org/10.1002/cae.22227

Davis, F. D., Bagozzi, R. P., & Warshaw, P. R. (1989). User acceptance of computer technology: A comparison of two theoretical models. *Management Science, 35*(8), 982–1003. https://doi.org/10.1287/mnsc.35.8.982

De Kumang, V., Sudin, A., Dr, P., & Swanto, S. (2024). Enhancing ESL learners reading comprehension and motivation via AI-generated personalised reading texts. *International Journal on E-Learning Practices (IJELP).* https://doi.org/10.51200/ijelp.v7i1.5440

Deng, X., & Yu, Z. (2023). A meta-analysis and systematic review of the effect of chatbot technology use in sustainable education. *Sustainability, 15*(4), 29–40. https://doi.org/10.3390/su15042940

Dijkstra, R., Genç, Z., Kayal, S., & Kamps, J. (2022). Reading comprehension quiz generation using generative pre-trained transformers. In *iTextbooks@ AIED* (pp. 4–17). https://e.humanities.uva.nl/publications/2022/dijk_read22.pdf

Duong, N. H., Le, D. H., Nguyen, H. L., & Nguyen, T. L. (2024). Applying AI in teaching English through the Language Hub system at a vocational college in Hanoi from teachers' perspective. In *The 12th OpenTESOL International Conference 2024 Proceedings* (pp. 183–195). https://opentesol.org/wp-content/uploads/2024/08/FINALIZED-PROCEEDINGS-OF-THE-12TH-OPENTESOL-INTERNATIONAL-HYBRID-CONFERENCE-2024-final.pdf

Eichler, A. (2024). *Teachers' perceptions of integrating natural language AI tools in English language teaching.* University of Twente. Retrieved from https://essay.utwente.nl/100065/1/Eichler_Psychology_BMS.pdf

Familoni, B. T., & Onyebuchi, N. C. (2024). Advancements and challenges in AI integration for technical literacy: A systematic review. *Engineering Science & Technology Journal*, *5*(4), 1042. https://doi.org/10.51594/estj.v5i4.1042

Feng, W. (2023). Advancing Educational equality: Using AI technology in K-12 English language education in rural China. *Asian Conference on Education Official Conference Proceedings/ACE*, 875–902. https://doi.org/10.22492/issn.2186-5892.2023.68

Harry, A., & Sayudin, S. (2023). Role of AI in education. *Interdisciplinary Journal and Humanity (INJURITY), 2*(3), 260–268. https://doi.org/10.58631/injurity.v2i3.52

Hazaymeh, W., Bouzenoun, A., & Remache, A. (2024). EFL instructors' perspective on using AI applications in English as a foreign language teaching and learning. *Emerging Science Journal.* https://doi.org/10.28991/esj-2024-sied1-05

He, X. (2024). Enhancing reading comprehension with AI-generated adaptive texts. *International Journal of New Developments in Education.* https://doi.org/10.25236/ijnde.2024.060708

Hermagustiana, I. (2017). The incorporation of vocabulary teaching strategies into reading lessons in EFL context. In *The 1st international Conference on Language, Literature and Teaching* (pp. 220–233). https://publikasiilmiah.ums.ac.id/handle/11617/8898

Hieu, H., & Thao, L. (2024). Exploring the impact of AI in language education: Vietnamese teachers' views on using ChatGPT for fairy tale retelling tasks. *International Journal of Learning, Teaching and Educational Research.* https://doi.org/10.26803/ijlter.23.3.24

Hoang, N. T., Han, D. N., & Le, D. H. (2023). Exploring Chatbot AI in improving vocational students' English pronunciation. *AsiaCALL Online Journal, 14*(2), 140–155. https://doi.org/10.54855/acoj.231429

Jafarian, N., & Kramer, A. (2025). AI-assisted audio-learning improves academic achievement through motivation and reading engagement. *Computers and Education: Artificial Intelligence.* https://doi.org/10.1016/j.caeai.2024.100357

Katsarou, E., Wild, F., Sougari, A. M., & Chatzipanagiotou, P. (2023). A systematic review of voice-based intelligent virtual agents in EFL education. *International Journal of Emerging Technologies in Learning (iJET), 18*(10), 65–85.

Kaplan-Rakowski, R., & Grotewold, C. (2023). Exploring teacher attitudes toward AI-powered educational tools: A case study of Quillionz in the classroom. *Journal of Educational Technology Research and Development, 71*(2), 245–262. https://doi.org/10.1007/s11423-023-10123-4

Khan, S., Hamer, J., & Almeida, T. (2021). Generate: A NLG system for educational content creation. In *EDM.* https://finetunelearning.com/wp-content/uploads/2021/06/Generate_EDM2021.pdf

Konar, A. (2018). *Artificial intelligence and soft computing: Behavioral and cognitive modeling of the human brain.* CRC Press.

Kundi, M. (2024). Embracing AI as an additional aid in teaching: transforming education for the 21st Century. *Open Access Education and Leadership Review.* https://doi.org/10.59644/oaelr.2(1).2024.127

Lelkes, A. D., Tran, V. Q., & Yu, C. (2021). Quiz-Style question generation for news stories. *Proceedings of the Web Conference, 2021*, 2501–2511. https://doi.org/10.1145/3442381.3449892

Lestari, Z. (2017). The teaching of critical reading in an EFL classroom. *PEOPLE: International Journal of Social Sciences*, 1, 519–530. https://doi.org/10.20319/pijss.2015.s11.519530

Liang, J., Hwang, G., Chen, M., & Darmawansah, D. (2021). Roles and research foci of artificial intelligence in language education: An integrated bibliographic analysis and systematic review approach. *Interactive Learning Environments, 31*, 4270–4296. https://doi.org/10.1080/10494820.2021.1958348

Liu, M., Zhang, J., Nyagoga, L., & Liu, L. (2024). Student-AI question cocreation for enhancing reading comprehension. *IEEE Transactions on Learning Technologies, 17*, 815–826. https://doi.org/10.1109/TLT.2023.3333439

Mackey, A., & Gass, S. M. (2005). *Second language research: Methodology and design.* Lawrence Erlbaum Associates Publishers.

Moura, A., & Carvalho, R. (2024). *Teachers' views on AI in the classroom: Training and ethical considerations. ResearchGate.* Retrieved from https://www.researchgate.net/publication/378577721_Teachers%27_perceptions_of_the_use_of_artificial_intelligence_in_the_classroom

Nguyen, H. L., Le, D. H., Nguyen, T. L., & Duong, N. H. (2024). Students' perceptions towards AI application in English classes via the Language Hub system at a vocational College. In *The 12th OpenTESOL international conference 2024 proceedings* (pp. 196–210). https://opentesol.org/wp-content/uploads/2024/08/FINALIZED-PROCEEDINGS-OF-THE-12TH-OPENTESOL-INTERNATIONAL-HYBRID-CONFERENCE-2024-final.pdf

Nguyen, T. L., Nguyen, H. L., & Le, D. H. (2024). Teachers' perspectives on AI-driven Quillionz for generating EFL reading comprehension quizzes. *Proceedings of the AsiaCALL International Conference, 6*, 20–34. https://doi.org/10.54855/paic.2462

Özer-Altınkaya, Z., & Yetkin, R. (2025). Exploring pre-service English language teachers' readiness for AI-integrated language instruction. *Pedagogies an International Journal,* 1–17. https://doi.org/10.1080/1554480x.2025.2451299

Özkan, E., Erdemir, N., & Coşkun, D. (2024). EFL teachers' perspectives on artificial intelligence: A systematic review. *Ihlara Eğitim Araştırmaları Dergisi.* https://doi.org/10.47479/ihead.1535035

Park, Y.-J., & Doo, M. (2024). Role of AI in blended learning: A systematic literature review. *The International Review of Research in Open and Distributed Learning, 25*(1), 1–12. https://doi.org/10.19173/irrodl.v25i1.7566

Parviz, M. (2024). The double-edged sword: AI integration in English language education from the perspectives of Iranian EFL instructors. *Complutense Journal of English Studies.* https://doi.org/10.5209/cjes.97261

Pham, T. T., & Le, T. T. (2024). Exploring the impact of artificial intelligence on student creativity in vietnamese tertiary EFL classrooms: Teacher perspectives. *Jurnal Komunikasi Pendidikan, 8*(2), 116–128. https://doi.org/10.32585/jurnalkomdik.v8i2.5052

Pham, T. T., Nguyen, L. A. D., Dang, H. M., & Le, T. T. P. (2024). *Exploring tertiary Vietnamese EFL students' engagement in vocabulary learning through the use of an AI Tool.* In: Proceedings of the AsiaCALL international conference (vol. 4, pp. 129–149). https://doi.org/10.54855/paic.23410

Pornita, D., Maximilian, A., & Herlisya, D. (2023). Teaching EFL reading skill using reciprocal teaching strategy: A classroom action research. *Journal Smart.* https://doi.org/10.52657/js.v9i2.2113

Pratama, R., Lestari, L., Kirkgöz, Y., & Imaniar, F. (2024). Teachers' perceived perspective and self-efficacy in teaching EFL using Intelligent Computer-Assisted Language Learning (ICALL): A rigorous analysis. *The JALT CALL Journal.* https://doi.org/10.29140/jaltcall.v20n3.1634

Ruslim, M. I., & Khalid, F. (2024). The use of artificial intelligence in differentiated instruction classrooms. *International Journal of Academic Research in Business and Social Sciences, 14*(8). https://doi.org/10.6007/ijarbss/v14-i8/22435

Russell, S. J., & Norvig, P. (2016). *Artificial intelligence: A modern approach.* Pearson.

Salameh, W. A. K. (2024). The dual role of AI in personalized learning: Enhancements and hindrances for diverse learners. *International Journal of Science and Research Archive.* https://doi.org/10.30574/ijsra.2024.13.2.2057

Sangarsu, R. R. (2023). Enhancing student engagement in learning with modern web and AI technologies. *International Journal of Science and Research (IJSR), 12*(3), 1007. https://doi.org/10.21275/sr231017100712

Sanjaya, D., Rahmah, S., Sinulingga, J., Lubis, A., & Yusuf, M. (2014). Methods of teaching reading to EFL learners: A case study. *International Journal of Education and Literacy Studies, 2*, 9–14. https://doi.org/10.7575/AIAC.IJELS.V.2N.2P.9

Saravanakumar, A. R., Raja, G. P., & Sivakumar, P. (2023). Transforming education: Perceptions and challenges of technology-enabled teacher education programmes. *Open Access Research Journal of Engineering and Technology, 5*(2), 77. https://doi.org/10.53022/oarjet.2023.5.2.0077

Shin, M. H. (2018). How to use artificial intelligence in the English language learning classroom. *Indian Journal of Public Health Research & Development, 9*(9), 557–561. https://doi.org/10.5958/0976-5506.2018.01058.6

Siyam, N., Abdallah, S., & Latif, Y. (2022). Acceptance of artificial intelligence among pre-service teachers: A multigroup analysis. *International Journal of Educational Technology in Higher Education, 19*(23), 1–21. https://doi.org/10.1186/s41239-022-00316-4

Song, C., & Song, Y. (2023). Enhancing academic writing skills and motivation: assessing the efficacy of ChatGPT in AI-assisted language learning for EFL students. *Frontiers in Psychology, 14*. https://doi.org/10.3389/fpsyg.2023.1260843

Su, J., Lv, L., & Li, Z. (2024). AI-empowered college English blended teaching in China from the perspective of educational ecology. *Trends in Social Sciences and Humanities Research, 2*(1), 1–15. https://doi.org/10.61784/tsshr3121

Šumak, B., López-de-Ipiña, D., Dziabenko, O., Correia, S. D., Carvalho, L. M. S. de, Lopes, S., Simsek, I., Can, T., Ivanuša Kline, D., & Pusnik, M. (2024). AI-based education tools for enabling inclusive education: Challenges and benefits. *2024 47th MIPRO ICT and Electronics Convention (MIPRO)*. https://doi.org/10.1109/MIPRO60963.2024.10569714

Taufikin, M. S. I., Supa'At, S., Azifah, N., Nikmah, F., Kuanr, J., & Parminder. (2024). The impact of AI on teacher roles and pedagogy in the 21st century classroom. In *2024 International conference on knowledge engineering and communication systems (ICKECS)*. https://doi.org/10.1109/ICKECS61492.2024.10617236

Uygun, D. (2024). Teachers' perspectives on artificial intelligence in education. *Advances in Mobile Learning Educational Research, 4*(1), 931–939. https://doi.org/10.25082/AMLER.2024.01.005

Vaidya, B. (2024). Harnessing AI for STEM education in South Asia: Impact, opportunities, and challenges. *Journal of Development Innovations, 8*(2), 113. https://doi.org/10.69727/jdi.v8i2.113

Wang, X., Wrede, S., van Rijn, L., & Wöhrle, J. (2023). AI-based quiz system for personalised learning. In *ICERI2023 proceedings* (pp. 5025–5034). IATED. https://www.dfki.de/fileadmin/user_upload/import/14536_106756.pdf

Wang, Z., Harun, J. B., & Yuan, Y. (2024). Enhancing reading instruction through gamification: A systematic review of theoretical models, implementation strategies, and measurable outcomes (2020–2024). *Journal of Information Technology Education: Research, 23*, 28. https://doi.org/10.28945/5394

Wang, J., Hussain, Y., & Mao, C. (2025). Artificial intelligence-driven personalized learning: Psycho-logical implications and educational outcomes. *International Journal of Education, Humanities and Social Sciences, 2*(1), 1. https://doi.org/10.70088/3wnrs278

Widiati, U., Rusdin, D., Indrawati, I., M., & Govender, N. (2023). The impact of AI writing tools on the content and organization of students' writing: EFL teachers' perspective. *Cogent Education, 10*. https://doi.org/10.1080/2331186X.2023.2236469

Xin, J. (2024). Investigating EFL teachers' use of generative AI to develop reading materials: A practice and perception study. *Language Teaching Research*. https://doi.org/10.1177/13621688241303321

Zhang, Y., & Dong, C. (2024). Exploring the digital transformation of generative AI-assisted foreign language education: A socio-technical systems perspective. *Syst., 12*(1), 462. https://doi.org/10.3390/systems12110462

Zhou, C., & Hou, F. (2025). How do EFL teachers utilize AI tools in their language teaching? *Theory and Practice in Language Studies*. https://doi.org/10.17507/tpls.1502.10

Zhou, Q., Hashim, H., & Sulaiman, N. (2024). Digital Echoes: Crafting Chinese EFL teacher identity in the era of AI-Enhanced instruction—A qualitative exploration. *Forum for Linguistic Studies*. https://doi.org/10.30564/fls.v6i5.6864

Nguyen Thi-Luong is an English teacher at FPT University and FPT Polytechnic College in Vietnam. She specializes in teaching English communication and academic skills. Her research interests include integrating technology into education education and enhancing classroom management.

Nguyen Hai-Linh is an English teacher for non-English major students at FPT University and FPT Polytechnic College, Vietnam. Her research interest is language teaching methodology, especially teaching listening and speaking skills. She always tries her best to help non-English majors enhance their English competency.

Employing AI Tools for Vocabulary Acquisition and Autonomous Learning

Vu Phi Ho Pham and Que Quan Huynh

Abstract This study examines high school EFL students' perceptions of technology for vocabulary acquisition facilitated by artificial intelligence and its impact on learner autonomy. The research, employing a structured questionnaire administered to 185 twelfth-grade students in Vietnam, revealed that AI tools such as ChatGPT and Google Translate significantly improved motivation, goal-setting, and self-regulated learning behaviors. Students reported increased confidence and independence through the use of gamification, adaptive feedback, and progress-tracking tools. Concerns over excessive dependence on artificial intelligence, superficial work satisfaction, and insufficient support for profound learning and self-evaluation emerged; however, Students continued to value instructor guidance, indicating a preference for balanced integration despite the promotion of autonomy by AI tools. The fluctuation in student experiences underlined the limits of tailored and contextually relevant support given by artificial intelligence. The results imply that, when used sensibly, artificial intelligence technologies can improve vocabulary learning and learner autonomy; however, pedagogical supervision is required to guarantee important participation and continuous learner improvement.

Keywords AI tools · Artificial intelligence · Vocabulary acquisition · Autonomous learning

1 Background of the Study

Artificial intelligence (AI) in education has changed language learning by offering tools for interactive participation, adaptive support, and real-time feedback. Because they can solve issues including limited exposure, lack of motivation, and limited

V. P. H. Pham (✉)
Industrial University of Ho Chi Minh City, Ho Chi Minh City, Vietnam
e-mail: phamvuphiho@iuh.edu.vn

Q. Q. Huynh
Van Lang University, Ho Chi Minh City, Vietnam

V. P. H. Pham et al. (eds.), *Empowering Educators: Integrating AI Tools for Personalized Language Instruction*, Studies in Computational Intelligence 1228,
https://doi.org/10.1007/978-3-032-01348-4_10

practice opportunities, generative AI applications, including ChatGPT, Grammarly, and AI-based chatbots, have become popular in English as a Foreign Language (EFL) instruction (Chan & Hu, 2023; Ngo, 2024; Solak, 2024).

Many studies have shown that artificial intelligence tools enhance language learning outcomes, most especially learner confidence and vocabulary development. For instance, Thai EFL students who utilized ChatGPT exhibited notable rises in vocabulary, grammar, fluency, and motivation (Songsiengchai et al., 2023). Particularly for shy or self-directed students, AI tools also promote structured language acquisition by means of tailored and rapid feedback congruent with the Input Hypothesis and Cognitive Load Theory (Ngo, 2024; Werdiningsih et al., 2024).

Just as crucial is AI's ability to foster student autonomy. Self-monitoring tools, adaptive learning paths, and goal-setting support help students to independently regulate their education (Huynh, 2024; Pham, 2024). Li et al. (2025) claim that AI-supported platforms can enable students to reach agentic learning outcomes by motivating self-regulation and ownership of the learning process.

Notwithstanding these benefits, concerns about overreliance on AI tools, declining critical thinking, and shallow learning engagement surface. Zhai et al. (2024) warn that overreliance on AI systems may compromise analytical abilities and lower cognitive engagement. These factors especially apply in educational environments where individual learning is crucial.

Although the effectiveness of AI tools in language acquisition has been investigated in China, Indonesia, and Thailand (Solak, 2024), studies in Vietnam have mostly concentrated on university students. Still, high school students' experiences and impressions remain underrecorded. This disparity is particularly crucial given the higher academic expectations placed on Vietnamese secondary students getting ready for national assessments, which call for language mastery and learning autonomy.

Globally, the integration of artificial intelligence (AI) in language education has attracted more and more interest as various studies show how it could increase vocabulary learning, student engagement, and autonomy (Chan & Hu, 2023; Songsiengchai et al., 2023). Studies conducted in China, Thailand, and Indonesia, among other countries, have found that AI-powered tools like ChatGPT can boost language proficiency and encourage independent learning practices (Solak, 2024). Still, questions concerning ethical ramifications, over-reliance, and declining critical thinking abound (Zhai et al., 2024).

While several recent research in Vietnam has started to investigate artificial intelligence applications in tertiary EFL environments (Huynh, 2024; Pham & Le, 2024), little attention has been dedicated to the experiences of high school students—especially in vocabulary learning. This results in a knowledge disparity since secondary pupils have different developmental problems and academic demands than university students.

Students at Nguyen Binh Khiem High School are getting ready for high-stakes university admission tests, which call for autonomy in vocabulary acquisition within the research setting. Still understudied, nevertheless, how these students view and assess artificial intelligence systems. Developing pedagogically competent, student-centered methods for AI integration in Vietnamese high school classrooms depends on closing this divide. This study thus aims to determine how high school EFL students view the benefits and drawbacks of artificial intelligence technologies for vocabulary acquisition and their degree of support for autonomous learning.

2 Literature Review

With their real-time feedback, adaptive support, and interactive learning possibilities, artificial intelligence (AI) technologies have progressively changed language learning settings. Studies showing students' general positive impressions of AI tools such as ChatGPT, Grammarly, and AI-powered chatbots (Chan & Hu, 2023; Liang et al., 2024) are mounting. EFL students, in particular, have shown how well artificial intelligence supports vocabulary, grammar, and writing skills (Werdiningsih et al., 2024; Solak, 2024; Songsiengchai et al., 2023). For example, Songsiengchai et al. (2023) noted that Thai university students utilizing ChatGPT notably raised their vocabulary, grammar, and fluency, thereby indicating increased motivation and English learning engagement.

Another significant advantage is the use of artificial intelligence tools to promote learner autonomy. ChatGPT and Grammarly provide personalized feedback, flexible access, and support for students to self-regulate their studies. Ngo, 2024; Pham, 2024; Huynh, 2024. Based on the Input Hypothesis and Cognitive Load Theory, Ngo (2024) discovered that ChatGPT promotes learner independence through contextualized and incidental vocabulary learning. Though over-dependence remains a problem, Huynh (2024) investigated studies on EFL students' use of AI technologies and discovered that customized traits promote autonomous learning. These findings support Li et al.'s (2025) review, which found that AI chatbots promote agentic learning outcomes and self-regulated behavior, particularly in socioculturally informed pedagogical environments.

Students frequently recognize the advantages of AI technologies in vocabulary and writing, particularly their adaptability, individualized coaching, and feedback accuracy. For example, Pham and Le (2024) discovered that both Vietnamese and US EFL students utilized ChatGPT to improve idea generation and reading comprehension. Similarly, Benek (2025) found that Slovak students value the adaptability of AI tools. These findings highlight the cross-contextual attractiveness of AI-assisted language acquisition. Still, questions about over-reliance, accuracy, and authenticity linger. Solak (2024) and Werdiningsih et al. (2024) both underlined the loss of authenticity and possible reliance on artificial intelligence-generated outputs for pupils. Reiterating the need for human-guided usage of artificial intelligence, Zhai et al. (2024) went further and connected over-reliance to declining students' critical thinking and decision-making skills.

Conversely, teachers voiced pedagogical and ethical questions. While students were willing to use artificial intelligence tools, Benek (2025) discovered that professors stressed constraints on training, curriculum alignment, and ethical responsibility. Echoing similar worries, Dimitriadou and Lanitis (2023) highlighted systematic obstacles, including prejudice, privacy concerns, and high implementation costs in smart classrooms.

Academic and cultural settings affect the acceptance of artificial intelligence tools. While Slovakia, Portugal, and Spain students valued ChatGPT's value, Žáková et al. (2025) discovered that national education systems greatly influenced students' readiness to use it. This cultural diversity is also shown in Chan and Hu's (2023) research on Hong Kong university students who welcomed AI tools for their efficiency but stayed wary of ethical and privacy issues. Such contextual variations highlight the need for locally grounded research, especially in underdeveloped areas like secondary education in Vietnam.

Many academics warn against unquestioning acceptance of artificial intelligence despite rising excitement about it. Emphasizing the need to match artificial intelligence technologies with pedagogical objectives to prevent undesirable effects such as plagiarism, disinformation, or cognitive inactivity, Chinonso et al. (2023) Pham (2024) also underlined that although students thought ChatGPT was interesting, they did not perceive it as a replacement for human teachers, who offer contextual knowledge and emotional intelligence to the classroom. The literature thus promotes language education balanced, human-centered AI integration.

Despite the growing body of research on AI in academic settings, there is a dearth of information on high school EFL students' perceptions and evaluations of AI tools for vocabulary acquisition and independence. Although secondary school students may differ substantially in terms of needs, cognitive readiness, and learning autonomy, the majority of university student research (e.g., Liang et al., 2024) ignores them. The influence of AI on student autonomy has been noted in studies like Huynh (2024) and Ngo (2024), but there has been little investigation into students' perceptions of this influence or the characteristics of AI tools that aid in their development of independent vocabulary acquisition.

Some questions that this study aims to address are as follows.

2.1 Research Questions

RQ1: What are the high school students' perspectives on the advantages and disadvantages of using AI tools to learn vocabulary?

RQ2: To what extent do high school students evaluate the impacts of AI tools in enhancing their autonomous learning?

3 Research Methodology

3.1 Pedagogical Setting and Participants

Established in 1997 as one of the first private schools in Ho Chi Minh City, Vietnam, Nguyen Binh Khiem High School was the setting for this research. Typically ranging from A1–A2 on the CEFR scale, most pupils at the institution arrive with poor English competency.

Using a convenience sample technique, the researcher invited roughly 200 EFL 12th-grade students from seven classrooms to participate to discover how artificial intelligence tools affect students' autonomy in English vocabulary learning. 185 students in all agreed to participate in the study. These pupils were having intense English instruction in readiness for the national university admission test set for 2024–2025. The higher intellectual expectations and longer school hours demanded of students compelled them to participate more in self-regulated learning outside of the classroom. Considering this background, it is especially important to investigate how artificial intelligence supports learner autonomy. Every participant was told about the goal of the study and reassured that their answers would stay private and utilized just for research.

This study comprehensively explored students' perspectives on how AI tools affect their vocabulary learning and autonomy in language acquisition. This approach allowed the simultaneous gathering of quantitative data to ensure a complete awareness of the research subject (Creswell et al., 2006). An online questionnaire was sent to around 200 EFL 12th graders who responded to the Google Form questionnaires.

3.2 Research Instrument

The data collection method for this investigation was a structured questionnaire. After a study of the advantages of many questionnaire forms, the researchers chose a technique combining multiple-choice items (Muijs, 2010) with five-point Likert scale questions. This approach allowed us to get consistent responses from a sizable sample of 186 12th graders at Nguyen Binh Khiem High School, thereby helping us to capture their views of how artificial intelligence technologies affect their autonomy in language learning. Strong statistical analysis (Muijs, 2010; Wright, 2005) was made possible, and decreased probable biases were ensured by this approach.

The questionnaire includes 4 parts covering students' experiences with AI tools for vocabulary learning and autonomy. Section 1 includes 3 items (1–3) to explore the students' information about using AI tools and their purposes. Section 2 (items 4–15) explores students' perspectives on the benefits of using AI tools for vocabulary acquisition. Section 3 (items 16–19) investigates the students' attitudes toward the disadvantages of using AI tools for learning vocabulary. The final section (items 20–30) was employed to explore the students' evaluation of the impacts of AI tools on their learning autonomies. This questionnaire was created with Google Forms and sent to the 12-grader students at Nguyen Binh Khiem High School in Ho Chi Minh City, Vietnam.

4 Results/Findings

4.1 Participants' Experience with AI in Vocabulary Learning

Following the first section, which aimed to determine participants' demographic information, the second section (section B) investigated to what extent students experienced AI tools when learning vocabulary, including the AI tools they employed, the frequency of AI tools' usage, and the AI tools features they were benefited from in their vocabulary learning process.

Table 1 lists the artificial intelligence tools participants utilized for vocabulary development. Reflecting learners' taste for interactive and fast vocabulary guidance, ChatGPT was the most often chosen tool (73.5%), closely followed by Google Translate (67%). With modest usage, Duolingo (47%) and Quizlet (43.8%) point to organized, gamified platforms being likewise somewhat popular among students. Azota (30.2%) and Grammarly (24.1%) are less often used, perhaps suggesting their supposed limited importance, especially to vocabulary acquisition. The results show unequivocally a preference for solutions providing instantaneous, contextualized, and interactive vocabulary learning opportunities.

Table 2 shows participants' main goals for applying artificial intelligence techniques to vocabulary acquisition. Emphasizing their focus on comprehending word meanings and actively reviewing their vocabulary knowledge, most students used AI tools for word definition searches (84.9%) and vocabulary quizzes (70.8%), While finding sentence examples was less often chosen (45.4%), grammar correction was nevertheless a major factor (53%). These results imply that students mostly favor artificial intelligence technologies for quick self-evaluation and word mastery.

Table 1 The AI tools the participants used in vocabulary learning

Question	The AI tools	Percentages of participants
Which AI tools do you use in vocabulary learning? (You can select more than one)	ChatGPT	73.5
	Grammarly	24.1
	Quizlet	43.8
	Google translate	67
	Duolingo	47
	Azota	30.2

Table 2 The purpose of using AI tools

Purposes of Using AI tools	The AI tools	Percentages of participants
What do often use AI tools for? (You can select more than one)	Vocabulary quizzes	70.8
	Grammar corrections	53
	Word definition lookups	84.9
	Sentence examples	45.4

Table 3 lists participants who often utilized artificial intelligence methods for vocabulary learning. ChatGPT (62.2%) and Google Translate (58.9%) were the most often used tools reflecting students' demand for interactive and instantaneous translation support. With modest use rates, Duolingo (37.3%) and Quizlet (36.2%) suggested some appeal of structured and game-based learning environments. The least often selected were Grammarly (31.9%) and Azota (27%), implying they were thought to have a less direct bearing on language acquisition. These findings suggest that students mostly prefer artificial intelligence technologies with interactive features and fast vocabulary help.

RQ1: What are the high school students' perspectives on the advantages and disadvantages of using AI tools to learn vocabulary?

To respond to this research question, the descriptive statistics of SPSS vs. 22 were used to calculate for the mean scores to see the patterns of central tendencies. Table 4 presents the students' perspectives on the advantages of AI tools when they used for vocabulary acquisition.

Table 4 shows how students view the benefits of using tools driven by artificial intelligence for vocabulary acquisition. Students strongly agreed that artificial intelligence tools helped them properly plan their vocabulary learning ($M = 4.28$, $SD = 0.703$), so indicating that structured guidance given by these technologies greatly improved learners' organization and management of their study routines among the most important advantages reported. Closely associated with planning, the results also showed strong agreement that AI technologies motivated students to take more responsibility for their own vocabulary growth ($M = 4.24$,

Table 3 AI tools for learning vocabulary

Commonly used AI tools	The AI tools	Percentages of participants
Which AI tools do you use in vocabulary learning? (You can select more than one)	ChatGPT	62.2
	Grammarly	31.9
	Quizlet	36.2
	Google translate	58.9
	Duolingo	37.3
	Azota	27

Table 4 Advantages of AI tools on students' vocabulary learning

Items	Advantages of AI-powered tools	n	M	SD
4	AI tools help me learn vocabulary independently	186	4.11	0.582
5	Using AI tools makes it easier to track my learning progress	186	3.91	1.004
6	I feel more confident in learning new vocabulary with the help of AI tools	186	4.16	0.686
7	AI tools encourage me to take responsibility for my vocabulary learning	186	4.24	0.633
8	I can effectively plan my vocabulary learning with AI tools	186	4.28	0.703
9	AI tools motivate me to set personal learning goals	186	4.18	0.681
10	AI tools make vocabulary learning more accessible and convenient	186	4.11	0.440
11	I can control the pace of my learning when using AI tools	186	3.87	0.879
12	AI tools reduce my dependence on teachers in vocabulary learning	186	3.77	0.645
13	I can assess my vocabulary knowledge more accurately with AI tools	186	4.02	0.678
14	AI tools help me stay focused on my learning goals	186	3.98	0.525
15	Overall, AI tools have improved my autonomy in vocabulary learning	186	3.89	0.614

SD = 0.633). This outcome emphasizes how well artificial intelligence can promote independent learning behaviors—qualities absolutely essential for ongoing language development.

Moreover, students exhibited more confidence when learning a new language using artificial intelligence support (M = 4.16, SD = 0.686) and significantly felt inspired to set personal learning goals (M = 4.18, SD = 0.681). These results imply that interactive and tailored aspects of artificial intelligence technologies greatly increased learners' self-efficacy, engagement, and goal-oriented activities. Furthermore appreciated by participants were the chances for independent learning (M = 4.11, SD = 0.582) and the improved accessibility and convenience offered by artificial intelligence tools (M = 4.11, SD = 0.440), so helping to remove obstacles including limited teacher availability and logistical constraints.

Some elements, such as the decrease in reliance on teachers (M = 3.77, SD = 0.645) and control over learning pace (M = 3.87, SD = 0.879), did, however, score much lower. These lower scores suggest that students still view professors as helpful or even necessary to the learning process, even while artificial intelligence tools help independent learning. This emphasizes the requirement of balanced integration between artificial intelligence tools and teacher-led teaching since it implies that, in spite of technological developments, the human teacher's influence is still major in directing and supporting learners.

While still underlining the ongoing relevance of including AI tools inside a supportive educational environment that still depends on significant teacher-student interactions, overall these results underline the significant role of AI tools in improving learner autonomy, confidence, and motivation.

Despite AI tools' advantages, several disadvantages relating to their impacts on students' vocabulary learning remain, as presented in Table 5.

Table 5 shows how negatively some students view using AI-powered tools for vocabulary acquisition. Among these drawbacks, students voiced the most worry about depending too much on AI tools instead of applying their own expertise and techniques (M = 4.26, SD = 0.633). This suggests a great risk that students can grow unduly dependent on technology help, therefore compromising their capacity for critical thinking and autonomous learning. Students also reported difficulties precisely evaluating their real vocabulary increase depending on AI tools (M = 4.03, SD = 0.709), implying that AI feedback systems may not fully capture or reflect students' learning progress, complicating self-assessment and self-monitoring.

Other prominent issues were connected to the quality and dependability of vocabulary recommendations given by AI tools (M = 3.98, SD = 0.947), and the inclination of students to utilize AI just to complete activities without really comprehending the language (M = 3.98, SD = 0.812). These results suggest possible limits in the accuracy and efficacy of AI-generated help, which might cause students to interact superficially instead of with deep understanding and retention. Such problems underline

Table 5 Disadvantages of AI-powered tools on students' autonomy in vocabulary learning

Items	Disadvantages of AI-powered tools	n	M	SD
16	The vocabulary suggestions given by AI tools are sometimes not accurate and reliable	186	3.98	0.947
17	I tend to rely too much on AI tools rather than using my own knowledge to learn vocabulary	186	4.26	0.633
18	I often use AI tools to complete vocabulary exercises without fully understanding them	186	3.98	0.812
19	I find assessing my real vocabulary improvement when using AI tools difficult	186	4.03	0.709

the need for prudence in including artificial intelligence tools in vocabulary instruction and the necessity of cautious direction from teachers to avoid oversimplified learning approaches.

These drawbacks have important overall consequences for tool designers and teachers. Strategies and direction are obviously needed to reduce pupils' overdependence and improve significant interactions with language materials. Therefore, curriculum design and teaching strategies should concentrate mostly on juggling the ease of AI technologies with the encouragement of learner autonomy and critical thinking.

RQ2: To what extent do high school students evaluate the impacts of AI tools in enhancing their autonomous learning?

The mean scores of the descriptive statistics were also employed to examine participants' evaluations of the AI tools that impacted their autonomy in vocabulary learning, as presented in Table 6.

Table 6 shows how students believe artificial intelligence tools affect their autonomous vocabulary development. Among the positive effects, students ranked the inclusion of gamification elements as the most helpful (M = 4.27, SD = 0.678), stressing the motivating power these interactive aspects have in keeping interest and supporting learner autonomy. Emphasizing the need for fast corrections and modifications in promoting good self-monitoring and strategic learning practices, students also highly valued the immediate feedback given by AI tools (M = 4.25, SD = 0.662). Likewise, goal-setting elements were highly valued (M = 4.19, SD = 0.758), underlining how much students' capacity to lead their vocabulary acquisition processes is improved by well-defined, reasonable aims.

Positive responses (M = 4.12, SD = 0.736) from adaptive learning paths let students alter their learning emphasis depending on personal needs. This implies that students view artificial intelligence systems as successful in tailoring their educational experiences, enabling personal agency in educational decisions. Translation functions (M = 4.00, SD = 1.125), real-time error detection (M = 4.01, SD = 1.070), and progress tracking (M = 3.97, SD = 1.075) all assist learners in independently testing their knowledge and tracking their continuous vocabulary development.

Personalized learning recommendations, on the other hand, had a quite low rating (M = 3.59, SD = 1.224), maybe suggesting discrepancies or restrictions in how well these recommendations fit the needs and preferences of individual students. Likewise, elements like offering samples of word usage in several settings (M = 3.87, SD = 1.323) and diverse practice forms (M = 3.98, SD = 1.103) had somewhat more variability, implying mixed student experiences on their efficacy in supporting independent learning.

These results show that artificial intelligence systems greatly increase student autonomy by providing interesting, responsive, and motivating elements. Variability in some responses, however, emphasizes the continuous need to improve AI-based suggestions and contextual learning chances to completely fulfill their promise of promoting learner independence and efficacy in language learning environments.

Table 6 The impacts of AI tools on students' autonomy

Items	Impacts of AI tools on autonomous learning	n	M	SD
20	AI tools provide personalized learning recommendations, allowing me to select and manage my vocabulary learning process independently	186	3.59	1.224
21	AI tools provide adaptive learning paths, enabling me to take control of my learning focus based on my own needs	186	4.12	0.736
22	AI tools provide instant feedback, helping me self-monitor and adjust my vocabulary learning strategies	186	4.25	0.662
23	AI tools provide various practice formats, encouraging me to explore and engage in vocabulary learning at my own pace	186	3.98	1.103
24	AI tools provide progress tracking, allowing me to independently assess my development and set future learning goals	186	3.97	1.075
25	AI tools provide examples of word usage in different contexts, enabling me to infer meanings and apply vocabulary autonomously	186	3.87	1.323
26	AI tools provide goal-setting features promoting independent vocabulary learning	186	4.19	0.758
27	AI tools provide gamification elements, motivating my vocabulary learning progress	186	4.27	0.678
28	AI tools provide real-time error detection, helping me learn from mistakes	186	4.01	1.070
29	AI tools provide visual aids (e.g., images, videos), supporting my self-directed vocabulary learning	186	3.97	1.102
30	AI tools provide me with translation features, helping me independently verify and understand difficult words	186	4.00	1.125

5 Discussion

5.1 *The Benefits and Disadvantages of Using AI Tools to Learn Vocabulary*

Regarding the responses to the first research question about the benefits and disadvantages of AI tools for vocabulary learning, the findings of the current study reflect a significant alignment with previous research concerning the affordances of artificial intelligence (AI) tools in language learning, particularly in fostering learner autonomy, motivation, and self-efficacy. The strong agreement that AI supports structured planning and promotes learner responsibility aligns with Liu and Reinders' (2025) study, which found that generative AI chatbots significantly enhanced learners' motivation and encouraged the development of self-regulated learning (SRL) strategies. These outcomes suggest that AI fosters key motivational processes like goal-setting, self-monitoring, and reflection, which are crucial in vocabulary acquisition and broader language learning contexts (Zimmerman, 2008).

Moreover, the enhanced learner confidence and increased goal-setting behaviors support findings by Csizér and Tankó (2017), who identified a strong link between SRL strategy use and learners' motivational beliefs and self-efficacy in academic writing. The emphasis on independent learning and accessibility through AI tools resonates with earlier research showing how AI facilitates ubiquitous, individualized language learning experiences (Kohnke et al., 2023).

However, While students respect artificial intelligence support, the rather lower mean scores for reduced teacher dependency and control over learning pace show that they still value instructor engagement. This is consistent with the results of Benek's (2025) study, which showed that although 83.1% of EFL learners believed AI-powered tools are valuable, many teachers highlighted worries about over-reliance on technology (19.2%) and the lack of human interaction (9.6%). as major constraints. Furthermore, the study revealed that commonly perceived negative effects of AI use were insufficient to support higher-order thinking (17.3%) and cultural-linguistic nuance (11.5%), so underlines the need for human teachers to guide deep cognitive engagement and contextualized language learning. These common results underline the requirement for a balanced integration of artificial intelligence and human instruction, supporting the conclusion that AI tools should be considered supplements rather than replacements for teacher-led education.

Nevertheless, the results of this study show that although technologies driven by artificial intelligence help with vocabulary development, students express major worries over their usage. The risk of depending too much on artificial intelligence raises the most questions since it can compromise autonomous learning and critical thinking. This is consistent with research by Zhai et al. (2024), who noted that students' critical thinking and analytical skills may suffer from too great reliance on AI dialogue systems.

Moreover, pupils said they found it challenging to evaluate their vocabulary development using artificial intelligence techniques. This complicates self-assessment and self-monitoring since it implies that artificial intelligence feedback systems might not fully reflect students' actual development. Supporting this, research by Chan and Hu (2023) and by Nguyen and Pham (2024) revealed that although students value AI's tailored support, they also show worries about its accuracy and its influence on personal development.

Concerns also include the quality and dependability of AI-generated vocabulary recommendations and students' inclination to employ AI just to finish projects without real knowledge. These problems highlight how limited artificial intelligence systems are in promoting deep learning and the need for human supervision. As Zhai et al. (2024) point out, over-reliance on artificial intelligence can result in passive learning patterns in which pupils embrace AI outputs without question.

5.2 *The Impacts of AI Tools on Students' Autonomous Learning*

This study reveals that artificial intelligence technologies favorably affect autonomous vocabulary acquisition largely by offering gamification elements, fast feedback, goal-setting capabilities, and adaptable learning paths. These results support recent research stressing the benefits of gamification and personalized feedback in motivating and autonomous learning in language acquisition (Haoming & Wei, 2024; Zainuddin et al., 2020). Like this study, more recent studies show how well artificial intelligence (AI) helps students monitor their vocabulary practice and develop independent control over it, strengthening their autonomy (Liao, 2022). Conversely, the discovered constraints on customized recommendations and context-specific examples mirror the problems brought forth in previous studies. When students periodically questioned the accuracy of AI-driven word choices, Liu et al. (2024) saw, for instance, a decline in students' trust and participation levels. The variety in students' experiences underscored in this study indicates constant challenges in regularly adapting AI support to individual learner preferences, which corresponds with earlier research findings (Li et al., 2025).

First, AI tools significantly enhance students' autonomous vocabulary learning by offering engaging and responsive tools; second, continuous improvements in personalized learning recommendations and context-specific support remain indispensable for optimizing AI's educational effectiveness.

6 Conclusion

With an eye on their perceived advantages, disadvantages, and effects on learner autonomy, this study examined high school EFL students' impressions of AI-powered tools for vocabulary acquisition. Students showed a generally good attitude toward artificial intelligence technology since they realized they may improve learning motivation, offer individualized help, and enable autonomous language acquisition. Often used technologies were Google Translate and ChatGPT, which reflect a taste for tools with quick response and flexible learning possibilities.

Still, the study also revealed some really major issues. Many students claimed great reliance on artificial intelligence tools, using them to finish tasks without a thorough knowledge of the subject. This tendency begs questions about how artificial intelligence can affect important cognitive engagement, self-regulation, and critical analysis—problems clearly present in the present research. Moreover, children still value instructor involvement even with the help of artificial intelligence technologies in self-regulated learning, suggesting that a harmonic mix of human instruction with technology support is absolutely necessary.

These results highlight the possibilities and restrictions of artificial intelligence for language development. The findings suggest that teachers and legislators should intentionally integrate artificial intelligence techniques into language training to enhance, rather than supplant, instructor guidance. Moreover, the diversity in students' experiences with autonomy-enhancing attributes necessitates more targeted AI design and instructional assistance tailored to their requirements.

Future research should encompass many educational settings, including longitudinal studies, to examine the impact of artificial intelligence on learner autonomy and vocabulary development over time. Moreover, the advancement of ethical, educational, and contextual applications of artificial intelligence in secondary education should be emphasized.

References

AlTwijri, L., & Alghizzi, T. M. (2024). Investigating the integration of artificial intelligence in English as foreign language classes for enhancing learners' affective factors: A systematic review. *Heliyon, 10*, Article e31053. https://doi.org/10.1016/j.heliyon.2024.e31053

Akash, J. H., & Aram, I. A. (2022). A convergent parallel mixed method of study for assessing the role of communication in community participation towards sustainable tourism. *Environment, Development and Sustainability*, 1–19. https://doi.org/10.1007/s10668-021-01959-z

Baidoo-Anu, D., & Owusu Ansah, L. (2023). Education in the era of generative artificial intelligence (AI): Understanding the potential benefits of ChatGPT in promoting teaching and learning. *Journal of AI, 7*(1), 52–62.

Benek, K. (2025). EFL learners' and teachers' perceptions of AI-powered language learning technologies: Benefits and challenges. *International Journal of Instruction, 18*(2), 103–120. https://doi.org/10.29333/iji.2025.1827a

Chan, C. K. Y., & Hu, W. (2023). Students' voices on generative AI: Perceptions, benefits, and challenges in higher education. *International Journal of Educational Technology in Higher Education, 20*(1), 43. https://doi.org/10.1186/s41239-023-00411-8

Chinonso, O. E., Theresa, A. M.-E., & Aduke, T. C. (2023). ChatGPT for teaching, learning and research: Prospects and challenges. *Global Academic Journal of Humanities and Social Sciences, 5*(2), 33–40. https://doi.org/10.36348/gajhss.2023.v05i02.001

Creswell, J. W., Shope, R., Plano Clark, V. L., & Green, D. O. (2006). How interpretive qualitative research extends mixed methods research. *Research in the Schools, 13*(1), 1–11.

Csizér, K., & Tankó, G. (2017). English majors' self-regulatory control strategy use in academic writing and its relation to L2 motivation. *Applied Linguistics, 38*(3), 386–404. https://doi.org/10.1093/applin/amv033

Dimitriadou, E., & Lanitis, A. (2023). A critical evaluation, challenges, and future perspectives of using artificial intelligence and emerging technologies in smart classrooms. *Smart Learning Environments, 10*(12). https://doi.org/10.1186/s40561-023-00231-3

Haoming, L., & Wei, W. (2024). A systematic review on vocabulary learning in AR and VR gamification context. *Computers & Education: X Reality, 4*, Article 100057. https://doi.org/10.1016/j.cexr.2024.100057

Huynh, Q. Q. (2024). A literature review on EFL students' integration of AI-based tools in English learning and the perceived impact on autonomy. *International Journal of AI in Language Education, 1*(2), 30–51. https://doi.org/10.54855/ijaile.24123

Kohnke, L., Moorhouse, B. L., & Zou, D. (2023). ChatGPT for language teaching and learning. *RELC Journal, 54*(2), 537–550. https://doi.org/10.1177/00336882231162868

Li, Y., Zhou, X., Yin, H. B., & Chiu, T. K. (2025). Design language learning with artificial intelligence (AI) chatbots based on activity theory from a systematic review. *Smart Learning Environments, 12*(1), 24. https://doi.org/10.1186/s40561-025-00379-0

Liang, W., Zhang, Y., Cao, H., Wang, B., Ding, D. Y., Yang, X., Vodrahalli, K., He, S., Smith, D. S., Yin, Y., McFarland, D. A., & Zou, J. (2024). Can large language models provide useful feedback on research papers? A large-scale empirical analysis. *NEJM AI, 1*(8), AIoa2400196. https://doi.org/10.1056/AIoa2400196

Liao, L. (2022). Artificial intelligence-based English vocabulary test research on cognitive web services platforms: User retrieval behavior of English mobile learning. *International Journal of E-Collaboration (IJeC), 19*(2), 1–19. https://doi.org/10.4018/IJeC.316656

Liu, G. L., Darvin, R., & Ma, C. (2024). Exploring AI-mediated informal digital learning of English (AI-IDLE): A mixed-method investigation of Chinese EFL learners' AI adoption and experiences. *Computer Assisted Language Learning*, 1–29. https://doi.org/10.1080/09588221.2024.2310288

Liu, M., & Reinders, H. (2025). Do AI chatbots impact motivation? Insights from a preliminary longitudinal study. *System, 128*, Article 103544. https://doi.org/10.1016/j.system.2024.103544

Muijs, D. (2010). *Doing quantitative research in education with SPSS*. Sage.

Ngo, K. T. (2024). The use of ChatGPT for vocabulary acquisition: A literature review. *International Journal of AI in Language Education, 1*(2), 1–17. https://doi.org/10.54855/ijaile.24121

Nguyen, N. H. V., & Pham, V. P. H. (2024). AI chatbots for language practices. *International Journal of AI in Language Education, 1*(1), 56–67. https://doi.org/10.54855/ijaile.24115

Pham, V. P. H. (2024). Vietnamese graduate students' perspectives on the use of ChatGPT. In H. P. Bui & E. Namaziandost (Eds.), *Innovations in technologies for language teaching and learning* (pp. 171–185). Springer. https://doi.org/10.1007/978-3-031-63447-5_9

Pham, V. P. H., & Le, A. Q. (2024). ChatGPT in language learning: Perspectives from Vietnamese students in Vietnam and the USA. *International Journal of Language Instruction, 3*(2), 59–72. https://doi.org/10.54855/ijli.24325

Songsiengchai, S., Sereerat, B., & Watananimitgul, W. (2023). Leveraging artificial intelligence (AI): ChatGPT for effective English language learning among Thai students. *English Language Teaching, 16*(11), 68–79. https://doi.org/10.5539/elt.v16n11p68

Solak, E. (2024). Revolutionizing language learning: How ChatGPT and AI are changing the way we learn languages. *International Journal of Technology in Education, 7*(2), 353–372. https://doi.org/10.46328/ijte.732

Werdiningsih, I., Marzuki, & Rusdin, D. (2024). Balancing AI and authenticity: EFL students' experiences with ChatGPT in academic writing. *Cogent Arts & Humanities, 11*(1), 2392388. https://doi.org/10.1080/23311983.2024.2392388

Wright, K. B. (2005). Researching Internet-based populations: Advantages and disadvantages of online survey research, online questionnaire authoring software packages, and web survey services. *Journal of computer-mediated communication, 10*(3). Retrieved from https://doi.org/10.1111/j.1083-6101.2005.tb00259.x

Zainuddin, Z., Chu, S. K. W., Shujahat, M., & Perera, C. J. (2020). The impact of gamification on learning and instruction: A systematic review of empirical evidence. *Educational Research Review, 30*, Article 100326. https://doi.org/10.1016/j.edurev.2020.100326

Zimmerman, B. J. (2008). Investigating self-regulation and motivation: Historical background, methodological developments, and future prospects. *American Educational Research Journal, 45*(1), 166–183. https://doi.org/10.3102/0002831207312909

Žáková, K., Urbano, D., Cruz-Correia, R., Guzmán, J. L., & Matišák, J. (2025). Exploring student and teacher perspectives on ChatGPT's impact in higher education. *Education and Information Technologies, 30*, 649–692. https://doi.org/10.1007/s10639-024-13184-y

Zhai, C., Wibowo, S., & Li, L. D. (2024). The effects of over-reliance on AI dialogue systems on students' cognitive abilities: A systematic review. *Smart Learning Environments, 11*(1), 28. https://doi.org/10.1186/s40561-024-00316-7

Assoc. Prof. Dr. Vu Phi Ho Pham Faculty of Foreign Languages, Industrial University of Ho Chi Minh City, Vietnam, was Vice-President of Ba Ria–Vung Tau University and Vice-President at Van Hien University, Vietnam. Pham has published more than 70 research articles in both local and International Journals, such as Computer-Assisted Language Learning, SAGE Open, System, and Journal of Psycholinguist Research (*20* Scopus/*14 ISI*), and 10 books/course books, and 2 edited books (Springer and IGI Global). He is the Vice President for Administrative Affairs of AsiaCALL. He is the Editor-in-chief of the International Journal of TESOL & Education. He is now the managing editor of CALL-EJ (Scopus-Q1).

Que Quan Huynh is a student pursuing a master's program in arts of English studies at Van Lang University, Vietnam. She is experienced in the English language. Her main interest in language is research on classroom teaching and education. Her work relates to the effects of AI on student autonomy and the current adoption of AI in Vietnam.

AI Tools for Language Learners: The Promotion of Learning Independence or Reliance

Tin T. Dang

Abstract Technology has been significantly claimed to support language learners in various aspects, including accuracy of vocabulary pronunciation, recognition of grammatical features, memorization and retention of vocabulary written form, reading comprehension skills, and production of written texts. In contrast, many other studies have suggested several problems when learning with technology such as distraction, technical problems, frustration, cheating, and unauthenticity. The research reported in this chapter argues that Vietnamese students in higher education have become more reliant on technology since the more frequent introduction of large language model (LLM) AI tools in EFL classroom activities. They have also turned out to be less critical and collaborative during their in-class activity engagement. The interviews with some mid-career teacher participants who have allowed the use of LLM AI tools in class indicate a less positive learning climate and less facilitative opportunities for sustainable development of learner autonomy. The study urges the teachers' strategic attention to students' cognitive development process and learner autonomy capacity in the long term.

Keywords Learner autonomy · Independent learning · Critical thinking · LLM

1 Introduction

Technology, particularly AI, has become a dominant force in social life and language education, reshaping how individuals learn and interact. AI-driven tools, such as chatbots and numerous adaptive platforms, have transformed language learning by offering personalized, accessible experiences that integrate seamlessly into daily life (Strielkowski et al., 2025). These technologies leverage natural language processing and predictive analytics to tailor content, enabling learners to practice anytime, anywhere, reflecting the societal shift toward ubiquitous digital integration (Maity &

T. T. Dang (✉)
Ho Chi Minh City University of Technology and Education, Ho Chi Minh City, Vietnam
e-mail: tin.dang@hcmute.edu.vn

V. P. H. Pham et al. (eds.), *Empowering Educators: Integrating AI Tools for Personalized Language Instruction*, Studies in Computational Intelligence 1228,
https://doi.org/10.1007/978-3-032-01348-4_11

Deroy, 2024; Zhang et al., 2023). Web 2.0 tools, including blogs, forum, and wikis, empower users to create and share content, fostering active participation in global communication and aligning with social trends toward user-driven platforms (Dang & Robertson, 2010; Wang, 2014).

The prominence of AI is also evident in automated assessment tools that provide instant feedback, supporting learners' self-regulation in diverse contexts (Heilman et al., 2010). This overinfluential dominance raises concerns about equity, data privacy, and learning authenticity (Ladd, 2012; Lee et al., 2024; Rubel & Jones, 2016). Despite these challenges, the integration of AI into educational practices underscores its transformative potential, requiring careful management to ensure inclusive, autonomous learning (Godwin-Jones, 2024). This is one of the primary reasons for research on the support of technology for learner autonomy development in language education has been significantly increased over the last decade.

Learner autonomy is a multifaceted construct, central to language education (Dang, 2024) and defined as the ability to take charge of one's learning (Holec, 1981). It involves learners initiating, monitoring, and evaluating their learning processes (Dang, 2012), reflecting a capacity for self-regulation that encompasses setting goals, selecting strategies, and assessing progress (Little, 2003; Oxford, 2003). Autonomous learners are motivated, goal-oriented, and curious, balancing independence with collaboration (Barrett, 2007; Chan, 2001). This autonomy is shaped by technical, psychological, socio-cultural, and political-critical perspectives, which interact to foster agency within learning environments (Benson, 2006; Dang, 2010). Socio-cultural factors, such as peer support and interactions with resources, play a significant role in enabling learners to personalize their learning while remaining connected to broader cultural values (Chik et al., 2018; Healy, 2007). Autonomy is not about isolation but interdependence, requiring step-by-step guidance to develop skills like reflection and critical thinking (Benson, 2011).

Unfortunately, classroom observations indicate that students frequently rely on immediate responses from technology applications, particularly AI tools, when receiving the questions from teachers. This tendency often bypasses critical processes of reflection and information analysis, undermining meaningful and critical engagement with learning activities. Consequently, it is critical to assert that such a product-oriented approach designed by technology cultivates learner autonomy. This study seeks to examine students' interactions with technology from the teachers' perspective to determine whether their current practices with the AI tools, using LLMs and big data, such as ChatGPT, Google Translate, and Gemini, support or impede the development of learner autonomy.

2 Technology and Language Learning

This section offers an overview of the three strengths and two weaknesses of technology for language learning commonly reported in prior research to highlight the differences between high quality and low quality of learning engagement. Benefits of vocabulary memorization and retention stand out as a significant contribution from technology (Shadiev et al., 2020). The second support from technology is for learners' reading comprehension, and the third is for text production (e.g., Chen, 2016; Lysenko & Abrami, 2014). Meanwhile, the decrease of attention and increase of cheating are the two main challenges for language education of all levels (e.g., Lee et al., 2024; Murray et al., 2020).

2.1 *Supporting Vocabulary Learning*

Technology significantly enhances vocabulary acquisition by moving beyond traditional rote memorization to foster deeper, context-rich learning. While memorization has historically been a common method for learning lexical items (Pan, 2017), it often lacks depth, focusing on repetition rather than understanding (Tanaka, 2017; Wu, 2018). Technologies like mobile applications enable seamless learning, linking classroom instruction with real-world application (Shadiev et al., 2018; Wong, 2013). For instance, mobile-assisted programs incorporating multimedia (text, sound, and images) improve recall and reduce cognitive load, as seen in studies where learners used MMS messages with text-picture-sound modes (Lin & Yu, 2017). Such approaches align with dual-coding theory, where visual and verbal information processed together enhance memory through connections across brain channels (Paivio, 1986; Peker et al., 2018).

Mobile tools like Vine application (like TikTok) also allow learners to create and share content, such as short videos, promoting active engagement and contextual vocabulary use (Kurt & Bensen, 2017). Furthermore, game-based systems, like Wu's (2018) unblock vocabulary practice, increase motivation and effectiveness by integrating curriculum-aligned multimedia. These technologies support authentic learning environments, encouraging learners to apply vocabulary in meaningful, real-life contexts, thus improving retention and productive knowledge (Nation, 2007).

2.2 *Supporting Reading Comprehension*

Technology has been consistently suggested to enhance reading comprehension skills as it can offer interactive, engaging, and personalized learning experiences. Applications like Intelligent Tutoring System (ITS), 3D-Readers, and iSTART use narrative and expository texts to provide instructions for the development of metacognitive and cognitive strategies (Johnson-Glenberg, 2007; McNamara et al., 2006; Wijekumar et al., 2017). These applications offer extensive practice opportunities and tailored feedback, surpassing traditional classroom methods by allowing learners to regulate pacing and content (Azevedo & Bernard, 1995; Shafiee Rad et al., 2024). Research shows that ITSs produce greater effects than conventional instruction thanks to their limited time for access to diverse materials (Golan et al., 2018).

Multimedia tools, including visual media, support comprehension by contextualizing vocabulary and structures, boosting motivation, particularly among younger learners (Liu et al., 2002; Vogel et al., 2006). AI-driven platforms, while understudied for reading, show promise in adapting content to learners' proficiency levels, as seen in a study reporting a 70% improvement in Indian government schools (Srinivasan & Murthy, 2021). AI tools have better functionality in offering interactive experiences, improving learners' confidence and potentially enhancing their reading comprehension skills across varied contexts (McCarthy & Yan, 2024). Such technologies also promote learner autonomy by enabling students to monitor progress and access various language examples. They can then enhance students' engagement and positive attitudes toward reading activities (Hui, 2024; Kuperman et al., 2023). Students' motivation continues to be nurtured during the process, improving both time and quality of the learning (De Smedt et al., 2020).

2.3 Supporting Production of Written Texts

Automated writing evaluation (AWE) applications and generative AI like ChatGPT are reported to significantly enhance the production of second language (L2) texts as they can deliver precise and immediate feedback that fosters linguistic accuracy and autonomy. For example, research shows that Grammarly and Pigai can provide formative feedback on grammar, spelling, and coherence, enabling learners to revise texts independently and improve writing quality (Barrot, 2023; Ding & Zou, 2024). AWE is also indicated to positively impact L2 students' linguistic accuracy, reducing reliance on instructors (Huawei & Aryadoust, 2023; Zhai & Ma, 2023). ChatGPT extends these capabilities by offering comprehensive feedback across content, organization, and language, encouraging grammatical and word choice revisions (Bucol & Sangkawong, 2024; Wang et al., 2024). AI-driven tools also promote students' ability to set goals and monitor progress through detailed suggestions (Schunk & Zimmerman, 2013). ChatGPT, for instance, can offer scalable, accessible, and diverse feedback, allowing learners to practice extensively and build confidence in producing accurate, expressive texts, ultimately fostering greater control over their writing process (Hyland, 2019).

Further research suggests that AWE tools like Grammarly focus on surface-level errors, achieving high revision accuracy for grammar and spelling, which only supports learners in addressing straightforward issues by themselves (Thi & Nikolov, 2022). ChatGPT, however, offers more comprehensive feedback when properly prompted, including organization and content, with 91.8% precision in argumentative writing, encouraging better revisions (Wang et al., 2024). Other studies show that learners engage more effectively with the clear, directive feedback of AWE. Meanwhile, the comprehensive feedback approach of ChatGPT sometimes challenges lower-proficiency students (Guo & Wang, 2024; Ranalli, 2018) and even discourages them to continue with the learning engagement process.

2.4 *Inhibiting Learning Attention*

In contrast to several positive facilitations of technology for L2 learning, smartphones and social media are significantly reported to distract learners by disrupting the attention which is critical for language acquisition. Smartphones, tightly attached to almost every single student in higher education (Vorderer et al., 2016), including Vietnam, are pervasive in classrooms. Checking the phone during class time is inevitable. Notifications and apps deliver various reinforcements, akin to slot machines, match-3 games, and shopping alerts, encouraging compulsive checking that fragments attention (Skinner, 2014). This aligns with operant conditioning, where intermittent rewards, like social media likes, reinforce habitual device use, reducing focus on language tasks (Alter, 2017).

Research shows that mobile phone usage impairs memory and attention during lectures, with text messages particularly disruptive to processing language input (Mendoza et al., 2018). While L2 learning relies on sustained attention to internalize pronunciation and structures, smartphones, even when off, lower baseline attentional performance and hinder comprehension of students (Skowronek et al., 2023). Social media platforms like Facebook, used by almost every student, accelerate distraction because these platforms are always less stressful than learning. They easily take away more studying time from students, negatively impacting academic performance (Kirschner & Karpinski, 2010; Ortiz-Ospina, 2019). These interruptions scatter thoughts, weakening the cognitive engagement needed for effective L2 learning (Carr, 2011).

Students' pervasive access to digital devices further distracts them as these devices foster multitasking and procrastination, undermining the deep focus required for language processing. In classrooms, those with laptops or smartphones often engage in off-task activities like social media or texting, which significantly reduce comprehension (Patterson & Patterson, 2017; Rosen et al., 2013). Multitasking, encouraged by internet browsers with multiple tabs, disrupts learning, as students tend to switch tasks every six minutes on average, taking up to 30 min to refocus fully (Carrier et al., 2015; Gazzaley & Rosen, 2016). This is particularly detrimental for L2 learners, whose attentional systems struggle to process complex language input under distraction (Issa & Morgan-Short, 2019). Social media, especially Facebook, contributes to procrastination, increasing anxiety and distraction when used to delay studying, further impairing language acquisition (Feng et al., 2019; Sternberg et al., 2020).

In addition, virtual humans and spoken dialogue systems (SDSs) are reported to frustrate L2 students when it fails to meet their psychological needs, undermining motivation and communication intention. For example, low Spanish EFL proficiency students reflect their lack of confidence and interest when SDSs do not foster effective communication (Fernández-Agüero & Hidalgo-McCabe, 2022; Güneş, 2022). When students struggle with understanding sequential utterances, and SDSs lack emotional cues, they feel incompetent and disconnected (Bibauw et al., 2019; Jeon, 2024). This limitation hinders the negotiation of meaning, which is critical for fluency, leading to anxiety and embarrassment, the emotions that inhibit communicative intention (Dewaele & Pavelescu, 2021; Kruk, 2022). Students expecting authentic, engaging interactions, as supported by novelty needs, instead encounter restrictive conversational paths, resulting in hopelessness linked to perceived failure (González-Cutre et al., 2016; Holm et al., 2020). Such emotional blocks, if intensified by non-self-determined motivation from rigid systems, discourage students from persisting in language tasks, reducing their willingness to communicate and slowing down the progress in EFL mastery (Pekrun & Linnenbrink-Garcia, 2012; Tai & Chen, 2023).

2.5 Inhibiting Authentic Learning

Generative AI applications, which are based on LLMs, are consistently reported to encourage cheating in language learning as they offer students abundant opportunities to produce assignments without engaging in authentic language learning processes. Since its release in November 2022, ChatGPT has raised numerous concerns among educators, with 30% of surveyed undergraduates admitting to using it for assignments, bypassing the cognitive effort required to develop language skills (Intelligent, 2023; Tlili et al., 2023). L2 learning always values authentic production of original texts for mastering vocabulary, grammar, and discourse. Relying on AI-generated responses decays the development of these competencies.

Surveys in 2023 in the USA indicate that 58% teenagers between 12 and 18 years old have used ChatGPT, often for tasks meant to demonstrate personal proficiency, leading to inauthentic outcomes (Common Sense Media, 2023). This behavior aligns with historical cheating patterns, where 62% of students admitted to cheating on written assignments, but AI accelerates the problem by offering instant, human-like texts which are hard to detect (McCabe, 2005). Consequently, students may submit AI-generated essays or translations, missing opportunities for meaningful practice and feedback essential for language acquisition, thus eroding academic integrity and skill development (Gamage et al., 2020; Waltzer et al., 2023).

In addition, the shift to online learning, facilitated by Covid-19, has amplified cheating opportunities, perpetuating inauthentic learning by prioritizing grades and superficial satisfaction over genuine skill acquisition. Online learning space offers less oversight and greater access to tools like group messaging apps, which students use to share answers or obtain unauthorized assistance (Gamage et al., 2020). In language courses, where discussing and writing tasks require personal output to build fluency, students can exploit online resources to copy responses or use AI chatbots, ignoring the necessary practice for improvement. Research in 2013 shows that a vast majority of students surveyed admitted to cheating at least once, and they considered it to be necessary (Harbin & Humphrey, 2013). A higher percentage of students' cheating should be expected in the current situation of 2025. This opportunistic cheating can be driven by pressures of heavy workloads or perceived low assignment value, leading students to prioritize completion over learning (Waltzer et al., 2023).

3 Technology and Learner Autonomy

Technology has been significantly reported to enhance learner autonomy by enabling self-directed, personalized language learning experiences. Students can better manage their studies by using mobile applications to select vocabulary, create content, and share artifacts online, fostering initiative and reflection (Chai et al., 2016; Kondo et al., 2012). Applications for quizzes, simulations, and reflections also support students to self-regulate tasks, allowing them to set goals and monitor progress (Kondo et al., 2012). Similarly, mobile tools, like speech-to-text for pronunciation practice and video making for concept application, motivated students to take charge of their learning (Leis et al., 2015).

Adaptive platforms like Duolingo, Rosetta Stone, and Babbel use AI to analyze real-time performance, adjusting content and difficulty to match individual needs, which encourages learners to set goals and monitor progress independently (Heilman et al., 2010; Vesselinov & Grego, 2012). AI-driven chatbots, simulating real-life conversations, allow learners to practice speaking at their own pace, fostering confidence and learner autonomy without constant teacher intervention (Hapsari & Wu, 2022; Jeon, 2024). For writing, LLM tools like ChatGPT and automated essay scoring systems deliver instant feedback on grammar, coherence, and vocabulary, enabling learners to make corrections by themselves and engage in self-regulated learning (Alharbi, 2023; Tseng & Warschauer, 2023).

Similarly, AI-enabled grammar and vocabulary tools adapt to learners' levels, promoting self-corrections and personalized learning paths (Divekar et al., 2022; Fu et al., 2020). These technologies are claimed to be aligned with self-regulated learning principles, supporting metacognitive skills like self-reflection and assessment. However, these suggestions seem to be superficial as the research participants are usually taken care of well. They have already assumed a certain level of learning responsibility. In addition, these investigations do not seem to document the insights of the learning process, making the findings opposite to what is presented in the next section.

The development of learner autonomy requires complex skills and dispositions beyond mere access (Little, 2004). Without proper guidance, learners may struggle to use resources effectively, hindering self-regulation (Benson, 2007; Reinders, 2010). Students' independent use of computers often fails to integrate classroom processes essential for learner autonomy, suggesting a disconnect between technology and pedagogical support (Little, 2004). When the process of learning is not specifically designed and implemented, the success of technology access is merely incidental. Learners coming from disadvantaged or low-resource situations may feel negative towards learning as they lack devices or connectivity (Ladd, 2012; McGrath et al., 2024), hindering their motivation in learning engagement.

In addition, over-reliance on AI tools risks diminishing human interaction, potentially weakening collaborative and reflective skills which are critical for learner autonomy (Selwyn, 2019). Ethical concerns, such as data privacy in AI systems, may also undermine trust, discouraging learners from engaging fully with technology (Rubel & Jones, 2016). For technology to support autonomy, it must be paired with teacher training and equitable access to ensure learners can navigate tools meaningfully (Oxford, 2003). The process of learning must be central in every practice. Without these, technology may fail to cultivate the reflective and strategic capacities autonomy demands, leaving learners unsupported in their self-directed journeys.

4 AI Tools in a Context of Higher Education in Vietnam

Nearly all undergraduate students in Vietnam are inseparable from their smartphones for both academic and personal activities. They actively engage with Facebook for social networking, TikTok for video browsing, and Zalo (like Viber) for instant messaging. It is almost impossible to find any student who does not use these three platforms on a regular basis. Approximately 70% of students bring laptops or tablets to class, prioritizing access to power outlets when choosing seats. With the affordable mobile data and high-speed internet connection in Vietnam, students face constant temptation to stay connected, feeling isolated when disconnected from their devices. Classroom observations even show that some students wear wireless earphones during lessons to keep up with the notification sounds. Their attention is more frequently fixed on device screens than on the classroom environment. Lecturers' references to online resources during the lessons accelerate this issue, as students instinctively turn to Google or generative AI (GenAI) tools to answer questions from lecturers, often bypassing critical engagement with the material.

4.1 Instrument and Data Collection

To understand teachers' perspectives of students' use of GenAI tools such as ChatGPT, DeepSeek, Gemini, Copilot, Google Translate, Grammarly, Phrasely, and similar platforms that students regularly used in the class, this study designed an online survey to gather insights from mid-career EFL teachers. The survey employed open-ended questions to elicit natural, detailed narratives about classroom learning scenarios, minimizing participants' concerns about providing pedagogically "correct" responses (Cohen et al., 2018). No personal information was collected from participants to ensure anonymity. Seventeen teachers, each with 7–15 years of teaching experience at universities in Vietnam, participated voluntarily. The group included those teaching only English skills courses, only English for Specific courses, or a combination of both types. Their responses documented over a dozen distinct classroom scenarios.

4.2 Analysis of the Results

The participating teachers in the study reported that students were allowed to use and regularly used GenAI tools in class, as preventing their smartphone access was impractical. They recognized that allowing students to maximize smartphone use was preferable to enforcing restrictions, as students would likely find covert ways to access these tools without permission. This aligns with the global trend of integrating digital tools into classroom practices in higher education (Vorderer et al., 2016). Most teachers in this study acknowledged that GenAI tools made students more passive and reliant on tools, diminishing their learning opportunities and slowing down their language acquisition process. Only 3 of the 16 participants noted that these tools enhanced students' independence in language learning.

The most popular use of GenAI tools from students reported by the teachers is to copy a quickly generated response from LLM tools without studying anything from that response. When receiving a question requiring students to brainstorm the main ideas for a paragraph writing with their peers, they refused to work with their partners. They automatically copied the question to ChatGPT, copied the response from the tool, and showed it to the teacher. They have total trust in the response from GenAI tools. Teacher 7 said that:

> When the teacher gives students a translation task or a similar assignment, students put it into the [AI] tool right away. They got caught several times when they copied exactly everything from AI tools without any modification from their own.

The second type of students' learning scenarios is to use GenAI tools to answer the reading comprehension questions instead of reading the materials and figuring out the meaning presented in the materials. They do not seem to care if they have understood the materials or developed their thinking skills from the interactions with the materials. They simply want to get the answer as quickly as possible even when the answer is not from them. Teacher 9 wrote in the survey:

> When the teacher asks students to read the texts and answer the questions, many students take a photo of the texts and put it into Google Translate for the translation.

It is necessary to note that students in these situations do not suffer from any time or workload pressure. However, they still choose the faster way with less effort, regardless of its benefits for language learning and mental growth.

The third group of learning scenarios is to let GenAI do the learning, reflecting students' belief that AI tools can perform all academic tasks, and their role is to merely instruct GenAI to complete their study. Influenced by advertisements showcasing the amazing products generated by tools like ChatGPT or Grammarly, students eagerly adopt these technologies to handle their language learning assignments. This overreliance fosters a misconception that strategic learning plans are unnecessary, as AI can instantly produce satisfactory outputs. This is clearly reported by Teacher 6, who said:

> Because students believe AI tools, they are no longer active in making learning plans. […] They said that with only a few prompts, AI can do everything. Students do not look for

reading materials anymore. They even use AI tools to summarize the materials for them, instead of reading these materials by themselves for their language proficiency improvement.

4.3 Discussion of the Results

Analysis of the data in the previous section shows that students' use of GenAI tools in language classrooms significantly hinders the development of learner autonomy, a dynamic process cultivated through structured support and reflective practice (Little, 1991). Autonomy requires learners to actively control their learning process, setting goals, monitoring progress, and evaluating outcomes (Dang & Le, 2022). However, the use of AI tools like ChatGPT and Google Translate reported in the current study does the job of managing these processes, minimizing students' engagement to mere prompts. Students perceive participation in the learning process as unnecessary, believing AI can handle all academic tasks. This passivity undermines the scaffolding of facilitative feedback that sociocultural theory posits as essential for engaging learners at their proficiency level (Vygotsky, 1986). While AI tools are reported to offer scalable feedback to foster goal-setting (Hyland, 2019; Schunk & Zimmerman, 1994), its widespread misuse as presented in the current study leads to inauthentic learning, like when students submit AI-generated work without checking the details of the work or learning the linguistic structures (as reported in Gamage et al., 2020).

The students' common use of GenAI tools in the current study tends to restrict them from initiating learning as they devalue pre-learning activities like planning and material selection, eroding their ability to initiate learning opportunities. It seems that setting goals, making schedules, and looking for resources is no longer necessary as all learning tasks can be done with little effort. When they need any piece of reference materials, a simple search or prompt can offer them a lot. In many situations, they do not even care reading these references, therefore, there is no reason for them to look for these materials. In addition, they are unaware of the importance of preparation skills as their learning goals and strategies are different from the traditional notion, where language learning requires interactive communication, critical thinking, and reflection (Vygotsky, 1986). They believe that they are ready to deal with any learning challenge without preparation.

Their current use of GenAI tools also hinders their ability to monitor the learning process as it removes them from engaging with language materials and disconnects them from the reflective processes. Like what has been reported in Vorderer et al. (2016), when they use tools like Google Translate to answer reading comprehension questions without analyzing the texts, they disregard their learning process and diminish opportunities for language acquisition. While sociocultural theory emphasizes the role of feedback in scaffolding learning, students' unguided AI use skips this, leading to no quality learning achievement. Autonomy requires self-regulation where they need to continuously deal with the feedback from the tools (Hyland, 2019), yet their use of the tools lacks this pedagogical integration.

In addition, students' ability to evaluate their learning, which is essential for the development of their learner autonomy capacity is diminished as their use of the AI tools prevents them from judging and dialoging with the AI-generated answers. As they trust these tools implicitly, they always have a good sense of achievement and never question if they are successful with their own learning activities. They do not wonder if there is anything else they need to improve or attempt to figure out if there is any mistake from the responses of the AI tools. Therefore, they do not have any chance to correct the mistakes which can help them improve their evaluation skills. Previous surveys show that these activities are cheating (Common Sense Media, 2023), but students think that it is how their learning should be.

5 Conclusion

The investigation reported in the current study shows that Vietnamese university students have extensive access to smart devices and GenAI tools like ChatGPT, Gemini, and Google Translate during language learning. However, their use of these tools detaches them from the learning process, yielding only superficial products rather than fostering linguistic competence. This is contradictory to process-oriented objectives of education. These (mis)uses hinder learner autonomy development, which requires active control over learning. First, AI tools restrict students from initiating learning by devaluing planning and material selection. Students believe that AI handles all learning tasks, and achieving the learning goals does not require any well-planned activity. Second, their current use of AI tools prevents them from monitoring their learning process as they use tools like Google Translate to answer comprehension questions without engaging with texts, disregarding the opportunities to analyze, transform, and negotiate with the texts for language development. Third, students' use of AI tools impedes their ability to evaluate learning. As they implicitly trust AI outputs, they just submit inauthentic work without questioning accuracy, missing chances to develop self-assessment skills. To improve the students' use of AI tools, the teachers' practices are suggested to engage students in the learning process by encouraging them to analyze AI responses, compare these with their own authentic opinions, or ask the tools to generate more than one response for comparison, for example. Teachers should not let students deal with the tools alone, they need to give feedback to students when they work with the tools. In addition, students need to be aware that their learning is demonstrated by their ability to control their own learning process, not the answers to the questions facilitated by the teachers. The transactional product-oriented manner provided by the AI tools is not advised for quality education.

References

Alharbi, W. (2023). AI in the foreign language classroom: A pedagogical overview of automated writing assistance tools. *Education Research International, 2023*(1), 4253331. https://doi.org/10.1155/2023/4253331

Alter, A. (2017). *Irresistible: The rise of addictive technology and the business of keeping us hooked*. Penguin Press.

Azevedo, R., & Bernard, R. M. (1995). A meta-analysis of the effects of feedback in computer-based instruction. *Journal of Educational Computing Research, 13*(2), 111–127. https://doi.org/10.2190/9lmd-3u28-3a0g-ftqt

Barrett, H. C. (2007). Researching electronic portfolios and learner engagement: The REFLECT initiative. *Journal of Adolescent & Adult Literacy, 50*(6), 436–449. http://www.jstor.org/stable/40015496

Barrot, J. S. (2023). Using automated written corrective feedback in the writing classrooms: Effects on L2 writing accuracy. *Computer Assisted Language Learning, 36*(4), 584–607. https://doi.org/10.1080/09588221.2021.1936071

Benson, P. (2011). *Teaching and researching autonomy in language learning* (2nd ed.). Routledge.

Benson, P. (2006). Autonomy in language teaching and learning. *Language Teaching, 40*(1), 21–40. https://doi.org/10.1017/S0261444806003958

Benson, P. (2007). Autonomy and its role in learning. In J. Cummins & C. Davison (Eds.), *International handbook of English language teaching* (pp. 733–745). Springer.

Bibauw, S., Thomas, F., & Desmet, P. (2019). Discussing with a computer to practice a foreign language: Research synthesis and conceptual framework of dialogue-based CALL. *Computer Assisted Language Learning, 32*(8), 827–877. https://doi.org/10.1080/09588221.2018.1535508

Bucol, J. L., & Sangkawong, N. (2024). Exploring ChatGPT as a writing assessment tool. *Innovations in Education and Teaching International*. https://doi.org/10.1080/14703297.2024.2363901

Carr, N. (2011). *The shallows: What the Internet is doing to our brains*. Norton & Company.

Carrier, L. M., Rosen, L. D., Cheever, N. A., & Lim, A. F. (2015). Causes, effects, and practicalities of everyday multitasking. *Developmental Review, 35*, 64–78. https://doi.org/10.1016/j.dr.2014.12.005

Chai, C. S., Wong, L. H., & King, R. B. (2016). Surveying and modeling students' motivation and learning strategies for mobile-assisted seamless chinese language learning. *Journal of Educational Technology & Society, 19*(3), 170–180. http://www.jstor.org/stable/jeductechsoci.19.3.170

Chan, V. (2001). Readiness for learner autonomy: What do our learners tell us? *Teaching in Higher Education, 6*(4), 505–518. https://doi.org/10.1080/13562510120078045

Chen, T. (2016). Technology-supported peer feedback in ESL/EFL writing classes: A research synthesis. *Computer Assisted Language Learning, 29*(2), 365–397. https://doi.org/10.1080/09588221.2014.960942

Chik, A., Aoki, N., & Smith, R. (2018). *Autonomy in language learning and teaching: New research agendas*. Palgrave. https://doi.org/10.1057/978-1-137-52998-5

Cohen, L., Manion, L., & Morrison, K. (2018). *Research methods in education* (8th ed.). Routledge.

Common Sense Media. (2023). *New poll finds parents lag behind kids on AI and want rules and reliable information to help them*. Retrieved 15 March 2025 from https://www.commonsensemedia.org/press-releases/new-poll-finds-parents-lag-behind-kids-on-ai

Dang, T. T. (2010). Learner autonomy in EFL studies in Vietnam: A discussion from socio-cultural perspective. *English Language Teaching, 3*(2), 3–9. https://doi.org/10.5539/elt.v3n2p3

Dang, T. T. (2012). Learner autonomy: A synthesis of theory and practice. *The Internet Journal of Language Culture and Society, 35*, 52-67. https://aaref.com.au/wp-content/uploads/2018/05/35-08.pdf

Dang, T. T. (2024). Cultural and situational constraints on undergraduate students' performance of learner autonomy in EFL learning. *Journal of Language Teaching and Research, 15*(6), 1791–1799. https://doi.org/10.17507/jltr.1506.04

Dang, T. T., & Le, H. T. Q. (2022). Learning place control: Vietnamese EFL students' appreciation and trust. *International Journal of Language Education and Applied Linguistics, 11*(2), 56–63. https://doi.org/10.15282/ijleal.v11i2.6597

Dang, T. T., & Robertson, M. (2010). Pedagogical lessons from students' participation in Web 2.0. *TESOL in Context*, *20*(2), 5-26. https://www.learntechlib.org/p/52471

De Smedt, F., Rogiers, A., Heirweg, S., Merchie, E., & Van Keer, H. (2020). Assessing and mapping reading and writing motivation in third to eight graders: A self-determination theory perspective [original research]. *Frontiers in Psychology*. https://doi.org/10.3389/fpsyg.2020.01678

Dewaele, J.-M., & Pavelescu, L. M. (2021). The relationship between incommensurable emotions and willingness to communicate in English as a foreign language: A multiple case study. *Innovation in Language Learning and Teaching, 15*(1), 66–80. https://doi.org/10.1080/17501229.2019.1675667

Ding, L., & Zou, D. (2024). Automated writing evaluation systems: A systematic review of Grammarly, Pigai, and Criterion with a perspective on future directions in the age of generative artificial intelligence. *Education and Information Technologies, 29*(11), 14151–14203. https://doi.org/10.1007/s10639-023-12402-3

Divekar, R. R., Jaimie, D., Samuel, C., Yalun, Z., Hui, S., Yue, C., & Braasch, J. (2022). Foreign language acquisition via artificial intelligence and extended reality: Design and evaluation. *Computer Assisted Language Learning, 35*(9), 2332–2360. https://doi.org/10.1080/09588221.2021.1879162

Feng, S., Wong, Y. K., Wong, L. Y., & Hossain, L. (2019). The internet and Facebook usage on academic distraction of college students. *Computers & Education, 134*, 41–49. https://doi.org/10.1016/j.compedu.2019.02.005

Fernández-Agüero, M., & Hidalgo-McCabe, E. (2022). CLIL students' affectivity in the transition between education levels: The effect of streaming at the beginning of secondary education. *Journal of Language Identity & Education, 21*(6), 363–377. https://doi.org/10.1080/15348458.2020.1795864

Fu, S., Gu, H., & Yang, B. (2020). The affordances of AI-enabled automatic scoring applications on learners' continuous learning intention: An empirical study in China British. *Journal of Educational Technology, 51*(5), 1674–1692. https://doi.org/10.1111/bjet.12995

Gamage, K. A. A., Silva, E. K. D., & Gunawardhana, N. (2020). Online delivery and assessment during covid-19: Safeguarding academic integrity. *Education Sciences, 10*(11), 301. https://doi.org/10.3390/educsci10110301

Gazzaley, A., & Rosen, L. D. (2016). *The distracted mind: Ancient brains in a high-tech world*. The MIT Press.

Godwin-Jones, R. (2024). Distributed agency in language learning and teaching through generative AI. *Language Learning & Technology, 28*(2), 5–30. https://doi.org/10125/73570

Golan, D. D., Barzillai, M., & Katzir, T. (2018). The effect of presentation mode on children's reading preferences, performance, and self-evaluations. *Computers & Education, 126*, 346–358. https://doi.org/10.1016/j.compedu.2018.08.001

González-Cutre, D., Sicilia, Á., Sierra, A. C., Ferriz, R., & Hagger, M. S. (2016). Understanding the need for novelty from the perspective of self-determination theory. *Personality and Individual Differences, 102*, 159–169. https://doi.org/10.1016/j.paid.2016.06.036

Güneş, Ö. (2022). Failure attributions and metacognitive awareness of EFL learners. *Language Awareness, 31*(1), 53–72. https://doi.org/10.1080/09658416.2021.1960538

Guo, K., & Wang, D. (2024). To resist it or to embrace it? Examining ChatGPT's potential to support teacher feedback in EFL writing. *Education and Information Technologies, 29*(7), 8435–8463. https://doi.org/10.1007/s10639-023-12146-0

Hapsari, I. P., & Wu, T. T. (2022). AI chatbots learning model in English speaking skill: Alleviating speaking anxiety, boosting enjoyment, and fostering critical thinking. In Y.-M. Huang, S.-C. Cheng, J. Barroso, & F. E. Sandnes (Eds.), *Innovative Technologies and Learning*.

Harbin, J. L., & Humphrey, P. (2013). Online cheating: The case of the emperor's clothing, elephant in the room, and the 800 lb. Gorilla. *Journal of Academic and Business Ethics, 7*, 1–6. https://www.aabri.com/manuscripts/131450.pdf

Healy, D. (2007). Theory and research: autonomy and language learning. In J. Egbert & E. Hanson-Smith (Eds.), *CALL environments: research, practice, and critical issues* 2nd ed., (pp. 377–388). Teachers of English to Speakers of Other Languages.

Heilman, M., Collins-Thompson, K., Callan, J., Eskenazi, M., Juffs, A., & Wilson, L. (2010). Personalization of reading passages improves vocabulary acquisition. *International Journal of Artificial Intelligence in Education, 20*(1), 73–98. https://doi.org/10.3233/JAI-2010-0003

Holec, H. (1981). *Autonomy in foreign language learning*. Pergamon.

Holm, M. E., Björn, P. M., Laine, A., Korhonen, J., & Hannula, M. S. (2020). Achievement emotions among adolescents receiving special education support in mathematics. *Learning and Individual Differences, 79*, 101851. https://doi.org/10.1016/j.lindif.2020.101851

Huawei, S., & Aryadoust, V. (2023). A systematic review of automated writing evaluation systems. *Education and Information Technologies, 28*(1), 771–795. https://doi.org/10.1007/s10639-022-11200-7

Hui, B. (2024). Scaffolding comprehension with reading while listening and the role of reading speed and text complexity. *The Modern Language Journal, 108*(1), 183–200. https://doi.org/10.1111/modl.12905

Hyland, K., & Hyland, F. (2019). Contexts and issues in feedback on L2 writing. In K. Hyland & F. Hyland (Eds.), *Feedback in second language writing: contexts and issues* 2 ed., (pp. 1–22). Cambridge University Press. https://doi.org/10.1017/9781108635547.003

Intelligent. (2023). *One-third of college students used ChatGPT for schoolwork during the 2022–23 academic year*. Retrieved 5 April 2025 from https://www.intelligent.com/one-third-of-college-students-used-chatgpt-for-schoolwork-during-the-2022-23-academic-year

Issa, B. I., & Morgan-Short, K. (2019). Effects of external and internal attentional manipulations on second language grammar development: An eye-tracking study. *Studies in Second Language Acquisition, 41*(2), 389–417. https://doi.org/10.1017/S027226311800013X

Jeon, J. (2024). Exploring AI chatbot affordances in the EFL classroom: Young learners' experiences and perspectives. *Computer Assisted Language Learning, 37*(1–2), 1–26. https://doi.org/10.1080/09588221.2021.2021241

Johnson-Glenberg, M. C. (2007). Web-based reading comprehension instruction: Three studies of 3D-readers. In D. S. McNamara (Ed.), *Reading comprehension strategies: Theories, interventions, and technologies* (pp. 293–324). Lawrence Erlbaum Associates Publishers.

Kirschner, P. A., & Karpinski, A. C. (2010). Facebook® and academic performance. *Computers in Human Behavior, 26*(6), 1237–1245. https://doi.org/10.1016/j.chb.2010.03.024

Kondo, M., Ishikawa, Y., Smith, C., Sakamoto, K., Shimomura, H., & Wada, N. (2012). Mobile assisted language learning in university EFL courses in Japan: Developing attitudes and skills for self-regulated learning. *ReCALL, 24*(2), 169–187. https://doi.org/10.1017/S0958344012000055

Kruk, M. (2022). Dynamicity of perceived willingness to communicate, motivation, boredom and anxiety in second life: The case of two advanced learners of English. *Computer Assisted Language Learning, 35*(1–2), 190–216. https://doi.org/10.1080/09588221.2019.1677722

Kuperman, V., Siegelman, N., Schroeder, S., Acartürk, C., Alexeeva, S., Amenta, S., & Usal, K. A. (2023). Text reading in English as a second language: Evidence from the multilingual eye-movements corpus. *Studies in Second Language Acquisition, 45*(1), 3–37. https://doi.org/10.1017/S0272263121000954

Kurt, M., & Bensen, H. (2017). Six seconds to visualize the word: Improving EFL learners' vocabulary through VVVs. *Journal of Computer Assisted Learning, 33*(4), 334–346. https://doi.org/10.1111/jcal.12182

Ladd, H. F. (2012). Education and poverty: Confronting the evidence. *Journal of Policy Analysis and Management, 31*(2), 203–227. https://doi.org/10.1002/pam.21615

Lee, V. R., Pope, D., Miles, S., & Zárate, R. C. (2024). Cheating in the age of generative AI: A high school survey study of cheating behaviors before and after the release of ChatGPT. *Computers and Education: Artificial Intelligence, 7*, 100253. https://doi.org/10.1016/j.caeai.2024.100253

Leis, A., Tohei, A., & Cooke, S. D. (2015). Smartphone assisted language learning and autonomy. *International Journal of Computer-Assisted Language Learning and Teaching (IJCALLT), 5*(3), 75–88. https://doi.org/10.4018/IJCALLT.2015070105

Lin, C.-C., & Yu, Y.-C. (2017). Effects of presentation modes on mobile-assisted vocabulary learning and cognitive load. *Interactive Learning Environments, 25*(4), 528–542. https://doi.org/10.1080/10494820.2016.1155160

Little, D. (1991). *Learner autonomy 1: Definitions, issues, and problems.* Authentik.

Little, D. (2003). Learner autonomy and second/foreign language learning. *Guide to good practice.* Retrieved 30 December 2024, from http://www.llas.ac.uk/resources/gpg/1409

Little, D. (2004). Constructing a theory of learner autonomy: Some steps along the way. In K. Makinen, P. Kaikkonen, & V. Kohonen (Eds.), *Future perspectives in foreign language education* (pp. 15–25). Oulu University.

Liu, M., Zena, M., Leah, G., & Lee, S. (2002). A look at the research on computer-based technology use in second language learning. *Journal of Research on Technology in Education, 34*(3), 250–273. https://doi.org/10.1080/15391523.2002.10782348

Lysenko, L. V., & Abrami, P. C. (2014). Promoting reading comprehension with the use of technology. *Computers & Education, 75*, 162–172. https://doi.org/10.1016/j.compedu.2014.01.010

Maity, S., & Deroy, A. (2024). Generative AI and its impact on personalized intelligent tutoring systems. *arXiv*. https://doi.org/10.48550/arXiv.2410.10650.

McCabe, D. L. (2005). Cheating among college and university students: A North American perspective. *International Journal for Educational Integrity, 1*(1) https://doi.org/10.21913/IJEI.v1i1.14

McCarthy, K. S., & Yan, E. F. (2024). Reading comprehension and constructive learning: policy considerations in the age of artificial intelligence. *Policy Insights from the Behavioral and Brain Sciences, 11*(1), 19–26. https://doi.org/10.1177/23727322231218891

McGrath, C., Farazouli, A., & Cerratto-Pargman, T. (2024). Generative AI Chatbots in higher education: A review of an emerging research area. *Higher Education*. https://doi.org/10.1007/s10734-024-01288-w

McNamara, D. S., O'Reilly, T. P., Best, R. M., & Ozuru, Y. (2006). Improving adolescent students' reading comprehension with iSTART. *Journal of Educational Computing Research, 34*(2), 147–171. https://doi.org/10.2190/1ru5-hdtj-a5c8-jvwe

Mendoza, J. S., Pody, B. C., Lee, S., Kim, M., & McDonough, I. M. (2018). The effect of cell phones on attention and learning: The influences of time, distraction, and nomophobia. *Computers in Human Behavior, 86*, 52–60. https://doi.org/10.1016/j.chb.2018.04.027

Murray, L., Giralt, M., & Benini, S. (2020). Extending digital literacies: Proposing an agentive literacy to tackle the problems of distractive technologies in language learning. *ReCALL, 32*(3), 250–271. https://doi.org/10.1017/S0958344020000130

Nation, P. (2007). The four strands. *Innovation in Language Learning and Teaching, 1*(1), 2–13. https://doi.org/10.2167/illt039.0

Ortiz-Ospina, E. (2019). *The rise of social media.* Our World in Data. Retrieved 10 April 2025 from https://ourworldindata.org/rise-of-social-media

Oxford, R. (2003). Toward a more systematic model of L2 learner autonomy. In D. Palfreyman & R. Smith (Eds.), *Learner autonomy across cultures: language education perspectives* (pp. 75–91). Palgrave Macmillan.

Paivio, A. (1986). *Mental representations: A dual coding approach.* Oxford University Press.

Pan, W. F. (2017). The effects of using the Kinect motion-sensing interactive system to enhance English learning for elementary students. *Educational Technology & Society, 20*(2), 188–200.

Patterson, R. W., & Patterson, R. M. (2017). Computers and productivity: Evidence from laptop use in the college classroom. *Economics of Education Review, 57*, 66–79. https://doi.org/10.1016/j.econedurev.2017.02.004

Peker, H., Regalla, M., & Cox, T. D. (2018). Teaching and learning vocabulary in context: Examining engagement in three prekindergarten French classrooms. *Foreign Language Annals, 51*(2), 472–483. https://doi.org/10.1111/flan.12338

Pekrun, R., & Linnenbrink-Garcia, L. (2012). Academic emotions and student engagement. In S. L. Christenson, A. L. Reschly, & C. Wylie (Eds.), *Handbook of research on student engagement* (pp. 259–282). Springer. https://doi.org/10.1007/978-1-4614-2018-7_12

Ranalli, J. (2018). Automated written corrective feedback: How well can students make use of it? *Computer Assisted Language Learning, 31*(7), 653–674. https://doi.org/10.1080/09588221.2018.1428994

Reinders, H. (2010). Towards a classroom pedagogy for learner autonomy: A framework of independent language learning skills. *Australian Journal of Teacher Education, 35*(5), 40–55.

Rosen, L. D., Mark Carrier, L., & Cheever, N. A. (2013). Facebook and texting made me do it: Media-induced task-switching while studying. *Computers in Human Behavior, 29*(3), 948–958. https://doi.org/10.1016/j.chb.2012.12.001

Rubel, A., & Jones, K. M. L. (2016). Student privacy in learning analytics: An information ethics perspective. *The Information Society, 32*(2), 143–159. https://doi.org/10.1080/01972243.2016.1130502

Schunk, D., & Zimmerman, B. J. (1994). *Self-regulation of learning and performance: Issues and educational applications.* Erlbaum.

Schunk, D. H., & Zimmerman, B. J. (2013). Self-regulation and learning. In W. M. Reynolds, G. E. Miller, & I. B. Weiner (Eds.), *Handbook of psychology: Educational psychology* (pp. 45–68). John Wiley & Sons Inc.

Selwyn, N. (2019). *Should robots replace teachers? AI and the Future of Education* (1st ed.). Polity Press.

Shadiev, R., Hwang, W.-Y., & Liu, T.-Y. (2018). Investigating the effectiveness of a learning activity supported by a mobile multimedia learning system to enhance autonomous EFL learning in authentic contexts. *Educational Technology Research and Development, 66*(4), 893–912. https://doi.org/10.1007/s11423-018-9590-1

Shadiev, R., Wu, T.-T., & Huang, Y.-M. (2020). Using image-to-text recognition technology to facilitate vocabulary acquisition in authentic contexts. *ReCALL, 32*(2), 195–212. https://doi.org/10.1017/S0958344020000038

Shafiee Rad, H., Javad, A., Aliakbar, J., & Hashemian, M. (2024). Crafting with AI: Personalized pathways to boost critical language awareness and spark creativity in writing through digital adaptive learning. *Language Awareness*. https://doi.org/10.1080/09658416.2024.2431071

Skinner, B. F. (2014). *Science and human behavior*. The B. F. Skinner Foundation. (Original work published 1953).

Skowronek, J., Seifert, A., & Lindberg, S. (2023). The mere presence of a smartphone reduces basal attentional performance. *Scientific Reports, 13*(1), 9363. https://doi.org/10.1038/s41598-023-36256-4

Srinivasan, V., & Murthy, H. (2021). Improving reading and comprehension in K-12: Evidence from a large-scale AI technology intervention in India. *Computers and Education: Artificial Intelligence, 2*, 100019. https://doi.org/10.1016/j.caeai.2021.100019

Sternberg, N., Luria, R., Chandhok, S., Vickers, B., Kross, E., & Sheppes, G. (2020). When Facebook and finals collide—Procrastinatory social media usage predicts enhanced anxiety. *Computers in Human Behavior, 109*, 106358. https://doi.org/10.1016/j.chb.2020.106358

Strielkowski, W., Grebennikova, V., Lisovskiy, A., Rakhimova, G., & Vasileva, T. (2025). AI-driven adaptive learning for sustainable educational transformation. *Sustainable Development, 33*(2), 1921–1947. https://doi.org/10.1002/sd.3221

Tai, T.-Y., & Chen, H.H.-J. (2023). The impact of google assistant on adolescent EFL learners' willingness to communicate. *Interactive Learning Environments, 31*(3), 1485–1502. https://doi.org/10.1080/10494820.2020.1841801

Tanaka, M. (2017). Examining EFL vocabulary learning motivation in a demotivating learning environment. *System, 65*, 130–138. https://doi.org/10.1016/j.system.2017.01.010

Thi, N. K., & Nikolov, M. (2022). How teacher and Grammarly feedback complement one another in Myanmar EFL students' writing. *The Asia-Pacific Education Researcher, 31*(6), 767–779. https://doi.org/10.1007/s40299-021-00625-2

Tlili, A., Shehata, B., Adarkwah, M. A., Bozkurt, A., Hickey, D. T., Huang, R., & Agyemang, B. (2023). What if the devil is my guardian angel: ChatGPT as a case study of using chatbots in education. *Smart Learning Environments, 10*(1), 15. https://doi.org/10.1186/s40561-023-00237-x

Tseng, W., & Warschauer, M. (2023). AI-writing tools in education: if you can't beat them, join them. *Journal of China Computer-Assisted Language Learning, 3*(2), 258–262. https://doi.org/10.1515/jccall-2023-0008

Vesselinov, R., & Grego, J. (2012). Duolingo effectiveness study. *City University of New York, 28*, 1–25.

Vogel, E. K., Woodman, G. F., & Luck, S. J. (2006). The time course of consolidation in visual working memory. *Journal of Experimental Psychology: Human Perception and Performance, 32*(6), 1436–1451. https://doi.org/10.1037/0096-1523.32.6.1436

Vorderer, P., Krömer, N., & Schneider, F. M. (2016). Permanently online—Permanently connected: Explorations into university students' use of social media and mobile smart devices. *Computers in Human Behavior, 63*, 694–703. https://doi.org/10.1016/j.chb.2016.05.085

Vygotsky, L. S. (1986). *Thought and language* (A. Kozulin, Trans. ed.). The MIT Press.

Waltzer, T., DeBernardi, F. C., & Dahl, A. (2023). Student and teacher views on cheating in high school: Perceptions, evaluations, and decisions. *Journal of Research on Adolescence, 33*(1), 108–126. https://doi.org/10.1111/jora.12784

Wang, L., Chen, X., Wang, C., Xu, L., Shadiev, R., & Li, Y. (2024). ChatGPT's capabilities in providing feedback on undergraduate students' argumentation: A case study. *Thinking Skills and Creativity, 51*, 101440. https://doi.org/10.1016/j.tsc.2023.101440

Wang, Y.-C. (2014). Using wikis to facilitate interaction and collaboration among EFL learners: A social constructivist approach to language teaching. *System, 42*, 383–390. https://doi.org/10.1016/j.system.2014.01.007

Wijekumar, K. K., Meyer, B. J. F., & Lei, P. (2017). Web-based text structure strategy instruction improves seventh graders' content area reading comprehension. *Journal of Educational Psychology, 109*(6), 741–760. https://doi.org/10.1037/edu0000168

Wong, L.-H. (2013). Analysis of students' after-school mobile-assisted artefact creation processes in a seamless language learning environment. *Journal of Educational Technology & Society, 16*(2), 198–211.

Wu, T.-T. (2018). Improving the effectiveness of English vocabulary review by integrating ARCS with mobile game-based learning. *Journal of Computer Assisted Learning, 34*(3), 315–323. https://doi.org/10.1111/jcal.12244

Zhai, N., & Ma, X. (2023). The effectiveness of automated writing evaluation on writing quality: A meta-analysis. *Journal of Educational Computing Research, 61*(4), 875–900. https://doi.org/10.1177/07356331221127300

Zhang, C., Schießl, J., Plößl, L., Hofmann, F., & Gläser-Zikuda, M. (2023). Acceptance of artificial intelligence among pre-service teachers: A multi group analysis. *International Journal of Educational Technology in Higher Education, 20*(1), 49. https://doi.org/10.1186/s41239-023-00420-7

Tin T. Dang is an EFL and TESOL lecturer at both undergraduate and postgraduate levels in Vietnam. He currently works as a Faculty of Foreign Languages dean at Ho Chi Minh City University of Technology and Education. He has also been supervising research students at several institutions. His research primarily focuses on learner autonomy, teaching methodology, curriculum development, and technology in education. He has published in TESOL in Context, The Journal of Asia TEFL, The Asian EFL Journal, The Internet Journal of Language, Culture and Society, and a few others. He has served on the board of directors of the VietTESOL Association since its establishment in 2018, chairing the academic committee, which is responsible for designing the content of the association events, leading the 8 special interest groups, and collaborating with different government sections for the sustainable development of the teachers' community in Vietnam. He has chaired the Language Teaching and Learning Today Conference (LTLT) in 2017, 2018, 2019, and 2023.

Exploring the Impact of ChatGPT on Non-native Learners of Arabic Language: Challenges and Opportunities

Alif Sismat, Rafidah Abdullah, Kujaimah Abdul Kahar, Rafizah Abdullah and Amalena Jarudin

Abstract Artificial intelligence (AI) based chatbots have been widely used as they offer great potential for personalized instruction. However, many AI models, including ChatGPT, are primarily trained on English-language data, raising concerns about their effectiveness in non-English contexts. Therefore, this study aims to explore the impact of using ChatGPT on Arabic language learning, primarily focusing on non-native speakers of Arabic and its potential for personalized instruction. This qualitative study gathered data through a focus group discussion with seven Malay learners of Arabic language at Universiti Islam Sultan Sharif Ali. Before the discussion, the participants completed eight language exercises using ChatGPT: grammar, morphology, paraphrasing, diacritization, error analysis, sentiment analysis, translation, and summarization. The study addresses the challenges and opportunities of using ChatGPT to complete tasks. While students benefited significantly from ChatGPT's assistance in paraphrasing, summarization, and translation tasks, challenges arose in grammar and morphology due to accuracy limitations. The study also underscores the importance of crafting precise prompts to maximize ChatGPT's effectiveness. Additionally, concerns such as overreliance on AI, ethical considerations, and technological limitations emerged. Despite these challenges, students recognized ChatGPT's value as a

A. Sismat (✉) · R. Abdullah · K. Abdul Kahar · R. Abdullah · A. Jarudin
Faculty of Arabic Language, Universiti Islam Sultan Sharif Ali, Begawan, Brunei
e-mail: alif.sismat@unissa.edu.bn

R. Abdullah
e-mail: rafidah.abdullah@unissa.edu.bn

K. Abdul Kahar
e-mail: kujaimah.kahar@unissa.edu.bn

R. Abdullah
e-mail: rafizah.abdullah@unissa.edu.bn

A. Jarudin
e-mail: amalena.jarudin@unissa.edu.bn

V. P. H. Pham et al. (eds.), *Empowering Educators: Integrating AI Tools for Personalized Language Instruction*, Studies in Computational Intelligence 1228,
https://doi.org/10.1007/978-3-032-01348-4_12

supplementary tool for personalized learning. This study underscores the importance of refining AI training data and developing clear guidelines for its responsible use in language education, offering valuable insights for educators and learners seeking to integrate AI-driven tools into personalized Arabic language instruction.

Keywords ChatGPT · Arabic · Non-native learners · Challenges · Opportunities

1 Introduction

The Arabic language is considered one of the most difficult languages to learn as it has a very complex morphological system (Holes, 2004). It is also known for its diglossia, which Ferguson (1959, p.335) defines as:

> A relatively stable language situation in which, in addition to the primary dialects of the language (which may include a standard or regional standard), there is a very divergent highly codified (often grammatically more complex) superposed variety, the vehicle of a large and respected body of written literature, either of an earlier period or of another speech community, which is learned largely by formal education and is used for most written and formal spoken purposes, but is not used by any sector of the community for ordinary conversation.

The Arabic language has its Modern Standard Arabic (MSA) and Non-Standard Arabic (NSA), also known as Colloquial Arabic (CA). MSA is derived from Classical Arabic which is the oldest form of Arabic dating back to the seventh and ninth centuries (Alanazi, 2024; van Putten, 2020). It is currently taught at schools and universities and used in the media, such as newspapers and magazines. CA, on the other hand, refers to regional dialects used in daily conversation (Cote, 2009) and media such as radio, television and social media platforms. For example, if a person asks, "What are you doing?" in MSA, he will say "ماذا تفعل؟" (*Mādhā taf'al?*). However, it is "بتعمل إيه" (*Bita 'mal Eīh)* in Egyptian CA and "أش كادير" (*Ash kāddīr*) in Moroccan CA. Various forms of the Arabic language may pose challenges, particularly to non-native learners of Arabic, as they may have to learn at least one CA to converse with native speakers in daily communication in addition to the MSA taught in the classrooms. As a result, it doubles the vocabulary they need to learn (Van Mol, 2014) and forces them to learn two different pronunciation systems (Abu-Hatab, 1992).

Advancements in technology have made Arabic language learning become more accessible, interactive and engaging (Pikri, 2022). Recent years have seen rapid growth in the utilisation of Generative Artificial Intelligence (AI) chatbots, such as Chat Generative Pre-Trained Transformer (ChatGPT), in various fields, and they have increasingly become of interest to researchers and stimulated interdisciplinary collaborations globally. Since the emergence of ChatGPT, many similar generative AI chatbots have emerged, such as Google Gemini (previously known as Google Bard), Microsoft Copilot, Anthropic's Claude and many others.

The debates on the application of ChatGPT in Education have been ongoing since then. Some studies highlighted its usefulness for adaptive and personalised learning (Rathore, 2023; Zhai, 2022) as it can provide instant feedback, corrections, and explanations (Baidoo-Anu, 2023; Fauzi et al., 2023; Haensch et al., 2023). However, some studies (Azaria, 2022; Farrokhnia et al., 2024; Mhlanga, 2023) also address concerns related to its data reliability, the risk of biases and a lack of higher-order thinking skills. In the field of second language (L2) education, similar studies also have reported positive findings such as increased students' motivation (Ali et al., 2023; Muñoz et al., 2023) and problem-solving skills (Urban et al., 2024), saving more time designing assessments, such as tests, quizzes, rubrics and prompt feedback, and reducing teachers' workloads (Hashem et al., 2024; Huang et al., 2022; Ji et al., 2023). However, there are some concerns about its threat to academic integrity (Kartal et al., 2023; Yan, 2023), linguistic and cultural biases (Fleisig et al., 2024; Zheng & Stewart, 2024), and over-reliance on the tool (Gao et al., 2024; Karataş et al., 2024).

The positive and negative findings of these studies are generally drawn from the perspective of education in general, and L2 education in particular. However, these studies on L2 education, particularly Arabic education for non-native speakers, remain scarce, demanding more empirical research to validate any conclusions drawn from concrete data and evidence. Therefore, this study aims to gain more insight into the impact of using ChatGPT on non-native learners of Arabic, pinpointing the challenges and opportunities in completing Arabic language exercises. Hence, it also contributes to the growing discourse on the integration of AI in language learning, primarily Arabic in this context.

2 Literature Review

2.1 Generative Artificial Intelligence for Personalised Language Learning

Personalised learning is "an educational approach that tailors learning experiences to individual students' needs, preferences, and interests" (Naznin, 2025). The concept of personalized learning enables technology-supported learning design and implementation to transition from a standardized approach to one that is adaptive and student-centred. (Hoic-Bozic et al., 2016). Recent empirical studies have shown that integrating ChatGPT into personalized learning can improve student learning and engagement. (Albdrani & Al-Shargabi, 2023; Owoseni et al., 2024). Karataş and Yüce (2024) reported that while ChatGPT enhances personalized learning and optimizes learning processes, challenges persist regarding information accuracy and data security. Despite the reported positive outcomes, Agbong-Coates (2024) addresses limitations such as technology accessibility, measurement bias, and the necessity of ongoing assessment when implementing AI-driven personalized learning initiatives. Policymakers should take these findings into consideration when developing and funding educational programs to ensure that AI integration remains equitable and accessible for all students. The present study differs from previous research by focusing specifically on non-native Arabic learners and evaluating ChatGPT's effectiveness in completing language tasks. The study aims to provide a detailed and context-specific analysis of ChatGPT's potential and limitations in personalized Arabic learning.

2.2 Generative Artificial Intelligence in Arabic Language Learning

As previously mentioned, research on the use of Generative Artificial Intelligence (GenAI) in Arabic language learning is scarce compared to the number of existing studies on the application of ChatGPT in education and L2 education in general. Lelepary et al. (2023) reported positive results in their research on integrating ChatGPT in Arabic language learning, such as improved reading skills, motivation and enthusiasm, and efficiency in completing their assignments. Sa'idah et al. (2024) investigated the AI's influence on Arabic learning and student engagement. The study reported that training teachers is essential to encourage AI usage in the classrooms. As a result, it significantly increased the achievement of the learning outcomes.

Nasaruddin (2024) explored the use of ChatGPT from the perspective of Arabic language teachers and reported that ChatGPT can generate educational materials in the form of texts, questions and images with precise prompts. As a result, this can reduce teachers' workloads, as preparing materials for teaching languages can be time-consuming. Fitrianto et al. (2024) examined the utilisation of AI in designing personalised Arabic language learning plans. The study reported that the approach can enhance the learning experience and foster inclusivity and accessibility for Arabic language learners. While the previous studies reported positive outcomes of utilising ChatGPT in Arabic language learning, there is still a need for more comprehensive research that addresses its benefits and limitations. Therefore, if ChatGPT is used as an assisting tool for Arabic language learner, the present study aims to evaluate its application in Arabic language learning based on Natural Language Processing tasks so that teachers and students could understand its linguistic capabilities and determine its suitability for practical use in the language classroom.

2.3 ChatGPT Evaluation for Arabic Language Tasks

Alyafeai et al. (2023) evaluated ChatGPT models (GPT 3.5 and GPT 4.0) based on seven Arabic Natural Language Processing (NLP): sentiment analysis, translation, transliteration, paraphrasing, part of speech tagging, summarisation, and diacritization. The study reported that GPT 4.0 outperformed GPT 3.5 in all tasks except summarisation and diacritization. Khondaker et al. (2023) also conducted a similar approach to evaluate ChatGPT. However, their study also compares its performance with BLOOMZ, a finetuned variant model of pre-trained multilingual language models (Muennighoff, 2022), and two other fine-tuned models: MARBERT v2 (Abdel-Mageed et al., 2020) and AraT5 (Nagoudi et al., 2021), revealing that ChatGPT were outperformed when compared to the smaller fine-tuned models.

Even though diacritics are often omitted from Arabic texts, they are used to denote short vowels and indicate grammatical functions (Hallberg, 2022; Rahmouni, 2024) so that readers can read a text correctly, primarily non-native speakers. Rahmouni (2024) and Khoshafah (2023) examined the use of ChatGPT in providing Arabic diacritics and revealed that ChatGPT often struggled to provide accurate diacritical marks. Therefore, such inefficiency may pose a challenge for non-native speakers, particularly beginners. Aljohani et al. (2025) evaluated GPT-4 performance in the summarisation task. The results indicate that GPT-4 can provide correct Arabic summaries while highlighting the need for further refinement to support non-English languages. Khondaker et al. (2023) also reported similar findings when comparing ChatGPT to other models, suggesting further refinement for improving the model.

Jiao et al. (2023) compared the performance of ChatGPT with commercial machine translation (MT) engines such as Google Translate and DeepL, revealing that ChatGPT can be as good as the other MT engines. Similarly, Nagi et al. (2024) also compared the translation quality of ChatGPT and Google Translate for scientific texts using an error analysis approach. The findings indicate that Google Translate outperforms ChatGPT even though both systems require more training. Nagi et al. (2024) experimented with ChatGPT using informed prompts to improve the English to Arabic translations. The study reported a high number of errors when translating complex English sentences into Arabic, particularly fluency errors. However, when retranslated using the informed prompts, the results indicate significant improvement in the quality of the translation.

While the findings of the previous studies show promise in some areas, ChatGPT is outperformed in specialised task. Therefore, the present study investigates its linguistic capabilities from the perspectives of non-native language learners as end-users. For this study, it only focuses on five out of the seven NLP tasks that Alyafeai et al. (2023) employed in their evaluation study: sentiment analysis, translation, paraphrasing, summarisation, and diacritisation. Transliteration and part of speech tagging were omitted as they are less likely to be used in language learning compared to the other five tasks. However, the study added three more tasks to understand ChatGPT's linguistic capabilities: grammar, morphology and error analysis. The selection of the eight tasks will be further explained in the methodology section.

2.4 Research Questions

As mentioned previously, there is limited research on the application of ChatGPT in Arabic language learning. While the studies addressed several strengths and weaknesses, the findings are not definite and generalizable as further investigation can evaluate its capabilities from different perspectives and contexts. The present study explores the impact of using ChatGPT among non-native learners of the Arabic language based on the above-mentioned eight language tasks: sentiment analysis, translation, paraphrasing, summarisation, and diacritisation, grammar, morphology and error analysis. Therefore, it aims to investigate the following questions:

- To what extent can ChatGPT support personalized learning for non-native Arabic learners across eight specific language tasks?
- What challenges do non-native Arabic learners encounter when using ChatGPT as a personalized learning tool to improve their proficiency in the language tasks?

Therefore, the findings of this study aim to give insight to Arabic language educators on how to integrate the use of GenAI chatbots in their classes. The findings can also be used to advance research in Arabic NLP and encourage further development of these chatbots in terms of the Arabic dataset in ChatGPT, as it can potentially help enhance Arabic language learning, primarily among non-native speakers.

3 Methods

3.1 Pedagogic Setting and Participants

The present study involves seven Bruneian students who were randomly sampled, majoring in the Arabic language and translation at Universiti Islam Sultan Sharif Ali as shown in Table 1. The students are Malay learners of the Arabic language. The students were also randomly sampled from each year of study to represent the demographic data of the students enrolled in the Arabic language and translation program. The study adopted focus group discussion, a qualitative technique to further understand the students' attitudes towards using ChatGPT for learning the Arabic language and get a more thorough grasp of the impact of using the tool on their learning process in terms of challenges and opportunities for improvements based on their experience using the tool in the experiment.

Table 1 Demographics of participants

Name	Gender	Age	Race	Major	Year of study
P1	Female	19	Malay	Arabic language and translation	Year 1
P2	Female	19	Malay	Arabic language and translation	Year 1
P3	Female	20	Malay	Arabic language and translation	Year 2
P4	Male	20	Malay	Arabic language and translation	Year 2
P5	Male	21	Malay	Arabic language and translation	Year 3
P6	Female	21	Malay	Arabic language and translation	Year 3
P7	Male	22	Malay	Arabic language and translation	Year 4

3.2 Design of the Study

Given the emerging role of GenAI in Arabic language learning and the limited existing research on its application, this study adopts an exploratory research design. While existing studies have shown examined ChatGPT's performance in various NLP tasks, there remains a gap in understanding its effectiveness for non-native Arabic language learners, primarily in the context of Bruneian Malay students. This study involves two processes: completing Arabic language exercises and focus group discussion. The first process requires the students to utilise ChatGPT-4o to complete eight language exercises individually: grammar, morphology, paraphrasing, diacritics, error analysis, sentiment analysis, translation, and summarisation, as shown in Fig. 1. The questions were carefully designed by the researchers, who are experts in translation studies and teaching the Arabic language to non-native speakers.

The second process requires them to participate in a focus group discussion and express their opinions based on their experience of using ChatGPT when answering the questions for each task. The discussion was conducted in Malay to ensure that the participants could express their thoughts in their mother tongue freely to enhance data quality by ensuring clarity, comfort, and depth of responses. The semi-structured interview items were designed in Malay to ensure that the participants could express their opinions easily cover three main areas as follows:

1. Effectiveness in Arabic language learning
    a. Can you describe your experience using ChatGPT in learning Arabic language?
    b. To what extent do you find the language generated by ChatGPT comprehensible and suitable for learning Arabic?
    c. How accurately does ChatGPT respond to your Arabic prompts?
2. Experience in completing each language task
    a. Can you describe your experience using ChatGPT to complete the (specific) task?

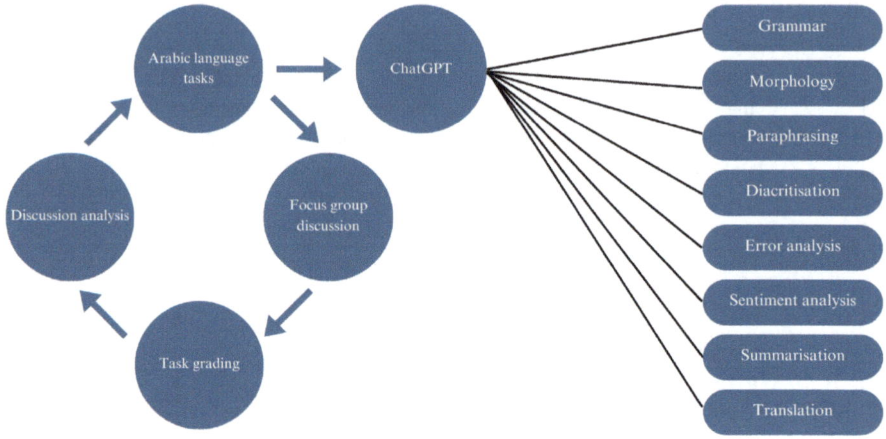

Fig. 1 Methodology flowchart

b. To what extent does ChatGPT provide accurate responses to your queries?
c. How clear and comprehensible do you find ChatGPT's explanations of its responses?

3. Benefits, risks and opportunities for improvements

a. In what ways has ChatGPT supported your learning of Arabic?
b. Which specific language tasks have you found ChatGPT to be most helpful with?
c. What challenges have you encountered when using ChatGPT for Arabic language learning?
d. What are your main concerns regarding the integration of ChatGPT into Arabic language learning?
e. What recommendations do you have for enhancing ChatGPT's effectiveness in Arabic language learning?

The language tasks and interview items were tested in a pilot test with a small group of students and subject-matter experts in the field prior to conducting the exploratory study. The questions were then refined based on their feedback. Triangulation was used to strengthen the overall validity by comparing findings of the participants' scores and answers in the language tasks, focus group discussion and existing literature. The study also ensured member checking to ensure that the participants' responses are accurately represented in the findings.

Previous studies (Abdelali et al., 2023; Ahuja et al., 2023; Alyafeai et al., 2023; Elmadany et al., 2022) have shown positive findings in evaluating the performance of generative AI models in Arabic NLP tasks. Similarly, the present study only uses all Arabic NLP tasks except part of speech tagging and transliteration, as Arabic language learners may not use ChatGPT for the two tasks daily. However, the grammar, morphology and error analysis tasks were added to the list as they are more beneficial for enhancing the Arabic language competencies.

3.3 Data Collection and Analysis

Before starting the data collection, students were informed regarding the privacy of the information, confidentiality, and audio recording and they could leave the discussion if they decided not to continue. The study was conducted on 2nd May 2024 in the university's computer lab. The duration of completing the tasks was 60 min while the discussion was conducted between 60 and 90 min. The interview was audio recorded and transcribed verbatim. The students' tasks were also graded accordingly by the researchers. The study examined their answers and performance in each task and then attempted to see if there was any correlation between their performance and findings from the interview.

4 Results/Findings

Results in Table 2 show the students' performance in eight tasks: grammar, morphology, paraphrasing, diacritisation, error analysis, sentiment analysis, translation and summarising. Each task was assessed on a scale ranging from 0 to 10 based on each task's rubric. As can be seen from Table 1, the students did best in the translation and summarising tasks while doing well in four tasks: sentiment analysis, error analysis, diacritics, and paraphrasing. On the other hand, they seem to perform poorly in grammar and morphology tasks. This section will address their performance respectively.

4.1 Grammar

In the grammar task, students were required to answer 10 questions on various grammar topics, such as rephrasing sentences into different forms (active, passive, nominal, verbal, etc.…), circumstantial (*ḥāl*) clause, grammatical cases (*i'rāb*), and many others. According to Table 1, the results showed that only one student performed well, scoring a 6. Meanwhile, three students scored below average, with scores ranging from 3.5 to 4.5, and three students underperformed, with marks between 1.5 and 2. Their scores indicate that ChatGPT is not ready to be used to learn Arabic grammar and needs major improvement.

Table 2 Students' individual scores in each task

Student	Grammar	Morphology	Paraphrasing	Diacritization	Error analysis	Sentiment analysis	Translation	Summarisation
1	1.5	2.5	6.5	2	6	8.3	8.9	9
2	2	2	6.5	8	6	8.3	9.8	9
3	3.5	3	8	9	6	7.3	9.6	9
4	4.5	2.5	5	8	7	6.3	9.6	9
5	6	6	6	8	9	7.3	9.8	9
6	4.5	4	6	4	7	7.3	9.6	9
7	2	1.5	6.5	9	6	7.3	9.4	9
Total	3.43	3.07	6.36	6.86	6.71	7.44	9.53	9

4.2 Morphology

In the morphology exercise, students were required to answer 10 questions on different morphology topics, such as derivations, clitics, and affixes. As shown in Table 1, the results revealed that only one student achieved a score of 6. Meanwhile, two students received below-average scores of 3 and 4, and the other four achieved scores of 1.5 and 2. Similar to the grammar task, their performance indicates that ChatGPT's responses to morphology-related questions are not reliable and require major improvement.

4.3 Paraphrasing

In the paraphrasing task, the students paraphrased two texts of different genres: media and tourism. The two texts are of similar lengths: 84 words for the first and 104 for the latter. The results in Table 1 indicate that most students achieved overall good results, scoring 6–6.5. A student performed notably, scoring 8, while another performed fairly, only scoring 5. Nevertheless, their good performance indicates that ChatGPT could assist them in the paraphrasing task. It has incredible potential to become a powerful paraphrasing tool if further evolved.

4.4 Diacritization

In the diacritization task, students were required to provide diacritics in 10 simple sentences. As shown in Table 1, the results revealed that seven students achieved excellent scores, ranging from 8 to 9. However, two students underperformed, scoring 2 and 4, respectively, due to incomplete diacritics in the sentences. Nevertheless, the overall performance suggests that ChatGPT could provide substantial support in diacritics exercises, particularly for students who are weak at diacritization or uncertain about which diacritics should be applied.

4.5 Error Analysis

In the Error Analysis task, the students were instructed to correct mistakes in 10 short sentences. The results in Table 1 indicate that most students achieved overall good results, scoring 6–9. One student achieved a notable score of 9, while many scored an average of 6. The students' good performance indicates that ChatGPT could assist them in conducting an error analysis, and it helps them understand the errors in their answers. However, ChatGPT requires further improvement regarding this task, as it has great potential to become a powerful writing assistant tool for students to ensure the quality of their writing. At the same time, it can help them learn from their mistakes and how to improve their writing and error analysis skills.

4.6 Sentiment Analysis

In the sentiment analysis task, the students were required to provide a sentiment analysis on 10 different words. The results in Table 1 indicate that most students achieved overall good results, scoring 6.3–7.3. Two students achieved a notable score of 8. The students' good performance indicated that ChatGPT could assist them in conducting a sentiment analysis and help them further understand the connotation of a term.

4.7 Translation

In the translation task, the students were required to translate Malay terms and simple short and long Malay sentences into Arabic. The results in Table 1 indicate that all students achieved excellent scores, ranging from 8.9 to 8.8. When looking further into individual questions, the students made similar translation mistakes in Questions 9 and 10, which required them to translate long sentences. However, the students' excellent performance indicates that ChatGPT could assist them considerably in translation exercises, suggesting that ChatGPT is a good translation assistant tool to enhance their productivity and quality.

4.8 Summarization

In the summarization task, students were asked to summarise a short paragraph of approximately 120 words into 30 words. As shown in Table 1, the results demonstrate that all students achieved excellent scores of 9. The results indicate that most students successfully summarize tasks with the assistance of ChatGPT. Their summaries also showed that they did not fully copy and paste the summary given by ChatGPT as they are different from one another.

5 Discussion

This section will address the challenges the participants faced in the tasks and opportunities for improvements based on their task grades and interview in the focus group discussion.

5.1 *Grammar*

In Sect. 4.1, the results showed that only one student achieved good scores, while the rest scored below 5. Upon analysing individual answers, it was found that most students refer to ChatGPT to obtain answers. However, some of the answers were inaccurate. For example, the answer given by ChatGPT for the question of converting the sentence from a verbal sentence: يذهب ريان وصفوان إلى معرض الكتب بالحافلة (*Yadhhab rayyān wa ṣafwān ilā ma 'raḍ al-kutub bi al-ḥāfila*) to a nominal sentence: ذهاب ريان وصفوان إلى معرض الكتب بالحافلة (*Dhihāb rayyān wa ṣafwān ilā ma 'raḍ al-kutub bi al-ḥāfila)*, whereas the correct answer is ريان وصفوان يذهبان إلى معرض الكتب بالحافلة (*Rayyān wa ṣafwān yadhhabān ilā ma 'raḍ al-kutub bi al-ḥāfila)*. Many students copied the answer provided by ChatGPT entirely. Some expressed that they noticed the mistake and gave the correct answer based on their knowledge. Two students also voiced concerns that using ChatGPT may not be an appropriate method for learning Arabic grammar, as they believe it requires guidance from a teacher, primarily for beginners.

Regarding the *i 'rab* questions, most students either did not refer to ChatGPT or simply copied its responses without selecting the correct information for their answers. Additionally, some students expressed frustration with ChatGPT's responses, even when they attempted to refine their queries for more accurate answers. Overall, the absence of accurate information on Arabic grammar may be a concern for teachers, particularly when designing personalized learning plans for their students as ChatGPT could potentially provide misleading or incorrect instruction. Therefore, researchers and developers should address this gap and develop sustainable solutions to ensure that students can effectively use ChatGPT for learning Arabic grammar.

5.2 *Morphology*

In Sect. 4.2, the findings indicate that only one student achieved a high score of 6, while the others scored below 5. Upon reviewing individual answers, it became clear that most students did not rely on ChatGPT for certain morphology questions, as their answers differed from the correct ones provided by ChatGPT. For instance, regarding the Arabic diminutives of زَيْنُ العارفين (*zayn al- ʻārifīn*), only one student gave the correct answer, which aligned with ChatGPT's response of زُيَيْنُ العَارفين (*zuyayn al- ʻārifīn*).

The results also showed that many students copied ChatGPT's answers entirely without filtering out irrelevant parts for specific questions. For example, when asked to identify the broken plural in a sentence, students listed all plural forms, including sound female and masculine plurals, as ChatGPT provided, without focusing on the specific plural form needed for the question. This highlights the importance of students being more selective and ensuring their answers are tailored to the requirements of each question. In the interview, all students acknowledged that some of ChatGPT's answers to morphology questions were incorrect. Some students preferred learning from books as they believed books can provide accurate information and answers. Others, who felt weak in Arabic morphology, were unsure of the correctness of the answers and thus resorted to copying them. Similar to concerns regarding the Arabic grammar, ChatGPT also lacks correct information on Arabic morphology. Therefore, it is worth investigating it in more comprehensive research that can address improvements or solutions for this issue so that teachers can provide their students with guidelines when designing personalized learning for them.

5.3 Paraphrasing

In Sect. 4.3, the results show that the students achieved overall good scores. In this section. The present study further discusses the challenges the students faced in the paraphrasing task and opportunities for improvements in further research. In the focus group discussion, all students agreed that the text that ChatGPT paraphrased was better than the original text. Some expressed that the paraphrased text was easier to understand because ChatGPT used simpler terms. Some also expressed that the good quality of the paraphrased text indicates the reliability of using it in paraphrasing texts effectively in a shorter amount of time. This finding contradicts Alyafeai et al. (2023) evaluation of ChatGPT, where both versions 3.5 and 4.0 received low scores. However, a possible explanation for this discrepancy is the use of different prompts. While this may not be the sole determining factor, it is noteworthy that the authors used English prompts, whereas the participants in this study used Arabic prompts. This suggest that ChatGPT's responses may vary depending on the language of interaction, particularly when prompts include specific requirements. For instance, in this task, the students were required to paraphrase a newspaper article and an example of their prompts is أعد الصياغة للنص الصحفي الآتي (*ʼaʻid al-ṣiyāga li al-naṣ al-ʼātī*), which translates to "Paraphrase this news article" rather than using general prompts, such as "Paraphrase the following text".

The findings also showed that some students were confused between paraphrasing and summarising tasks. They summarised the texts instead of paraphrasing them. As a result, they were penalised with a points deduction. Nevertheless, the study suggests that students should be provided clear guidelines on paraphrasing, summarising, and comparing the two tasks, primarily for non-native learners of Arabic.

5.4 *Diacritization*

In Sect. 4.4, the results show that all students achieved good scores, except for two who did not fully apply diacritics to the questions, resulting in scores below 5. Upon analyzing individual questions, it was found that most students answered correctly, except for Question 7, which was: رأينا عشرين سمكا في البركة (*ra'aynā 'ishrīna samakan fī al-birka*). The students made an error with the word البركة (*al-birka*), as there are three possible diacritics for this word: البَرَكة (*al-baraka*), البُركة (*al-burka*), and البِركة (*al-birka*), each with a different meaning. The first means blessing, the second means mallard, and the last means pond. This highlights the importance of precise prompts in obtaining accurate responses from ChatGPT. In this task, most students used a similar prompt: "ضع تشكيلات تامة في الجملة الآتية" (*ḍa' tashkīlāt tāmma fī al-jumla al-'ātiya*), which translates to "Please diacritise the entire following sentence". A comparison between the low and high scorers revealed that the low scorers omitted the word "entire" in their prompts, which may have contributed to less accurate responses.

Overall, students expressed that they would use ChatGPT for diacritics tasks in the future, as it could save time and is generally accurate. However, to achieve better results, students must review the answers and ensure that clear and precise instructions are provided to receive correct responses. The finding of this study contradicts the studies of Rahmouni (2024) and Khoshafah (2023), which reported that ChatGPT often struggled with diacritic accuracy. A possible explanation for this discrepancy is that the present study utilised the latest version of ChatGPT, which may have yielded more accurate responses.

5.5 *Error Analysis*

In Sect. 4.5, the results show that the students achieved overall good scores. In this section, some students expressed uncertainty about the accuracy of ChatGPT's responses. In this task, the students used a common prompt: "صحح الأخطاء في الجملة الآتية" (*ṣaḥḥiḥ al-akṭā' fī al-jumla al-'ātiya*), which translates to "Please correct the mistakes in the following sentence". While ChatGPT provided correct answers for some questions, errors persisted in certain sentences, highlighting the need for users to exercise caution when relying on ChatGPT for error analysis.

The following question is the only one that all students almost answer correctly: يقرأ الطلاب المدرسية ورجوع الكتب العملية.

(*yaqraʾu al-ṭullāb al-madrasiyya wa rujūʿ al-kutub al-ʿamaliyya*)

Most students provided the incorrect answer:

يقرأ الطلاب المدرسية ويرجعون الكتب العملية.

(*yaqraʾu al-ṭullāb al-madrasiyya wa yarjiʿūna al-kutub al-ʿamaliyya*)

The students managed to change the noun رجوع (*rujūʿ*) to the verb يرجعون (*yarjiʿūna*). However, the correct verb is يراجعون (*yurājiʿūna*) because it means revise, and the previous one means return.

Some students also did not refer to ChatGPT and provided their answers, as seen in the following example:

هذا الطالبات يدرسن في المدرسة الثانوية.

(*hādhā al-ṭālibāt yadrusna fī al-madrasa al-thānawiyya*)

The students knew that the error here was the gender and number of the demonstrative pronoun هذا (*hādhā*) but some students could not provide the correct one, which is هؤلاء (*hāʾulā*). Nevertheless, their overall good scores in the task indicate that they did not copy and paste the answers given by ChatGPT, suggesting that they answered the questions critically even though they almost provided the correct one. They also stated that they would use ChatGPT for error analysis in the future, particularly if they need to confirm that the words are correct or not. The high scores in this task also correlate with the findings of Alyafeai et al. (2023).

5.6 Sentiment Analysis

In Sect. 4.6, the results show that the students achieved overall good scores, indicating that the answers generated in ChatGPT helped them understand the connotations of the words. However, they could have provided more than one answer. As a result, all of them could not give a complete answer to several questions. For example, Question 3 required them to carry out a sentiment analysis for an Arabic word يحتاج (*yaḥtāj*), which means to need or require. The students used a similar prompt: "حلل المشاعر في الكلمة الآتية" (*ḥallil al-mashāʿir fī al-kalima al-ʾātiya*), which translates to "Please analyse the sentiments for the following word". The sentiment analysis for the word يحتاج can be as follows:

- Neutral: أحتاج إلى قلم للكتابة (*aḥtāj ilā qalam lil-kitāba*, which means I need a pen to write), which states a fact or necessity.
- Positive: أحتاج إلى تطوير مهاراتي لتحقيق أهدافي (*aḥtāj ilā taṭwīr mahārātī li-taḥqīq ahdāfī*, which means I need to improve my skills to achieve my goals), which expresses a desire for personal growth or ambition)
- Negative: أحتاج إلى المزيد من الوقت ولكن فات الأوان الآن (*aḥtāj ilā al-mazīd min al-waqt walākin fāt al-awān al-ān*, which means I need more time, but it is too late now), which expresses feeling of lack or regret.

Overall, most students felt that the given answers were inaccurate. Their good scores suggest that they did not copy and paste the given answers and tried to provide the answers using their critical thinking skills. They also stated that they would use ChatGPT for sentiment analysis in the future, particularly if they need to confirm that their prior knowledge of a word's connotation is correct.

5.7 Translation

In Sect. 4.7, the results show that the students achieved overall excellent scores, indicating that ChatGPT can provide quality translations. However, when further analysing their answers to individual questions, the results showed that most answered correctly except Questions 9 and 10. The two questions required them to translate longer sentences. This finding aligns with that of Nagi et al. (2024), who also identified errors in translating complex sentences. The analysis also showed that most of them provided literal translations and made some grammatical mistakes, such as the definite nouns using ال (al) and indefinite article without ال, as can be seen in the following example:

Original text: Universiti tersebut telah mengadakan program khidmat masyarakat di Kampong Ayer (The university organised a community service program in Kampong Ayer).

Arabic translation: نظمت الجامعة البرنامج لخدمة المجتمع في كامبونغ أير.

(*nazzamat al-jāmiʿah al-barnāmij li-khidmat al-mujtamaʿ fī kāmbong ayir*).

In this task, the students used a similar prompt: "ترجم الجملة الآتية إلى العربية" (*tarjim al-jumla al-ʾātiya ilā al-ʿarabiyya*), which translates to "Please translate the following sentence into Arabic". As can be seen in the example, the translator should have translated the Malay indefinite noun "program" similarly into Arabic برنامج (*barnāmij*) or برنامجا (*barnāmijan*) in this context. A possible explanation for this mistake is singular nouns may not require indefinite articles in Malay to indicate that they are indefinite nouns, unlike English singular nouns that require indefinite articles "a" and "an".

Generally, the students stated that the translations were of good quality and comprehensible. This finding correlates with the study of Jiao et al. (2023). However, they also expressed their preference for other existing translation tools, such as Google Translate, Context Reverso and al-Maany. However, some students also suggested that the translations need further revision, indicating that they did not copy and paste the answers provided by ChatGPT. Their critical thinking skills were reflected in their comments as follows:

- The translation quality varies in terms of language pairs and directionality.
- Human translators need to be well-versed with the source and target cultures.

The translators would also use ChatGPT for translation tasks in the future as the translations did not require major revisions and could save time.

5.8 Summarisation

In Sect. 4.8, the results showed that the students achieved excellent scores, suggesting that ChatGPT can effectively assist with producing quality summaries. This finding correlates with the studies of Al-Johani et al. (2025) and Khondaker et al. (2023), which also emphasized the need for further refinement. A deeper analysis of their responses to individual questions shows that most students successfully summarised the text. Most students could convey the same key points as in the original text.

When students were asked about their use of ChatGPT for the summarisation tasks, the following key points emerged from their feedback:

- ChatGPT makes summarising easier and is particularly beneficial for last-minute tasks. The responses were clear and generated quickly.
- ChatGPT's outputs capture the intended meaning and meet the required word count, while effectively including all the key points.
- ChatGPT does not always provide the specific words requested, making it less suitable for assignments that demand precision. Quillbot was recommended as an alternative for better control over the text length and specificity.
- Some users are hesitant to rely on ChatGPT or other internet sources for references due to concerns about reliability and the possibility of errors.
- ChatGPT is perceived as effective and helpful for short summarisation tasks, although less satisfying for tasks that require greater accuracy.

Overall, most students agreed that ChatGPT is a useful tool and planned to continue using it, although there is still room for improvement.

5.9 General Comments

This section reports general comments in the focus group discussion that are not related to any specific tasks, highlighting the challenges and opportunities for improvement. The comments are categorized as follows:

- **Overreliance on ChatGPT:** The students expressed their concern regarding excessive dependency on the tool, which can impair their critical thinking skills (Amoozadeh et al., 2024; Duhaylungsod & Chavez, 2023; Gao et al., 2024; Karataş et al., 2024; Pham & Le, 2024; Valova et al., 2024) and recommended to resort to reliable references first. Some of the students' comments are as follows:

> I am afraid that students may rely too much on ChatGPT and do not use their critical thinking skills when they face a problem.

> Students may depend too much on ChatGPT and are less likely to refer books. On contrary they should refer these books as they are more reliable.

- **Ethical Concerns in Language Learning:**: Some students blindly trusted ChatGPT and copied its answers, particularly when they are uncertain of the accuracy of the responses. This can be seen in some of the tasks. The uncertainty may pose risks to academic credibility and linguistic development (Baskara, 2023; Ibrahim et al., 2023; Kartal et al., 2023; Yan, 2023).

> Students would be more likely to copy ChatGPT's responses without thinking, especially when they are not sure if the answers are correct.

> Copying the responses without analysing it may lead to plagiarism and thus, hinder developing their language skills.

Some students also highlighted the importance of enhancing AI literacy among students through proper guidelines and policy (Jarrah et al., 2023; Perkins, 2023), which should be provided by the university.

> The university must provide proper guidelines and policy on how to use AI, like ChatGPT, so that students would use it wisely and will not attempt to plagiarise or cheat in their assessments.

- **Lack of accurate data:** Students felt uncertain about the accuracy of ChatGPT's responses, especially in grammar and morphology exercises. It is recommended that further research should focus on the two linguistic aspects to enhance the responses, as improvements in these areas would greatly benefit teachers, particularly when designing personalized learning plans for students.
- **Inaccurate responses:** Using vague prompts often resulted in general or imprecise answers. The responses may also vary significantly when similar prompts are given repeatedly (Kohnke et al., 2023). Therefore, users should include detailed and clear prompts to obtain more accurate responses. In the interview, the students also suggested that additional training should be provided for educators and students on how to formulate effective prompts would be beneficial (Kasneci et al., 2023; Lee & Park, 2024; Lo, 2023; Nguyen, 2023).
- **One size does not fit all:** The lack of accurate data and inaccurate responses require the foundational Arabic linguistic knowledge and critical thinking. Therefore, ChatGPT may not be ideal for beginners as they may struggle to assess the accuracy of the responses. If introduced to beginners, it should be used under the teacher's supervision and strictly used as a supplementary language learning aid. Nevertheless, the students generally agreed that ChatGPT is a valuable assistant tool for personalized learning.

6 Conclusion and Implication

The present study aims to investigate the challenges and opportunities for improvement when integrating ChatGPT in Arabic language learning for non-native learners. Overall, the findings partially align with previous studies, such as Alyafeai et al. (2023), while also presenting new insights. The present study excluded transliteration and part of speech tagging while incorporating additional tasks, such as grammar, morphology and error analysis, thereby expanding the understanding of ChatGPT's linguistic capabilities and its potential of use when designing personalized learning plans for non-native learners of Arabic.

Overall, the students performed well across the eight Arabic language exercises, particularly in the translation and summary tasks, indicating that ChatGPT can be useful for non-native learners of Arabic when used effectively. Students noticed that ChatGPT's paraphrased texts were often more refined than the original versions. The study also revealed that the quality of the ChatGPT translations was good and required minimal revisions, indicating its effectiveness as a supportive tool for language learners. However, most students performed poorly in the grammar and morphology exercises. Therefore, further improvements and precise data training are required to improve accuracy in these areas. Overall, the present study extends the existing literature by offering a more detailed, task-oriented, and context-specific analysis of ChatGPT's role in personalized Arabic language learning.

Some students pointed out that correct prompts are crucial in getting accurate responses from ChatGPT. Therefore, further research should be conducted on precise prompts to obtain accurate responses. Despite existing challenges, the students are aware of them. They would still use ChatGPT, indicating that they recognise its value for personalised language learning. The present study also reported useful prompts that can be used in academic and research settings. Future research should explore the impact of using different prompts to optimise ChatGPT's effectiveness, as they can be beneficial for tailoring personalised language learning plans.

The findings also revealed other challenges such as overreliance on ChatGPT, ethical concerns regarding its use in language learning, limitations in data accuracy, inaccurate responses, and its unsuitability for all language learners. However, the findings also emphasized potential solutions, such as consulting reliable sources beyond ChatGPT, establishing clear guidelines and policies for its use, enhancing the system with more accurate data, providing additional training to improve AI literacy, and exercising caution when using the tool as a supplementary language learning tool rather than a primary learning resource.

However, the study also addresses its limitations. The data should be interpreted with cautions. While this study provides valuable insights into the use of ChatGPT for Arabic language learning among non-native speakers, several limitations should be acknowledged. The small sample size of seven Malay learners limits the generalizability of the findings, and the qualitative nature of the study, while insightful, lacks quantitative data to measure the tool's effectiveness. Furthermore, ethical concerns such as plagiarism and overreliance on AI tools were not explored in depth. Future research should address these limitations by incorporating larger and more diverse samples, employing mixed-methods approaches, and investigating broader linguistic skills and responsible AI integration in language learning.

References

Abdelali, A., Mubarak, H., Chowdhury, S. A., Hasanain, M., Mousi, B., Boughorbel, S., El Kheir, Y., Izham, D., Dalvi, F., Hawasly, M., Nazar, N., Elshahawy, Y., Ali, A., Durrani, N., Milic-Frayling, N., & Alam, F. (2023). LAraBench: Benchmarking Arabic AI with large language models. arXiv [Preprint]. https://arxiv.org/abs/2305.14982

Abdul-Mageed, M., Elmadany, A., & Nagoudi, E. M. B. (2020). ARBERT & MARBERT: Deep bidirectional transformers for Arabic. arXiv [Preprint]. https://arxiv.org/abs/2101.01785

Abu-Hatab, W. (1992). Discourse error analysis of compositions written by community college students. *Unpublished master's thesis, University of Jordan, Jordan.*

Agbong-Coates, I. J. G. (2024). ChatGPT integration significantly boosts personalized learning outcomes: A Philippine study. *International Journal of Educational Management and Development Studies, 5*(2), 165–186.

Ahuja, K., Diddee, H., Hada, R., Ochieng, M., Ramesh, K., Jain, P., Nambi, A., Ganu, T., Segal, S., Axmed, M., Bali, K., & Sitaram, S. (2023). Mega: Multilingual evaluation of generative AI. arXiv [Preprint]. https://arxiv.org/abs/2303.12528

Alanazi, M. S. (2024). The use of modern standard Arabic and colloquial Arabic in translation tasks: A new perspective. *Cogent Arts & Humanities, 11*(1), 2366572.

Albdrani, R. N., & Al-Shargabi, A. A. (2023). Investigating the effectiveness of ChatGPT for providing personalized learning experience: A case study. *International Journal of Advanced Computer Science & Applications, 14*(11)

Ali, J. K. M., Shamsan, M. A. A., Hezam, T. A., & Mohammed, A. A. (2023). Impact of ChatGPT on learning motivation: Teachers and students' voices. *Journal of English Studies in Arabia Felix, 2*(1), 41–49.

Aljohani, A., Alharbi, R., Alkhaldi, A., & Aljedaani, W. (2025). Evaluating LLMs for Arabic code summarization: Challenges and insights from GPT-4. In *2025 8th International Conference on Data Science and Machine Learning Applications (CDMA)* (pp. 67–72). IEEE.

Alyafeai, Z., Alshaibani, M. S., AlKhamissi, B., Luqman, H., Alareqi, E., & Fadel, A. (2023). Taqyim: Evaluating arabic nlp tasks using chatgpt models. arXiv [Preprint]. https://arxiv.org/abs/2306.16322

Amoozadeh, M., Nam, D., Prol, D., Alfageeh, A., Prather, J., Hilton, M., Ragavan, S. S., & Alipour, A. (2024, November). Student-AI interaction: A case study of CS1 students. In *Proceedings of the 24th Koli Calling International Conference on Computing Education Research* (pp. 1–13).

Azaria, A. (2022). ChatGPT usage and limitations. Preprint. https://hal.science/hal-03913837v1

Baidoo-Anu, D., & Ansah, L. O. (2023). Education in the era of generative artificial intelligence (AI): Understanding the potential benefits of ChatGPT in promoting teaching and learning. *Journal of AI, 7*(1), 52–62.

Baskara, R. (2023). Exploring the implications of ChatGPT for language learning in higher education. *Indonesian Journal of English Language Teaching and Applied Linguistics, 7*(2), 343–358.

Cote, R. A. (2009). Choosing one dialect for the Arabic speaking world: A status planning dilemma. *Journal of Second Language Acquisition and Teaching, 16*, 75–97.

Duhaylungsod, A. V., & Chavez, J. V. (2023). ChatGPT and other AI users: Innovative and creative utilitarian value and mindset shift. *Journal of Namibian Studies, 33*(2023), 4367–4378.

Elmadany, A., Nagoudi, E. M. B., & Abdul-Mageed, M. (2022). ORCA: A challenging benchmark for Arabic language understanding. arXiv [Preprint]. https://arxiv.org/abs/2212.10758

Farrokhnia, M., Banihashem, S. K., Noroozi, O., & Wals, A. (2024). A SWOT analysis of ChatGPT: Implications for educational practice and research. *Innovations in Education and Teaching International, 61*(3), 460–474.

Fauzi, F., Tuhuteru, L., Sampe, F., Ausat, A. M. A., & Hatta, H. R. (2023). Analysing the role of ChatGPT in improving student productivity in higher education. *Journal on Education, 5*(4), 14886–14891. https://doi.org/10.31004/JOE.V5I4.2563

Ferguson, C. A. (1959). Diglossia. *Word-Journal of the International Linguistic Association, 15*(2), 325–340.

Fitrianto, I., Setyawan, C. E., & Saleh, M. (2024). Utilizing artificial intelligence for personalized Arabic language learning plans. *International Journal of Post Axial: Futuristic Teaching and Learning, 201*, 32–142.

Fleisig, E., Smith, G., Bossi, M., Rustagi, I., Yin, X., & Klein, D. (2024). Linguistic bias in ChatGPT: Language models reinforce dialect discrimination. arXiv [Preprint]. https://arxiv.org/abs/2406.08818

Gao, Y., Wang, Q., & Wang, X. (2024). Exploring EFL university teachers' beliefs in integrating ChatGPT and other large language models in language education: A study in China. *Asia Pacific Journal of Education, 44*(1), 29–44.

Haensch, A. C., Ball, S., Herklotz, M., & Kreuter, F. (2023). Seeing ChatGPT through students' eyes: An analysis of TikTok data. *ArXiv Preprint*. https://arxiv.org/abs/2303.05349v1

Hallberg, A. (2022). Principles of variation in the use of diacritics (taškīl) in Arabic books. *Language Sciences, 93*, 1–15.

Hashem, R., Ali, N., El Zein, F., Fidalgo, P., & Khurma, O. A. (2024). AI to the rescue: Exploring the potential of ChatGPT as a teacher ally for workload relief and burnout prevention. *Research & Practice in Technology Enhanced Learning, 19*, 23.

Hoic-Bozic, N., Dlab, M. H., & Mornar, V. (2015). Recommender system and web 2.0 tools to enhance a blended learning model. *IEEE Transactions on Education, 59*(1), 39–44.

Holes, C. (2004). *Modern Arabic: Structures, functions, and varieties*. Georgetown University Press.

Huang, W., Hew, K. F., & Fryer, L. K. (2022). Chatbots for language learning—Are they really useful? A systematic review of chatbot-supported language learning. *Journal of Computer Assisted Learning, 38*(1), 237–257.

Ibrahim, H., Liu, F., Asim, R., Battu, B., Benabderrahmane, S., Alhafni, B., Adnan, W., Alhanai, T., Alshebli, B., Baghdadi, R., Bélanger, J. J., Beretta, E., Celik, K., Chaqfeh, M., Daqaq, M. F., El Bernoussi, Z., Fougnie, D., de Soto, B. G., Gandolfi, A., & Zaki, Y. (2023). Perception, performance, and detectability of conversational artificial intelligence across 32 university courses. *Scientific Reports, 13*(1), 12187.

Jarrah, A. M., Wardat, Y., & Fidalgo, P. (2023). Using ChatGPT in academic writing is (not) a form of plagiarism: What does the literature say. *Online Journal of Communication and Media Technologies, 13*(4), Article e202346.

Ji, H., Han, I., & Ko, Y. (2023). A systematic review of conversational AI in language education: Focusing on the collaboration with human teachers. *Journal of Research on Technology in Education, 55*(1), 48–63.

Jiao, W., Wang, W., Huang, J. T., Wang, X., & Tu, Z. (2023). Is ChatGPT a good translator? A preliminary study. arXiv [Preprint]. https://arxiv.org/abs/2301.08745

Karataş, F., Abedi, F. Y., Ozek Gunyel, F., Karadeniz, D., & Kuzgun, Y. (2024). Incorporating AI in foreign language education: An investigation into ChatGPT's effect on foreign language learners. *Education and Information Technologies, 29*(15), 19343–19366.

Karataş, F., & Yüce, E. (2024). AI and the future of teaching: Preservice teachers' reflections on the use of artificial intelligence in open and distributed learning. *International Review of Research in Open and Distributed Learning, 25*(3), 304–325.

Kartal, G. (2023). Contemporary language teaching and learning with ChatGPT. *Contemporary Research in Language and Linguistics, 1*(1), 2980–2253.

Kasneci, E., Seßler, K., Küchemann, S., Bannert, M., Dementieva, D., Fischer, F., Gasser, U., Groh, G., Günnemann, S., Hüllermeier, E., Krusche, S., Kutyniok, G., Michaeli, T., Nerdel, C., Pfeffer, J., Poquet, O., Sailer, M., Schmidt, A., Seidel, T., & Kasneci, G. (2023). ChatGPT for good? On opportunities and challenges of large language models for education. *Learning and Individual Differences, 103*, Article 102274.

Khondaker, M. T. I., Waheed, A., Nagoudi, E. M. B., & Abdul-Mageed, M. (2023). Gptaraeval: A comprehensive evaluation of Chatgpt on Arabic nlp. arXiv [Preprint] https://arxiv.org/abs/2305.14976

Khoshafah, F. (2023). ChatGPT for Arabic-English translation: Evaluating the accuracy.

Kohnke, L., Moorhouse, B. L., & Zou, D. (2023). ChatGPT for language teaching and learning. *Relc Journal, 54*(2), 537–550.

Lee, S., & Park, G. (2024). Development and validation of ChatGPT literacy scale. *Current Psychology, 43*(21), 18992–19004.

Lelepary, H. L., Rachmawati, R., Zani, B. N., & Maharjan, K. (2023). ChatGPT: Opportunities and challenges in the learning process of Arabic language in higher education. *Journal International of Lingua and Technology, 2*(1), 11–23.

Lo, C. K. (2023). What is the impact of ChatGPT on education? A rapid review of the literature. *Education Sciences, 13*(4), 410.

Mhlanga, D. (2023). Open AI in education, the responsible and ethical use of ChatGPT towards lifelong learning. In D. Mhlanga, (Eds.), *FinTech and artificial intelligence for sustainable development: The role of smart technologies in achieving development goals* (pp. 387–409). Cham: Springer Nature. https://doi.org/10.1007/978-3-031-37776-1_17

Muennighoff, N., Wang, T., Sutawika, L., Roberts, A., Biderman, S., Scao, T. L., Saiful Bari, M., Shen, S., Yong, Z., Schoelkopf, H., Tang, X., Radev, D., Aji, A. F., Almubarak, K., Albanie, S., Alyafeai, Z., Webson, A., Raff, E., & Raffel, C. (2022). Crosslingual generalization through multitask finetuning. arXiv [Preprint]. https://arxiv.org/abs/2211.01786

Muñoz, S. A. S., Gayoso, G. G., Huambo, A. C., Tapia, R. D. C., Incaluque, J. L., Aguila, O. E. P., & Arias-Gonzáles, J. L. (2023). Examining the impacts of ChatGPT on student motivation and engagement. *Social Space, 23*(1), 1–27.

Nagi, K. A., Alzain, E., & Naji, E. (2024). Informed prompts and improving ChatGPT English to Arabic translation. *Al-Andalus Journal for Humanities Social Sciences, 11*(98)

Nagoudi, E. M. B., Elmadany, A., & Abdul-Mageed, M. (2021). AraT5: Text-to-text transformers for Arabic language generation. arXiv [Preprint]. https://arxiv.org/abs/2109.12068

Nasaruddin, N. (2024). Using ChatGPT in teaching Arabic as a foreign language. *Arabiyatuna Journal Bahasa Arab, 8*(1), 1–24.

Naznin, K., Al Mahmud, A., Nguyen, M. T., & Chua, C. (2025). ChatGPT integration in higher education for personalized learning, academic writing, and coding tasks: A systematic review. *Computers, 14*(2), 53.

Nguyen Thi Thu, H. (2023). EFL teachers' perspectives toward the use of ChatGPT in writing classes: A case study at Van Lang University. *Nguyen, TTH EFL Teachers' Perspectives toward the Use of ChatGPT in Writing Classes: A Case Study at Van Lang University International Journal of Language Instruction, 2*(3), 1–47.

Owoseni, A., Kolade, O., & Egbetokun, A. (2024). Enhancing personalised learning and student engagement using generative AI. In A. Owoseni, O. Kolade, & A. Egbetokun, (Eds.), *Generative AI in higher education: innovation strategies for teaching and learning* (pp. 123–150). Cham: Springer Nature.

Perkins, M. (2023). Academic Integrity considerations of AI large language models in the post-pandemic era: ChatGPT and beyond. *Journal of University Teaching and Learning Practice, 20*(2), 1–24.

Pham, V. P. H., & Le, A. Q. (2024). ChatGPT in language learning: Perspectives from Vietnamese students in Vietnam and the USA. *International Journal of Language Instruction, 3*(2), 10–54855.

Pikri, F. (2022). Utilization of information and communication technology as Arabic learning media. *International Journal of Demos (IJD), 4*(2), 890–897.

Rahmouni, K. (2024). Exploring the use of ChatGPT in teaching Arabic case endings: Effectiveness, challenges and recommendations. *Journal of Educational Technology and Innovation, 6*(4).

Rathore, B. (2023). Future of AI & generation alpha: ChatGPT beyond boundaries. *EDUZONE: International Peer Reviewed/Refereed Multidisciplinary Journal (EIPRMJ), ISSN.*

Sa'idah, M. A., Diantoro, K., Mahmudah, U., Dolan, E., Santoso, N. A., & Junaedi, S. R. P. (2024). Enhancing Arabic language teaching through artificial intelligence: Assessing effectiveness and educational implications. In *2024 3rd International Conference on Creative Communication and Innovative Technology (ICCIT)* (pp. 1–8). IEEE.

Urban, M., Děchtěrenko, F., Lukavský, J., Hrabalová, V., Svacha, F., Brom, C., & Urban, K. (2024). ChatGPT improves creative problem-solving performance in university students: An experimental study. *Computers & Education, 215*, Article 105031.

Valova, I., Mladenova, T., & Kanev, G. (2024). Students' perception of ChatGPT usage in education. *International Journal of Advanced Computer Science & Applications, 15*(1).

Van Mol, M. (2014). Arabic receptive language teaching: A new CALL approach. In K. Wahba, Z. A. Taha, & L. England (Eds.), *Handbook for Arabic language teaching professionals in the 21st century* (pp. 305–314). Routledge.

Van Putten, M. (2020). Classical and modern standard Arabic. *Arabic and Contact-Induced Change, 1*, 57–82.

Yan, D. (2023). Impact of ChatGPT on learners in a L2 writing practicum: An exploratory investigation. *Education and Information Technologies, 28*(11), 13943–13967.

Zhai, X. (2022). ChatGPT user experience: Implications for education. *SSRN Electronic Journal.* https://doi.org/10.2139/ssrn.4312418

Zheng, Y. D., & Stewart, N. (2024). Improving EFL students' cultural awareness: Reframing moral dilemmatic stories with ChatGPT. *Computers and Education: Artificial Intelligence, 6*, Article 100223.

Alif Sismat is an assistant professor at the Faculty of Arabic Language, Universiti Islam Sultan Sharif Ali (UNISSA). He obtained his PhD from the University of Leeds in the United Kingdom, specializing in applied translation studies. While remaining active in teaching and research, he also holds the Director of Strategic Development and Sustainability Office position.

Rafidah Abdullah is an assistant professor at the Faculty of Arabic Language, Universiti Islam Sultan Sharif Ali (UNISSA). She obtained her PhD from the International Islamic University Malaysia, specializing in Arabic literature. While remaining active in teaching and research, she is also currently the Dean of the faculty.

Kujaimah Abdul Kahar is a lecturer at the Faculty of Arabic Language, Universiti Islam Sultan Sharif Ali (UNISSA). She recently obtained her PhD from the International Islamic University Malaysia, specializing in Arabic grammar. While remaining active in teaching and research, she is currently the Head of the Arabic Language Enhancement Programme.

Rafizah Abdullah is a lecturer at the Faculty of Arabic Language, Universiti Islam Sultan Sharif Ali (UNISSA). She recently obtained her PhD from UNISSA, specializing in teaching Arabic to speakers of other languages (TESOL). In addition to her academic responsibilities, she currently holds the position of deputy director of the Centre for Research and Publication at the university.

Amalena Jarudin is a tutor at the Faculty of Arabic Language, Universiti Islam Sultan Sharif Ali (UNISSA). She obtained her Master's in Arabic language from UNISSA and currently teaches university-required Arabic language courses.

Using Python and ChatGPT to Create Chatbots for Language Practices

Vu Phi Ho Pham and Ngoc Hoang Vy Nguyen

Abstract This article offers a comprehensive road map for language teachers who want to use Python and ChatGPT to develop AI-powered chatbots to raise students' language proficiency and communication skills. AI-driven chatbots are a terrific supplement since traditional language learning methods may lack real-time contact, tailored feedback, and constant speaking possibilities. Teachers might create dynamic, interactive chatbots that imitate conversations, provide rapid feedback, and change learners' competency degrees by using Python's programming tools and ChatGPT's strong Natural Language Processing (NLP). This work presents a thorough handbook for creating chatbots ensuring accessibility for teachers with varying degrees of technological ability. By means of daily assignments, these chatbots help students raise fluency, daily practice, and confidence in the target language. Teachers can enhance their teaching toolset by means of this practical, technologically driven method, therefore providing pupils with a more immersive, interesting, and efficient language learning environment.

Keywords Python · ChatGPT · ChatBot · Language practices

V. P. H. Pham (✉)
Industrial University of Ho Chi Minh City, Ho Chi Minh City, Vietnam
e-mail: phamvuphiho@iuh.edu.vn

N. H. V. Nguyen
University of North Texas, Denton, USA
e-mail: NgocHoangVyNguyen@my.unt.edu

V. P. H. Pham et al. (eds.), *Empowering Educators: Integrating AI Tools for Personalized Language Instruction*, Studies in Computational Intelligence 1228,
https://doi.org/10.1007/978-3-032-01348-4_13

1 The Rationale of the Study

Language acquisition is a difficult and complicated process that calls for regular practice and meaningful connection. Although they have significant benefits, traditional language instruction and learning strategies sometimes lack enough chances for real-time communication for their students. The conventional classroom approach emphasizes grammar rules and vocabulary acquisition while focusing less on communicative competence (Richards & Rodgers, 2014). Consequently, learners may develop theoretical knowledge of the language without acquiring the practical skills necessary for spontaneous and fluent communication. This gap between knowledge and application can hinder learners' ability to function effectively in real-world linguistic contexts (Bygate, 1998).

A major limitation of traditional language instruction is the delayed and generalized nature of feedback. In classroom settings, teachers often provide feedback after a considerable delay, making it difficult for students to correct mistakes in real-time (Littlewood, 1981). Additionally, feedback is usually directed at the entire class rather than personalized to individual students' specific challenges, reducing its impact on language improvement (Ellis, 2009). Personalized, immediate feedback is critical in language learning, as it allows learners to adjust their use of language structures and refine pronunciation, ultimately leading to improved fluency and accuracy.

Self-study methods, while offering flexibility, also present significant challenges. Many learners opt for self-directed study to supplement their language learning, using textbooks, apps, and recorded lessons. However, these methods often lack the dynamic interaction needed for meaningful language acquisition (Dörnyei, 2001). Without chances for real-time communication, students find it difficult to grow in confidence and spontaneity in speech. As Swain's (1985) Output Hypothesis highlights the part speech plays in cognitive processing, a fundamental idea of language learning is the need for output and engagement. Self-study without an interactive component could restrict students' capacity to practice using language and create necessary communicative methods.

Moreover, self-directed learning might cause isolation, therefore lowering motivation and involvement. Learning a language is naturally social. Hence, a lack of cooperative learning opportunities could impede development. Studies indicate that social connection is essential for preserving student motivation since it promotes responsibility and group growth (Thornbury & Slade, 2006). Lack of social interaction in self-study environments usually leads to lower motivation, which causes uneven practice and, finally, stagnation in language ability.

These constraints of conventional classroom education and self-study techniques clearly call for creative solutions like real-time contact, tailored feedback, and more student involvement. Artificial intelligence (AI)–powered chatbots, notably those created using Python and ChatGPT, are one such method. AI-driven chatbots present a viable answer by giving students an interactive and adaptive language learning environment. These chatbots provide instantaneous, customized grammar, pronunciation, and fluency feedback, so students are involved in simulated chats. Unlike conventional teaching approaches, AI-powered chatbots let students practice their language abilities anywhere and at any time, therefore removing the restrictions of classroom scheduling and the availability of native speakers.

By modeling human-like dialogues, artificial intelligence chatbots solve the difficulty of real-time interaction. Thanks to developments in natural language processing, chatbots can interact with students in meaningful conversations so they may practice their language in risk-free surroundings. AI chatbots give a nonjudging environment where students may experiment with new language and phrase structures, unlike conventional classroom environments where students may feel uncomfortable about making mistakes. This is consistent with Krashen's (1982) Affective Filter Hypothesis, which holds that lowering anxiety in the course of learning improves acquisition. Chatbots create the best setting for language development by reducing the pressure related to public speaking.

Moreover, chatbots driven by artificial intelligence can be taught to provide tailored comments, therefore eliminating one of the main drawbacks of conventional education approaches. These chatbots offer instantaneous adjustments, ideas, and explanations as they examine human input in real-time. For instance, the chatbot can instantly point out mistakes and offer direction for development if a student mispronounces a word or creates a grammatically wrong sentence. This function guarantees that students obtain focused help, enabling them to hone their abilities properly. Furthermore, chatbots are available around the clock, so students have endless chances to practice, strengthening their knowledge through constant interaction.

The possibility to improve motivation and learner involvement is another important benefit of chatbot-assisted learning. Unlike fixed self-study resources, chatbots bring an interactive and gamified element to language learning. Studies on artificial intelligence chatbots in education find that making learning more interesting and customized can inspire students (Liu & Reinders, 2025). Learners who interact with chatbots get instant answers, have goal-oriented discussions, and get encouragement—all of which help to keep them motivated going forward. Furthermore, chatbots' interactive character fits the self-determination theory (Ryan & Deci, 2000), which emphasizes the motivation of the need for autonomy, competency, and relatedness. AI chatbots provide these motivating goals by letting students pace their learning, get immediate feedback, and participate in realistic discussions.

Moreover, chatbot-based learning can enable cooperative experiences, therefore addressing the problem of isolation in self-directed study. Group learning activities include artificial intelligence chatbots so that students can participate in interactive debates, role-playing games, and peer feedback sessions. This method reflects the advantages of group learning, in which pupils grow by means of mutual feedback and experience. Research on peer feedback and group writing in digital contexts has revealed that social engagement improves learning results by means of critical thinking and linguistic awareness (Pham, 2021). When students interact with chatbots alongside their peers, they benefit from both automated support and human contact, therefore creating a whole language learning environment.

The limitations of traditional classroom learning and self-study methods highlight the necessity of innovative, technologically sophisticated substitutes in language acquisition. AI-powered chatbots, particularly those developed using Python and ChatGPT, provide a transformational approach by means of real-time communication, tailored feedback, and higher engagement. Chatbots could close the knowledge acquisition-practical application gap by addressing significant challenges in language acquisition, hence enhancing learners' fluency and confidence in real-world communication. Future research should examine how chatbot-assisted learning influences long-term results and look at how artificial intelligence may enhance language education to meet different student needs.

1.1 Technological Innovations in Language Learning

Modern artificial intelligence (AI), natural language processing (NLP), machine learning (ML), and chatbot technologies have presented innovative concepts to improve language acquisition using the limitations of conventional and self-directed language education methodologies. AI-driven chatbots in language instruction have overcome significant challenges by offering personalized feedback, real-time involvement, and more student autonomy. These chatbots allow users to communicate at their own speed and convenience, therefore facilitating more flexible and easily available language practice (AbuShawar & Atwell, 2015; Fryer & Carpenter, 2006). Unlike conventional methods that provide delayed feedback, artificial intelligence chatbots provide instantaneous, adaptive responses that let trainees correct mistakes in real time and therefore enhance their language skills.

One of the key components of artificial intelligence-powered chatbots is Natural Language Processing (NLP), which focuses on the interaction between computers and human languages. In a substantial and useful manner, NLP allows machines to create, understand, and analyze human language (Bird et al., 2009). In language education, NLP enables chatbots to have reasonable dialogues, detect user intent, and provide contextual answers. Grammatical accuracy, speaking fluency, and language comprehension all seem to improve considerably here.

Another fundamental tool driving artificial intelligence chatbots is machine learning (ML), which helps systems learn from data and improve their performance over time without explicit programming for every task (Russell & Norvig, 2016). In language learning applications, ML helps chatbots to adapt to varying degrees of expertise of individual pupils, hence enhancing the accuracy and personalizing of their responses over numerous encounters. By analyzing more user inputs, this data-driven learning approach ensures that chatbots become more successful and hence a beneficial tool for long-term language progress.

Among the most widely used tools for natural language processing and artificial intelligence chatbot development is the Natural Language Toolkit (NLTK), a whole Python package designed for this usage. Development of intelligent chatbots rely on NLTK's facilities for tokenizing, sentiment analysis, text analysis, and speech tagging. Python is the advised programming language for chatbot development also because of its simplicity, readability, and extensive library support (Van Rossum, 2007). The easy syntax of Python lets developers create sophisticated chatbots with little coding complexity, hence increasing the accessibility of AI-powered language learning tools.

Launched in November 2022, ChatGPT is a breakthrough invention in this field since it creates human-like writing depending on user input. ChatGPT is a great tool for language instruction since it can interact in meaningful conversation, help with writing, scripting, and answering challenging questions. Its capacity to replicate realistic dialogue helps students to engage in interactive and interesting real-world language use.

These artificial intelligence and natural language processing technological developments have transformed language education, filling in for self-study approaches and shortcomings in conventional classroom instruction. Learners gain from instant feedback, more engagement, and more autonomy by including chatbots into language instruction, therefore promoting more efficient language acquisition.

1.2 Challenges in Teaching Pronunciation and Achieving Native-Like Proficiency

Teaching pronunciation in English as a Foreign Language (EFL) or English as a Second Language (ESL) offers ongoing difficulties mostly related to the lack of exposure to native speakers (Derwing & Munro, 2015). Because they do not routinely hear or practice native-like pronunciation patterns, many students find English phonetics difficult. Many EFL/ESL teachers also lack specific phonetic and pronunciation instruction, which hinders their capacity to properly fix pronunciation mistakes (Murphy, 2014). Learners who lack appropriate direction and feedback may grow to have fossilized mispronunciations, which would make it more difficult for them to be understood in practical settings.

Beyond pronunciation, achieving native-like proficiency is another significant challenge in EFL/ESL education. Many teachers themselves are non-native speakers who were taught by non-native instructors, leading to potential gaps in pronunciation and spoken fluency instruction. Traditional language teaching methods have historically placed greater emphasis on grammar, reading, and writing skills over oral communication and pronunciation practice (Nguyen & Newton, 2020). Furthermore, the unrealistic expectation for learners to attain native-like proficiency can create frustration and demotivation, as many struggle to mimic native pronunciation without the right support and tools.

1.3 AI Chatbots as an Innovative Solution

One promising approach to overcoming these limitations is AI-powered chatbots, such as ChatGPT and Gemini, which can be developed using Python to enhance pronunciation and conversational skills. These chatbots simulate native-like conversations, provide real-time feedback, and adapt to learners' proficiency levels (Haristiani, 2019). Unlike traditional methods, chatbots engage users in interactive dialogues, correct pronunciation mistakes, suggest alternative phrasing, and provide grammatical explanations, making language learning more dynamic and personalized (Fryer & Carpenter, 2006; Kerly et al., 2007). By incorporating AI-driven pronunciation training, learners gain consistent, immediate feedback, allowing them to refine their speaking skills effectively in a low-pressure environment.

1.4 Issues in Creating Chatbots for Language Practices

While AI-powered chatbots offer promising solutions for language learning, developing effective and reliable systems presents several challenges.

From an objective perspective, chatbots must be able to understand and generate responses that are both grammatically correct and contextually appropriate. This requires advanced Natural Language Processing (NLP) and Machine Learning (ML) models capable of interpreting user intent, managing complex conversations, and avoiding incorrect or misleading responses. The chatbot's capacity to adjust interactions depending on the learner's degree of competency presents another important difficulty since it guarantees that responses are neither too simple nor too sophisticated. Furthermore, a good chatbot has to spot linguistic mistakes in vocabulary, grammar, and pronunciation, so provide insightful comments to improve knowledge. Beyond conversational accuracy, data storage and security are absolutely vital since chatbots must retain privacy and comply with data protection rules while storing and processing user interactions.

From a subjective standpoint, there is continuous worry that chatbots driven by artificial intelligence could oversimplify the learning process or reduce the value of teachers (AbuShawar & Atwell, 2015). Although extremely crucial for social and cultural aspects of communication, some educators worry that leaning too much on chatbots could reduce human connection in language instruction. Moreover, good implementation depends on enough technological literacy and training for teachers and students to correctly introduce chatbots into their courses.

2 Review of Literature

Emphasizing both the benefits of their integration into the classroom and the difficulties in their use, current study has thoroughly examined the ways in which ChatGPT and AI-powered chatbots could be used in language instruction. Even if chatbots provide customized interaction, quick feedback, and accessibility for self-directed learning, issues connected to teacher-student relationships, over-reliance on artificial intelligence, and ethical dilemmas remain heated topics of debate.

Especially in non-Western learning environments like Vietnam, Nguyen and Pham (2024) investigated how artificial intelligence chatbots might reduce student anxiety and improve speaking skills. Their findings underlined that chatbots, including ChatGPT—offer instantaneous feedback and flexible learning opportunities, which qualifies them as a valuable complement to traditional classroom training. The study also underlined how artificial intelligence avatars might enable students to practice natural discussions, lower stress, and increase fluency. The writers did note, though, that chatbots sometimes lack emotional and cultural sensitivity, which would affect their capacity to sustain motivation and interest.

Annamalai et al. (2023) investigated how Self-Determination Theory (SDT) using Chatbots helps students see their competency by providing instantaneous feedback, validating the hypothesis that tools driven by artificial intelligence can help students always raise their language competency. Moreover, chatbots promote autonomy by letting students study at their own pace, which is particularly important for self-regulated learning. This is consistent with earlier studies showing that self-regulated learning improves long-term memory and application of language abilities. The results support the reasoning behind including chatbots in language instruction since they can provide independent and customized learning environments problematic for traditional classroom settings.

Likewise, Fryer et al. (2020) investigated how chatbots maintained task interest and drive in language-learning environments. Their research showed that chatbots' dynamic, responsive character greatly raised student attention, highlighting the possibilities of artificial intelligence-driven technology to make language learning livelier and more fun. Conventional classroom environments cannot maintain consistent attention, especially in repeated practice activities including grammar exercises and pronunciation drills. On the other hand, chatbots offer gamification, adaptive interactions, and real-time conversations—qualities that would draw students more than others. These results support the claim that chatbots can be a useful addition to classroom education, therefore solving one of the main issues noted in the justification—maintaining learner motivation in language acquisition.

Ericsson and Johansson (2023) investigated their conversational AI use for English-speaking practice by means of a longitudinal study including Swedish lower-secondary students. The study indicated that students—especially female students and those with less ability—felt more comfortable utilizing AI chatbots than in traditional classroom environments. This outcome is crucial in verifying the hypothesis that chatbots can give students a low-stakes, judgment-free setting in which they might become confident in spoken English and fluency. The study highlights how artificial intelligence chatbots might reduce language learning-related anxiety, therefore addressing a main problem in conventional teaching.

Kim and Su (2024) enhanced this study by looking at chatbots with both voice and text capabilities, finding that they significantly increase communication proficiency by inspiring involvement and, therefore, raising motivation. While it also stressed the fact that chatbots offer improved language input—which is essential for language acquisition, their research underlined the requirement of extra language-specific chatbot programs customized to learners' needs. Since Python and ChatGPT may be changed to fit specific language goals and learner profiles, this helps justify their usage in creating customized chatbots.

In order to gain knowledge from Vietnamese and American students, Pham and Le (2024) looked at how they felt about using ChatGPT for language instruction. Based on their research, ChatGPT is typically seen as a helpful tool for language acquisition, especially in improving student engagement and offering fast comments. Students reported ChatGPT facilitates self-directed learning by letting them practice their language at their own pace. The study also underlined over-reliance on ChatGPT, which can limit critical thinking and creativity, so to help offset this, the writers propose a blended method combining artificial intelligence-based learning with conventional classroom instruction.

Nguyen (2020) met with EFL teachers at Van Lang University in Vietnam about their opinions on using ChatGPT in writing courses. The study showed that ChatGPT's ability to enhance writing teaching highly excites teachers, especially in terms of immediate feedback, customized learning experiences, and automated writing evaluations. Nguyen (2020), however, also raised important issues, including the requirement for professional training, growing awareness of ChatGPT's shortcomings, and worries about student over-reliance on AI-generated feedback). These results support earlier research emphasizing the need for ethical artificial intelligence applications and teacher readiness in the classroom.

In a Second Language Acquisition (SLA) course, Pham (2024) asked Vietnamese graduate students about their impressions of ChatGPT as a language learning tool. Students said ChatGPT was a helpful learning tool, especially in enhancing engagement, self-confidence, and classroom participation. The findings fit up with Annamalai et al. (2023) and Fryer et al. (2020), who stressed how chatbots and AI-assisted technologies keep students involved in task-based learning environments, hence promoting learner motivation. Pham (2024) also affirmed that ChatGPT complements past studies, including Nguyen and Pham (2024) and Pham and Le (2024), who underlined the advantages of AI-driven feedback and self-regulated learning, helping students produce ideas, clarify concepts, and reinforce acquired information.

Although chatbots offer several benefits, as shown in the systematic evaluation of 25 studies by Huang et al. (2022) constraints still exist. Chatbots, they discovered, find it difficult to offer emotionally and culturally sensitive interactions—a fundamental element of good language instruction. Although personalization, speed, and simplicity of use are great benefits, chatbots' lack of emotional intelligence and cultural flexibility lowers their efficacy in some situations. This emphasizes the need of more developments in AI-driven language learning technologies, therefore supporting the justification that the creation of chatbots should include NLP developments to better replicate human-like interactions.

In line with cognitive flexibility, critical thinking, and inclusive interactions, Chauncey and McKenna (2023) have suggested an ethical framework for the responsible use of artificial intelligence in education). They underlined that chatbots should be made with cultural sensitivity in mind so that students from many language backgrounds get fair and efficient language support. This supports the need of ethical AI chatbot design in language learning in line with the larger conversation of the function of artificial intelligence in education.

These empirical investigations taken together reinforce the justification for this study by showing that chatbots solve important obstacles in language acquisition like motivation, accessibility, and individualized feedback. They also draw attention, nevertheless, the constant need for developments in ethical considerations, cultural sensitivity, and chatbot flexibility. This emphasizes the need of creating AI-powered chatbots utilizing Python and ChatGPT to close these gaps, therefore guaranteeing that language learners get interactive, customized, and culturally relevant support in their learning path.

2.1 Steps to Develop an AI Chatbot for Language Practice Using Python and ChatGPT

Building an AI-powered chatbot for language learning calls for enrolling for a ChatGPT API account, configuring a suitable development environment, and Python code integration of chatbot functionalities. Use these guidelines to create an elementary level English speaking chatbot to help students in their practice.

2.1.1 Step 1: Install Python

Python is the primary programming language used for developing AI chatbots due to its readability, simplicity, and extensive library support. To install Python:

1. Visit https://python.org
2. Download the latest version of Python for your operating system (Windows, macOS, or Linux).
3. Follow the installation instructions and ensure that Python is added to the system PATH during installation (Fig. 1).

After installation, verify Python by opening a terminal (MacOS) or command prompt (Window) and running:

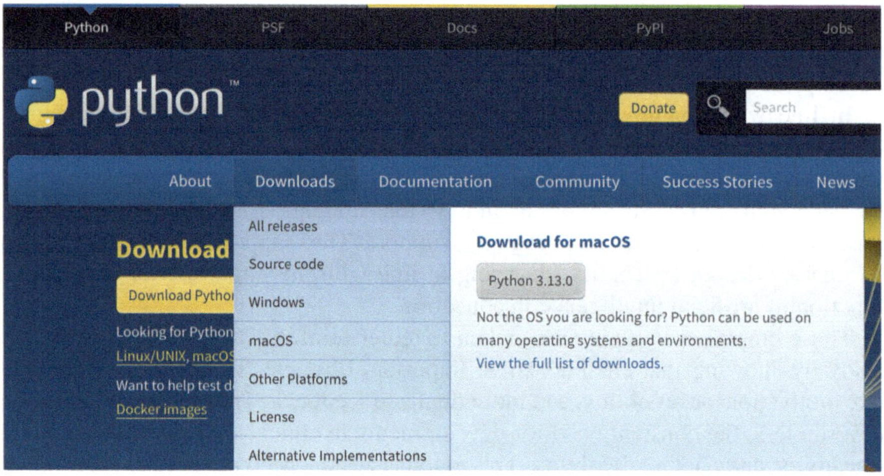

Fig. 1 Install python

```sh
python --version
```

If installed correctly, this command should return the Python version number.

2.1.2 Step 2: Install Visual Studio Code (VS Code)

VS Code is a lightweight, user-friendly integrated development environment (IDE) for writing and running Python code.

1. Download and install VS Code from https://code.visualstudio.com
2. Install the Python extension in VS Code to enable Python syntax highlighting and debugging.

Once installed, open VS Code and set up a workspace for your chatbot project (Fig. 2).

2.1.3 Step 3: Register for a ChatGPT Account

To integrate ChatGPT into the chatbot, you need an API key from OpenAI.

1. Visit https://chatgpt.com
2. Sign up for an account (if you don't already have one).
3. Navigate to the API section and generate an API key for your chatbot.

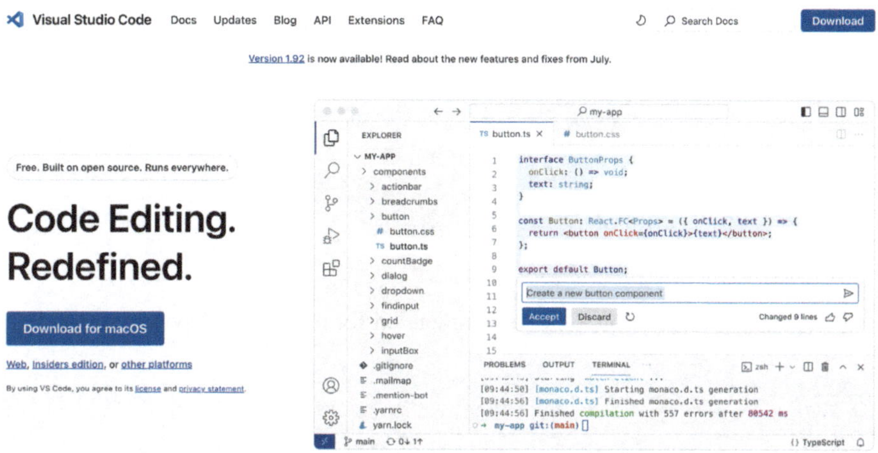

Fig. 2 Install visual studio code

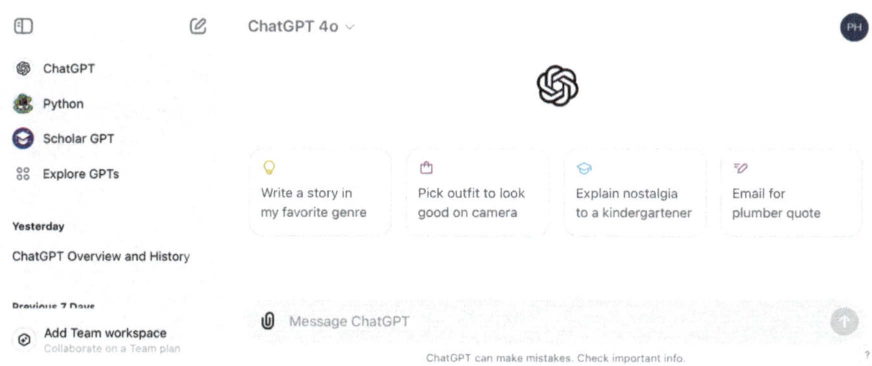

Fig. 3 Sign up for a ChatGPT account

Keep this API key secure, as it will be required to authenticate requests to ChatGPT (Fig. 3).

2.1.4 Step 4: Set Up Your Development Environment

Before writing code, set up your Python environment in VS Code.

1. Run Visual Studio Code.
2. Create a new folder for your chatbot project. Name it something like "Chatbot_Project".
3. Open a new terminal inside VS Code:
   - Click on Terminal → New Terminal

- Navigate to the project directory using the following command (replace Chatbot_Project with your actual folder name):

```sh
cd path/to/Chatbot_Project
```

4. Create a virtual environment (recommended for managing dependencies):

```sh
python -m venv chatbot_env
```

5. Activate the virtual environment:
   - On Windows:

```sh
chatbot_env\Scripts\activate
```

   - On macOS/Linux:

```sh
source chatbot_env/bin/activate
```

6. Install the required dependencies:
7. Install open AI and speech recognition (for voice interaction):

```sh
pip install openai speechrecognition
```

2.1.5 Step 5: Generate a Chatbot Code Using ChatGPT

To leverage ChatGPT's capabilities in Python programming, you can use the following ChatGPT prompt to generate your chatbot script:

ChatGPT Prompt:

Can you help write a Python code to create a Chatbot to practice English speaking at the elementary level?

Install Required Libraries

Before running the chatbot, install the necessary dependencies:

```sh
pip install openai speechrecognition pyttsx3 pyaudio
```

2.2 Python Code for an AI-Powered English Speaking Chatbot

See Fig. 4.

2.3 How to Run the Chatbot

1. Save the script as chatbot.py.
2. Run the script in a terminal or command prompt:

```sh
python chatbot.py
```

Speak into your microphone, and the chatbot will respond in both text and voice.

```python
import nltk
from nltk.stem import WordNetLemmatizer
import numpy as np
import random
import string

# Initialize the lemmatizer
lemmatizer = WordNetLemmatizer()

# Define a simple set of intents and responses
intents = {
    "greeting": {
        "patterns": ["hello", "hi", "hey", "good morning", "good evening"],
        "responses": ["Hello! How can I help you today?", "Hi there! Want to
    },
    "farewell": {
        "patterns": ["bye", "goodbye", "see you", "exit"],
        "responses": ["Goodbye! Have a great day!", "See you later! Keep prac
    },
    "age": {
        "patterns": ["how old are you", "what is your age", "age?"],
```

Fig. 4 Python code for a Chatbot

3 Chatbot Versus ChatGPT: Key Differences in Language Learning

Although AI is used in both ChatGPT and custom-built chatbots to produce human-like interactions, their purposes in language learning settings are somewhat different. Operating based on pre-defined lesson content, a custom chatbot meant for language practice uses a disciplined approach to instruction and evaluation. While teachers design a chatbot to follow a specific curriculum, ChatGPT generates responses dynamically, relying on a big database. Thus, the chatbot guides students through courses so that they practice grammar, pronunciation, and important vocabulary in line with a given schedule.

Teachers can also set up every class to further their goals of learning. Depending on the objectives of the lesson, the chatbot may correct mistakes, ask pre-defined questions, and provide focused activities. Teachers' ability to track student reactions and development over time is one main benefit. Moreover, by means of controlled chatbot interactions, pupils can practice often, thereby enhancing their learning. Unlike ChatGPT, which provides unrestricted interactions, a chatbot promises targeted, goal-oriented learning sessions. Though ChatGPT is great for general conversation practice, a custom-built chatbot basically provides a controlled learning environment where students follow pre-planned courses and get organized feedback.

4 Conclusion

By offering dynamic, personalized, and easily available language practice, Python and ChatGPT applied in chatbot development present a different method of language learning. AI-driven chatbots greatly help to improve fluency, grammar accuracy, and pronunciation since traditional language learning approaches may lack real-time feedback and regular speaking chances. Using Natural Language Processing (NLP) and Machine Learning (ML), chatbots can replicate real-world interactions, provide fast feedback, and adapt to suit students' degrees of competency, guaranteeing ongoing development. Artificial intelligence chatbots inspire regular practice in a low-risk environment, unlike more traditional self-study techniques, therefore lowering students' fear and raising their motivation.

Moreover, certain chatbots let professors create courses, track student development, and guarantee regulated learning—all of which ChatGPT cannot achieve. This control guarantees that students participate in focused activities matching their academic path. The simplicity of Python and strong library support enable educators and developers to design AI-driven chatbots suitable for particular learning requirements quickly. Chatbots will keep redefining language acquisition as artificial intelligence develops and closes the distance between classroom instruction and practical conversation. Future research should investigate how sophisticated pronunciation evaluation and multimodal artificial intelligence learning settings spanning text, audio, and video interactions coupled with emotional intelligence in artificial intelligence chatbots. These developments will close the distance separating human-led from AI-assisted language education, therefore guaranteeing a comprehensive learning experience.

References

AbuShawar, B., & Atwell, E. (2015). ALICE chatbot: Trials and outputs. *Computación y Sistemas, 19*(4), 625–632. https://doi.org/10.13053/CyS-19-4-2326

Annamalai, N., Eltahir, M. E., Zyoud, S. H., Soundrarajan, D., Zakarneh, B., & Al Salhi, N. R. (2023). Exploring English language learning via Chabot: A case study from a self determination theory perspective. *Computers and Education: Artificial Intelligence, 5*, 100148. https://doi.org/10.1016/j.caeai.2023.100148

Bird, S., Klein, E., & Loper, E. (2009). *Natural language processing with Python: Analyzing text with the natural language toolkit.* "O'Reilly Media, Inc."

Bygate, M. (1998). Theoretical perspectives on speaking. *Annual Review of Applied Linguistics, 18*, 20–42.

Chauncey, S. A., & McKenna, H. P. (2023). A framework and exemplars for ethical and responsible use of AI Chatbot technology to support teaching and learning. *Computers and Education: Artificial Intelligence, 5*, 100182. https://doi.org/10.1016/j.caeai.2023.100182

Derwing, T. M., & Munro, M. J. (2015). *Pronunciation fundamentals: Evidence-based perspectives for L2 teaching and research.* John Benjamins.

Dörnyei, Z. (2001). New themes and approaches in second language motivation research. *Annual Review of Applied Linguistics, 21*, 43–59.

Ellis, R. (2009). Corrective feedback and teacher development. *L2 Journal: an Electronic Refereed Journal for Foreign and Second Language Educators, 1*(1), 3–18. https://doi.org/10.5070/l2.v1i1.9054

Ericsson, E., & Johansson, S. (2023). English speaking practice with conversational AI: Lower secondary students' educational experiences over time. *Computers and Education: Artificial Intelligence, 5*, 100164. https://doi.org/10.1016/j.caeai.2023.100164

Fryer, L., & Carpenter, R. (2006). Emerging technologies bots as language learning tools. *Language Learning & Technology, 10*(3), 8–14.

Fryer, L. K., Coniam, D., Carpenter, R., & Lapusneanu, D. (2020). Bots for language learning now: Current and future directions. *Language Learning & Technology, 24*(2), 8–22.

Haristiani, N. (2019). Artificial Intelligence (AI) chatbot as language learning medium: An inquiry. *Journal of Physics: Conference Series, 1387*(1), 012020. https://doi.org/10.1088/1742-6596/1387/1/012020

Huang, W., Hew, K. F., & Fryer, L. K. (2022). Chatbots for language learning—Are they really useful? A systematic review of chatbot-supported language learning. *Journal of Computer Assisted Learning, 38*(1), 237–257. https://doi.org/10.1111/jcal.12610

Kerly, A., Ellis, R., & Bull, S. (2007, December). CALMsystem: a conversational agent for learner modelling. In *International conference on innovative techniques and applications of artificial intelligence* (pp. 89–102). London: Springer.

Kim, A., & Su, Y. (2024). How implementing an AI chatbot impacts Korean as a foreign language learners' willingness to communicate in Korean. *System, 122*, 103256. https://doi.org/10.1016/j.system.2024.103256

Krashen, S. D. (1982). *Principles and practice in second language acquisition.* Pergamon Press.

Littlewood, W. (1981). Communicative language teaching. *Cambridge UP.*

Liu, M., & Reinders, H. (2025). Do AI chatbots impact motivation? Insights from a preliminary longitudinal study. *System, 128*, 103544. https://doi.org/10.1016/j.system.2024.103544

Murphy, J. (2014). Teacher training programs provide adequate preparation in how to teach pronunciation. *Pronunciation Myths: Applying Second Language Research to Classroom Teaching, 21*, 188–224.

Nguyen, L. T., & Newton, J. (2020). Pronunciation teaching in tertiary EFL classes: Vietnamese teachers' beliefs and practices. *TESL-EJ, 24*(1), n1.

Nguyen, N. H. V., & Pham, V. P. H. (2024). AI Chatbots for language practices. *International Journal of AI in Language Education, 1*(1), 56–67.

Pham, V. P. H. (2024). Vietnamese graduate students' perspectives on the use of ChatGPT. In H. P. Bui, E. Namaziandost (Eds.) Innovations in technologies for language teaching and learning. Studies in Computational Intelligence, vol. 1159. Cham: Springer. https://doi.org/10.1007/978-3-031-63447-5_9

Pham, V. P. H. (2021). The impacts of collaborative writing on individual writing skills: A case study in EFL classrooms. *Journal of Psycholinguistic Research, 50*(4), 817–830. https://doi.org/10.1007/s10936-023-09939-2

Pham, V. P. H., & Le, A. Q. (2024). ChatGPT in language learning: Perspectives from Vietnamese students in Vietnam and the USA. *International Journal of Language Instruction, 3*(2), 59–72. https://doi.org/10.54855/ijli.24325

Richards, J. C., & Rodgers, T. S. (2014). *Approaches and methods in language teaching.* Cambridge University Press.

Van Rossum, G. (2007, June). Python programming language. In *USENIX annual technical conference* vol. 41, no. 1, pp. 1–36.

Russell, S. J., & Norvig, P. (2016). *Artificial intelligence: a modern approach.* Pearson.

Ryan, R. M., & Deci, E. L. (2000). Self-determination theory and the facilitation of intrinsic motivation, social development, and well-being. *American Psychologist, 55*(1), 68–78.

Swain, M. (1985). Communicative competence: Some roles of comprehensible input and comprehensible output in its development. *Input in Second Language Acquisition/newbury House, 15*, 165–179.

Thornbury, S., & Slade, D. (2006). *Conversation: From description to pedagogy.* Cambridge University Press.

Vu Phi Ho Pham Faculty of Foreign Languages, Industrial University of Ho Chi Minh City, Vietnam, was Vice-President of Ba Ria–Vung Tau University and Vice-President at Van Hien University, Vietnam. Pham has published more than 70 research articles in both local and International Journals, such as Computer-Assisted Language Learning, SAGE Open, System, and Journal of Psycholinguist Research (20 Scopus/14 ISI), and 10 books/course books, and 2 edited books (Springer and IGI Global). He is the Vice President for Administrative Affairs of AsiaCALL. He is the Editor-in-chief of the International Journal of TESOL & Education. He is now the managing editor of CALL-EJ (Scopus-Q1).

Ngoc Hoang Vy Nguyen is a PhD student at the University of North Texas, USA. She works as a Lecturer in the Department of English at Ho Chi Minh University of Industry and Trade, Vietnam. She graduated in TESOL from PuKyeong National University. Her research interests include using technology to enhance learning, teaching methodology, task-based language teaching, and the incorporation of technology in language education. Nguyen has authored articles in international journals and participated in numerous academic conferences. She is presently engaged in a study investigating the application of AI tools to improve language instruction in higher education.

AI in Translation and Support Systems

Application of AI Tools in Translation Practices: Benefits and Challenges

Le Thi Ngoc Phan

Abstract Artificial Intelligence (AI) is one of the hottest buzzwords in the technology world today. With the continuous development of information technology, AI has become an important factor in most fields, including the translation industry. As a powerful assistant to humans, AI has had very positive impacts on the development of the translation industry. This chapter sheds light on the role of AI in translation, as well as the benefits and challenges it brings to educators and learners. Combining both quantitative and qualitative methods through questionnaires, interviews and translation quality evaluation, the study was conducted with the participation of 100 students from translation classes I directly taught at Vietnam National University (VNU). The findings revealed that the use of AI in translation practices brought both benefits and challenges to educators and learners. Some of the potential and prospects of AI translation can be mentioned such as higher speed, more complex language translation, and application in many disciplinary fields. However, some undeniable challenges are lack of ability to translate naturally and lack of contextual awareness. Despite numerous obstacles remaining to overcome, the advancement of AI will present numerous prospects and chances and support university educators in their translation teaching.

Keywords AI translation tools · Translation practices · Benefits · Challenges · Vietnamese educators and students

1 Introduction

In the digital age, translation has become important in connecting countries and cultures. Professional translators no longer have exclusive responsibility for finding, evaluating, and translating information from around the globe. Translation is not

L. T. N. Phan (✉)
VNU University of Languages and International Studies, Vietnam National University, Hanoi, Vietnam
e-mail: phanthingocle@vnu.edu.vn

V. P. H. Pham et al. (eds.), *Empowering Educators: Integrating AI Tools for Personalized Language Instruction*, Studies in Computational Intelligence 1228,
https://doi.org/10.1007/978-3-032-01348-4_14

simply converting words from one language to another; it also requires a deep understanding of the language and culture, as well as knowledge of the two languages (House, 2018). Therefore, translators always face challenges such as ensuring accuracy, precision, and grammar for the translation.

Artificial intelligence (AI) technology has offered powerful tools to help us address the challenges of the translation industry. The translation industry has undergone a transformation. AI applications like ChatGPT and Google Translate offer quick, reliable, and affordable solutions (Language Insight, 2024). The introduction of artificial intelligence-powered language tools has, in fact, been shown in numerous studies to be successful in raising the quality of students' translation performance (Adams & Chuah, 2022; Chen & Wei, 2021; Kornfeld & Roy, 2021; Sari, 2024; Song & Song, 2023; Tran, 2024). Despite their strength, these tools raise significant concerns over their capacity to maintain contextual richness and linguistic variation, both of which are critical for nuanced communication (U.S. EUATC, 2023; Translation Company, 2023). According to Okpor (2014), there are advantages and disadvantages to professional students' training. Even though AI translation is a widely used and highly convenient tool, the phenomenon of people depending on it has grown increasingly serious and has affected translation positions to some degree.

In Vietnam, the incorporation of AI technology has emerged as a crucial component in the ever-changing field of translation training (Nguyen, 2020; Nguyen & Tran, 2019). As the area develops, cutting-edge language models like ChatGPT, DeepL, and Microsoft Translator (Ho, 2024; Pham & Cao, 2025) coexist with more established systems like Google Translate (Tran, 2020). These resources mark a new frontier by offering several approaches of AI-powered translation. Besides, it also enhances the complexity of the learning process for students (Nguyen & Ho, 2021; Nguyen & Pham, 2024). Tran and Nguyen (2017) claimed that it provides useful benefits like cost-effectiveness, uniform terminology, and the ability to handle high translation quantities.

Language tutors and learners clearly have a high opinion of AI applications in translation. Their functions go beyond merely serving as educational tools; they also advance more general social development (Nguyen et al., 2025a, 2025b). However, little is known about their complex roles and the difficulties students encounter when putting these applications into practice, particularly in the Vietnamese context (Nguyen & Ho, 2021). That fact inspired me to undertake this study to delve deeper into both the benefits and challenges when AI tools such as Google Translate, ChatGPT are used in their English-Vietnamese translation practice course. In the context of rapid technological development, AI-powered translation is reshaping the future of the translation industry. I hope the research results will have practical significance. With new technological breakthroughs, AI tools can help improve the quality and efficiency of translation.

2 Literature Review

2.1 *Overview of AI in Translation*

Throughout human history, translation has played a crucial role. It is now used in a wide range of circumstances, from religious settings to language instruction (Köksal & Yürük, 2020). AI Translation has emerged as a key component of this progress. AI in translation refers to the modification of an algorithm that translates texts using machine learning and neural networks. The models now employed in the translation industry are the result of four stages of artificial intelligence research (Zhang & Lu, 2021).

Significant turning points have occurred in the history of AI translation. First, the 1950s and 1960s saw the development of rule-based systems, culminating in the Georgetown-IBM experiment in 1954, which demonstrated machine translation in practice. During the 1970s and 1980s, early work in statistical machine translation (SMT) expanded, and this methodology was compared to earlier AI techniques. The 1990s and 2000s witnessed an improvement in translation quality due to SMT's increased smoothness. AI-based translation software, like Google Translate, became commercially available in 2006. In 2016, Google adopted neural network translation using the Transformer model, marking the shift from SMT to neural machine translation.

In the translation industry, there are many types of artificial intelligence used to enhance the efficiency and accuracy of the translation process (Mohamed et al., 2024). Here are some of these types of artificial intelligence: (1) *Natural Language Processing (NLP)*: it is a type of artificial intelligence used to help computers understand and process natural human language. NLP is used to determine the grammar, sentence structure, and meaning of text to create more accurate translations. (2) *Machine Learning*: artificial intelligence is used to enable computers to automatically learn from data and improve their performance. Machine learning can be used to build translation models to translate different languages. (3) *Neural Machine Translation (NMT)*: it is a type of artificial intelligence that uses neural networks to translate texts. NMT is considered one of the most modern translation technologies, allowing translations to achieve high accuracy and automatically adjust over time.

2.2 *AI Translation Tools*

According to Charles-Kenechi (2024), some current AI translation tools are ChatGPT, Google Translate, Microsoft Translator, and DeepL. Each application has its own pros and cons, which are reviewed below.

First, ChatGPT is considered to be a useful translation tool. Studies revealed that ChatGPT can translate text with high accuracy and reliability, just like a human (Alkhawaja, 2024; Sahari et al., 2023). As Dong et al. (2022) noted, ChatGPT can employ input prompts to integrate extra information, such as human interactions, in contrast to conventional machine translation systems (Dong et al., 2022). There may be several benefits to using ChatGPT in classrooms for language learning (Pham, 2025; Pham & Nguyen, 2024; Pham & Le, 2024). AI-generated translations are more contextually accurate than Google Translate translations since AI can understand natural language and write academically, according to Hidayati and Nihayah (2024). Besides, Sahari et al. (2023) also claimed that ChatGPT reduces the initial translation time, allowing human translators to focus on accuracy assurance and improvement. Although ChatGPT has several benefits, its translation features might be restricted. The translations produced by ChatGPT are understandable; however, it seems to be useless when it comes to separable phrasal verbs (Alosaimi & Alawad, 2024) and users tend to become overly reliant on using it in their learning process (Nguyen et al., 2025a, 2025b). In addition, according to Pham and Nguyen (2024), some people are worried about how ChatGPT would affect language learning and knowledge acquisition, while others see it as a limitation on accuracy and individualized learning. Additionally, Banat and Adla (2023) claimed that ChatGPT cannot translate culturally sensitive communications that require context-rich processing data. Furthermore, the over-reliance on critical thinking skills is also a concern for some researchers (Marzuki et al., 2023; Neji et al., 2023).

Second, as one of the most popular machine translation tools today, Google Translate (GT) uses AI technologies such as deep learning and natural language processing to translate texts quickly and accurately. GT, as explained by Bahri and Mahadi (2016), is a free machine translation tool created by the Google team that allows text to be translated across languages in less than another second. According to Aulia et al. (2024), GT is a popular and widely used machine translation program for anyone who needs translation help or is learning a second language. Given that it is available for free on websites and in mobile apps for iOS and Android, GT is among the most widely used machine translation programs. Besides, from students' perspectives, Amna (2022) revealed that time savings and immediate outcomes are the benefits of adopting GT. Besides translations, GT offers many other advantages. GT is capable of instantly translating text on the screen into graphics after identifying text in a user-taken snap. The pronunciation, dictionary, and translation audio are also provided by GT (Hamood & Al-Bagoa, 2021). Despite its obvious benefits, GT also has drawbacks, some of which may include grammatical problems, difficult sentence translation, pragmatically meaningless idioms, and limited internet connection (Aulia et al., 2024). The majority of English instructors thought that using GT during the language learning process degrades the process itself (Groves & Mundt, 2015). Moreover, according to Amna (2022), students often translate nearly every sentence in their projects, get less motivated to learn how to translate using the techniques provided to them, and grow more uninformed about grammar and language compositions. Do (2023) also investigated the negative impact of GT on basic language learning among students. It is revealed that learning a new language through uncontrolled use of GT will only cause information to be stored in short-term memory. Without regular study and application, this knowledge will be forgotten, and students will no longer be able to recall it (Do, 2023).

Third, Microsoft Translator uses AI technologies to support real-time translation of documents, emails, and messages. According to Koehn and Knowles (2017), Microsoft Translator use artificial intelligence to translate automatically between over 70 languages, including the most widely spoken ones worldwide. Additionally, it supports the eleven speech translation systems that enable the Microsoft Translator Apps for iOS and Android, Skype Translator, Skype for Windows Desktop, and the Microsoft Translator live chat feature. The features offered by Microsoft Translator include cross-platform access, the ability to translate text, audio, and video files, and the capability to translate messages in real-time while conversing with someone, even if you do not speak the same language (Fitria, 2021). Besides, Matviienko et al. (2024) claimed that its open API also makes it simple to incorporate Microsoft Translator into other programs or services. This enables developers to add machine translation capabilities to their own goods and services. For general translations of reliable and acceptable quality, Microsoft Translator may be a decent choice (Specia et al., 2018). However, compared to GT, it has some restricted features such as the inability to translate photos. Moreover, the quality of translations might vary depending on the circumstances and particular languages (Matviienko et al., 2024). In agreement, Yudiarti (2019) stated that the machine translation technique does not consistently provide accuracy. In contrast to human translators, it is unable to focus on a context, resolve ambiguity, or draw on experience or mental imagery (Gen, 2016).

Fourth, as a new machine translation tool, DeepL uses AI technologies such as neural machine translation to generate high-quality translations and automatically adjusts to improve accuracy over time. In the study of Amanda (2024), students mentioned some advantages of DeepL such as improved text quality, improved error detection, and ease of use. Besides, DeepL Translator encourages students writing strategies during revisions (Amanda, 2024). In addition, according to Matviienko et al. (2024), DeepL has some benefits in excellent translation quality and more accurate translations of technical and specialized terms. Studies by Deng and Yu (2022) also demonstrated that, in addition to generating translations that were more syntactically accurate, DeepL translated more naturally and readable than human translations. According to Ahmadnia et al. (2019) and Rivera-Trigueros (2021), DeepL's translations need less post-editing effort than those produced by Google Translate. This drastically reduces the time and cost required to complete a translation project, which is crucial given that translation is a business. Besides the advantages, Amanda (2024) also pointed out difficulties, especially when it came to technical language and complex examples. Even though DeepL wrote better, it is still crucial to carefully check the translations. Some users still have trouble, especially when translating texts that require extensive cultural understanding or are highly contextualized (Kamaluddin et al., 2024). Furthermore, Matviienko et al. (2024) also claimed that DeepL has limited choice of languages compared to Google Translate and lacks some additional functions, such as photo translation or translation of web pages.

2.3 Review of Studies on Benefits and Challenges of AI Application in Translation Practices in the World

There are numerous recent studies in the world discussing the benefits of AI application in translation. Sutopo and Hastuti (2020) investigated the function of machine translation in scholarly translation instruction. The results demonstrated the far greater beneficial impact that machine translation had on students. Over 50% of students use machine translation to assist them in rendering materials, including articles, or other assignments (Sutopo & Hastuti, 2020). According to Wang (2023), people gradually get used to the convenience that AI translation offers, and many professors and students have acknowledged that AI even fosters the growth of English major learning in real-world applications. Besides, AI integration in translation procedures has promise for improving translation effectiveness, removing linguistic obstacles, and increasing information accessibility (Soysal, 2023). Bohatyrets (2023) claimed that machine translation systems are now much more accurate and efficient due to the quick development of AI technology, which has increased their use in a variety of industries. The vast majority of participants (75%) in the study of Khasawneh (2023) were fast to confirm that AI translation tools ease cross-cultural communication amongst people with diverse cultural backgrounds. Moreover, in his assessment of the advantages and difficulties of AI in translation research, Charles-Kenechi (2024) proposed that AI tools might be used to improve translation in a number of areas, such as speed and efficiency, cost-effectiveness, high consistency and accuracy, and scalability. According to the research by Mohamed et al. (2024), artificial intelligence, specifically, neural machine translation, is at the forefront of this revolutionary shift. Because of enhanced comprehension of context, idioms, and subtleties, translation accuracy has reached unprecedented levels. Besides, Atarchi et al. (2024) conducted a study on the role of AI translation tools such as DeepL, Google Translate, Grammarly, and Quilbot in academic translation. The participants in this study were convinced that these tools enable them to enhance the papers' coherence and clarity while also lowering the quantity of mistakes they made (Atarchi et al., 2024).

Despite the inevitable efficiency of AI translation tools, researchers also identified their unavoidable limitations. In the study of Sutopo and Hastuti (2020), many students make linguistic mistakes when they translate by typing long sentences into the tool. It requires authentication as a result, which adds delay. Moreover, AI systems frequently fail to grasp the variety of expressions and contextual nuances that are essential for good communication, which could result in translations that are shallow and unoriginal (AI Technology Reviews, 2023; Mills, 2023). As observed in educational contexts when AI tools are employed for language learning, an over-reliance on standardized language may lead to a loss of expressive richness (TrueLanguage, 2023). According to Loureiro and Ferreira (2023), there were errors in the translations produced by the AI tools that the students used, particularly with regard to punctuation, gender and person number correspondence, verb tenses, and the fittingness of the context to the language level. Additionally, the authors pointed out how these tools tended to use literal translations and how ChatGPT tended to soften some slang (Loureiro & Ferreira, 2023). Soysal (2023) also revealed that the use of AI in translation also brings up significant ethical issues, including the value of human translation skills, the precision and cultural suitability of translations, and the effects of AI on the labor force. Therefore, according to Bohatyrets (2023), post-editing is still essential to guarantee the quality and context-specific details of translated material. For fully autonomous machine translation, obstacles including linguistic subtleties, cultural context, and domain-specific terminology still exist (Bohatyrets, 2023). In addition, one of the limitations mentioned in Khasawneh's (2023) study is that AI translation tools cannot comprehend complicated language, including idiomatic idioms. Besides, it is acknowledged that AI translation has flaws and technological problems that stem from natural language processing (Charles-Kenechi, 2024). Human language is more complex than only grammar and vocabulary (Downie, 2020). Thus, AI systems frequently have trouble understanding the nuances of context, cultural allusions, and emotions that are ingrained in communication (Sanusi, 2024).

2.4 *Review of Studies on Benefits and Challenges of AI Application in Translation Practices in Vietnam*

Although the application of AI translation tools is a hot topic worldwide, in Vietnam this issue has only attracted moderate attention from researchers in recent years. Some authors emphasized the positive aspects of AI-powered translation applications. Nguyen et al. (2021) claimed that AI-based machine translation has greatly outperformed conventional techniques, and a machine translator is a great tool for accurately translating speech or text between languages. In addition, in the study of Nguyen and Do (2023), the participants mainly used Google Translate and Im Translator to translate single words and difficult paragraphs. The findings revealed that these tools benefited students due to their accuracy, free expenses, and easy access, which could help students improve reading comprehension and vocabulary enhancement. Besides, Tran et al. (2024) examined various AI translation tools like Google Translate, Translator Online, Chat GPT and other AI-powered aids and mentioned some main benefits including the adoption of innovative translation techniques and the effective handling of lengthy materials. In agreement, Dinh's (2024) study investigated the widespread use of AI tools like ChatGPT and Google Translate and showed that these tools can improve translation efficiency because of their substantial speed and consistency advantages. In addition, according to Nguyen (2024a, 2024b), the most obvious benefit that the majority of students acknowledged was that, in comparison to employing experienced translators, using online technical tools for translation work could enable them to complete their assignments more quickly and affordably.

However, a few Vietnamese researchers also discussed the challenging aspects of AI tools in translation. According to Nguyen and Do (2023), people may become discouraged from learning new words and phrases and from reading written English if these AI-powered translators become widely used. Besides, some participants expressed their doubts about whether these AI tools could improve their English speaking skills, and some encountered trouble connecting to the Internet, which is required to utilize these services (Nguyen & Do, 2023). Besides, Truong (2023) also investigated the use of Google Translate in translating Vietnamese texts into English ones and found that by using Vietnamese as the source language, this application failed to produce a high-quality output. The difficulties students encounter fall into two primary categories: grammatical level (the context, sentence structure, and phrase structure of the source text) and vocabulary level (words, technical terms, and cultural references) (Truong, 2023). Challenges such as idiomatic language, context awareness deficiencies, and persistent errors requiring human intervention are also covered in the study of Tran et al. (2024). Similarly, Dinh (2024) claimed that AI technologies that rely on standardized terminology frequently homogenize expressions by reducing its richness, especially for less widely spoken languages like Vietnamese. Through the analysis of noun phrases in AI-generated translations and a comparison with translations recommended by a business translation course textbook, this study reveals significant variations in contextual accuracy, lexical variety, and translation quality. The results showed how limited they are in providing a variety of contextually relevant word selections, underscoring the significance of human judgment in the translation process (Dinh, 2024). In addition, when using AI translation tools, most participants in Nguyen's (2024) study frequently encountered problems with grammar and vocabulary. When terminology from source language texts delivers abstract ideas, AI translation systems fail to provide proper word choice and grammar structures (Nguyen, 2024).

2.5 Research Gap

As demonstrated by the literature review, the use of AI in translation has garnered significant interest from scholars worldwide. Studies have shown different types of AI translation tools with both their advantages and disadvantages. In addition, reviewing the application of AI tools to translation practices in the classroom has revealed that in addition to providing students with great benefits, AI tools also create challenges for students in the translation process. It is evident, though, that this has only recently become a popular topic in Vietnam. This is a new subject at Vietnam National University (VNU), and there is not any study on employing AI in translation-related classroom activities. Consequently, I believe that a study is required to give a general overview of the benefits and difficulties of teaching and learning translation when students employ AI applications in their translation practices. Whether the benefits and challenges that Vietnamese students face are similar or different from those mentioned in other studies when students study in different learning environments is a topic that needs to be further explored. From there, the study can identify an unexplored aspect of AI translation, such as its pedagogical applications in university settings and future directions in AI translation for teaching and learning. These objectives can be obtained through the following two research questions:

1. What benefits does the application of AI tools bring to teaching and learning translation?
2. What challenges does the application of AI tools cause to teaching and learning translation?

An overview of AI in translation has shown the benefits and potential of this technology in assisting translators. However, translation is not simply a matter of converting words from one language to another, but also requires a deep understanding of the language, culture, as well as disciplinary knowledge of the two languages. Therefore, translators always face challenges such as ensuring the accuracy, precision, and grammar of the translation. With such characteristics of the role of AI in translation practices, I conducted this study with the subject and methods presented below.

3 Methodology

3.1 Research Study Design

3.1.1 Background

100 students from Basic English-Vietnamese Translation and Interpretation classes I directly taught at Vietnam National University (VNU) participated in this study. Students must have English proficiency at level B2 in accordance with the Common European Framework of Reference for Languages (Level 4 in accordance with the 6-level Foreign Language Competency Framework) to enroll in the course.

The Basic English-Vietnamese Translation and Interpretation course provides students with basic knowledge of translation and consecutive interpretation. Through activities and experiential exercises on the topic of general economics and society, students can expand their background knowledge and improve their vocabulary on the topics learned in the program; at the same time, they are equipped with basic skills for professional translation and interpretation work. The course also aims to create interest in learning and give students the right orientation towards translation and interpretation work. In the course, I provided students with instructions on how AI tools were introduced and assessed in the classroom.

In the first step, I helped students to get acquainted with the potential, constraints, and moral implications of utilizing AI in translation practices in the classroom. I also got started with the most popular AI translation tools, as reviewed above, like ChatGPT, Google Translate, and Microsoft Translator.

In the second step, I specified clear learning objectives for this AI-integrated activity for students. I clarified that AI translation tools could serve as additional teaching and learning resources, assisting learners in translating texts from English to Vietnamese. In addition, these tools also assist teachers in checking grammar, paraphrasing, detecting plagiarism, creating content and providing suggestions to improve the clarity and coherence of students' writing. This ensures that teachers' communication to learners goes beyond mere theoretical knowledge, encapsulating the practical applications of AI tools in real-life teaching situations.

In the third step, to achieve the learning objectives, I designed interesting and instructive activities that make use of AI translation tools. Specifically, each lesson is structured into four main parts: Reading, Vocabulary, Grammar, and Translation into Vietnamese. (1) Reading: includes articles with a variety of topics in socio-economic themes such as cultures, history, tourism and other articles and books. (2) Vocabulary: includes vocabulary by topic, fixed expressions, phrases, words in context and word structure in English. (3) Grammar: provides related grammatical phenomena, how to use new words in specific sentence contexts. (4) Translation into Vietnamese is an activity to assess students' level of understanding, vocabulary, structure and ability to express themselves in English. In all of the above learning content, students could use AI tools to save time looking up words and finding answers.

In the fourth step, I taught students how to critically evaluate information produced by AI and on the limitations of AI. For example, I chose one English article on a socioeconomic theme (approximately 350–400 words long) and distributed it to every group. The entire article had to be translated into Vietnamese by the students using one AI translation tool (like Google Translate). I had a discussion about how AI operates and why it could produce inaccurate information prior to the activity. Following that, students had to identify and analyze problems in GT translations and give recommendations.

In the last step, I held a post-activity session to evaluate the AI's contribution to the learning process, discuss the results, and reflect on the experience. In this activity, students were encouraged to share their analysis of the article translation (for example, what are the errors in this translation? What better translation version does the group have?). The remaining groups observed the presenting group's performance and offered feedback. The lesson was then summarized by discussing the implications of AI in future academic and professional settings. I also highlighted its ethical application and the value of human oversight for students to overcome their challenges in their translation practices.

3.1.2 Ethical Considerations for the Study

Ethical issues were taken carefully in my investigation. In the first place, all of my students were informed about the course goals and how different AI tools were used to help them with translation exercises from the first class of the semester. I described to them the goals and procedures of the study as well as how the information gathered from questionnaires and interviews would be integrated and used. After that, each participant signed a consent form committing them to assist me with this study. I further assured them that I would be the only one with access to and use of the data gathered from the surveys and interviews. Each participant was also given a pseudonym to ensure his/ her identity and the confidentiality of his/ her data.

3.2 Data Collection

In this study, the data were collected through questionnaires, interviews, and translation quality evaluation.

3.2.1 Questionnaire

Questionnaire was adopted as the main method in this study because according to Kuphanga (2024), by providing researchers with accessibility, affordability, and the capacity to contact a wide range of people, questionnaires allow for the effective collection of thorough insights. According to the research questions, there are two parts in the questionnaire related to both the benefits and challenges of AI translation tools for learning and teaching. The questionnaire was designed based on the classification of benefits and challenges of AI in translation studies by Charles-Kenechi (2024). There are 10 statements related to the benefits of AI tools in translation practices in part 1, and 10 statements related to challenges in using AI translation tools in part 2. The questionnaire adopted the 5-point Likert scale (strongly disagree, disagree, neutral, agree, strongly agree) for all statements in both two parts because both survey administrators and respondents would find the 5-point Likert scale easy to use and comprehend. Compared to higher-point scales, the 5-point Likert scale requires less time and effort to complete and respondents are not overloaded with options (Perzynska, 2024).

3.2.2 Interviews

I conducted semi-structured in-depth interviews with 20 students to find out further information that surfaced from the questionnaire questions. Semi-structured qualitative research interviews, according to Brinkmann (2015), are predicated on the interviewer's intention to learn; they center on the interviewee's descriptions, which are typically about real-world occurrences as they are experienced, and deciphering the meaning of the descriptions requires some form of interpretation. Besides, Xu (2024) also claimed that investigating intricate societal phenomena and complex human experiences in-depth can be made easier via semi-structured interviews. This is partly due to its emphasis on first-person narratives, the dynamic balance between appropriate structure and relative flexibility, and the open-ended and flexible nature of its interview questions (Xu, 2024).

Based on the two research topics and the issues that surfaced from the questionnaire, the interview form consists of ten questions. All in-person interviews were done in plain English to get more information about students' expectations and opinions as well as to triangulate the data collected from questionnaires. I obtained permission from each participant to videotape the interview before we began. It was also explained to them that they were not required to register their names. I also recorded the session, made notes to follow the speaker, and documented any additional questions that came up during the interview. Each interview lasted an average of fifteen minutes.

3.2.3 Translation Quality Evaluation

To evaluate the effectiveness of AI tools for translation practices more accurately, I combined the translation quality evaluation method with the two methods (questionnaire and interview) mentioned above. According to Postan (2023), translation quality assessment method is the process of analyzing translated text systematically to determine how accurate, acceptable, and readable it is in relation to the original. In the field of translation practices, it is essential to make sure that the final product corresponds with the desired goals and target audience. Beyond language precision, translation quality also takes into account context, cultural quirks, and the overall coherence of the text (Postan, 2023). The students' translation assignments were evaluated by me based on the translation quality evaluation rubric adapted from Ustaszewski (2014) which includes 4 criteria: meaning; functional and textual adequacy; target language mechanics; style, register and idiomaticity (Appendix).

3.3 Data Analysis

3.3.1 Questionnaire

The data obtained from the questionnaire were organized according to the issues from the two research questions. Standard deviation and mean scores were used to characterize the data from the Likert questionnaire. Data analysis employed two primary statistical techniques: inferential statistics, which use statistical tests to draw inferences from data, and descriptive statistics, which use indexes like mean and median to characterize data. Then, data were synthesized and presented in tables. After that, comments were made regarding the relevant information covered in the literature review.

The reliability coefficient was confirmed using a split-half method based on the Spearman-Brown formula to guarantee data reliability. Because Spearman-Brown reliability (Rsb) of part 1 is 0.81 and that of part 2 is 0.83, the Rsb is strong in this instance, above the requirement of 0.7. It means that the information gathered is reliable.

3.3.2 Interviews

The analysis of the interviews was broken into three small steps. The first step is to transcribe the interviews after they have all been completed. I proceeded and arranged the audio files such that they accurately represented the person who had been questioned. I then began the process of turning the audio files and related notes into a logical written text while locating and eliminating any unnecessary records. Once step 1 was finished, each interview's transcript was split into two halves based on the two questions listed in the question list. These covered both the advantages and drawbacks of AI translation technologies. In the end, the replies were categorized according to the two main research questions that served as the study's direction. In the last step—interpreting the data, when the data had been organized and completed, I compared and contrasted them with the results of both local and international studies to better understand the response that the study participants had provided. Additionally, by incorporating new viewpoints and questions that surface throughout the interview process, this method allowed me to uncover new parts of the subject that would have been missed by previous research.

4 Research Results and Discussions

4.1 Research Question 1: What Benefits Does the Application of AI Tools Bring to Teaching and Learning Translation?

To investigate the effectiveness of using AI tools to support translation practices, I used translation quality assessment to preliminarily evaluate translation assignments from students based on Ustaszewski's (2014) rubric which includes 4 criteria: meaning; functional and textual adequacy; target language mechanics; style, register and idiomaticity. The percentage of translations that met the above criteria on 4 levels (excellent, adequate, deficient, unacceptable) is shown in Table 1.

Table 1 Translation quality evaluation

Translation quality evaluation

Criteria	Meaning (%)	Functional and textual adequacy (%)	Target language mechanics (%)	Style, register, and idiomaticity (%)
Excellent	5	30	27	2
Adequate	32	53	58	33
Deficient	48	14	19	46
Unacceptable	15	3	4	19

Table 1 shows that with the advancement of today's AI tools, the quality of translation has increased significantly in aspects such as functional and textual adequacy, target language mechanics. The translation approximates the intended communicative function and to the needs and characteristics of the target audiences with excellent and adequate levels of 83%. Besides, the translations contain few violations of target language mechanics (grammar, spelling, punctuation,...) with excellent and adequate levels of 85%. It can be seen that before the advent of AI, translation activities were all performed by humans, from analyzing the original text, determining the meaning, to translating and editing. However, this process often takes a lot of human time and effort, especially for documents with difficult specialties or texts with many repetitive phrases. However, with the development of AI, machine translation systems (MT) have been designed to automatically analyze, process and translate texts quickly and accurately. Using technologies like deep learning and natural language processing, machine translation systems can learn and improve every day, making the translation process more efficient.

To further explore the benefits of AI tools in learning and teaching translation, I combined the above translation evaluation results with the learner's opinions in the survey, which are shown in Table 2.

Table 2 shows that AI translation tools bring many benefits to students' translation learning with 6/10 statements having mean scores > 4 and the remaining statements having mean scores > 3.5. Additionally, each factor showed a small standard deviation (SD < 0.7), indicating that the data were distributed closely around the mean. The main benefits can be illustrated as below.

Table 2 Benefits of AI translation tools

Benefits of AI translation tools		
Statements	Mean	Standard deviation
1. AI tools assist translators in effectively handling large amounts of content	4.36	0.51
2. AI tools help improve the accuracy and fluency of translations	3.61	0.56
3. AI tools enable translators to complete their work more quickly	4.58	0.50
4. AI tools have the ability to translate more complex languages	3.52	0.47
5. AI translation tools can be employed at any time and are available online	4.53	0.53
6. AI translation tools can arrange and comprehend information from a variety of fields	4.28	0.47
7. AI translation tools help optimize the proofreading and editing process	3.75	0.63
8. AI tools can make translation more efficient and cost-effective	4.48	0.68
9. AI tools can handle multiple languages, making translation flexible and diverse	3.64	0.51
10. AI tools can perform continuous translation, assisting in quick-response situations	4.56	0.62

4.1.1 High Speed

First, the 3 statements (3, 5, 10) that gained the highest mean scores (M > 4.5) are all related to increasing the speed of completing the translation. All students agreed that AI tools enabled them to complete their work more quickly (M = 4.58) and assisted them in quick-response situations (M = 4.56). In the interviews, students also confirmed these benefits. One student said, "*Compared to manual translation, AI translation saves time by processing and producing translations rapidly*" (S1). In agreement, another student explained this fact in detail:

> When we receive a translation assignment, we just use some AI-powered tools like Google translate or ChatGPT. These tools help us translate texts in a very short time and suggest many good sentence structures. I think if we only used dictionaries, we could not complete the translation so quickly. (S2)

This finding is aligned with the results mentioned by Nguyen (2024) who stated that the most notable benefit that the majority of students concurred with was that employing online technical tools for translation work might enable them to complete their assignments more quickly. Similarly, 94% of respondents in Khasawneh's (2023) study agreed with the claim that using AI translation technologies improves task efficiency and promptness. As shown by Katan and Taibi (2021), the current finding is consistent with earlier research that showed the benefits of AI-supported translation in reducing delays and increasing productivity. Moreover, in the study of Jakobsen (2017), it is explained that the traditional method of translating uses a human translator, which is frequently slow when translating a lot of texts or when real-time translation is needed. According to Liu and Chen (2023), some AI tools like Google Translate and DeepL can translate millions of words per minute. Besides, the speed of AI translation tools was also emphasized in the study of Charles-Kenechi (2024) in which AI tools were proven to translate text virtually instantly. This speed is preferable when instant access to information and/or materials is necessary, as in the case of live broadcasts, overseas sales and purchases, or disaster response (Charles-Kenechi, 2024). Sharing the same opinions, Bozkurt et al. (2023) revealed that AI translation technologies could quickly translate product descriptions, marketing materials, and customer support information for companies operating in cross-border marketplaces to meet local requirements.

4.1.2 Accessibility

These benefits were followed by the fact that AI translation tools can be employed at any time and are available online (M = 4.53). In the interview, all students shared the same thought with this beneficial aspect. One student said, "*You can use AI translation tools online at any time and from any location as long as you have an Internet connection*" (S3). In agreement, the participants in the study of Nguyen (2024) also shared their opinions about AI translation tools like ChatGPT, stating that it was a primary instrument for translation support. Its notable attributes include availability and time-saving (Nguyen, 2024). In my study, the participants also highly appreciated the assistance of ChatGPT in their translation practices and regarded ChatGPT as the most useful online tool to use. One student admitted:

> ChatGPT can understand and arrange knowledge from a variety of areas, including disciplinary language, because it has been trained on an enormous amount of data. Despite the formal language used in the Vietnamese text, ChatGPT can comprehend the original source and carry out its translation duty well. (S4)

4.1.3 Efficiency and Cost-Effectiveness

Besides the benefits related to speed of completing tasks, all students agreed with the aspect of AI tools related to dealing with large amounts of content (M = 4.36) and being efficient and cost-effective (M = 4.48). One student shared her thought:

> With the help of AI tools, I feel more confident and less stressed when dealing with long translations and completing many translation assignments in a semester. I think if I used a dictionary, the efficiency would not be as good. (S5)

This opinion is similar to that of the participants in the study of Khasawneh (2023), who agreed that using AI translation technologies reduces their workload. Besides, according to Charles-Kenechi (2024), a large number of documents can be translated thanks to the scalability of AI translation systems. Sharing the same idea, Sin-wai (2014) claimed that due to non-proportionality of time or cost, AI systems could be modified to allow for an upscaling of translation, which converts into efficiency. For large-scale and varied content needs, AI translation technologies are therefore most appropriate for enterprise-level organizations, such as governments, media outlets, and multinational corporations (Sin-wai, 2014). Besides, in the interview, students also shared their ideas about the cost-effectiveness of AI tools in the translation industries. One student said that:

> Professional human translators have important uses due to their unique knowledge, but they can also be expensive, particularly for small businesses or individuals. For some tasks, using AI translation instead of hiring qualified human translators can be more affordable. (S6)

This result is consistent with Brooks' (2020) theories regarding machine translation, according to which employing AI tools is more economical than engaging qualified translators. Similarly, according to Benbada and Benaouda (2023), machine translation, which is an application of artificial intelligence, can be classified as a cost-effective alternative to human translation services. Liu (2022) also gave an example of cloud-based AI translation services from Microsoft and Amazon, which assist organizations in implementing translation at a cost-effective rate. When cross-lingual communication is required but costs cannot be prohibitively high, this is highly beneficial for small businesses, non-profit organizations, and educational institutions. Moreover, according to Brynjolfsson et al. (2019), AI solutions are usually free or significantly less expensive than human translators are. In a sense, this lowers the cost of the service, increasing its market reach and enabling more individuals and companies to use translation services.

4.1.4 Flexibility

In addition, students also shared their agreement with the fact that AI translation tools can arrange and comprehend information from a variety of fields (M = 4.28). This confirms the flexibility of AI tools in translating different fields. One student shared that:

> When studying disciplinary subjects, translation skills play an important role because we often have to refer to documents in different languages about our majors. AI tools have really helped us a lot in grasping information from various fields. This is very useful for us to learn our majors. (S7)

This was also reported by Soysal (2023) who stated that AI integration in translation procedures has promise for improving translation effectiveness, removing linguistic obstacles, and increasing information accessibility.

4.1.5 Accuracy Improvements

An interesting thing is that through the survey results, students also expressed hesitation with some features of AI tools in ensuring the accuracy, complexity, and diversity of language with statements 2, 4, 9 ranging the mean scores from 3.5 to 3.6. In the interviews, there are also conflicting opinions regarding the reliability of the AI tools. A few students said that using a translation tool driven by artificial intelligence produced a more accurate translation than they could have done themselves. One student explained:

> With the help of AI, my translation will be more accurate in terms of structure and vocabulary. If I translate by myself by looking up the dictionary, sometimes I will make mistakes in complex sentence structures and word forms in sentences. (S8)

This opinion is consistent with a number of students trusting translations from Vietnamese to English by AI tools in the study of Nguyen and Do (2023). More specifically, students in Nguyen's (2024) study utilized Cambridge Translate (GT) from Cambridge Dictionary Online to convert brief Vietnamese sentences into English. Although this application can automatically translate sentences that are less than 160 words, the students reported that the program's translation accuracy was fairly high. Additionally, the participants expressed their trust in the accuracy of AI tools by using Microsoft tools to check grammar and spelling mistakes when translating a source language text (Nguyen, 2024). Furthermore, Charles-Kenechi (2024) also revealed that the reliability of producing AI translations with neural machine translation has significantly increased. According to Yuan (2018), DeepL is one of the apps that stand out due to the coherence and fluency of the translations it provides, which are extremely similar to those of human quality. These make use of enormous datasets and sophisticated neural networks to interpret proverbs, context, and colloquial language processing, which improves translation quality.

However, besides the positive opinions mentioned above, in this aspect, there are still some students expressing doubts about the accuracy of AI translation tools. This result is consistent with the results obtained from the translation quality evaluation above where although the student's translation contained relatively few errors in language mechanics and readability, the translation still contains frequent inappropriate style/ register choices or frequent unidiomatic wording, which may obscure or change meaning. In addition, based on the review of previous studies mentioned above, it can be seen that there are inevitable limitations when applying AI to translation practices. Those challenges are presented in more depth in the next section.

4.2 Research Question 2: What Challenges Does the Application of AI Tools Cause to Teaching and Learning Translation?

First, through analyzing translation assignments presented in Table 1, I also found that they still have problems with two aspects: meaning, and style, register, and idiomaticity. In terms of meaning, it can be seen that the translations almost show some misunderstanding of the original texts, and they contain more than occasional changes in meaning or unwarranted omissions/ additions (63%). As regards style, register, and idiomaticity, 65% of translations contain frequent inappropriate style/ register choices or frequent unidiomatic wording. Such errors can obscure or change the meaning of the translations. From the initial analysis of the students' translations, it can be seen that although the development of AI has brought many benefits to the translation industry, it is undeniable that it also brings many challenges. One of those challenges is assessing the accuracy of AI systems. As machines, these systems are not capable of understanding cultural factors or communication language like humans, leading to them being able to produce inconsistent or incorrect translations.

To re-exam these above limitations and to investigate more deeply into the difficulties of using AI translation tools, some challenges are suggested in part 2 of the questionnaire, which are shown in the Table 3.

Table 3 shows that the main challenges of AI translation tools include lack of ability to understand cultural factors ($M = 4.65$), lack of ability to communicate naturally ($M = 4.63$), lack of contextual awareness ($M = 4.56$), and lack of regional language understanding ($M = 4.30$). This shows that despite being able to translate grammatically accurately, AI translation tools still show many limitations in situations where it is necessary to understand hidden meanings related to context or cultures.

4.2.1 Contextual Misunderstandings

First, as regards unnatural translation, based on the results of the translation quality assessment, I found that one of the main reasons why artificial intelligence has not yet been able to completely replace human translators is because AI is only capable

Table 3 Challenges of AI translation tools

Challenges of AI translation tools		
Statements	Mean	Standard deviation
1. Lack of ability to communicate naturally	4.63	0.46
2. Lack of contextual awareness	4.56	0.59
3. Lack of sense of humor	3.55	0.61
4. Lack of regional language understanding	4.30	0.50
5. Lack of understanding of nonverbal language	3.79	0.47
6. Lack of ability to understand cultural factors	4.65	0.57
7. Lack of ability to produce a high-quality product	3.58	0.65
8. Making learners lazy to think and to use effort in translating	2.08	0.52
9. Requiring access to the internet	3.25	0.61
10. Tendency to employ literal translations	3.68	0.56

of translating languages based on pre-programmed algorithms and processes. These algorithms often follow the rules of formal communication, not everyday communication. This makes AI translation rigid and unnatural, especially in the context of flexible listening-speaking communication where creativity is the most crucial factor. According to Harris (1977), natural translation is the translation performed by bilinguals in routine situations without any specialized instruction. The idea of natural translation is similar to Toury's idea of a native translator (Toury, 1982), but it differs in that Toury views translation as a skill that develops through socialization processes, whereas natural translation assumes an intuitive competence that is coextensive with all bilingualism at any age and regardless of the level of proficiency in the two languages. In this study, naturalness in language is often related to the ability to use words appropriately in context. This also explains why students emphasized this challenge in their interviews. One student explained:

> Today's translation AI systems have rich memories of vocabulary, semantics, and grammar, but lack adaptation to context. A single sentence or word, when applied in different situations, can have different meanings. To overcome these errors, it is necessary to have humans involved in the process of proofreading the translation to make it more accurate. (S9)

Agreeing with this, another student added that, "*When it comes to complex or ambiguous statements, AI translation technologies may have trouble understanding context, which could lead to errors or mistranslations*" (S10). These students' comments are quite consistent with what I witnessed in the translations obtained from students. It can be difficult to navigate cultural nuances because AI tools lack context awareness, which results in inaccurate information that ignores the subtleties. In some contexts, to be able to translate the source texts accurately, the translator needs to have an understanding of the culture and needs to use descriptive equivalent techniques. This is something that AI tools cannot yet provide. As one student gave a specific example to illustrate:

> In a translation, I was asked to translate the phrase "lễ tế Nam Giao". If I use AI tools, the phrase will simply be translated as "Nam Giao ceremony". However, many readers will not know about this ceremony in Vietnam, so the translator needs to add cultural knowledge that is not available in the target language: "the national ceremonial service at Nam Giao where kings offered their thanks to heaven". (S10)

4.2.2 Cultural Nuances

In addition, AI tools are often pre-programmed so they are only optimized for general conversational translation, making them difficult to approach regional slang. One student shared her thought:

> Nowadays, young people always have new languages, or special words that are only used in a certain region. The rigidity of AI is that it cannot understand the "slang" of young people or cultural changes in communication. I think this is a major limitation of AI tools. (S11)

It can be seen that the lack of understanding of these languages makes AI face huge challenges when interacting with humans, not only in terms of translation but also in terms of cultural understanding and context awareness. According to Alexopoulos et al. (2016), context is any information that can be used to describe the state of an item, such as a person, location, or physical or digital object. In multilingual interactions involving many turns, Pombal et al. (2024) defined context as information that goes beyond the current turn and is essential for minimizing ambiguity and preserving coherence between turns. Thus, context-awareness is the capacity to adapt a component's behavior based on the context in which it operates to make it more applicable or efficient for the scenario (Lucke et al., 2013).

The absence of context awareness is consistent with earlier studies that highlighted the subtle cultural differences that automated systems could overlook (Zhang et al., 2019). Thus, for translations that go beyond simple linguistic accuracy, Zhang et al. (2019) emphasized the significance of overcoming cultural differences. In agreement, Tran et al. (2024) claimed that the lack of context awareness in machine translation techniques is a challenge faced by English-Vietnamese translation majors. According to participants in Tran et al. (2024) study, the cultural context is frequently difficult for machine translation to understand; it is like having a conversation without knowing the cultural cues that are not spoken. Nguyen (2024) stated that the differences between Vietnamese and English could cause difficulties for translators. According to Chan (2004), a translation that ignores cultural nuances leads to distortion; thus, programs for training translators should incorporate cultural competency as a key element to address this. To maintain high-quality translation standards, prior research also highlighted the ongoing necessity of human control (Och, 2003; Wu et al., 2018).

4.2.3 Idiomatic Expressions

Additionally, based on my evaluation of student translations, I found that these limitations of AI tools might be a cause of indomaticity-related errors. In the interview, one student also emphasized, "*Idiomatic phrases pose a difficult problem for us to deal with when using AI translation tools because these tools frequently fail to capture their complexities, resulting in translation errors*" (S12). The challenges with idiomatic expressions are consistent with other research showing that AI tools have trouble capturing subtle linguistic features (Specia et al., 2018). Moreover, this finding also supports Wang's (2020) research and shows that these tools have not yet been developed to adequately capture important linguistic features like cultural nuances. Stated differently, an understanding of the cultural context in which a language is used is necessary to appreciate the relevance of linguistic components like idiomatic idioms. However, it is insufficient to simply acknowledge these difficulties; translation-training programs must take proactive measures to overcome them. According to Specia et al. (2018), human interpreters play a crucial role in understanding the complexities of idiomatic idioms. In agreement, to overcome this specific difficulty, Othman and Ismail (2023) suggested using specialized artificial intelligence (AI) tools, training AI models on datasets that include cultural diversity, using human translators as editors or post-editors, and incorporating cultural dialogue into the translation process.

4.2.4 Over-Reliance

It is interesting to find that almost no students agreed with the view that AI tools make learners lazy to think and to use effort in translating (M = 2.08). In the interview, the student shared his thoughts on this issue, "*I think AI has a supporting role in translation practices, but they cannot replace humans because to have a high-quality translation we need to spend time on proofreading*" (S13). Similarly, another student said, "*I think students will not be lazy when using AI tools because the limitations of AI are very obvious. This requires translators to pay more attention to edit some errors of AI tools to get the best translation*" (S14). This finding is also consistent with that of Yolifi et al. (2025) who proved that students found translation AI tools helpful for improving their English skills, but they did not depend on it entirely with nearly all students disagreeing that it made them lazy or less motivated. Sharing the same opinions, most students in the study of Laksana and Komara (2024) had neutral responses about possible over-reliance or dependence on DeepL. In agreement, according to Sidiq and Syafryadin (2024), the majority of students did not believe that utilizing AI tools made them less motivated to learn; instead, it provided them with a good language structure. Similarly, according to Pham and Le (2024), ChatGPT, or an AI chatbot, was a good tool for helping people learn languages. Additionally, ChatGPT was viewed as a useful tool to promote students' learning and expand their knowledge, and it was found to help engage students in the learning process (Pham & Le, 2024). Moreover, Nguyen (2024) also stated that beyond the cognitive realm, AI tools are crucial for learners' emotional and psychological experiences, such as increased motivation or decreased worry.

However, it can be seen that this study result is in contrast to that of several other studies. According to Mardiah and Nissa (2024), students believed that artificial intelligence (AI) technology made them sluggish and uninteresting since they were too reliant on it and were too lazy to study and fully understand the material. Furthermore, students' critical thinking skills may deteriorate (Mardiah & Nissa, 2024). Pham and Le (2024) revealed that an excessive amount of interaction with ChatGPT may inhibit students' ability to think critically and creatively. Moreover, in the study of Dakakni and Safa (2023), some educators who participated in the interviews even went so far as to claim that AI discourages creativity and originality and makes students lazy by encouraging them to cheat. The finding also contrasts with the claims made by Viktorivna et al. (2022) that students are no longer motivated to read or complete assignments due to AI. Besides, Abalkheel (2022) contended that AI technology not only reduces student motivation to learn but also results in less creativity in tasks that are assigned and may cause learning boredom. Moreover, according to Wogu et al. (2018), students who switch back to using AI will be psychologically and mentally removed from their subject of study. These results support worries expressed in the literature regarding the necessity of a balanced use of machine translation systems in educational contexts and the possible barriers to the development of autonomous language skills (Alammar & Abdel-Reheem Amin, 2023; Lee, 2021). This difference shows the positive attitude of students in my study with the support of AI tools in their translation practices. In the teaching and learning process, it is evident that both teachers and students are always aware of the advantages and disadvantages of AI tools. This, in my opinion, is a positive outcome since it allows both teachers and students to fully benefit from AI's contributions to the teaching and learning process.

5 Conclusion

5.1 Major Findings

The purpose of this study is to explore the benefits and challenges that AI tools bring to educators and learners in translation practices. I conducted the study in translation classes that I directly taught at VNU with 100 students. The data were collected from both quantitative and qualitative methods through questionnaires, interviews and translation quality evaluation. The findings show that some of the potential and opportunities of AI translation include increased speed, the ability to translate more complicated languages, and its use in a wide range of disciplines. Nonetheless, there are certain indisputable difficulties, such as a lack of contextual understanding, cultural considerations, and the inability to translate naturally. One interesting point different from most other studies is that students do not feel that AI tools make them lazier in their learning. This shows that students are always aware of both the strengths and weaknesses of AI tools and are always conscious of taking an active role in proofreading to get the best quality translation. Although there are still many challenges to be solved, the development of AI will offer many opportunities for both educators and learners in translation studies.

5.2 Pedagogical Implications for Educators and Learners

The study emphasizes how crucial it is to balance human monitoring in language instruction with AI translation capabilities. Even though AI can translate texts in an understandable and reliable manner, teachers still need to incorporate cultural context and sophisticated comprehension into their lessons. This guarantees that students understand the language and its cultural context, both of which are essential for real linguistic competency. Given these results, a number of research implications are recommended for both educators and learners.

5.2.1 Selecting AI Tools

In terms of selecting AI tools for different translation tasks, as the use of AI in many industries grows, we need to make sure that the AI tool we select complements the goals of our translation tasks, which often include text translation and audio translation practices. First, for text translation which is the process of translating written material from one language into another while maintaining its original meaning and substance, learners can choose some AI-powered translation tools such as Google Translate, DeepL, and ChatGPT because they can process vast quantities of text much faster than human translators. Furthermore, instant cross-language communication is made possible by AI-powered real-time translation tools. This is evident in features such as Google's "Interpreter Mode" and other language translation applications. Second, for translating spoken language, one way is through speech recognition. The transcribed material can be translated into the target language using machine translation tools like Speechify and FluentU. These tools are helpful for activities like live speech interpretation, translating audio content in foreign languages, and supporting multilingual interactions because they can translate continuously and in real time. In short, the choice of AI tool depends on having a thorough grasp of the translation task's goal and the type of data being used. This alignment creates the conditions for successful outcomes and guarantees the effective use of AI capabilities.

5.2.2 Incorporating AI into Lesson Plans

As regards best practices for incorporating AI into lesson plans, careful preparation and planned implementation are necessary for the effective integration of AI into translation instruction. First, educators can begin by integrating AI into specific tasks, such as practicing pronunciation or grammar. For instance, ELSA Speak can assist with pronunciation drills, while Grammarly can be introduced for writing projects. Second, before implementing AI tools across the curriculum, schools and educators might start pilot projects to evaluate them with smaller groups. This makes it possible to recognize possible obstacles and improve tactics. After the initial deployment is successful, educators can extend AI integration to incorporate more complex exercises, such interactive listening assignments or conversational practice with AI chatbots. With such gradual integration, a smoother transition to technology-enhanced instruction can be achieved, which increases familiarity and confidence between teachers and students.

5.2.3 Incorporating AI into Assessment Strategies

AI can offer opportunities for educators to create more responsive, individualized, and efficient assessment experiences. First, educators can use AI for pre-assessment and diagnostic activities. For example, before introducing a new idea, teachers can utilize AI to create diagnostic tests. Then, AI can help teachers to evaluate results to find probable misconceptions and past knowledge. These findings allow them to modify lesson plans in light of students' prior knowledge. Second, AI tools can provide initial feedback for students' submitted work before teachers review. Students can make revisions based on AI recommendations. Reviewing both the AI feedback and student revisions can enable teachers to identify learning patterns. Third, AI can also help teachers design customised practice sets targeting specific skills. Depending on each student's needs, teachers might offer various practice resources. Fourth, teachers can use AI to support self-assessment for students. For instance, teachers can create self-check questions for their students and then offer AI-generated examples for students to evaluate their own work. Then, using AI-recommended prompts, teachers assist students in reflecting on their learning.

5.2.4 Addressing AI-Related Challenges

Concerning ways to address AI-related challenges in the classroom, both educators and learners have a significant role to play. For students' roles, they should actively take the initiative, offer comments, and contribute to the development of AI tools. Being proficient with AI technologies is only one aspect of this; another is managing the linguistic, cultural, and ethical issues surrounding automatic translation. Besides, it should be a top priority for students to strengthen their critical thinking abilities to assess AI translations. To help students get an accurate assessment of the effectiveness of AI translation tools, the teacher's involvement should be emphasized. Teachers are of great significance in adopting AI successfully in classes. They are able to customize AI technologies to fit the unique demands of their students because of their knowledge and experience with classroom dynamics. Therefore, it should be possible for teachers to customize AI technologies to suit the learning objectives. An instructor who specializes in vocabulary development, for example, might create customized vocabulary lists, quizzes, or flashcards utilizing AI platforms. Teachers also play a vital role in balancing technology with pedagogy. While AI can be a great help, educators need to combine technology with more conventional approaches. Instead of depending only on automated suggestions, they should help students understand the fundamental concepts by guiding them in evaluating AI-generated feedback. Besides, by using AI analytics, teachers may identify patterns in student performance and modify their teaching to tackle prevalent problems.

5.3 Limitations and Suggestions for Further Research

The study has limitations because it only looks at the classes I taught directly and has a small sample size. Future studies could examine a wider range of participants and explain the discrepancy between the AI-induced "laziness" findings of this study and contrasting findings from other countries. Besides, these constraints could be addressed by broadening the diversity of participant groups, performing comparative analyses in various linguistic and cultural contexts, and investigating a wider range of AI techniques. In addition, researchers can investigate efficient ways to teach critical thinking in translation classes and how it affects students' use of AI tools. Moreover, studies related to the role of AI in more advanced linguistic translation tasks, such as literary or legal translation, are also areas that require further research. Such studies can aid in improving translation efficiency and productivity to open up new markets and generate employment prospects. Even though there are numerous obstacles to overcome, effective usage of AI will open up a lot of possibilities for the translation sector in the future.

Appendix

Translation Quality Evaluation Rubric (Ustaszewski, 2014)

Meaning	Functional and textual adequacy	Target language mechanics	Style, register, and idiomaticity	Overall rating
The translation accurately reflects the content of the source text. Slight nuances and shades of meaning have been rendered adequately. The translation contains few or no transfer errors, and those present have only a minot effect on meaning	The translation accurately addresses the target audience by fully taking its needs and characteristics into consideration. It also fully accomplishes the intended communicative function. Minor or no edits needed	The translation contains few or no violations of the rules and conventions of target language mechanics (grammar, spelling, punctuation, etc.). It reads similarly to texts originally written in the target language for the same purpose	Style and register are appropriate for the text type in the target language and for the target audience. The translation reads smoothly and the wording is idiomatic. Any errors have only a minor effect on meaning	Excellent
The translation contains occasional and/or minor transfer errors that slightly obscure or change meaning	The translation approximates to the intended communicative function and to the needs and characteristics of the target audience. Can be repaired with edits	The translation contains occasional errors in target language mechanics	The translation contains occasional and/ or minor inappropriate style/register choices or occasional unidiomatic wording. Such errors may slightly obscure meaning	Acceptable
The translation shows some misunderstanding of the original and/or the translation brief. It contains more than occasional changes in meaning and/or unwarranted omissions/additions	The translation gives some consideration to the intended communicative function and the needs of the target audience but misses some important aspects of it. Repair requires considerable effort	The translation is hard to comprehend because it contains frequent and/or obvious errors in target language mechanics. The structure of the source language shows up in the translation and affects its readability	The translation contains frequent inappropriate style/register choices or frequent unidiomatic wording. Such errors may obscure or change meaning	Deficient

(continued)

(continued)

Meaning	Functional and textual adequacy	Target language mechanics	Style, register, and idiomaticity	Overall rating
The translation reflects or contains important unwarranted deviations from the original. It contains inaccurate renditions and/or important omissions or additions that cannot be justified by the translation brief. Very defective comprehension of the original text	The translation disregards the intended communicative function and fails to address the target audience. Cannot be repaired with revisions	The text is extremely difficult to read bordering on being incomprehensible. The translation reveals serious language proficiency issues. Un-grammatical use of the target language	The translation contains excessive inappropriate style/register choices or disruptive unidiomatic wording. Such errors obscure or change meaning	Unacceptable

References

Adams, D., & Chuah, K. (2022). Artificial intelligence-based tools in research writing: Current trends and future potentials. *Artificial Intelligence in Higher Education, 9*, 1–16. https://doi.org/10.1201/9781003184157-9

Ahmadnia, B., Haffari, G., & Serrano, J. (2019). Round-trip training approach for bilingually low-resource statistical machine translation systems. *International Journal of Artificial Intelligence, 17*(1), 167–185. http://www.ceser.in/ceserp/index.php/ijai/article/view/5959

AI Technology Reviews. (2023). *How AI translation is breaking down language barriers*. Retrieved from https://aitechnologyreviews.com

Alammar, A., & Abdel-Reheem Amin, E. (2023). EFL students' perception of using AI paraphrasing tools in English language research projects. *Arab World English Journal, 14*(3), 166–181. https://doi.org/10.24093/awej/vol14no3.11

Albalkheel, A. (2022). Amalgamating bloom's taxonomy and artificial intelligence to face the challenges of online EFL learning amid post covid-19 in Saudi Arabia. *International Journal of English Language and Literature Skills, 11*(1), 16–30. https://doi.org/10.18488/519v1it4409

Alexopoulos, K., Makris, S., Xanthakis, V., Sipsas, K., & Chryssolouris, G. (2016). A concept for context-aware computing in manufacturing: The white goods case. *International Journal of Computer Integrated Manufacturing, 29*(8), 839–849. https://doi.org/10.1080/0951192X.2015.1130257

Alkhawaja, L. (2024). Unveiling the new frontier: ChatGPT-3 powered translation for Arabic-English language pairs. *Theory and Practice in Language Studies, 14*(2), 347–357. https://doi.org/10.17507/tpls.1402.05

Alosaimi, A., & Alawad, A. (2024). Evaluation of the translation of separable phrasal verbs generated by ChatGPT. *Arab World English Journal, 1*(1), 282–291. https://doi.org/10.24093/awej/chatgpt.19

Amanda, K. (2024). *The impact of using DeepL translator on EFL students' writing*. Masters thesis, UIN Sumatera Utara Medan.

Amna, S. (2022). English learners' perceptions using google translate for doing assignments: Advantages and disadvantages. *Journal of Language Education Development, 4*(2), 1–16. https://ejournal.ummuba.ac.id/index.php/pbi/article/view/328/745

Atarchi, K., Abdelkarim, E., & Mohamed, M. (2024). The role of artificial intelligence translation tools in academic translation: Faculties of pure sciences as a case study. *International Journal of Translation and Interpretation Studies, 4*(3), 7–17. https://doi.org/10.32996/ijtis.2024.4.3.2

Aulia, R., Destari, D., & Komariah, A. (2024). Students' perception of using google translate at English education department UINSI Samarinda. *El-Syaker: Samarinda International Journal of Language Studies, 1*(1), 33–41. https://journalweb.org/ojs/index.php/El-Syaker/article/view/10/23

Bahri, H., & Mahadi, T. S. T. (2016). Google translate as a supplementary tool for learning Malay: A case study at University Saint Malaysia. *Journal of Advances in Language and Literary Studies, 7*(3), 161–167. https://journals.aiac.org.au/index.php/alls/article/view/2305

Banat, M., & Abu Adla, Y. (2023). Exploring the effectiveness of GPT-3 in translating specialized religious text from Arabic to English: A comparative study with human translation. *Journal of Translation and Language Studies, 4*(2), 1–23. https://doi.org/10.48185/jtls.v4i2.762

Benbada, M. L., & Benaouda, N. (2023). *Investigation of the role of artificial intelligence in developing machine translation quality. Case study: Reverso context and google translate translations of expressive and descriptive texts. Language combination: Arabic English/English-Arabic* (doctoral dissertation, faculty of letters and languages-department of English).

Bohatyrets, V. (2023). Artificial intelligence and machine translation post-editing: Prospects and challenges (insights for international students). *Mediaforum Analytics Forecasts Information Management, 13*, 195–209. https://doi.org/10.31861/mediaforum.2023.13.198-209

Bozkurt, A., Junhong, X., Lambert, S., Pazurek, A., Crompton, H., Koseoglu, S., & Romero-Hall, E. (2023). Speculative futures on ChatGPT and generative artificial intelligence (AI): A collective reflection from the educational landscape. *Asian Journal of Distance Education, 18*(1), 53–130. https://www.asianjde.com/ojs/index.php/AsianJDE/article/view/709

Brinkmann, S. (2015). Qualitative interviewing. *Oxford University Press*. https://doi.org/10.1093/acprof:osobl/9780199861392.001.0001

Brooks, R. (2020). *A Brief History of Machine Translation Technology*. Retrieved from https://www.k-international.com/blog/history-machine-translation

Brynjolfsson, E., Hui, X., & Liu, M. (2019). Does machine translation affect international trade? Evidence from a large digital platform. *Management Science, 65*(12), 5449–5460. https://doi.org/10.1287/mnsc.2019.3388

Chan, S. W. (2004). *A dictionary of translation technology*. Chinese University Press.

Charles-Kenechi, S. (2024). Artificial intelligence in translation studies: Benefits and challenges. Cascades, *Journal of the Department of French & International Studies, 2*(1), 5–15. https://cascadesjournal.com/index.php/cascades/article/view/31

Chen, W., & Wei, H. (2021). Effect of an AI-powered writing assistant on writing quality and idea generation. *Journal of Educational Technology & Society, 24*(3), 84–97.

Dakakni, D., & Safa, N. (2023). Artificial intelligence in the L2 classroom: Implications and challenges on ethics and equity in higher education: A 21st century Pandora's box. *Computers and Education: Artificial Intelligence, 5*, 1–10. https://doi.org/10.1016/j.caeai.2023.100179

Deng, X., & Yu, Z. (2022). A systematic review of machine-translation-assisted language learning for sustainable education. *Sustainability, 14*(13), 7598. https://doi.org/10.3390/su14137598

Dinh, H. M. T. (2024). Navigating the convenience trap with ChatGPT and google translate: The risks of homogenization in translation teaching for Vietnamese students. *International Journal of Linguistics Literature and Translation, 7*(8), 244–255. https://doi.org/10.32996/ijllt.2024.7.8.28

Do, T. H. (2023). The negative impact of google translate on basic language learning among students at Hoa Binh University. *Journal of Science and Technology, Hoa Binh University, 8*, 79–85. https://vjol.info.vn/index.php/hoabinh/article/view/85684

Dong, Q., Li, L., Dai, D., Zheng, C., Wu, Z., Chang, B., & Sui, Z. (2022). A survey for in-context learning. arXiv preprint arXiv:2301.00234

Downie, J. (2020). *Interpreters versus machines. Can interpreters survive in an AI-dominated world?* Routledge.

EUATC. (2023). *The future of translation—a nuanced perspective.* https://euatc.org

Fitria, T. N. (2021). A review of machine translation tools: The translation's ability. *Language Circle Journal of Language and Literature, 16*(1), 162–176. https://doi.org/10.15294/lc.v16i1.30961

Gen, Tr. I. T. (2016). The advantages and disadvantages of Machine Translation. *Writing Systems and Language Discussion List.* http://www.omniglot.com/language/articles/machinetranslation.htm

Groves, M., & Mundt, K. (2015). Friend or foe? Google translate in language for academic purposes. *Journal of English for Specific Purposes, 37*, 112–121. https://doi.org/10.1016/j.esp.2014.09.001

Hamood, M. I., & Al-Bagoa, M. A. K. (2021). The translation of adverbial beta clause functions by using google translate. *International Journal of English Linguistics, 11*(2), 118–125. https://doi.org/10.5539/ijel.v11n2p118

Harris, B. (1977). *The importance of natural translation.* University of Ottawa, School of Translators and Interpreters.

Hidayati, N. N., & Nihayah, D. H. (2024). Google translate, ChatGPT or google bard AI: A study toward Non-English department college students' preference and translation comparison. *Inspiring English Education Journal, 7*(1), 14–33. https://doi.org/10.35905/inspiring.v7i1.8821

Ho, P. X. P. (2024). Using ChatGPT in English language learning: A study on I.T. students' attitudes habits and perceptions. *International Journal of TESOL & Education, 4*(1), 55–68. https://doi.org/10.54855/ijte.24414

House, J. (2018). *Translation: The basics.* Routledge.

Jakobsen, A. L. (2017). *Translation process research.* The handbook of translation and cognition, (pp.19–49).

Kamaluddin, M. I., Rasyid, M. W. K., Abqoriyyah, F. H., & Saehu, A. (2024). Accuracy analysis of DeepL: Breakthroughs in machine translation technology. *Journal of English Education Forum (JEEF), 4*(2), 122–126. https://doi.org/10.29303/jeef.v4i2.681

Katan, D., & Taibi, M. (2021). *Translating cultures: An introduction for translators, interpreters and mediators.* Routledge.

Khasawneh, M. A. S. (2023). The potential of AI in facilitating cross-cultural communication through translation. *Journal of Namibian Studies: History Politics Culture, 37*, 107–130. https://doi.org/10.59670/jns.v37i.4654

Koehn, P., & Knowles, R. (2017). Six Challenges for Neural Machine Translation. In *Proceedings of the first workshop on neural machine translation* (pp. 28–39). Vancouver. Association for Computational Linguistics. https://doi.org/10.18653/v1/W17-3204

Köksal, D., & Yürük, N. (2020). A critical review on machine translation in the digital age. *Journal of Computer Science and Technology, 20*(1), 25–34. https://doi.org/10.31539/jcst/764006

Kornfeld, L., & Roy, D. (2021). Educational implications of AI writing tools for academic writing. *British Journal of Educational Technology, 52*(1), 248–262. https://doi.org/10.1111/bjet.12973

Kuphanga, D. (2024). Questionnaires in research: Their role, advantages, and main aspects. *ActionAid International.* https://doi.org/10.13140/RG.2.2.15334.64325

Laksana, K. N., & Komara, C. (2024). Indonesian EFL students' perceptions of DeepL machine translation tool: Utilization, advantages, and disadvantages. *Journal of Language and Literature Studies, 4*(2), 256–2766. https://doi.org/10.36312/jolls.v4i2.1931

Lee, M. (2021). The effectiveness of machine translation in foreign language education: A systematic review and meta-analysis. *Computer Assisted Language Learning, 36*, 103–125. https://doi.org/10.1080/09588221.2021.1901745

Liu, B. (2022). *Artificial intelligence and machine learning capabilities and application programming interfaces at amazon, google, and Microsoft*, (Doctoral dissertation, Massachusetts Institute of Technology).

Liu, P. L., & Chen, C. J. (2023). Using an AI-based object detection translation application for English vocabulary learning. *Educational Technology & Society, 26*(3), 5–20.

Loureiro, A. S., & Ferreira, P. (2023). Students' perceptions of the use of artificial intelligence in translation practices classes. *Pratica, 7*(2), 33–49.

Lucke, S., Lachnit, H., Koenig, S., & Uengoer, M. (2013). The informational value of contexts affects context-dependent learning. *Learning and Behaviour, 41*, 285–297. https://doi.org/10.3758/s13420-013-0104-z

Language Insight. (2024). *2024 trends in the translation industry*. https://languageinsight.com

Mardiah, H., & Nissa, K. (2024). Generation Z students' perspectives on artificial intelligence (AI) technology in English language learning. *Journal of Literature Linguistics and Language Teaching, 5*(1), 1–11. https://doi.org/10.26740/nld.v5n1.p1-11

Marzuki, Widiati, U., Rusdin, D., Darwin, & Indrawati, I. (2023). The impact of A.I. writing tools on the content and organization of students' writing: EFL teachers' perspective. *Cogent Education, 10*(2), 2236469. https://doi.org/10.1080/2331186X.2023.2236469

Matviienko, L., Khomenko, L., Denysovets, I., Horodenska, K., Nikolashyna, T., & Pavlova, I. (2024). Comparative analysis of online translators in the machine translation system. *Revista Romaneasca Pentru Educatie Multidimensionala, 16*(3), 101–118. https://doi.org/10.18662/rrem/16.3/885

Mills, O. (2023). *Context idioms and nuances: How AI grapples with translation challenges*. Retrieved from https://oliviermills.com/articles/context-idioms-nuances-ai-grapples-translation-challenges

Mohamed, Y. A., Khanan, A., Bashir, M., Mohamed, A. H. H. M., Adiel, M. A. E., & Elsadig, M. A. (2024). The impact of artificial intelligence on language translation: A review. *IEEE Access, 12*, 25553–25579. https://doi.org/10.1109/ACCESS.2024.3366802

Neji, W., Boughattas, N., & Ziadi, F. (2023). Exploring new AI-based technologies to enhance students' motivation. *Issues in Informing Science & Information Technology, 20*, 95–110. https://doi.org/10.28945/5149

Nguyen, T. T. T., & Tran, T. H. (2019). Teaching translation technology: A case study in a Vietnamese University. In *Proceedings of the 5th International Conference on Linguistics, Literature and Culture*, pp 1–6.

Nguyen, T. T. T. (2020). The integration of technology in translation education: A case study in a Vietnamese university. In *The 8th International Conference on Foreign Language Teaching and Applied Linguistics*, pp. 47–57.

Nguyen, T. T. T., & Ho, T. T. T. (2021). The use of machine translation tools in English-Vietnamese translation practice: A case study in a Vietnamese university. In *The 9th International Conference on Foreign Language Teaching and Applied Linguistics*, pp. 43–53.

Nguyen, M. T., Meesad, P., & Nguyen, H. H. C. (2021). English-Vietnamese machine translation using deep learning. In: P. Meesad, D. S. Sodsee, W. Jitsakul, S. Tangwannawit, (Eds.) *Recent advances in information and communication technology 2021. IC2IT 2021. Lecture notes in networks and systems*, vol. 251. Cham: Springer. https://doi.org/10.1007/978-3-030-79757-7_10

Nguyen, T. T. H., & Do, T. T. Y. (2023). Utilizing google translate and I'm translator as intelligent artificial tools in EFL classes. *Ho Chi Minh City University of Education Journal of Science, 20*(10), 1873–1884. https://vjol.info.vn/index.php/sphcm/article/view/88824

Nguyen, H. A. (2024a). Harnessing AI-based tools for enhancing English speaking proficiency: Impacts, challenges, and long-term engagement. *International Journal of AI in Language Education, 1*(2), 18–29. https://doi.org/10.54855/ijaile.24122

Nguyen, M. T. (2024b). Common online technical tools for translation: Students' choices, perceptions, and translation strategies used. *European Journal of Multilingualism and Translation Studies, 4*(1), 155–171. https://doi.org/10.46827/ejmts.v4i1.533

Nguyen, N. H. V., & Pham, V. P. H. (2024). AI Chatbots for language practices. *International Journal of AI in Language Education, 1*(1), 56–67. https://doi.org/10.54855/ijaile.24115

Nguyen, T. K. C., Le, P. T., Nguyen, T. T. H., & Nguyen, T. M. H. (2025a). Using computer-assisted language learning to improve interpretation skills for fourth-year English majors at Hanoi open University. *International Journal of AI in Language Education, 2*(1), 1–19. https://doi.org/10.54855/ijaile.25211

Nguyen, T. Y. P., Nguyen, N. T., & Phan, N. K. H. (2025b). The challenges of applying ChatGPT in the academic writing of postgraduate students in English major at IUH. *International Journal of AI in Language Education, 2*(1), 20–37. https://doi.org/10.54855/ijaile.25212

Och, F. J. (2003). Minimum error rate training in statistical machine translation. *Proceedings of the 41st Annual Meeting of the Association for Computational Linguistics*, pp. 160–167.

Okpor, M. D. (2014). Machine translation approaches: issues and challenges. *International Journal of Computer Science Issues (IJCSI), 11*(5), 159–165. https://doi.org/10.13140/RG.2.2.12055.38561

Othman, A. P. D. F., & Ismail, A. P. D. S. (2023). Revolutionizing medical education with artificial intelligence (AI)—The new norm. *IIUM Medical Journal Malaysia, 22*(2), 1–2. https://journals.iium.edu.my/kom/index.php/imjm/article/view/2356

Perzynska, K. (2024). What is the likert scale? Everything You Need To Know in 2024. *Survey*. https://survicate.com/customer-feedback/likert-scale

Pham, V. P. H., & Nguyen, M. T. (2024). Chatgpt va hoat dong giang day: Cac thach thuc moi cua giang vien. *Tap Chi Khoa hoc va Cong nghe Dai hoc Cong nghe Dong Nai, 1*, 115–123. https://vjol.info.vn/index.php/dntu/article/view/91869

Pham, M. T., & Cao, T. X. T. (2025). The practice of ChatGPT in English teaching and learning in Vietnam: A systematic review. *International Journal of TESOL & Education, 5*(1), 50–70. https://doi.org/10.54855/ijte.25513

Pham, N. N. H. (2025). The use of ChatGPT in EFL students as a learning assistant in their writing skills: A literature review. *International Journal of AI in Language Education, 2*(1), 38–54. https://doi.org/10.54855/ijaile.25213

Pham, V. P. H., & Le, A. Q. (2024). ChatGPT in language learning: Perspectives from Vietnamese students in Vietnam and the USA. *International Journal of Language Instruction, 3*(2), 59–72. https://doi.org/10.54855/ijli.24325

Pombal, J., Agrawal, S., Zaranis, E., Fernandes, P., & Martins, A. F. T. (2024). A context-aware framework for translation-mediated conversations. *Computation and Language, 12*, 1–20. https://doi.org/10.48550/arXiv.2412.04205

Postan, L. (2023). *Quality assessment of translations*. https://www.getblend.com/blog/quality-assessment-translations/

Rivera-Trigueros, I. (2021). Machine translation systems and quality assessment: A systematic review. *Language Resources and Evaluation, 56*(2), 593–619. https://doi.org/10.1007/s10579-021-09537-5

Sahari, Y., Al-Kadi, A. M. T., & Ali, J. K. M. (2023). A cross sectional study of ChatGPT in translation: Magnitude of use, attitudes, and uncertainties. *Journal of Psycholinguistic Research, 52*(6), 2937–2954. https://doi.org/10.1007/s10936-02310031-y

Sanusi, R. A. (2024). Leveraging artificial intelligence for enhanced translation and interpretation practice. In *Conference: Leveraging Artificial Intelligence for Enhanced Translation and Interpretation.* Abuja.

Sari, A. N. (2024). Exploring the potential of using AI language models in democratising global language test preparation. *International Journal of TESOL & Education, 4*(4), 111–126. https://doi.org/10.54855/ijte.24447

Sidiq, F. A., & Syafryadin, S. (2024). Students' perception of using DeepL for translating English text. *Journal of English Language Teaching in Indonesia, 12*(1), 139–148. https://e-journal.stkipsiliwangi.ac.id/index.php/eltin/article/view/4685

Sin-wai, C. (2014). The development of translation technology 1967–2013. In *Routledge Encyclopedia of Translation Technology* (pp. 2–31). Routledge.

Song, C., & Song, Y. (2023). Enhancing academic writing skills and motivation: Assessing the efficacy of ChatGPT in AI-assisted language learning for EFL students. *Frontiers in Psychology, 14*, 1260843. https://doi.org/10.3389/fpsyg.2023.1260843

Soysal, F. (2023). Enhancing translation studies with artificial intelligence (AI): Challenges, opportunities, and proposals. *Karamanoğlu Mehmetbey Üniversitesi Uluslararası Filoloji Ve Çeviribilim Dergisi, 5*(2), 177–1915. https://doi.org/10.55036/ufced.1402649

Specia, L., Turchi, M., & Rajendran, S. (2018). Quality estimation for machine translation. *Synthesis Lectures on Human Language Technologies, 11*(3), 1–123.

Sutopo, A., & Hastuti, D. M. (2020). The role of Machine Translators in academic translation teaching. *International Journal of Scientific Engineering and Science, 4*(5), 29–31.

Toury, G. (1982). Transfer as a universal of verbal performance of L2 learners in situations of communication in translated utterances. *Finlance, 2*, 63–78.

Tran, T. H., & Nguyen, T. T. T. (2017). Machine translation and its implications for translation teaching in Vietnam. In *Proceedings of the 4th International Conference on Linguistics, Literature and Culture*, pp. 1–8.

Tran, T. H. (2020). The role of machine translation in translation education: A case study in a Vietnamese university. In *The 8th International Conference on Foreign Language Teaching and Applied Linguistics*, pp. 171–183.

Tran, T. T. P., Tran, T. T. S., & Le, T. N. U. (2024). Using machine translation in English-Vietnamese translation: Perspectives from English-Vietnamese translation major students. *Hue University Journal of Science: Social Sciences and Humanities, 133*(6B), 107–126. https://jos.hueuni.edu.vn/index.php/hujos-ssh/article/view/7406

Tran, T. (2024). AI tools in teaching and learning English academic writing skills. *Proceedings of the AsiaCALL International Conference, 4*, 170–187. https://doi.org/10.54855/paic.23413

TrueLanguage. (2023). *Globalization cultural awareness translations and AI*. Retrieved from https://www.truelanguage.com

Truong, H. (2023). Using Google translate effectively and efficiently in translating Vietnamese texts into English ones. *IntechOpen*. https://doi.org/10.5772/intechopen.1003009

U.S. Translation Company. (2023). *Translation accuracy: Why does it matter?* Retrieved from https://ustranslation.com

Ustaszewski, M. (2014). *Towards a methodology for intercomprehension-based language instruction in translator training*. Doctor of Philosophy in Linguistics and Media Studies, University of Innsbruck.

Viktorivna, K. L., Oleksandrovych, V. A., Oleksandrivna, K. I., & Oleksandrivna, K. N. (2022). Artificial intelligence in language learning: What we are afraid of. *Arab World English Journal, 8*, 262–273. https://doi.org/10.24093/awej/call8.18

Wang, Y. (2020). When artificial intelligence meets educational leaders' data-informed decision-making: A cautionary tale. *Educational Policy Studies Faculty Publications, 40*. https://scholarworks.gsu.edu/eps_facpub/40

Wang, L. (2023). The impacts and challenges of artificial intelligence translation tool on translation professionals. In *8th International Conference on Social Sciences and Economic Development (ICSSED 2023)*, pp. *163*, 1–6. https://doi.org/10.1051/shsconf/202316302021

Wogu, I. A. P., Mistra, S., Olu-Owolabi, E. F., Assibong, P. A., & Udoh, O. D. (2018). Artificial intelligence, artificial teachers and the fate of learners in the 21st century education sector: Implications for theory and practice. *International Journal of Pure and Applied Mathematics, 119*(16), 2245–2259.

Wu, D., Zhang, L., Zhang, H., & Zhou, M. (2018). Recent advances in neural machine translation: A survey. *IEEE Transactions on Artificial Intelligence, 2*(4), 55–75.

Xu, J. B. (2024). *Conducting semi-structured interviews in social service research: A practical guide*. National University of Singapore Social Service Research Centre. https://fass.nus.edu.sg/ssr/wp-content/uploads/sites/8/2024/07/SSR-Research-Guide-2024-Conducting-Semi-Structured-Interviews-in-Social-Service-Research.pdf

Yolifi, F. W., Afrianto, A., & Masyhur, M. (2025). Students' views on the use of google translate in English language learning. *Professional Journal of English Education, 8*(1), 239–249. https://journal.ikipsiliwangi.ac.id/index.php/project/article/view/26242
Yuan, Y. (2018). *Human translation quality estimation: feature- based and deep learning-based* (Doctoral dissertation, University of Leeds).
Yudiarti, I. (2019). *The analysis of Microsoft translator quality in translating complex sentence Indonesia into English of the text.* Undergraduate Thesis. Education and Teacher Training Faculty, State Institute of Islamic Studies of Ponorogo. https://etheses.iainponorogo.ac.id/8453/
Zhang, Z., Lan, Y., Zhai, Y., & Huang, L. (2019). *Customization of neural machine translation for domain adaptation.* arXiv preprint ar Xiv:1902.07127.
Zhang, C., & Lu, Y. (2021). Study on artificial intelligence: The state of the art and future prospects. *Journal of Industrial Information Integration, 23*, Article 100224. https://doi.org/10.1016/j.jii.2021.100224

Phan Thi Ngoc Le is an English lecturer at VNU University of Languages and International Studies, Vietnam National University, Hanoi. Her research interests include English Linguistics, Language and Technology, Translation, EMI, and ESP. She has contributed to numerous publications in journals such as the Interdisciplinary Journal of Problem-based Learning and the Journal of Mekong Societies.

Evaluating Academic Support Services in the Age of AI: A Framework for Design Effectiveness and Digital Integration

Mengly Ky and Ania Lian

Abstract This paper investigates how academic support services in higher education can be more effectively evaluated and redesigned in light of growing digitalisation and the potential of artificial intelligence (AI). Rather than collecting new empirical data, the study focuses on designing and applying an evaluative framework to guide future research and service development. Drawing on a case study of a regional Australian university's Language and Learning Centre (L&LC), the study develops and introduces a three-layer evaluation framework encompassing inclusivity, academic performance, and student satisfaction. Through qualitative analysis of literature and institutional resources, the study applies the framework to identify both strengths and limitations in the existing support model. To bridge gaps identified in design, responsiveness, and accessibility, the paper proposes seven actionable policy recommendations. These recommendations aim to support the ethical and pedagogically sound integration of AI into academic literacy services—highlighting tools such as chatbots, usage analytics, and adaptive feedback platforms as complementary to human-led support. The study offers a structured and scalable approach to improving academic support in diverse and digitally mediated learning environments.

Keywords Academic support services · Artificial intelligence · Student satisfaction · Inclusivity framework

M. Ky · A. Lian (✉)
Charles Darwin University, Casuarina, Australia
e-mail: Ania.Lian@cdu.edu.au

M. Ky
e-mail: mengly.ky@students.cdu.edu.au

V. P. H. Pham et al. (eds.), *Empowering Educators: Integrating AI Tools for Personalized Language Instruction*, Studies in Computational Intelligence 1228,
https://doi.org/10.1007/978-3-032-01348-4_15

1 Introduction

The global shift towards mass higher education has led to a significant increase in university enrolments worldwide over the past few decades (Hawkins et al., 2018; Schofer & Meyer, 2005). In Australia, transformative reforms introduced in the 1980s by then Education Minister John Dawkins fundamentally reshaped the higher education landscape. These reforms, detailed in *Higher Education: A Policy Statement*, commonly known as the Dawkins White Paper, introduced a unified national system, merging smaller institutions and incorporating Tertiary and Further Education (TAFE) into the university framework (Dawkins, 1988). This expansion brought a more diverse student cohort, requiring universities to develop specialised academic support services to address a wide range of learning needs (Barthel et al., 2021).

Over the past two decades, the rise of digital learning has added further complexity to how universities design and deliver academic support. In today's educational landscape, online learning has emerged as a flexible and popular solution to meet diverse student needs, a trend significantly accelerated by the COVID-19 pandemic (Cavaleri & Tran, 2021). However, while universities have expanded their digital academic support services, ensuring these services are accessible, interactive, and pedagogically sound remains a persistent challenge. Research has shown that students in online education settings often require structured support in developing academic literacy skills, particularly in writing, research, and critical thinking (Rotar, 2022).

More recently, the emergence of artificial intelligence (AI) in education has introduced both new possibilities and uncertainties. Tools such as ChatGPT, automated feedback generators, and adaptive writing platforms are increasingly being used by students to support their learning, particularly in academic English. These tools can provide real-time feedback, assist in refining written work, and guide students through academic processes. However, the role of AI in formal academic support services remains poorly defined, with few universities developing systematic strategies for integration.

Despite the availability of AI technologies that can complement traditional services—such as automated tutoring systems, intelligent writing advisors, and learning analytics dashboards—academic support centres continue to rely heavily on conventional delivery models, including one-on-one consultations and static online resources. This raises critical questions: How can AI be effectively incorporated into English language and literacy support without displacing essential human interaction? What roles can AI play in enhancing academic outcomes and ensuring equitable access to support?

This paper addresses these questions by critically evaluating the academic support services at a regional Australian university's Language and Learning Centre. It builds upon a structured framework developed through a critical literature review to assess service effectiveness and considers how AI tools might be incorporated within this framework. By identifying current strengths and limitations, and highlighting opportunities for AI-driven innovation, this study aims to inform a more strategic, data-informed, and inclusive model for academic support in the digital age.

1.1 Issues in Academic Support Services

As enrolments in online programs increase, students encounter new challenges that demand not only self-regulation and motivation, but also the ability to locate and engage with academic support independently. Brindley (2014) describes the essential skills required for online learners as the capacity to manage time effectively, access and use educational resources, and remain goal-oriented—traits not all students possess (Martin & Bolliger, 2018).

In response to these challenges, academic support must be continuous and responsive, not simply a one-off intervention. Barnes et al. (2024) argue that effective academic support services must be regularly evaluated and adapted to meet students' evolving needs. Yet, this ongoing adaptation is made difficult by the persistent problem of low student engagement in feedback processes. Chanock (2007), Leckey and Neill (2010), and Watson (2003) have all emphasised the centrality of student feedback in shaping support services, but Luaces et al. (2018) highlight the practical barriers to collecting it—particularly the administrative burden and low response rates. Berk (2012) further critiques the reliability and validity of small feedback samples, noting that inadequate data significantly weakens institutional decision-making.

This situation has prompted some researchers to call for alternative approaches to evaluation. Rather than relying solely on student surveys, institutions can develop structured frameworks based on core pedagogical objectives and evidence-based criteria. These frameworks allow services to be reviewed against intended outcomes, independent of direct student commentary.

In this context, AI offers promising solutions. By using AI-powered analytics tools to monitor resource usage, click patterns, and learner progress, support centres can generate a more comprehensive and less intrusive understanding of student engagement. AI-driven sentiment analysis, for example, could detect student satisfaction through patterns in language used in open-text feedback. These tools do not replace student input but rather complement it, especially when response rates are low.

Nonetheless, few institutions have explored these opportunities. Academic support literature continues to emphasise the implementation of good practice models without providing the detailed benchmarks needed for meaningful evaluation. Brindley (2014) and Walsh et al. (2024) point to the importance of aligning support strategies with institutional values but stop short of articulating criteria for success. Even where data is available, as in Hendriksen et al. (2005), there is often a lack of clarity around interpretation. To address this gap, the current study develops a three-layer framework—focusing on inclusivity, academic performance, and satisfaction—to guide support centres in self-evaluating their services.

As digital transformation accelerates and AI becomes more embedded in students' learning practices, the question is not whether academic support should adapt, but how. This study takes a step in that direction by offering a flexible, evidence-based framework that can accommodate both traditional practices and emerging technologies, ensuring academic support services remain relevant, effective, and inclusive.

1.2 Study Context

This study was conducted at a regional Australian university that primarily serves remote, online, international, and Indigenous student populations. The university's geographic isolation has led to a strong emphasis on digital learning environments and related academic support systems. In alignment with its strategic plan, the university aims to provide inclusive, responsive, and accessible services that cater to all students across learning modalities. The Language and Learning Centre (L&LC), which operates under the university's library division, plays a central role in delivering academic support tailored to diverse learning contexts.

The L&LC's support services are largely delivered online and are designed to be flexible and self-directed. However, a significant challenge emerged during the author's research internship: a lack of meaningful student feedback made it difficult to assess the quality and relevance of these support services. This study responds to that challenge by evaluating the design of the L&LC's services through a structured, literature-informed framework, rather than relying solely on direct student feedback.

Additionally, this evaluation was carried out within the scope of a research unit focused on educational institutions and learning communities. Given the three-month timeframe of the internship, the study employed desk-based research methodologies to critically examine publicly available materials from the L&LC and to develop an evaluative framework. The framework, built through thematic synthesis of academic literature, provides a structured approach to assessing academic support services and their alignment with quality standards. To address these gaps, this study undertakes the design of a structured evaluative framework that can guide future data collection and service development. By focusing on the L&LC as a case study, the research aims to provide both a practical tool for internal evaluation and broader insights for academic support units navigating digital transformation.

1.3 Research Questions

To guide this study, the following research questions were formulated:

1. What specific criteria do different academic learning centres use to evaluate the quality of their support services?

2. Based on these evaluation criteria, how well do the L&LC's academic support services and resources align with best practices and institutional objectives?
3. In the absence of direct student feedback, what alternative methods—particularly those involving AI and digital analytics—can academic support centres use to evaluate the quality of online support services and resources?

These questions aim to bridge current knowledge about academic support effectiveness with the emerging role of artificial intelligence in shaping more responsive, inclusive, and scalable academic services.

2 Methodology

The study adopts a desk-based research approach, shaped by the scope and objectives of a coursework research unit on organisational learning. Rather than collecting empirical data, the primary aim of the study was to explore and design a robust framework that could guide future data collection and evaluation of academic support services. This responds to a common limitation in existing studies (Ashton-Hay & Doncaster, 2021; Nallaya & Hobson, 2021; Wilson, 2016), which tend to collect data without sufficiently critical or integrated frameworks to interpret their findings meaningfully. Given the limited timeframe of the author's research internship, the focus was placed on synthesising existing literature to construct an evaluative framework and then testing its practical relevance by applying it to the services provided by the L&LC.

According to Snyder (2019), as knowledge production in research accelerates, it often becomes fragmented, making it challenging to maintain a comprehensive understanding of current findings. This fragmentation is particularly evident in the domain of academic support services, where insights are dispersed across education, language learning, technology, and management studies. The literature review of the present study offers a method for consolidating findings and identifying consistencies that can be translated into evaluative criteria. Building on this rationale, the methodology proceeded in two phases.

2.1 *Phase One*

The first phase involved conducting a critical literature review focused on academic support services, particularly in online and hybrid learning contexts. Following Carnwell and Daly's (2001) model of critical review, four steps were taken: (1) defining the scope of the review, (2) identifying relevant sources, (3) synthesising the literature, and (4) applying insights to the study context. Peer-reviewed articles from journals such as the *Journal of Academic Language and Learning* and the *Journal of*

Further and Higher Education were reviewed, alongside interdisciplinary sources addressing resource design, academic literacies, and digital pedagogy.

Where explicit evaluation criteria were not specified, the study applied Morse's (2006) inference technique to identify implicit standards embedded within descriptions of support services. In total, 56 relevant sources were curated using Zotero software for iterative analysis. These findings were inductively synthesised to construct a three-layer evaluation framework.

To strengthen the neutrality and applicability of the framework, Scriven's (1991) Goal-Free Evaluation (GFE) model was adapted. GFE encourages evaluators to focus on what a program *actually* delivers, rather than being swayed by its stated goals—a particularly relevant strategy for academic support services, where objectives are often broad or undefined. By examining service functions in practice, especially regarding inclusivity, academic performance, and student satisfaction, the study was able to extract grounded evaluative criteria. Significantly, while many studies prioritise outcome measures, this phase deliberately emphasised *design principles* as the focal point. This orientation aligns with the study's purpose: to create a framework capable of guiding future empirical data collection and analysis, rather than prematurely focusing on impact assessment. This design-centric focus also enables the framework to remain adaptable for future integration of emerging AI tools, which operate at the intersection of design features (e.g., chatbots, feedback systems) and user experience.

2.2 Phase Two

In the second phase, the constructed framework was applied to the L&LC's publicly accessible online resources, covering five core service domains: (1) Online Tutoring (via a third-party provider), (2) Peer Study Programs, (3) Recorded Workshops, (4) Individual Consultations and Workshops, and (5) Study Skills Online Resources. These services were reviewed descriptively, focusing on how their design aligned with, or diverged from, the framework's criteria. This application followed Sullivan-Bolyai and Bova's (2021) method of Qualitative Description (QD), which supports the evaluation of diverse, non-numeric resources. QD enabled rich documentation of how each service addressed key dimensions of inclusivity, academic performance support, and student satisfaction.

Additionally, this phase considered the potential for AI integration, although the L&LC does not currently deploy such technologies. The analysis explored possibilities for enhancing services with AI tools—such as real-time learning analytics, chatbot-based guidance, and AI-driven writing assistants—to improve responsiveness and personalisation.

2.3 Summary of Methodological Approach

The combined methodological strategy—literature synthesis, framework development, and descriptive application using QD—ensured a comprehensive yet adaptable approach appropriate to the scope of the project. Importantly, the study did not seek to evaluate outcomes based on direct data collection. Instead, it prioritises the design of an evaluation framework that can guide future data gathering and analysis, thus addressing a significant gap in the field where empirical data is often collected without adequate theoretical framing. The resulting framework positions future research to conduct well-grounded, critical evaluations of academic support services, with the flexibility to incorporate technological advancements such as AI tools.

3 Designing a Framework for Evaluating Academic Support Services

This section outlines the conceptual and analytical process through which the evaluative framework for academic support services was constructed. Rather than functioning as a traditional literature review, this phase of the study synthesises empirical findings and theoretical insights from a diverse body of research, applying a qualitative, design-oriented lens to inductively identify core principles and practical benchmarks for evaluating the quality and impact of academic support services across institutions and modalities. Particular attention is given to the dimensions of inclusivity, academic performance, and student satisfaction, which underpin the framework and inform its relevance to both current service evaluation and future integration of artificial intelligence tools.

3.1 The Need to Serve All

Historical perspectives underscore the foundational role of academic support units in responding to student diversity. Chanock (2011) notes that these services were originally developed to support non-traditional student cohorts—such as Indigenous, mature-aged, and non-English-speaking background students—who faced structural barriers in navigating higher education. In contemporary contexts, supporting diversity has grown to encompass cultural understanding and internationalisation (Nallaya & Hobson, 2021; Ryan, 2020).

Academic support that is sensitive to learners' sociocultural contexts must integrate both cultural responsiveness and practical personalisation. Lim and Symons (2018) emphasise that materials designed solely from a staff perspective risk missing critical learner needs. Norman and Newham (2018) advocate for the use of student profiles and help-seeking records to better customise services. Hay et al. (2018)

propose tracking students' digital interactions as a proxy for engagement and to identify resource utilisation patterns.

From a design standpoint, Sinclair et al. (2017) recommend using multimedia, interactive tools, and clear learning outcomes to boost learner engagement. Immediate feedback is also essential. Dihoff et al. (2004) and Hatziapostolou and Paraskakis (2010) argue that timely, formative feedback can improve retention and confidence. Barber (2020) further argues for the use of third-party support providers to offer extended service hours.

Emerging technologies can expand the reach and responsiveness of such design features. For instance, AI-powered platforms can provide tailored academic support based on real-time analysis of user behaviour. Machine learning algorithms can adapt feedback to the user's performance level, and chatbots can offer immediate responses to frequently asked questions, improving both accessibility and satisfaction. Despite these opportunities, few studies have explicitly integrated AI into evaluations of academic support services, revealing a significant research and practice gap that this paper seeks to address.

3.2 Enhancing Academic Performance

Improving academic outcomes is a core objective of support services. Hitch et al. (2012) recommend aligning services with learners' contexts rather than enforcing rigid academic norms. Miller (2015) proposes a multi-literacies framework encompassing institutional, digital, cultural, critical, language, and academic literacies. Each of these domains is integral to enabling student success.

O'Neill et al. (2022) and Ashton-Hay and Doncaster (2021) further demonstrate that academic support positively correlates with student confidence, academic literacy, and GPA performance. However, they also caution that self-reported success does not necessarily translate into measurable retention outcomes.

AI has the potential to enhance this domain significantly. Digital writing assistants, such as ChatGPT or Grammarly, can scaffold student writing with grammar checks, paraphrasing support, and citation suggestions. AI-supported tutoring systems can also offer adaptive learning paths based on diagnostic assessments, ensuring students receive appropriate levels of challenge. Moreover, these tools can collect real-time data on usage patterns and learning trajectories, offering academic support teams actionable insights into students' needs.

3.3 Fostering Student Satisfaction

Student satisfaction remains a vital component in evaluating service effectiveness. Chahal (2015), drawing on Parasuraman et al. (1988) SERVQUAL model, outlines five indicators of satisfaction: understanding user needs, effective communication, timely responses, reliability, and staff competence. Walters-Archie (2018) emphasises immediacy and responsiveness, especially for online learners.

McCarthy and Tutty (2011) identify two practical challenges to satisfaction: poor visibility of support services and inefficient navigation. They argue that students are more likely to engage with well-promoted, easily accessible resources. However, resource constraints—such as staff availability and budget limitations—often impede the delivery of timely and satisfactory services.

Here too, AI can offer support. Intelligent recommendation systems can help students discover relevant resources based on their course enrolment or previous interactions. Virtual assistants can reduce staff workload by handling routine queries. These technologies, when embedded thoughtfully, could raise service visibility, streamline access, and improve students' overall satisfaction.

3.4 Summary of Themes

Across the literature, three core objectives emerge as essential to the effective design of academic support services:

1. Inclusivity—ensuring support resources are adaptable, engaging, and culturally sensitive.
2. Academic Performance—enhancing literacies and academic outcomes through targeted, flexible support.
3. Student Satisfaction—providing clear, responsive, and reliable services that are easily accessible.

Table 1 summarises this framework. Its dimensions form the foundation of the evaluative framework applied in this study. Notably, while the literature identifies best practices, few studies explore how AI could systematically address persistent challenges in each domain. By incorporating AI-enabled possibilities, the framework developed in this paper not only reflects current best practices but also anticipates future directions for academic support services in digitally mediated environments.

Table 1 Framework for evaluating academic support services

Objective	Criteria
Inclusivity	Student-centred design, multimodal resources, multicultural responsiveness, third-party extension of services, tracking user profiles and patterns
Academic performance	Alignment with literacies (institutional, digital, social/cultural, critical, academic), learner confidence, GPA improvement, performance feedback
Student satisfaction	Clarity, responsiveness, accessibility, reliability, timely assistance, intuitive navigation, service discoverability

4 Study Findings

This section presents the study's findings organised according to the three research questions: (1) What criteria are used by academic support centres to evaluate service quality? (2) How well do the L&LC's offerings align with these criteria? (3) What alternative, AI-informed methods can be used when direct student feedback is lacking?

4.1 RQ1: What Specific Criteria Do Different Academic Learning Centres Use to Evaluate the Quality of Their Support Services?

The literature review revealed that effective academic support services aim to:

- Promote **inclusivity** by tailoring support to diverse student needs.
- Enhance **academic performance** through development of multiple literacies.
- Improve **student satisfaction** via responsive, accessible, and clearly communicated services.

Each objective is supported by specific criteria, including:

- Designing student-centred, interactive, and multimodal resources.
- Tracking usage patterns and personalising content.
- Extending service hours through third-party providers.
- Offering timely, formative feedback.
- Ensuring discoverability and reliability of support services.

These criteria form the basis of the three-layer evaluation framework employed in this study.

4.2 RQ2: How Effectively Do the L&LC's Services Align with These Evaluation Criteria?

The L&LC demonstrates several strengths:

- Its online Study Skills platform is student-centred and includes multimodal content (e.g. videos, handouts, self-evaluation quizzes).
- Tutor.com integration extends support beyond office hours.
- Clear section objectives improve transparency in many areas.

However, gaps were also noted:

- No explicit focus on cultural or intercultural awareness.

- Inconsistent provision of feedback and self-assessment tools across resource sections.
- Limited visibility and accessibility of services; users often encounter multiple steps before locating resources.
- No system in place to track student interaction or gather immediate feedback.

These limitations suggest that while the L&LC meets many inclusivity and academic performance criteria, it falls short in consistently supporting satisfaction and responsiveness. The integration of AI could address these gaps:

- AI-based analytics tools could track usage patterns and personalise learning experiences.
- AI chatbots could provide instant support, improving responsiveness and discoverability.
- Sentiment analysis and adaptive feedback tools could capture and interpret student reactions in real time (Table 2).

4.3 *RQ3: What Alternative Methods—Especially AI-Informed Ones—Can Support Evaluation in the Absence of Direct Feedback?*

Given the difficulty of collecting meaningful student feedback, the study explored indirect methods for evaluating support effectiveness. These include:

- Analysing help-seeking records (Norman & Newham, 2018).
- Tracking engagement via digital platforms (Hay et al., 2018).
- Using performance analytics to identify usage trends.

AI technologies provide powerful extensions of these methods:

- Learning analytics dashboards can aggregate student interactions, identifying high- and low-engagement areas.
- AI-generated usage reports can inform iterative improvements.
- Feedback bots embedded within resources can offer students real-time channels for rating usefulness.

In sum, the findings suggest that integrating AI into the framework can help academic support centres achieve greater precision and responsiveness in service evaluation. This would not only mitigate the absence of direct feedback but also enhance the inclusivity and adaptability of academic support in a digital era.

Table 2 Evaluation of L&LC services against the framework

Objective	Presence	Absence
Inclusivity of academic support services and resources	– **Student-centredness:** The Study Skills webpage connects content to the curriculum through real-text examples and intuitive, self-explanatory exercises – **Flexibility in navigation**: Students can skip materials and engage directly with quizzes, though reviewing materials enhances comprehension – **Multimodality of resources**: Resources include videos, games, and interactive aids to sustain interest and effectively present key concepts – **Self-assessment for retention**: Pre- and post-learning quizzes help students reflect on understanding and apply knowledge – **Extension of services**: Tutor.com offers flexible 24/7 academic support, extending coverage beyond regular hours	– **Guideline and outcome indication**: Most pages lack consistent formatting and explicit learning outcomes tied to macro and micro-skills – **Student feedback mechanisms**: Feedback is placed at the end of sections and may not gather meaningful input; real-time in-page prompts (e.g., yes/no) are lacking
Positive impact on students' academic performance	– **Peer-assisted-study-session** (PASS) testimonials highlight increased confidence and academic performance – **Digital, academic, and language literacies** are clearly addressed in respective online sections	– **No content supporting students' understanding of CDU systems** (e.g., library tools) – **Lack of sociocultural literacy support** (e.g., content promoting multiculturalism) – **No clear link to retention:** The testimonials visible on the L&LC pages do not specify whether the services helped students remain enrolled in their programs, leaving the impact on retention unclear
Providing satisfactory services for students	– **Clear communication of information and instructions:** Each section of the Study Skills website clearly states its objectives and provides guidance to help students engage with and achieve these learning goals effectively	– **Booking system complexity** and short consultation times reduce responsiveness – **One consultation per week** limit can hinder progress – **Navigation** through the library site is cumbersome, reducing visibility and access

5 Discussion

The findings of this study reaffirm the importance of a structured, multi-layered framework for evaluating academic support services. In particular, they underscore the need to balance traditional pedagogical criteria with the dynamic opportunities offered by AI-driven technologies.

First, the study demonstrates that while many academic support centres, including the L&LC, make considerable efforts to promote inclusivity and student success, they often fall short in terms of responsiveness, adaptability, and systematic evaluation—particularly in digital environments. These limitations are not necessarily due to lack of commitment, but rather to reliance on traditional models that are ill-equipped for real-time, scalable, and personalised student engagement.

Second, the three-layer framework developed here—based on inclusivity, academic performance, and student satisfaction—offers a practical and comprehensive tool for evaluating existing services and identifying strategic improvements. The L&LC's resources align well with inclusivity goals, particularly through student-centred design, multimodal content, and extended service coverage via third-party providers. However, the absence of mechanisms for continuous feedback, limited visibility of services, and inconsistent support for intercultural and institutional literacies diminish their overall impact.

To further clarify how the study's findings align with its original research objectives, the following reflections consolidate the framework's contribution and its practical implications. While, as noted by the reviewer, the study does not report statistically significant findings, its contribution lies in the systematic development and application of an evaluative framework grounded in the study's three research objectives: inclusivity, academic performance, and student satisfaction. By inductively synthesising existing literature and applying the resulting framework to the L&LC's support services, the study demonstrates clear alignment between the framework's dimensions and the practical needs of academic support units. The framework effectively surfaces both strengths (such as multimodal resources and extended service hours) and gaps (including limited cultural responsiveness and absence of real-time feedback mechanisms) in relation to these objectives. This alignment affirms the framework's relevance and practical utility as a diagnostic tool, offering structured guidance for academic support centres aiming to enhance their services. Importantly, the framework provides a foundation for future empirical research that can test its applicability and effectiveness through quantitative methods, including statistical analysis, across broader institutional contexts.

Despite the strengths identified through this framework, persistent challenges remain in both the design and evaluation of support services. Artificial intelligence presents a promising frontier for addressing these needs. AI tools such as chatbots, usage analytics, adaptive feedback systems, and virtual assistants offer scalable ways to personalise support, monitor user engagement, and collect actionable insights—thereby reducing reliance on traditional feedback mechanisms. For example, implementing AI-enabled tracking systems could help academic centres like the L&LC identify patterns in resource usage and adapt services based on student behaviour.

Furthermore, the integration of AI aligns well with the evolving expectations of digital-native learners who value instant feedback, accessible guidance, and tailored support. Yet, caution is required to ensure these technologies are pedagogically sound, ethically implemented, and do not replace the human interaction that remains vital for many students—particularly those from underserved communities.

In this context, the study advocates for a dual strategy: (1) refining traditional services using the evaluative framework developed here, and (2) piloting and integrating AI tools that enhance interactivity, inclusivity, and real-time responsiveness. Such an approach enables academic support centres to move beyond reactive service models and toward proactive, data-informed, and learner-centred practices.

Overall, the findings support the view that academic support services must evolve in tandem with technological advancements and shifting student needs. By embedding AI into their strategic planning and evaluation frameworks, universities can foster more effective, inclusive, and engaging learning environments.

6 Policy Recommendations: Enhancing Academic Support Services Through AI Integration

Drawing on the findings from this study, which evaluated academic literacy support services at a regional Australian university, the following policy recommendations are proposed to guide institutions seeking to improve their services through structured frameworks and ethical use of artificial intelligence (AI). These policies are intended for higher education administrators, academic support leaders, and education policymakers.

- Establish institutional frameworks for evaluating support services

Policy Action: Require academic support centres to implement structured, evidence-based evaluation frameworks, such as the proposed three-layer model encompassing inclusivity, academic performance, and student satisfaction.

Rationale: This study demonstrated that reliance on sporadic student feedback is insufficient for capturing the complexity and effectiveness of academic support services. A structured evaluative approach allows for consistent and holistic assessment, even in the absence of comprehensive feedback.

- Embed ethical AI into academic support policies

Policy Action: Develop institution-wide policies that promote the responsible integration of AI technologies—such as chatbots, automated feedback systems, and AI-enhanced writing tools—into academic support services.

Rationale: AI tools can improve responsiveness, personalisation, and accessibility of academic support, especially for remote and diverse learners. However, integration must prioritise pedagogical soundness, student privacy, and ethical safeguards.

- Enforce standards for visibility, accessibility, and multimodal design

Policy Action: Mandate that all academic support platforms meet standards for online accessibility, including intuitive navigation, high visibility, and multimedia content designed for varied learning styles.

Rationale: The study identified challenges in locating and accessing academic support resources, which undermines service equity and effectiveness. User-centred and multimodal design principles promote inclusivity and student engagement.

- Introduce real-time feedback mechanisms

Policy Action: Require academic support services to embed real-time feedback prompts (e.g., in-page rating buttons, micro-surveys) into all digital resources.

Rationale: Timely and specific feedback mechanisms offer actionable data for continuous improvement and overcome the limitations of delayed or under-reported student evaluations.

- Fund analytics dashboards for usage monitoring

Policy Action: Provide funding and technical support for academic support units to implement analytics dashboards that track user engagement, access patterns, and resource utility.

Rationale: Learning analytics offer a valuable alternative to direct feedback, enabling data-informed decision-making and better alignment between support services and student needs.

- Promote cultural and linguistic inclusivity

Policy Action: Make it a policy requirement for academic support materials to reflect intercultural communication standards and address the needs of multilingual and Indigenous learners.

Rationale: The study found minimal content focused on cultural inclusivity. Inclusive practices improve access, relevance, and effectiveness for diverse student cohorts.

- Encourage human-AI hybrid service models

Policy Action: Develop institutional strategies for combining AI-enhanced services with human-led academic support, ensuring that each complements the other.

Rationale: Rather than replacing educators, AI can extend the reach and timeliness of academic support. A hybrid model ensures human empathy and judgement are retained while expanding capacity.

7 Study Limitations

While this study contributes to the development of a structured, future-oriented framework for evaluating academic support services, several limitations should be acknowledged. These limitations are primarily shaped by the scope, methodology, and timeframe of the research internship.

First, the study did not involve direct empirical data collection from students or staff. Instead, it deliberately prioritised the design and testing of an evaluative framework to guide future data-driven research. This approach was chosen in recognition of a persistent gap in existing studies, where data is often collected without sufficient critical framing. As such, while the framework has been conceptually validated through application to institutional materials, its full potential can only be realised once it is employed in empirical contexts.

Second, the analysis of the L&LC relied exclusively on publicly available online resources. This scope limitation means that internal processes, staff perspectives, and unpublished service data were beyond reach. Consequently, certain aspects of service delivery—such as internal decision-making, staff training practices, or informal student interactions—remain unexplored.

Third, given the evolving nature of AI technologies and their integration into higher education, the study could not fully capture the dynamic innovations that may emerge beyond its completion. While the framework anticipates the use of AI tools and provides policy recommendations for their integration, it does not include empirical testing of AI-enhanced services within the L&LC. To situate the proposed framework within current research on AI-enhanced academic support, it is important to consider recent studies examining ChatGPT's role in academic writing and feedback provision (Fang et al., 2023; Guo et al., 2022; Mahapatra, 2024; Wilson & Billam, 2023). These studies illustrate how ChatGPT can complement traditional support services by enhancing proofreading accuracy, simulating peer interactions, and providing formative feedback, thereby addressing key challenges in accessibility, responsiveness, and scalability of academic support units.

Lastly, the study was constrained by the three-month timeframe of the research internship. A longer duration would have allowed for deeper engagement with stakeholders and potential pilot testing of the framework in practice.

Despite these limitations, the study lays important groundwork by offering a structured approach for future evaluations. The framework developed here provides a critical lens through which future studies can systematically assess academic support services, integrating both human and AI-driven interventions to enhance service effectiveness in increasingly digital learning environments.

8 Conclusion

This study highlights the urgent need for universities to rethink how academic support services are evaluated and delivered in increasingly digital environments. It demonstrates the value of structured, multi-layered frameworks that prioritise inclusivity, academic outcomes, and student satisfaction—especially when direct feedback from students is limited or unavailable.

Building on these insights, the study presents a set of practical policy recommendations that translate the framework into actionable strategies for higher education institutions. These include embedding ethical AI, promoting real-time feedback, improving access and visibility, and fostering hybrid human-AI service models.

In doing so, the paper contributes to an emerging conversation about how artificial intelligence can enhance—not replace—academic literacy support. Crucially, the development and application of the evaluative framework provide a replicable model for academic support centres seeking to integrate both human-led and AI-enabled services. By anchoring AI within pedagogically sound and ethically responsible frameworks, institutions can more effectively serve diverse student cohorts and adapt to the demands of a rapidly evolving digital learning landscape.

Looking ahead, future research should focus on empirically testing the framework's applicability across varied institutional contexts, using both qualitative insights and quantitative validation. Such studies will be essential to refining the framework and ensuring its scalability, helping academic support services remain both responsive and inclusive in an era of accelerating digital transformation.

References

Anderson, D. S., & Eaton, E. (1982). Australian higher education research and society: PART I: Post-war reconstruction and expansion: 1940–1965. *Higher Education Research & Development, 1*(1), 5–32. https://doi.org/10.1080/0729436820010102

Ashton-Hay, S. A., & Doncaster, N. (2021). Student success and retention: What's academic skills got to do with it? *Journal of Academic Language and Learning, 15*(1), 102–116.

Australia Bureau of Statistics. (1990). *Year book Australia.* ABS. https://www.ausstats.abs.gov.au/ausstats/free.nsf/0/68F657F55DAB6077CA257AFA0010CC41/$File/13010_1990_bk73.pdf

Australian Government Department of Education, Skills and Employment. (2021). *2021–2023 Mission based compact between the commonwealth of Australia and Charles Darwin university.* https://www.education.gov.au/higher-education-funding/resources/charles-darwin-university-compact-20212023

Barber, R. (2020). The good, the bad and the interesting: Integrating a third-party provider into ALL services at a regional university. *Journal of Academic Language and Learning, 14*(1), 54–67.

Barnes, N., Fischer, S., & Kilpatrick, S. (2024). Going above and beyond: Realigning university student support services to students. *International Journal of Educational Research, 124*, Article 102270. https://doi.org/10.1016/j.ijer.2023.102270

Barthel, A., Bartlett, A., Chanock, K., & Moore, T. (2021). Changing identities: A history of academic language and learning in Australia. *Journal of Academic Language and Learning, 15.*

Barton, G., & Lumley, A. (2020). Academic support online: Developing an integrated academic support environment at the University of the Arts London. In C. Dennis, S. Abbott, R. Matheson, & S. Tangney (Eds.), *Flexibility and pedagogy in higher education* (pp. 123–144). BRILL. https://doi.org/10.1163/9789004438118_010

Berk, R. A. (2012). Top 20 strategies to increase the online response rates of student rating scales. *International Journal of Technology in Teaching and Learning, 8*(2), 10.

Brindley, J. E. (2014). Learner support in online distance education: Essential and evolving. In O. Zawacki-Richter & T. Anderson (Eds.), *Online distance education: Towards a research agenda* (pp. 287–310). Athabasca University Press. https://doi.org/10.15215/aupress/9781927356623.01

Carnwell, R., & Daly, W. (2001). Strategies for the construction of a critical review of the literature. *Nurse Education in Practice, 1*(2), 57–63. https://doi.org/10.1054/nepr.2001.0008

Cavaleri, M., & Tran, K. (2021). Online academic support during the COVID-19 pandemic: Reflections on unexpected outcomes that challenge assumptions. *Journal of Academic Language and Learning, 15*(1), R1–R11.

Chahal, D. (2015). The student rover mentor program: Inclusion, satisfaction and perceived impact. *Journal of Academic Language and Learning, 9*(2), A46–A61.

Chanock, K. (2007). Valuing individual consultations as input into other modes of teaching. *Journal of Academic Language and Learning, 1*(1), 9.

Chanock, K. (2011). A historical literature review of Australian publications in the field of academic language and learning in the 1980s: Themes, schemes, and schisms: Part One. *Journal of Academic Language and Learning, 5*(1), A36–A58.

Charles Darwin University. (2014). *Professional placement in global learning.* Internal document. https://docs.google.com/document/d/1sEWxyPC3uqZeEEdMHbWHema01GCppF8E/edit

Charles Darwin University. (2021). *Strategic plan 2021–2026.* https://editorial.cdu.edu.au/charles-darwin-universitystrategic-plan/#article

Charles Darwin University. (n.d.). *Study skills: Open access to academic resources and practical study help.* https://www.cdu.edu.au/library/language-and-learning-support/study-skills

Dawkins, J. S. (1988). *Higher education: A policy statement.* Australian Government Publishing Service.

Dihoff, R. E., Brosvic, G. M., Epstein, M. L., & Cook, M. J. (2004). Provision of feedback during preparation for academic testing: Learning is enhanced by immediate but not delayed feedback. *The Psychological Record, 54*(2), 207–231. https://doi.org/10.1007/BF03395471

Fang, T., Yang, S., Lan, K., Wong, D. F., Hu, J., Chao, L. S., & Zhang, Y. (2023). Is ChatGPT a highly fluent grammatical error correction system? A comprehensive evaluation. https://doi.org/10.48550/ARXIV.2304.01746

Guo, K., Wang, J., & Chu, S. K. W. (2022). Using chatbots to scaffold EFL students' argumentative writing. *Assessing Writing, 54*, Article 100666. https://doi.org/10.1016/j.asw.2022.100666

Gurney, L., & Grossi, V. (2019). Performing support in higher education: Negotiating conflicting agendas in academic language and learning advisory work. *Higher Education Research & Development, 38*(5), 940–953. https://doi.org/10.1080/07294360.2019.1609916

Hanover Research. (2018). *Global benchmarking and best practices analysis of online student supports.* https://cdn2.hubspot.net/hubfs/3409306/Global%20Benchmarking%20and%20Best%20Practices%20in%20Online%20Student%20Supports.pdf

Harvey, A., & Russell-Mundine, G. (2016). Modelling interdisciplinary collaboration to build cultural competence and academic literacy. *Journal of Academic Language and Learning, 10*(1), 17.

Hatziapostolou, T., & Paraskakis, I. (2010). Enhancing the impact of formative feedback on student learning through an online feedback system. *Electronic Journal of E-Learning, 8*(2), 111–122.

Hawkins, J. N., Mok, K. H., & Neubauer, D. (2018). The many faces of Asia Pacific higher education in the era of massification. In *Higher education in Asia* (pp. 1–8). https://doi.org/10.1007/978-981-13-0248-0_1

Hay, S. A., Yin, Z., & Ross, A. S. (2018). Ask a question: Student use and misuse of online academic skills support. *Journal of Academic Language and Learning, 12*(1), A81–A96.

Hendriksen, S. I., Yang, L., Love, B., & Hall, M. C. (2005). Assessing academic support: The effects of tutoring on student learning outcomes. *Journal of College Reading and Learning, 35*(2), 56–65. https://doi.org/10.1080/10790195.2005.10850173

Hitch, D., et al. (2012). Academic skills and beyond: A resource-based approach to support student success in higher education. *Journal of Academic Language and Learning, 6*(2), 13.

Huang, L.-J.D. (2021). Developing intercultural communicative competence in foreign language classrooms. *International Journal of Intercultural Relations, 83*, 55–66. https://doi.org/10.1016/j.ijintrel.2021.04.015

Jacobi, L. (2023). Shifting gears in a pandemic: The impact of online academic support for international and domestic students. *Journal of Comparative & International Higher Education, 15*(2), 219–242. https://doi.org/10.32674/jcihe.v15i2.4467

Kecskes, I. (2015). Intracultural communication and intercultural communication: Are they different? *International Review of Pragmatics, 7*(2), 171–194. https://doi.org/10.1163/18773109-00702002

Ky, M. (2023, September). *Measuring success in silence: Evaluating online academic support services without direct student feedback*. https://drive.google.com/file/d/1c3jydMKR9FT9cJxI_teZmsL8sBpydSfV/view?usp=sharing

Leckey, J., & Neill, N. (2010). Quantifying quality: The importance of student feedback. *Quality in Higher Education, 7*(1), 19–32. https://doi.org/10.1080/13538320120045058

Lim, N., & Symons, C. (2018). A step towards putting the students back into the academic language support model. *Journal of Academic Language and Learning, 12*(2), A39–A54.

Luaces, O., Díez, J., & Bahamonde, A. (2018). A peer assessment method to provide feedback, consistent grading and reduce students' burden in massive teaching settings. *Computers & Education, 126*, 283–295. https://doi.org/10.1016/j.compedu.2018.07.016

Mahapatra, S. (2024). Impact of ChatGPT on ESL students' academic writing skills: A mixed methods intervention study. *Smart Learning Environments, 11*(1), 9. https://doi.org/10.1186/s40561-024-00295-9

Martin, F., & Bolliger, D. U. (2018). Engagement matters: Student perceptions on the importance of engagement strategies in the online learning environment. *Online Learning, 22*(1), 205–222. https://doi.org/10.24059/olj.v22i1.1092

McCarthy, S. L., & Tutty, J. (2011). Strategies for developing effective ALL websites. *Journal of Academic Language and Learning, 5*(2), A23–A34.

Miller, A. (2015). A multi-literacies framework for university teaching. *Journal of Academic Language and Learning, 9*(5), A19–A31.

Morse, J. M. (2006). Insight, inference, evidence, and verification. *International Journal of Qualitative Methods, 5*(1), 93–100. https://doi.org/10.1177/160940690600500108

Nallaya, S., & Hobson, J. E. (2021). A division-wide framework to scaffold the development of English language and intercultural learning. *Journal of Academic Language and Learning, 15*(1), 162–186.

Norman, E. A., & Newham, E. C. (2018). The role of learning advisors and support staff within an increasingly differentiated student community. *Journal of Academic Language and Learning, 12*(1), A128–A140.

O'Neill, R., et al. (2022). The impact of an embedded academic literacy approach on international student transition to an Australian university. *Journal of Academic Language and Learning, 16*(1), 35–58.

Rotar, O. (2022). Online student support: A framework for embedding support interventions into the online learning cycle. *Research and Practice in Technology Enhanced Learning, 17*(1), 2. https://doi.org/10.1186/s41039-021-00178-4

Ryan, J. (2020). Transforming academic cultures. *Journal of Academic Language and Learning, 14*(2), 1–19.

Schofer, E., & Meyer, J. W. (2005). The worldwide expansion of higher education in the twentieth century. *American Sociological Review, 70*(6), 22. https://doi.org/10.1177/000312240507000602

Scriven, M. (1991). *Evaluation thesaurus* (4th ed.). Sage Publications.

Sinclair, P. M., et al. (2017). High engagement, high quality: A guiding framework for developing asynchronous e-learning. *Nursing & Health Sciences, 19*(1), 126–137. https://doi.org/10.1111/nhs.12322

Snyder, H. (2019). Literature review as a research methodology: An overview and guidelines. *Journal of Business Research, 104*, 333–339. https://doi.org/10.1016/j.jbusres.2019.07.039

Stewart, B. L., Goodson, C., Miertschin, S., Norwood, M., & Ezell, S. (2013). Online student support services: A case based on quality frameworks. *MERLOT Journal of Online Learning and Teaching, 9*(2), 290–303.

Stone, C., Freeman, E., Dyment, J. E., Muir, T., & Milthorpe, N. (2019). Equal or equitable? The role of flexibility within online education. *Australian and International Journal of Rural Education, 29*(2), 26–40.

Sullivan-Bolyai, S., & Bova, C. (2021). Qualitative description a "how-to" guide. *UMass Chan Medical School*. https://doi.org/10.13028/8VWE-XC61

Walsh, C., et al. (2024). A systematic literature review of online academic student support in higher education. *Online Learning, 28*(2). https://doi.org/10.24059/olj.v28i2.3954

Walters-Archie, A. (2018). Academic support for online students in the English-speaking Caribbean. *Journal of Further and Higher Education, 42*(6), 868–878. https://doi.org/10.1080/0309877X.2017.1332353

Watson, S. (2003). Closing the feedback loop. *Tertiary Education and Management, 9*(2), 145–157. https://doi.org/10.1080/13583883.2003.9967099

Westra, K. (2018, October 20). Online student services: What, where, who, when, how, and most importantly, why. *EDUCAUSE Review*. https://er.educause.edu/articles/2018/10/online-student-services-what-where-who-when-how-and-most-importantly-why

Wilson, K. (2016). Critical reading, critical thinking: Delicate scaffolding in English for academic purposes (EAP). *Thinking Skills and Creativity, 22*, 256–265. https://doi.org/10.1016/j.tsc.2016.10.002

Wilson, O., & Billam, J. (2023). ChatGPT in June 2023: An annotated bibliography for ALL professionals. *Journal of Academic Language and Learning, 17*(1), 7.

Youker, B. W. (2024). Scriven's goal-free evaluation. *Journal of MultiDisciplinary Evaluation, 20*(47). https://doi.org/10.56645/jmde.v20i47.1005

Mengly Ky is a recipient of a prestigious Australia Awards Scholarship, which supported his Master's studies at Charles Darwin University.

Ania Lian is a Senior Lecturer at Charles Darwin University, where she plays a leading role in supervising PhD and research students and contributes to the development of a vibrant and inclusive research culture.

GPSR Compliance

The European Union's (EU) General Product Safety Regulation (GPSR) is a set of rules that requires consumer products to be safe and our obligations to ensure this.

If you have any concerns about our products, you can contact us on ProductSafety@springernature.com

In case Publisher is established outside the EU, the EU authorized representative is:

Springer Nature Customer Service Center GmbH
Europaplatz 3
69115 Heidelberg, Germany

Batch number: 09019511

Printed by Printforce, the Netherlands